Hidden Hands

The Douglass Series
On Women's Lives
and the
Meaning of Gender

Hidden Hands

An Anthology of American Women Writers, 1790–1870

Edited by Lucy M. Freibert and Barbara A. White

Rutgers University Press · New Brunswick, New Jersey

Library of Congress Cataloging in Publication Data
Main entry under title:

Hidden hands.

(Douglass series on women's lives and the meaning of gender)
Bibliography: p.
Includes index.
  1. American fiction—Women authors. 2. American fiction—19th century.
I. Freibert, Lucy M., 1922–. II. White, Barbara Anne, 1942–. III. Series.
PS647.W6H5 1984   810'.8'09287   84–22884
ISBN 0–8135–1088–0
ISBN 0–8135–1089–9 (pbk.)

Permission has been generously granted to reproduce excerpts from the following works:

Nina Baym, *Woman's Fiction: A Guide to Novels by and about Women in America, 1820–1870*, copyright © 1978. Used by permission of Cornell University Press.

A. Cowie, *The Rise of the American Novel*, copyright © 1948. Reprinted by permission of D. C. Heath and Company.

Helen Waite Papashvily, *All the Happy Endings*, copyright © 1956 by Helen Waite Papashvily. Used by permission of the author and Harper & Row, Publishers, Inc.

Jane P. Tompkins, *Sensational Designs: The Cultural Work of American Fiction, 1790–1860*, copyright © 1985. Used by permission of the author and Oxford University Press.

Ann Douglas Wood, "The 'Scribbling Women' and Fanny Fern: Why Women Wrote," from *American Quarterly* 23 (1971): 5–7, 8–12, copyright © 1971, Trustees of the University of Pennsylvania. Used by permission of the author and the University of Pennsylvania.

TO OUR MOTHERS
Amelia Stich Freibert
Mary Elizabeth Busacker White
(1919–1979)

Contents

Preface

Hidden Hands: An Anthology of American Women Writers, 1790–1870 is a collection of popular writings. We have prepared it especially for classroom use, hoping it will prove valuable as a reader in women's studies, American studies, and literature and history courses that treat the period between American independence and the Civil War. In recent years educators have noted the absence of both women writers and popular writers from the American canon. Many teachers have read some of the important historical and critical studies of the past ten years, such as Ann Douglas's *The Feminization of American Culture,* Nina Baym's *Woman's Fiction,* and Mary Kelley's *Private Woman, Public Stage.** In the process they have been reminded that Hawthorne and Melville were not the only—and certainly not the most popular—writers in mid-nineteenth-century America; in fact, the writings of their despised contemporaries, "scribbling women" like Susan Warner and Martha Finley, exerted a more powerful cultural influence.

Unfortunately, the primary works discussed in the recent critical studies have not been readily available. Students, and probably most of their teachers, know this material only by report; they have heard of Fanny Fern but have not read her. Many works by early-nineteenth-century American women are out of print, and the few available in reprints are too expensive for classroom use. Moreover, the key writings of the period, best sellers of the century such as Susan Warner's *The Wide, Wide World* (1850) and Augusta Evans Wilson's *St. Elmo* (1866), happen to be novels rather than poems or short stories. Our ancestors were fond of the doubledecker novel, the longer the better, and most are too lengthy for survey courses.

Hidden Hands thus consists of excerpts from novels. As teachers, we ordinarily dislike using excerpts; we shudder at Reader's Digest condensed books and tend to choose, from the standard anthologies, the complete works in preference to the excerpts. But in this case there is no logical recourse. A sampling of the doubledecker novels may provide the only sure way for students to see for themselves what was written by nineteenth-century American women other than Margaret Fuller and Harriet Beecher Stowe. We have tried to make the excerpts substantial enough to give a clear sense of an author's style and the content and tone of her novel.

In preparing this volume, we have included only women writers because we realize how hard it is for teachers to provide gender balance in the early American period. Since the current anthologies contain so few women, and no novelists other than Stowe, teachers need a large and

---

*See the Bibliography for complete citations of works of criticism mentioned in the text.

varied selection of women writers from which to choose. We have had some reservations, however, about restricting a collection of popular fiction to women. We do not want to help perpetuate, as many of the recent historical and critical studies have done, traditional myths about nineteenth-century women writers. The central myth is that women wrote "popular" novels (trash for the crowd), while men wrote "serious" novels (literature for posterity); women earned pots of money, men starved for the sake of art. This myth appears to contain some truth if one compares Nathaniel Hawthorne to Fanny Fern, as is usually done. But Hawthorne should more justly be paired with Margaret Fuller, who was not wildly popular either, and Fern with Sylvanus Cobb, T. S. Arthur, or J. H. Ingraham. In fact, men wrote popular novels and earned money also. If women authored the top three sellers of the century, men out-numbered women on the best-seller list three to one.*

Men also wrote in the "sentimental" vein that is so often ridiculed in criticism of nineteenth-century popular fiction. In a recent talk on early women writers, one of the editors coerced her audience into playing "guess the author" of the following passage. An alcoholic staggers home from the bar just in time to receive a religious book from his dying sister:

> The inebriate—his mind sobered by the deep solemnity of the scene—stood there, and leaned over to catch the last accents of one, who, in ten minutes more, was to be with the spirits of heaven.
>
> All was the silence of deepest night. The dying child held the young man's hand in one of hers; with the other, she slowly lifted the trifling memorial she had assigned especially for him, aloft in the air. Her arm shook—her eyes, now becoming glassy with death-damps, were cast toward her brother's face. She smiled pleasantly, and as an indistinct gurgle came from her throat, the uplifted hand fell suddenly into the open palm of her brother's, depositing the tiny volume there. Little Jane was dead.
>
> From that night, the young man stepped no more in his wild courses, but was reformed.

The guesses were reasonable enough—Susan Warner, Fanny Fern—but the passage is from *Franklin Evans* (1842), a temperance novel by Walt Whitman. Interestingly, Whitman thought enough of this episode from his novel to reprint it separately as "Little Jane" in the Brooklyn *Daily Eagle*.

Many of the selections we have included may strike the reader as little "better" than Whitman's. By modern standards the popular nineteenth-century novels contain many flaws: their plots range from trite and pre-

---

*According to "Over-All Best Sellers in the United States," Appendix A in Frank Luther Mott's *Golden Multitudes*, 303–322. Problems in assessment of popularity are discussed in Nina Baym's *Woman's Fiction*, 300–301. We have taken estimates of sales and earnings for particular authors from standard sources, but it is sometimes questionable whether these sources are entirely accurate.

dictable to wildly improbable; characters lack individuality and are all good or all bad; style is undistinguished; sense of place is almost always lacking. Twentieth-century readers are likely to find children's dying gurgles positively distasteful and to resent being drowned in tears. As Whitman's little Jane departs this world, the rest of the family cries "thick tears."

In any attempt to evaluate the fiction included in this collection, the reader should remember that not only did men write the same type of fiction but the standards by which people judge literature are changeable and open to debate. Most of the critics listed in our bibliographies take a condescending, if not hostile, attitude; the only ones to claim any literary merit are Wellesley students in the Nineteenth-century American Women's Fiction Project (see "A Patchwork Piece" in Bibliography) and Jane P. Tompkins in "Sentimental Power: *Uncle Tom's Cabin* and the Politics of Literary History." For a discussion of literary standards we recommend Tompkins's article and Deborah S. Rosenfelt's "The Politics of Bibliography: Women's Studies and the Literary Canon."

Another myth we have tried to combat in *Hidden Hands* is that women wrote exclusively "sentimental" or "domestic" novels. A novelist like E. D. E. N. Southworth is usually placed in one of the above categories although she was more satirical than sentimental and had little interest in domesticity. In *Woman's Fiction* Baym criticizes both terms, noting that they are judgmental rather than descriptive and imply falsely that the authors elevate feeling and domesticity above all else. Baym uses the term *woman's fiction* to characterize the fiction she examines in her book. Yet she intentionally discusses only one "genre," as she puts it, and not the whole of nineteenth-century fiction by women; she restricts her study to fiction that tells a particular story (for the story, see the Criticism section). Some of the novels we include tell this story, but some do not. We have tried to emphasize the variety in writings by women in the period 1790–1870. If women often wrote novels that lend themselves to the labels "sentimental" and "domestic," or that tell Baym's story of a young girl winning her own way in the world, they also pioneered in realistic fiction, ventured into satire and humor, and wrote frontier romance, the forerunner of our modern western. The comprehensive history that American literature badly needs will have to include all of these contributions.

In a further attempt to offer a broad representation of women's writing during the early American period, we have included authors from the North, South, East, and what was then West. Nevertheless, wherever they lived and whatever type of fiction they wrote, the novelists are alike in some ways. Most are white and even though some started out poor, they are middle class in family background, education, and values, if not economic status. In general, only middle-class white women had both the education and motivation to write and the access to the publishing world necessary to get a novel printed and distributed. Most of these women reveal in their writings prejudices that modern readers will find as unsavory as child deathbed scenes. Some of the authors worked for social justice and seemed radical to their contemporaries, but they still believed in the superiority of whites (usually WASPs), men, married heterosexuals, and the upper and middle classes. We have not censored these biases in the selections, believing that the writers should be read and evaluated as they are.

Limitations of space have prevented us from including many writers we consider significant. It was necessary to excerpt certain novels, such as *St. Elmo, The Wide, Wide World,* and *Ruth Hall* (1855), because they are essential for an understanding of the period. For the space remaining we chose works like Sally Barrell Wood's *Dorval* (1801) and Metta Fuller Victor's *The Senator's Son* (1853) that are less well known but widely representative of their era. The fiction of the most famous writers of the time—Harriet Beecher Stowe, Louisa May Alcott, and Rebecca Harding Davis—is available elsewhere. Ideally, the growing interest in early literature by American women will lead to the reprinting or anthologizing of works by writers we regretfully omitted, writers such as Alice Cary, Martha Griffith Browne, Caroline Howard Gilman, Alice Bradley Neal Haven, Mary Jane Hawes Holmes, Charlotte A. Fillebrown Jerauld, Emily Chubbock Judson ("Fanny Forester"), Sara Clarke Lippincott ("Grace Greenwood"), Elizabeth Stuart Phelps and her daughter Elizabeth Stuart Phelps Ward, Ann Sophia Stephens, Elizabeth Drew Stoddard, and Mary Virginia Hawes Terhune ("Marion Harland"). The first novel known to have been written by an American black woman, *Our Nig* (1859) by Harriet E. Adams Wilson, was discovered after we had completed our manuscript or we would have included it; fortunately, it is available in an inexpensive edition.

Like everyone who has worked with nineteenth-century women's fiction, we have had some difficulty with our authors' names. A novelist like Augusta Jane Evans Wilson, who wrote her most important works before she married Wilson, would most reasonably be called Augusta Evans; but she is found in most biographical sources and literary histories under Wilson. What is one to do with the writer who adopted the pseudonym "Fanny Fern"? She collected a number of names, the full list being Grata Payson Sara Willis Eldredge Farrington Parton. We have chosen to keep the authors' married names, since these are most frequently used in bibliographic sources, but have also restored their family names—thus, Augusta Evans Wilson, Caroline Stansbury Kirkland. When a middle name has become an integral part of the name by which an author is known, we have kept it—thus, Lydia Maria Francis Child, Sarah Josepha Buell Hale. "Fanny Fern" becomes Sara (her preferred first name) Willis (family name) Parton (married name by which she is most often known).

Hidden Hands begins with an introduction that tries to set the novels in context for a survey course. We have attempted to relate them chronologically and thematically to the standard (male) American literary canon. More specific information about the novels and authors included may be found in the general introductions to each of the seven sections in the body of the volume: Early Didacticism: The Novel of Seduction; Melodrama; Frontier Romance; Satire and Humor; Early Realism; Later Didacticism: The Novel of Education; and Polemic: Slavery, Temperance, and Women's Rights. We are not completely satisfied with these terms since twentieth-century critics tend to exalt some types of literature, such as realism and satire, and devalue others, using "didactic" and "polemic" to denigrate socially conscious fiction. We were tempted to create our own less value-laden terms; however, we chose immediate intelligibility and kept to the designations most often used to characterize early American fiction. With the possible exception of the novel of seduction, we do not consider any form intrinsically superior or inferior.

For every author included in a section, we have provided a brief biographical sketch and a discussion of her novel against which the excerpts may be understood. Whenever possible, we have excerpted from the text of the first edition of the novel. To make the excerpts more readable, we have modified certain eighteenth-century practices to conform to modern usage. We have modernized the long-tailed s (f), used capitals and lower-case type for some words originally printed in all capitals, removed excessive quotation marks, and corrected obvious typographical errors. Otherwise, we have preserved individualities of spelling and punctuation. Omitted portions within paragraphs are indicated by ellipses and longer omissions by an entire line of dots.

At the end of the anthology we have included a representative selection from criticism of nineteenth-century women's fiction; these selections are intended to provide highlights of the criticism for students and teachers who need a quick overview. The bibliography that follows should help readers who want to pursue particular topics in greater depth.

Hidden Hands exists, in large part, because books like Helen Papashvily's *All the Happy Endings* and Baym's *Woman's Fiction* have intrigued their readers and shown the significance of early American women's fiction. We acknowledge our indebtedness to the critics who have kept this fiction alive and wish to credit the many authors included in the critical and bibliographic sections at the end of this volume. We owe particular thanks to Josephine Donovan for her efforts on behalf of this book. We have profited from the assistance of the staffs at the University of New Hampshire Library, the University of Louisville Library, and the Lilly Library of Indiana University. We are especially grateful to Theresa MacGregor, Jane Russell, Delinda Buie, and Elizabeth Elam.

Hidden Hands

Introduction

"An American novel is such a moral, sentimental thing, that it is enough to give any body the vapours to read one," complains a character in Hannah Webster Foster's *The Boarding School* (1798). American readers of the day were apparently willing to risk the vapours; even though they regularly purchased European works, they read American novels avidly. During the national period, Foster's *The Coquette* (1797), along with Susanna Haswell Rowson's *Charlotte, A Tale of Truth* (1794) and William Hill Brown's *The Power of Sympathy* (1789), headed the best-seller list. In 1870 Rowson's biographer, Elias Nason, could write of *Charlotte:*

> It has stolen its way alike into the study of the divine and into the workshop of the mechanic; into the parlor of the accomplished lady and the bed-chamber of her waiting maid; into the log-hut on the extreme border of modern civilization and into the forecastle of the whale ship on the lonely ocean. It has been read by the grey-bearded professor after his "divine Plato;" by the beardless clerk after balancing his accounts at night; by the traveler waiting for the next conveyance at the village inn; by the school girl stealthfully in her seat at school.*

Nason's account could be applied as well to many of the works represented in *Hidden Hands,* for they sold by the hundreds of thousands. In the 1820s James Fenimore Cooper's publisher explained that 6,500 copies was "the utmost limits to which the sale of a popular book can be pushed," but by the middle of the century books had become big business. According to Frank L. Mott in *Golden Multitudes*, the number of fictional works appearing each year had increased tenfold, and the sales kept pace. When Augusta Evans Wilson's *St. Elmo* was published in 1866, it quickly sold 300,000 copies; between 1860 and 1870 E. D. E. N. Southworth produced three novels that matched that record. Works by Rowson, Foster, Wilson, Southworth, Susan Warner, and Maria Cummins appear on Mott's list of "over-all best sellers," and those of Tabitha Gilman Tenney, Frances Miriam Berry Whitcher, Sarah Josepha Buell Hale, Lydia Maria Francis Child, Sara Willis Parton ("Fanny Fern"), and Metta Fuller Victor rank among the "better sellers." Warner's *The Wide, Wide World* (1850) was the first American novel to reach the million mark.

The success of these women in attracting readers and joining men on the best-seller lists did not put an end to the long-standing debate over whether women should write. In the 1850s Nathaniel Hawthorne shuddered at the thought of his wife as a "female author," and A. W. Abbot feared that "the appetite for bookmaking notoriety" might be

*Elias Nason, *A Memoir of Mrs. Susanna Rowson* (Albany, N.Y.: Joel Munsell, 1870), 50.

"alarmingly on the increase among our fair friends" (see Criticism section). The popular success of some women novelists made it easier, however, for others to pursue a writing career, and it also shifted the focus of the debate from whether women should write to what they should write. All the authors included in *Hidden Hands* were restricted in what they could write; they were limited, not only by their own conditioning or by the need to sell books and thus retain permission to write, but also by cultural conventions. In her 1860 essay "How Should Women Write?" (see Criticism section), Mary E. Bryan complains that men, "after much demur and hesitation, have given women liberty to write; but they cannot yet consent to allow them full freedom." Metaphysics, non-orthodox religion, the "great social and moral problems"—anything beyond the surface of life—is considered "unfeminine." "Having prescribed these bounds to the female pen," Bryan concludes, "men are the first to condemn her efforts as tame and commonplace, because they lack earnestness and strength."

But, despite the restrictions placed upon them, early women writers achieved something more than notoriety. The novel was for women the genre most adaptable to their experience, and if they wrote much "tame and commonplace" fiction, they also made solid contributions to the development of the American novel. In certain areas, most notably realism, women seem to have been the pioneers. It is impossible at this point, when there is no American literary history that gives equal consideration to women writers, to assess the full extent of women's achievement. Nor can we yet give definitive answers to such frequently asked questions as "Did women and men write differently? Did they have different styles or pursue different themes?" We do know that women generally wrote the same types of novels as men in the period 1790–1870; they entered every area except sea fiction. The gender separation that marks popular fiction of the twentieth century (e.g., male westerns, female gothics) did not then obtain, and the categories into which this anthology is divided apply to both men's and women's writings. Whether or not women wrote substantially differently within these genres, they did bring specifically female experiences to their fiction, and they focused on women, just as men writers focused on men. A brief overview of the categories shows some differences in perspective.

Beginning in the sentimental mode popularized in England by Samuel Richardson, the American novel told the story of a virtuous young woman falling prey to a rake who abandons her when she becomes pregnant. Men who employed the seduction theme—for example, William Hill Brown, probable author of *The Power of Sympathy,* and James Butler, author of *Fortune's Football* (1797)—tended to emphasize the rake; they portrayed the seduction as only one part of his total experience. Women writers built the entire novel on the seduction, the experience that alone would destroy the heroine's life. Rowson's *Charlotte, A Tale of Truth* and Foster's *The Coquette* show, respectively, the naive and the willful woman victimized by the egotistic, irresponsible man. These au-

thors, like their British and American counterparts of both sexes, justified the racy content of the novels by characterizing them as warnings
that would save young readers from immorality.

Gradually the need to diversify plots and the profusion of wild American landscapes available as settings fostered the introduction of fantastic and improbable events and produced the gothic or melodramatic
novel. Writers like Charles Brockden Brown, John Neal, Sally Barrell
Wood, Southworth, and Wilson introduced into their works acts of theft,
swindling, kidnapping, murder, and incest. They placed their characters
in the midst of storms, shipwrecks, fires, and floods and exposed them
to villains whose physical and psychological aberrations spelled terror.
The women novelists, breaking sharply the victimization pattern of the
seduction novel, enabled their heroines to escape countless dangers;
they were allowed to triumph over violent men and sometimes even to
reform them in the process. Aurelia in Wood's *Dorval* (1801), Capitola in
Southworth's *The Hidden Hand* (1859), and Edna in Wilson's *St. Elmo*
save themselves and other characters against overpowering odds. Men
writers varied in their treatment of women. In *Ormond* (1799) Brown
depicted Constantia as a tower of moral strength who ultimately kills
her attacker with a penknife. The women in other works are less fortunate; for instance, in Neal's *Logan, A Family History* (1822) one heroine
is raped and the other falls dead upon her lover's body after he is shot.

The bizarre incidents of the melodramas were, in some instances, no
more strange and unbelievable than the real occurrences of settlement
life. The frontier romance, represented in this volume by Ann Eliza
Schuyler Bleecker's *The History of Maria Kittle* (1791), Child's *Hobomok* (1824), and Catharine Maria Sedgwick's *Hope Leslie* (1827), describes the harshness of the wilderness. None of these writers achieved
the cumulative effect of Cooper's *The Leather-Stocking Tales*; yet their
novels compare favorably to individual Cooper works. All three demonstrate more effectively than Cooper the fear and helplessness frontier
women suffered, as well as the strength and endurance they developed.
Consequently, their women characters are more alive than Cooper's "females." Bleecker, Child, and Sedgwick also employed lifelike details in
the manner of their contemporaries Hale and Caroline Stansbury Kirkland, who were among the earliest American realists.

By the beginning of the nineteenth century, America had attained sufficient cultural development to sustain the satiric and comic modes. At
the turn of the century, Hugh Henry Brackenridge successfully brought
out several volumes of political satire entitled *Modern Chivalry* (1792,
1793, 1797). Tenney won acclaim for her *Female Quixotism* (1801),
which spoofed sentimental novels and novel readers. And later in the
1800s, Whitcher, Seba Smith, and A. B. Longstreet delighted the public
by ridiculing customs and pieties that had endured from an earlier age.
All these humorists, the women as well as the men, frequently treated
their female characters more harshly than the male, making them the
butt of cruel jokes. But Tenney, for one, was not simply making fun of

women when she subjected her mock-heroine to endless indignities before bringing her to her senses. Like Whitcher in a later era, she attacked
the romantic illusions and genteel posturing she considered harmful to
women.

The attention to specific details incorporated in satire, humor, and, to
some degree, frontier romance reflects the expansion of realism taking
place in the novel generally at the time. The exact descriptions of places
and events of everyday life presented in Hale's *Northwood* (1827) and
Kirkland's *A New Home—Who'll Follow?* (1839) have parallels in earlier
works by Brackenridge and Royall Tyler and the later *Miss Ravenel's
Conversion* (1867) by John De Forest. But while Brackenridge, Tyler, and
De Forest set their works in the public and political sectors, Hale and
Kirkland focused on the individual and the family in the local settings,
thereby anticipating the form of realism that arose later in the century
in the works of Rose Terry Cooke, Sarah Orne Jewett, and Mary E. Wilkins Freeman.

Realism pointed the novel in a serious and practical direction. By mid
century its content had changed dramatically, and the novel of education emerged as a major trend in fiction. Men writers continued to stress
excitement and adventure, but, influenced by Goethe's *Wilhelm Meister*
(1795–1796, translated into English by Thomas Carlyle in 1824), they
experimented with the *Bildungsroman*. Herman Melville, for example,
turned from the exotic adventure of *Typee* (1846) and *Omoo* (1847) to
the education of the young man in *Redburn* (1849) and *White Jacket*
(1850). Women writers produced the novel of education by the scores.
Their works, represented here by Warner's *The Wide, Wide World*, Cummins's *The Lamplighter* (1854), and Martha Finley's *Elsie Dinsmore*
(1867), treated major concerns of women's lives: developing strength of
character and religious belief, finding love and security, managing a
home, rearing children, and facing death and adversity. The didacticism
that pervades these works differs greatly from that of the earlier period.
Instead of the negative cautions embedded in the novel of seduction, the
new didacticism offered positive guidance. In the pages of education
novels, several generations of women found practical advice and role
models after which to pattern their lives.

This positive didacticism carried over into the polemical novels of the
period. From the 1830s to the 1860s America seethed with the spirit of
reform, and novelists reflected that fact in their works. Some authors,
like Hale, Caroline Lee Whiting Hentz, and the later Cooper, were openly
anti-reform. Of those novelists who were attracted by prospects for social change, the best known men writers held out little hope for success.
Hawthorne in *The Blithedale Romance* (1852) and Bayard Taylor in
Hannah Thurston (1867) explore various reforms, such as communal
living, spiritualism, and women's rights; they find the reformers lacking
and conclude that individual selfishness prevents any effective social
change. Both authors portray their "new women" as falling in love and
speedily giving up the feminist cause; Hawthorne's Zenobia commits

suicide out of unrequited love, and Taylor's Hannah makes a traditional marriage, promising to depend wholly on her husband.

Women novelists tended to be less pessimistic about social change. They dealt with specific issues, particularly slavery, temperance, and women's rights, and presented reformers in a more flattering light. In *Uncle Tom's Cabin* (1851) Harriet Beecher Stowe exposes the evils of the slave system, and in *Incidents in the Life of a Slave Girl* (1861) Harriet Brent Jacobs ("Linda Brent") shows in shocking detail the horrors of slavery as it affected black women. Victor in *The Senator's Son* (1853) ponders the effects of intemperance on the family and puts her faith in the Maine laws. Caroline Chesebro' in *Isa, A Pilgrimage* (1852) portrays a woman successfully liberating herself from both religious and social conventions, while Parton in *Ruth Hall* (1855) traces her heroine's battle for social and economic justice.

In all these works, women endure hardships and agonies as great as those Hawthorne and Taylor imposed on their characters. Yet the women writers allowed their characters to endure in dignity. The women were less ambivalent toward reform; perhaps, through the personal experience of injustice, they had come to view reform as an absolute necessity. Whatever the source of their positive spirit, it enabled women to write prolifically and to form a community of writers who encouraged one another and projected a vision only now beginning to be realized.

As the works excerpted in *Hidden Hands* chronicle the development of the American novel, they also embody most of the themes critics and teachers have identified as central to the American canon. The "standard" themes—America as the New Eden, the American dream, religion, friendship, and the individual versus society—were also major concerns of the women writers. Again, however, the women worked from a different perspective based on their varying experiences.

The New Eden, to which men and women felt themselves led by a benevolent Providence, had an ambivalent character for both. Although it offered opportunity for religious, political, and economic freedom, it was also a "howling wilderness." Men writers, while noting the dangers and privations, focused more than the women on the adventure in conquest of the wilds. Women writers, ever conscious of the threats posed by both natural and human elements, often treated the fearful aspects of the New Eden. Many saw the loneliness of the frontier as detrimental to women's life and health. Rowson, for example, depicts Charlotte Temple's months of isolation in an unpopulated region of New York as contributing to her death in childbirth. Tenney blames isolation on a country estate, along with the early death of her mother, for the romantic imbalance of Dorcasina. Whitcher attributes the provincialism, stupidity, and pettiness of the inhabitants of Wiggletown and Scrabble Hill to isolation from civilization; through both the Widow Bedott and Aunt Maguire, she ridicules the crudity of rural life. Even writers like Bleecker and Child, who describe the natural beauty of the wilderness, interrupt paradisiacal scenes with accounts of violence.

The individual freedoms promised by the New Eden, along with the personal autonomy and material success that have come to be known as the American dream, were more accessible to men than to women. For men, upward mobility according to the pattern of Benjamin Franklin seemed a simple matter of hard work and honesty, a natural formula. For women, the path was less sure. Confined to the home, they received neither the academic nor the practical education allowed to men. Moreover, they were subject to the authority of parents, husbands, brothers, or sons and seldom had an opportunity to seek advancement in "the world." While some rebels, like Parton, managed to gain freedom and success on their own, other women, like Warner, Hentz, and Southworth, could begin to pursue the American dream only through the necessity of supporting their families. Their version of the dream, even at its best, was more limited than the male version.

Having surmounted a variety of barriers in their own lives, the women writers put their female characters through similar encounters. Nearly all the writers represented here provide their characters with some form of education. Sometimes it results in their destruction, as with Charlotte Temple, who is led astray by her French teacher, or Dorcasina Sheldon, who under her father's tutelage reads history and romance but chooses the latter as a guide. More often, education, even though painful, provides the basis for a rise in life, as in the case of Warner's Ellen Montgomery, Cummins's Gerty Amory, and Finley's Elsie Dinsmore. Each of these characters grows mentally and morally stronger and is rewarded with a kind and well-fixed husband.

Still other characters move beyond conventional lives. In *The Hidden Hand* Southworth's Capitola gets her real education in the streets dressed as a boy. Circumventing those who seek to restrain her, she succeeds in helping the good and punishing the evil. Parton's Ruth Hall, like Capitola, educates herself in the real world; she learns the ins and outs of the publishing business and becomes a financial success. In Wilson's *St. Elmo*, Edna Earl, who receives a classical education from the local minister despite her guardian's fear that she will become a "blue stocking," uses her exceptional knowledge to become a successful writer and governess in New York. Her independence and strength enable her to convert her lover St. Elmo and direct him into the ministry. Chesebro's Isa does the opposite—she educates herself away from orthodox religion and leads her guardian's son to change his career from theology to medicine—but she also becomes influential and financially independent through her writings.

In exposing the barriers that threatened to keep their characters from achieving the autonomy and success associated with the American dream, women writers identified the harshest deterrent as white male domination. Some of the novelists allied themselves with the most conservative social forces and openly opposed women's rights; they would have been horrified at being viewed as "anti-men" in any way. Nevertheless, the most obvious common thread in late-eighteenth- and early-nineteenth-century novels by women is their negative portrayal of men. It is not only that men are usually the villains, the thieves and murderers, in the novels, or that the respectable "nice" men in novels like *St. Elmo, The Wide, Wide World, The Lamplighter,* and *Ruth Hall* try to exercise an arbitrary and unjust authority over the women. In addition, from seducers like Rowson's Montraville and Foster's Sanford, who leave their pregnant victims to die, to drunken husbands like Parke Madison of *The Senator's Son,* demonic masters like Dr. Flint in *Incidents in the Life of a Slave Girl,* or dominating fathers like Horace Dinsmore, men regularly engage in psychological and physical violence toward women.

In their struggle to throw off male domination, women in both life and literature were alternately aided and hampered by religion. Theology assisted them by providing stable rather than arbitrary authority to which they could appeal in endeavoring to protect themselves and their children from abuse. When lonely and frustrated, they could turn to the solace of prayer; when threatened or thwarted, they could point to religious ideals and count on fear of divine punishment to bring the oppressor into line. Through persistence in faith and principle, Edna brings St. Elmo into the ministry, Ellen Montgomery converts Abraham Van Brunt, and Elsie Dinsmore rescues her father from "damnation." Religion was also what turned "bad girls" into "good girls." Cummins's Gerty Amory changes from a demon child into a model of patience and piety. As a vengeful youth, she throws rocks through windows, but as an adult, she exhibits her strong will only to develop her own character, advance her career, serve others, or withstand the tyranny of those who would keep her from fulfilling her duty. This transformation is effected by the religious ideals she learns at the side of the blind Emily Graham. Prayers, kindness, and the gift of a Bible from Ellen Montgomery convert the urchin Nancy in *The Wide, Wide World.*

But religion was also woman's enemy. By fostering the patristic model of God as father, it taught the daughter that she must submit to her father in every instance. It set rigid boundaries for young women, demanding of them an ideal of chastity not expected of their brothers. It reminded wives that they were subject to their husbands in all things and supported the state by recognizing the passage of a woman's property to her husband after marriage. Ministers advised wives of cruel and abusive husbands to be patient, promising that God would care for them and their children, and blamed women if their husbands were unfaithful or drank excessively. Most of the women in the novels excerpted here suffer at some point because of religious principles in which they have been schooled. The most dramatic (or melodramatic) example is Elsie Dinsmore's fall from the piano bench when she is psychologically torn between what she sees as conflicting duties to her heavenly and earthly fathers.

Apart from the mixed blessings of religious faith, women's only solace in the male-dominated world of the novels is female friendship. If, as many critics have pointed out, male characters in American literature

tend to avoid women and bond with each other in pairs—Brackenridge's
Captain Farrago and Teague O'Regan, Cooper's Natty Bumppo and Chingachgook, and Melville's Tom and Toby—female characters also seek
same-sex relationships. Women writers often created communities of
women within their works. Friends like Harriot Stanly in Tenney's *Female Quixotism*, Esther Downing in Sedgwick's *Hope Leslie*, Alice
Humphreys in *The Wide, Wide World*, the blind Emily Graham in *The
Lamplighter*, the grandmother in Jacobs's *Incidents in the Life of a Slave
Girl*, and Mary Irving in Chesebro's *Isa* support the respective heroines,
enabling them to become their best selves. Problems in the women's
novels usually occur when, like Charlotte Temple, the heroine is too
isolated to have close female friends, or when she is separated from her
friends. Since most nineteenth-century women did not get to choose
their place of residence, separation often occurs; in novels such as Foster's *The Coquette*, Child's *Hobomok*, and Victor's *The Senator's Son*, it
helps precipitate a crisis in the heroine's life.

In the novels included in *Hidden Hands*, isolation and separation are
almost never presented in a positive light. Women's handling of the traditional individual-versus-society theme thus differs significantly from
men's. In many works by men writers the hero appears in a confronta-
tional stance vis-à-vis the social world: he is Cooper's Natty Bumppo
battling desperately to hold back civilization, Hawthorne's Miles Cover-
dale detaching himself from community ideals, or Melville's Ahab or
Pierre raising a fist in mad defiance. These characters view themselves
as outsiders pitted against a civilization that is frequently symbolized
by women. In novels by women the same situation is often portrayed but
with the values reversed; in other words, the female novelists also see
women as representing civilization, but the better part of civilization,
their obligation being to contain the violent individualism of the men
and build a peaceful community for all. While the women's heroines are
true, rather than self-created, outsiders, their goal is to get inside, to at-
tain a secure position in the social fabric whereby they can work to
change it.

Thus the phrase "individual versus society" would not have made
sense to most nineteenth-century women writers, or they would at the
least have interpreted it differently. Individual heroines have to challenge society as they make their way against cultural restrictions, but
with the possible exception of Chesebro's Isa, they are not against society per se. It is perhaps this fact that has made the novels seem conservative to many modern readers. One of the larger critical issues regarding nineteenth-century women's fiction is in fact whether it is
"conservative," advocating submission for women and conformity to
their gender roles, or covertly "radical," providing as Helen Papashvily
puts it in *All the Happy Endings*, "handbooks of . . . feminine revolt"
(see Criticism section). Both positions have been argued very persua-
sively, suggesting a problem with the terms of the debate. Nina Baym
notes in *Woman's Fiction* that the novels often end with a changed hero-

ine beginning "the reformation of the world immediately around her." Since this reformation is "primarily affectional and domestic," it does not seem radical in modern terms (p. 20). Neither, though, is it entirely conservative because the novelists imagined their heroines' affectional and domestic values transforming a mercenary, alienated, and impersonal society. They espoused a "cult of domesticity," Baym concludes, "but not as that cult is generally analyzed, as a conservative or traditional ethos" (p. 20).

After 1870 the novelists' plans for domesticating the world came to seem naive and be increasingly misunderstood. Later generations of women writers rejected nearly everything in the fiction of their predecessors. Like Edith Wharton, they criticized the "laxities" of the language (A Backward Glance, p. 51); like Ruth Suckow, a novelist of the 1920s and 1930s, they saw the novels as "dreary tales of submission" marred by the authors' "teachery Sunday school attitude" ("Literary Soubrettes," p. 517). The women who immediately followed the novelists in Hidden Hands, "local colorists" such as Jewett and Kate Chopin, quickly dropped the standard Cinderella plot. With Wharton, Willa Cather, Zora Neale Hurston, and other writers they worked to create new plots and new heroines who would be as unlike as possible the nineteenth-century "tomb of female virtue."

Nevertheless, American women novelists of the first eighty years did leave a legacy. The "hidden hands" not only prepared the way for future generations of women to be able to write and get published but they also bequeathed their moral vision. Later women writers, however much they might disassociate themselves from the narrow world of Warner, would seldom allow their heroines to reject "sivilization" in the manner of Twain's Huck Finn or pursue the American dream with the ruthless single-mindness of a Jay Gatsby. Instead they would criticize rampant individualism, violence, and industrial capitalism, which they too associated with men, and promote the same "female" values of social responsibility and cohesion, peace, and affectional and domestic life.

Early Didacticism
The Novel of Seduction

Susanna Haswell Rowson

THE AMERICAN NOVEL has its origin in the seduction novel appropriated from the British sentimental tradition of Samuel Richardson and
his followers. To make the sensational story of the "ruin" of an innocent
girl palatable to readers steeped in Puritan thought, early novelists emphasized the factual and educative nature of their works. Alexander
Cowie in *The Rise of the American Novel* says that didacticism was, in
fact, a *"sine qua non* of the early novel" (p. 17).

Susanna Rowson and Hannah Foster, both of whom treated the seduction theme, sought acceptance by claiming that their stories were based
on true experience. They also cautioned against the reading of novels.
In *Mentoria* (1791), Rowson questioned the value of an education in
which a young woman's head becomes "well stored with sensibility and
all the delicate feelings gleaned from a circulating library, the contents
of which she has eagerly and indiscriminately perused." Foster, in *The
Boarding School* (1798), recorded her conviction that "novels are the fa-
vourite, and the most dangerous kind of reading, now adopted by the
generality of young ladies." This moralistic approach disarmed critics
and prepared readers to view the novel as a source of valuable lessons.
Since many of the readers were thought to be young working women deprived of parental guidance while living away from home, the didactic
aspect of the seduction novel seemed highly beneficial.

Later readers have been more critical. According to Leslie Fiedler
in *Love and Death in the American Novel*, Americans "debased" the
Richardsonian tradition by transforming the seduction theme "into a
feminist attack upon the male, a symbolic castration of the oppressing
sex" (p. 61). Other critics have emphasized the negative view of women
implied by the seemingly easy victory of the seducer and the obligatory
punishment of the victim by death in childbirth. Certainly, women
novelists after Rowson and Foster treated seduction very differently; like
Sally Barrell Wood in *Dorval* (1801) and Catharine Maria Sedgwick in
Hope Leslie (1827), they created strong heroines who confound seducer
types.

The novels excerpted here—Rowson's *Charlotte, A Tale of Truth* (London 1791; Philadelphia 1794) and Foster's *The Coquette, or the History
of Eliza Wharton* (Boston 1797)—were two of the three most popular
novels published in America during the national period; they are also
the most readable of the early efforts.

Susanna Haswell Rowson (1762–1824)

Susanna Rowson was one of the most resourceful and versatile women in early American letters. She became, in turn, governess, novelist, actress, playwright, poet, songwriter, schoolmistress, editor, and essayist. Born in Portsmouth, England, to Susanna Margrove and Lieutenant William Haswell, she endured an unsettled childhood and youth. Her mother having died in childbirth, Rowson lived with relatives in England until 1768, when her father brought her to Nantasket, Massachusetts. In 1778 her first American stay ended when Haswell, a Loyalist, was forced to forfeit his property and return to England in poverty.

Educated in music, rhetoric, and the classics, Rowson became governess in the household of the duchess of Devonshire, a patron of the arts who encouraged her in her literary endeavors. Within a relatively short time Rowson published three novels: *Victoria* (1786), *The Inquisitor: or, Invisible Rambler* (1788), and *Mary: or, The Test of Honor* (1789). In 1787 she married William Rowson, a hardware merchant and friend of her father. William Rowson, a charming but ineffectual person, soon failed in business. To support her family, which by this time included her husband's sister and his illegitimate child, Rowson continued to write. In 1791 she published her most successful novel, *Charlotte, A Tale of Truth*, printed in America three years later and popularized as *Charlotte Temple*. *Mentoria*, a volume of advice to young women, and *Rebecca, Fille de Chambre*, a semi-autobiographical novel, appeared in 1792.

For a short time the Rowsons worked with an English theatrical troupe. When the company dissolved, they came to America, where, from 1793 to 1797, they performed in various theaters in the East. During this period, Rowson composed songs and wrote and adapted plays, most of which incorporated patriotic and feminist themes. Her *Slaves in Algiers* (1794) became a popular stock piece. At the close of her theatrical career, Rowson opened a school near Boston. There, from 1797 until 1822, she taught young women "the common branches" as well as "embroiderie, geography and musicke." During her years as an educator, Rowson completed textbooks in geography, history, Bible studies, and spelling. She also served as contributing editor to the *Boston Weekly Magazine* and wrote for the *Monthly Anthology* and the *New England Galaxy*. She continued publishing novels and poetry, completing in her lifetime twenty-four books and plays. Her last novel, *Charlotte's Daughter*, was published posthumously in 1828. As Dorothy Weil (see Selected Bibliography) remarks, Rowson "seems to have been perpetually in motion" (p. 5) and to have "created a literary self that served as both model and mentor for her readers" (p. 10).

Selected Bibliography

OTHER WORKS
Trials of the Human Heart (1795); *Reuben and Rachel: or, Tales of Old Times* (1798); *Sarah, or the Exemplary Wife* (1804).

SECONDARY
McGrath, Kathleen Conway. "Popular Literature as Social Reinforcement: The Case of *Charlotte Temple*." In *Images of Women in Fiction*, edited by Susan Koppelman Cornillon, 21–27. Bowling Green, Ohio: Bowling Green University Popular Press, 1972.
Martin, Wendy. "Profile: Susanna Rowson, Early American Novelist." *Women's Studies* 2, no. 1 (1974): 1–8.
Nason, Elias. *A Memoir of Mrs. Susanna Rowson*. Albany, N.Y.: Joel Munsell, 1870.
Parker, Patricia L. "*Charlotte Temple*: America's First Best Seller." *Studies in Short Fiction* 13 (Fall 1976): 518–520.
Vail, R. W. G. *Susanna Haswell Rowson, the Author of Charlotte Temple*. Worcester: American Antiquarian Society, 1933.
Weil, Dorothy. *In Defense of Women: Susanna Rowson (1762–1824)*. University Park, Pa. and London: Pennsylvania State University Press, 1976.

Charlotte, A Tale of Truth (1794)

Charlotte, A Tale of Truth, Susanna Rowson's greatest achievement, was America's first best seller. In 1812 the American publisher Matthew Carey wrote to Rowson: "Charlotte Temple is by far the most popular and in my opinion the most useful novel ever published in this country and probably not inferior to any published in England." To date, *Charlotte* has gone through over 200 editions; at the middle of this century, it had sold more copies than any other novel in the history of American fiction.

While critics generally agree on the novel's historical significance, they disagree about the reasons for its success. Certainly some of its appeal came from the racy nature of the material. One unauthorized edition billed Charlotte as "the Fastest Girl in New York." Leslie Fiedler (*Love and Death in the American Novel*), who disparages *Charlotte*, attributes its success to "the bare bones of plot," claiming that it embodies "in its essential form the myth or archetype of seduction as adapted to the needs of the American female audience" (p. 68). Other critics, such as Alexander Cowie (*The Rise of the American Novel*), find value in *Charlotte*'s basic "sincerity and power" (p. 14).

Rowson professed a moral intent. In the preface she expresses the hope that her insights will benefit "the many daughters of Misfortune who, deprived of natural friends, or spoilt by a mistaken education, are thrown on an unfeeling world without the least power to defend themselves from the snares not only of the other sex, but from the more dangerous arts of the profligate of their own." The excerpts that follow illustrate Rowson's ability to write the didactic novel at its best/worst, to temper the account with a realism that gives the novel strength and direction, and to justify the depiction of a wide-ranging immorality by presenting it under the guise of preventing evil.

Other elements besides the didactic added to *Charlotte*'s appeal. As Constance Rourke points out in *The Roots of American Culture*, Rowson was a serious writer who turned out "one sentimental novel after another in an easy style that must have cost her some effort, none of them without some touch of originality, all of them with a [feminist] bias" (p. 79). Although the feminist touch is stronger in Rowson's plays and other later works, it is present in *Charlotte*. It shows up in the narrator's obvious sympathy for Charlotte and in the inclusion of many instances illustrating the precariousness of woman's plight in a male-dominated society.

Rowson's greatest achievement lies in the creation of the central characters. Charlotte, like the heroines of most seduction novels, is a model of beauty and goodness. She also displays intelligence, a certain ingenuity, and some assertiveness. Even so, she fails because of inexperience and lack of guidance. Montraville, her seducer, is more complex than the general run of his type. He does not make a career of seduction. He suffers pangs of conscience from time to time when he considers Charlotte's plight, and he shows sincere remorse when he learns of her death. Belcour, Montraville's companion and sometime friend, and La Rue, Charlotte's teacher and traveling companion, are stereotyped vice figures, but La Rue fills a special role on the didactic level. In Chapter VII the narrator explains La Rue's motivation: "once a woman has stifled the sense of shame in her own bosom, when once she has lost sight of the basis on which reputation, honor, everything that should be dear to the female heart rests, she grows hardened in guilt and will spare no pains to bring down innocence and beauty to the shocking level with herself." If seeing Charlotte's sufferings does not dissuade young readers from danger, surely the prospect of becoming like La Rue should do so. The use of such didactic techniques, combined with the excitement of the seduction theme, assured Rowson of a continuous readership.

Rowson claims to have learned the story of Charlotte from an old woman who knew her. Since at least 1845, a tombstone in Trinity Churchyard in New York has borne Charlotte's name. As Carl Van Doren points out, however, the grave probably contains the ashes of Charlotte Stanley, whom Colonel John Montrésor, Rowson's cousin, seduced from her home in England and deserted in New York (*The American Novel, 1789–1939*, pp. 8– 9).

The story opens in England in 1774, where Charlotte, an only child of fifteen, is attending Madame Du Pont's boarding school. There she comes under the influence of a French teacher, Mademoiselle La Rue, who betrays her into the power of Montraville, a soldier about to embark for America with his friend Belcour.

CHAPTER IX
We Know not What a Day May Bring Forth.

Various were the sensations which agitated the mind of Charlotte, during the day preceding the evening in which she was to meet Montraville. Several times did she almost resolve to go to her governess, show her the letter, and be guided by her advice: but Charlotte had taken one step in the ways of imprudence; and when that is once done, there are always innumerable obstacles to prevent the erring person returning to the path of rectitude: yet these obstacles, however forcible they may appear in general, exist chiefly in imagination.

Charlotte feared the anger of her governess: she loved her mother, and the very idea of incurring her displeasure, gave her the greatest uneasiness: but there was a more forcible reason still remaining: should she show the letter to Madame Du Pont, she must confess the means by

Charlotte, A Tale of Truth, 2 vols. in 1 (Philadelphia: Printed by D. Humphries for M. Carey, 1794), 170 pp. Excerpts are taken from 1: 49–65; 2: 72–81.

which it came into her possession; and what would be the consequence? Mademoiselle would be turned out of doors.

"I must not be ungrateful," said she. "La Rue is very kind to me; besides I can, when I see Montraville, inform him of the impropriety of our continuing to see or correspond with each other, and request him to come no more to Chichester."

However prudent Charlotte might be in these resolutions, she certainly did not take a proper method to confirm herself in them. Several times in the course of the day, she indulged herself in reading over the letter, and each time she read it, the contents sunk deeper in her heart. As evening drew near, she caught herself frequently consulting her watch. "I wish this foolish meeting was over," said she, by way of apology to her own heart, "I wish it was over; for when I have seen him, and convinced him my resolution is not to be shaken, I shall feel my mind much easier."

The appointed hour arrived. Charlotte and Mademoiselle eluded the eye of vigilance; and Montraville, who had waited their coming with impatience, received them with rapturous and unbounded acknowledgments for their condescension: he had wisely brought Belcour with him to entertain Mademoiselle, while he enjoyed an uninterrupted conversation with Charlotte.

Belcour was a man whose character might be comprised in a few words; and as he will make some figure in the ensuing pages, I shall here describe him. He possessed a genteel fortune, and had a liberal education; dissipated, thoughtless, and capricious, he paid little regard to the moral duties, and less to religious ones: eager in the pursuit of pleasure, he minded not the miseries he inflicted on others, provided his own wishes, however extravagant, were gratified. Self, darling self, was the idol he worshipped, and to that he would have sacrificed the interest and happiness of all mankind. Such was the friend of Montraville: will not the reader be ready to imagine, that the man who could regard such a character, must be actuated by the same feelings, follow the same pursuits, and be equally unworthy with the person to whom he thus gave his confidence?

But Montraville was a different character: generous in his disposition, liberal in his opinions, and good-natured almost to a fault; yet eager and impetuous in the pursuit of a favorite object, he staid not to reflect on the consequence which might follow the attainment of his wishes; with a mind ever open to conviction, had he been so fortunate as to possess a friend who would have pointed out the cruelty of endeavouring to gain the heart of an innocent artless girl, when he knew it was utterly impossible for him to marry her, and when the gratification of his passion would be unavoidable infamy and misery to her, and a cause of never-ceasing remorse to himself: had these dreadful consequences been placed before him in a proper light, the humanity of his nature would have urged him to give up the pursuit: but Belcour was not this friend; he rather encouraged the growing passion of Montraville; and being pleased

with the vivacity of Mademoiselle, resolved to leave no argument un-
tried, which he thought might prevail on her to be the companion of
their intended voyage; and he made no doubt but her example, added to
the rhetoric of Montraville, would persuade Charlotte to go with them.

Charlotte had, when she went out to meet Montraville, flattered herself that her resolution was not to be shaken, and that, conscious of the
impropriety of her conduct in having a clandestine intercourse with a
stranger, she would never repeat the indiscretion.

But alas! poor Charlotte, she knew not the deceitfulness of her own
heart, or she would have avoided the trial of her stability.

Montraville was tender, eloquent, ardent, and yet respectful. "Shall I
not see you once more," said he, "before I leave England? will you not
bless me by an assurance, that when we are divided by a vast expanse of
sea I shall not be forgotten?"

Charlotte sighed.

"Why that sigh, my dear Charlotte? could I flatter myself that a fear
for my safety, or a wish for my welfare occasioned it, how happy would
it make me."

"I shall ever wish you well, Montraville," said she; "but we must meet
no more."

"Oh say not so, my lovely girl: reflect, that when I leave my native
land, perhaps a few short weeks may terminate my existence; the perils
of the ocean—the dangers of war—"

"I can hear no more," said Charlotte in a tremulous voice. "I must
leave you."

"Say you will see me once again."

"I dare not," said she.

"Only for one half hour to-morrow evening: 'tis my last request. I
shall never trouble you again, Charlotte."

"I know not what to say," cried Charlotte, struggling to draw her
hands from him: "let me leave you now."

"And you will come to-morrow," said Montraville.

"Perhaps I may," said she.

"Adieu then. I will live upon that hope till we meet again."

He kissed her hand. She signed an adieu, and catching hold of Mademoiselle's arm, hastily entered the garden gate.

CHAPTER X

When We Have Excited Curiosity, It Is But an Act of Good Nature to Gratify It.

Montraville was the youngest son of a gentleman of fortune, whose family being numerous, he was obliged to bring up his sons to genteel professions, by the exercise of which they might hope to raise themselves
into notice.

.   .   .   .

When Montraville chose the profession of arms, his father presented him with a commission, and made him a handsome provision for his private purse. "Now, my boy," said he, "go! seek glory in the field of battle. You have received from me all I shall ever have it in my power to bestow: it is certain I have interest to gain you promotion; but be assured that interest shall never be exerted, unless by your future conduct you deserve it. Remember, therefore, your success in life depends entirely on yourself. There is one thing I think it my duty to caution you against: the precipitancy with which young men frequently rush into matrimonial engagements, and by their thoughtlessness draw many a deserving woman into scenes of poverty and distress. A soldier has no business to think of a wife till his rank is such as to place him above the fear of bringing into the world a train of helpless innocents, heirs only to penury and affliction. If, indeed, a woman, whose fortune is sufficient to preserve you in that state of independence I would teach you to prize, should generously bestow herself on a young soldier, whose chief hope of future prosperity depended on his success in the field—if such a woman should offer—every barrier is removed, and I should rejoice in an union which would promise so much felicity. But mark me, boy, if, on the contrary, you rush into a precipitate union with a girl of little or no fortune, take the poor creature from a comfortable home and kind friends, and plunge her into all the evils a narrow income and increasing family can inflict, I will leave you to enjoy the blessed fruits of your rashness; for by all that is sacred, neither my interest or fortune shall ever be exerted in your favour. I am serious," continued he, "therefore imprint this conversation on your memory, and let it influence your future conduct. . . ."

As this conversation passed but a few hours before Montraville took leave of his father, it was deeply impressed on his mind: when, therefore, Belcour came with him to the place of assignation with Charlotte, he directed him to enquire of the French woman what were Miss Temple's expectations in regard to fortune.

Mademoiselle informed him, that though Charlotte's father possessed a genteel independence, it was by no means probable that he could give his daughter more than a thousand pounds; and in case she did not marry to his liking, it was possible he might not give her a single *sous*; nor did it appear the least likely, that Mr. Temple would agree to her union with a young man on the point of embarking for the seat of war.

Montraville therefore concluded it was impossible he should ever marry Charlotte Temple; and what end he proposed to himself by continuing the acquaintance he had commenced with her, he did not at that moment give himself time to enquire.

CHAPTER XI
Conflict of Love and Duty.

Almost a week was now gone, and Charlotte continued every evening to meet Montraville, and in her heart every meeting was resolved to be the last; but alas! when Montraville at parting would earnestly intreat one more interview, that treachcrous heart betrayed her; and, forgetful of its resolution, pleaded the cause of the enemy so powerfully, that Charlotte was unable to resist. Another and another meeting succeeded; and so well did Montraville improve each opportunity, that the heedless girl at length confessed no idea could be so painful to her as that of never seeing him again.

"Then we will never be parted," said he.

"Ah, Montraville," replied Charlotte, forcing a smile, "how can it be avoided? My parents would never consent to our union; and even could they be brought to approve it, how should I bear to be separated from my kind, my beloved mother?"

"Then you love your parents more than you do me, Charlotte?"

"I hope I do," said she, blushing and looking down, "I hope my affection for them will ever keep me from infringing the laws of filial duty."

"Well, Charlotte," said Montraville gravely, and letting go her hand, "since that is the case, I find I have deceived myself with fallacious hopes. I had flattered my fond heart, that I was dearer to Charlotte than any thing in the world beside. I thought that you would for my sake have braved the dangers of the ocean, that you would, by your affection and smiles, have softened the hardships of war, and, had it been my fate to fall, that your tenderness would chear the hour of death, and smooth my passage to another world. But farewel, Charlotte! I see you never loved me. I shall now welcome the friendly ball that deprives me of the sense of my misery."

"Oh stay, unkind Montraville," cried she, catching hold of his arm, as he pretended to leave her, "stay and calm your fears. I will here protest that was it not for the fear of giving pain to the best of parents, and returning their kindness with ingratitude, I would follow you through every danger, and in studying to promote your happiness, insure my own. But I cannot break my mother's heart, Montraville; I must not bring the grcy hairs of my doating grand-father with sorrow to the grave, or make my beloved father perhaps curse the hour that gave me birth." She covered her face with her hands, and burst into tears.

"All these distressing scenes, my dear Charlotte," cried Montraville, "are merely the chimeras of a disturbed fancy. Your parents might perhaps grieve at first; but when they heard from your own hand that you was with a man of honour, and that it was to insure your felicity by an union with him, to which you feared they would never have given their assent, that you left their protection, they will, be assured, forgive an error which love alone occasioned, and when we return from America, receive you with open arms and tears of joy."

Belcour and Mademoiselle heard this last speech, and conceiving it a proper time to throw in their advice and persuasions, approached Charlotte, and so well seconded the entreaties of Montraville, that finding Mademoiselle intended going with Belcour, and feeling her own treacherous heart too much inclined to accompany them, the hapless Charlotte, in an evil hour, consented that the next evening they should bring a chaise to the end of the town, and that she would leave her friends, and throw herself entirely on the protection of Montraville.

"But should you," said she, looking earnestly at him, her eyes full of tears, "should you, forgetful of your promises, and repenting the engagements you here voluntarily enter into, forsake and leave me on a foreign shore—"

"Judge not so meanly of me," said he. "The moment we reach our place of destination, Hymen[1] shall sanctify our love; and when I shall forget your goodness, may heaven forget me."

"Ah," said Charlotte, leaning on Mademoiselle's arm as they walked up the garden together, "I have forgot all that I ought to have remembered, in consenting to this intended elopement."

"You are a strange girl," said Mademoiselle; "You never know your own mind two minutes at a time. Just now you declared Montraville's happiness was what you prized most in the world; and now I suppose you repent having insured that happiness by agreeing to accompany him abroad."

"Indeed I do repent," replied Charlotte, "from my soul: but while discretion points out the impropriety of my conduct, inclination urges me on to ruin."

"Ruin! fiddlestick!" said Mademoiselle; "am not I going with you? and do I feel any of these qualms?"

"You do not renounce a tender father and mother," said Charlotte.

"But I hazard my dear reputation," replied Mademoiselle, bridling.

"True," replied Charlotte, "but you do not feel what I do." She then bade her good night: but sleep was a stranger to her eyes, and the tear of anguish watered her pillow.

CHAPTER XII

Nature's last, best gift:
Creature in whom excell'd, whatever could
To fight or thought be nam'd!
Holy, divine! good, amiable, and sweet!
How thou art fall'n.!—

When Charlotte left her restless bed, her languid eye and pale cheek discovered to Madame Du Pont the little repose she had tasted.

1. The Greek god of marriage.

"My dear child," said the affectionate governess, "what is the cause of the languor so apparent in your frame? Are you not well?"

"Yes, my dear Madam, very well," replied Charlotte, attempting to smile, "but I know not how it was; I could not sleep last night, and my spirits are depressed this morning."

"Come chear up, my love," said the governess; "I believe I have brought a cordial to revive them. I have just received a letter from your good mama, and here is one for yourself."

Charlotte hastily took the letter: it contained these words—

"As to-morrow is the anniversary of the happy day that gave my beloved girl to the anxious wishes of a maternal heart, I have requested your governess to let you come home and spend it with us; and as I know you to be a good affectionate child, and make it your study to improve in those branches of education which you know will give most pleasure to your delighted parents, as a reward for your diligence and attention I have prepared an agreeable surprise for your reception. Your grand-father, eager to embrace the darling of his aged heart, will come in the chaise for you; so hold yourself in readiness to attend him by nine o'clock. Your dear father joins in every tender wish for your health and future felicity, which warms the heart of my dear Charlotte's affectionate mother,

L. Temple."

"Gracious heaven!" cried Charlotte, forgetting where she was, and raising her streaming eyes as in earnest supplication.

Madame Du Pont was surprised. "Why these tears, my love?" said she. "Why this seeming agitation? I thought the letter would have rejoiced, instead of distressing you."

"It does rejoice me," replied Charlotte endeavouring at composure, "but I was praying for merit to deserve the unremitted attentions of the best of parents."

"You do right," said Madame Du Pont, "to ask the assistance of heaven that you may continue to deserve their love. Continue, my dear Charlotte, in the course you have ever pursued, and you will insure at once their happiness and your own."

"Oh!" cried Charlotte, as her governess left her, "I have forfeited both for ever! Yet let me reflect:—the irrevocable step is not yet taken: it is not too late to recede from the brink of a precipice, from which I can only behold the dark abyss of ruin, shame, and remorse!"

She arose from her seat, and flew to the apartment of La Rue. "Oh Mademoiselle!" said she, "I am snatched by a miracle from destruction! This letter has saved me: it has opened my eyes to the folly I was so near committing. I will not go, Mademoiselle; I will not wound the hearts of those dear parents who make my happiness the whole study of their lives."

"Well," said Mademoiselle, "do as you please, Miss; but pray understand that my resolution is taken, and it is not in your power to alter it. I

shall meet the gentlemen at the appointed hour, and shall not be sur-
prized at any outrage which Montraville may commit, when he finds
himself disappointed. Indeed I should not be astonished, was he to come
immediately here, and reproach you for your instability in the hearing of
the whole school: and what will be the consequence? you will bear the
odium of having formed the resolution of eloping, and every girl of spirit
will laugh at your want of fortitude to put it in execution, while prudes
and fools will load you with reproach and contempt. You will have lost
the confidence of your parents, incurred their anger, and the scoffs of the
world; and what fruit do you expect to reap from this piece of heroism,
(for such no doubt you think it is?) you will have the pleasure to reflect,
that you have deceived the man who adores you, and whom in your heart
you prefer to all other men, and that you are separated from him for ever."

This eloquent harangue was given with such volubility, that Charlotte
could not find an opportunity to interrupt her, or to offer a single word
till the whole was finished, and then found her ideas so confused, that
she knew not what to say.

At length she determined that she would go with Mademoiselle to the
place of assignation, convince Montraville of the necessity of adhering
to the resolution of remaining behind; assure him of her affection, and
bid him adieu.

Charlotte formed this plan in her mind, and exulted in the certainty of
its success. "How shall I rejoice," said she, "in this triumph of reason
over inclination, and, when in the arms of my affectionate parents, lift
up my soul in gratitude to heaven as I look back on the dangers I have
escaped!"

The hour of assignation arrived: Mademoiselle put what money and
valuables she possessed in her pocket, and advised Charlotte to do the
same; but she refused; "my resolution is fixed," said she; "I will sacrifice love to duty."

Mademoiselle smiled internally; and they proceeded softly down the
back stairs and out of the garden gate. Montraville and Belcour were
ready to receive them.

"Now," said Montraville, taking Charlotte in his arms, "you are mine
for ever."

"No," said she, withdrawing from his embrace, "I am come to take an
everlasting farewel."

It would be useless to repeat the conversation that here ensued; suf-
fice it to say, that Montraville used every argument that had formerly
been successful, Charlotte's resolution began to waver, and he drew her
almost imperceptibly towards the chaise.

"I cannot go," said she: "cease, dear Montraville, to persuade. I must
not: religion, duty, forbid."

"Cruel Charlotte," said he, "if you disappoint my ardent hopes, by all
that is sacred, this hand shall put a period to my existence. I cannot—
will not live without you."

"Alas! my torn heart!" said Charlotte, "how shall I act?"

"Let me direct you," said Montraville, lifting her into the chaise.

"Oh! my dear forsaken parents!" cried Charlotte.

The chaise drove off. She shrieked, and fainted into the arms of her betrayer.

After their arrival in America, Charlotte languishes under Montraville's erratic attentions. Montraville regrets having seduced Charlotte, but he does not consider marrying her since that would mean losing his father's financial support. Instead, he sets Charlotte up in a country house and allows the perfidious Belcour, who wants Charlotte for himself, to convince him that she is unfaithful. Montraville then abandons Charlotte and marries a beautiful and wealthy American woman. When she is evicted from her residence, Charlotte appeals to La Rue (now the rich Mrs. Crayton) for help. La Rue orders her servant, John, to throw Charlotte out, but John takes her to his house, where Charlotte gives birth to her daughter.

In the following excerpt, a benefactor, Mrs. Beauchamp, reunites the dying Charlotte with her father, and Montraville and Belcour are duly punished. Later, La Rue also receives an appropriate chastisement. Separated from her wealthy husband, she engages in dissipation and suffers poverty and imprisonment. Shortly before her death she acknowledges the justness of her punishment to Charlotte's parents, who come upon her ill and starving on a street in London.

VOL. II

CHAPTER XXXIII

Which People Void of Feeling Need not Read.

When Mrs. Beauchamp entered the apartment of the poor sufferer, she started back with horror. On a wretched bed, without hangings and but poorly supplied with covering, lay the emaciated figure of what still retained the semblance of a lovely woman, though sickness had so altered her features that Mrs. Beauchamp had not the least recollection of her person. In one corner of the room stood a woman washing, and, shivering over a small fire, two healthy but half naked children; the infant was asleep beside its mother, and, on a chair by the bed side, stood a porrenger and wooden spoon, containing a little gruel, and a tea-cup with about two spoonfulls of wine in it. Mrs. Beauchamp had never before beheld such a scene of poverty; she shuddered involuntarily, and exclaiming—"heaven preserve us!" leaned on the back of a chair ready to sink to the earth. The doctor repented having so precipitately brought her into this affecting scene; but there was no time for apologies: Charlotte caught the sound of her voice, and starting almost out of bed, exclaimed—"Angel of peace and mercy, art thou come to deliver me? Oh, I know you are, for whenever you was near me I felt eased of half my sor-

rows; but you don't know me, nor can I, with all the recollection I am mistress of, remember your name just now, but I know that benevolent countenance, and the softness of that voice which has so often comforted the wretched Charlotte."

Mrs. Beauchamp had, during the time Charlotte was speaking, seated herself on the bed and taken one of her hands; she looked at her attentively, and at the name of Charlotte she perfectly conceived the whole shocking affair. A faint sickness came over her. "Gracious heaven," said she, "is this possible?" and bursting into tears, she reclined the burning head of Charlotte on her own bosom; and folding her arms about her, wept over her in silence. "Oh," said Charlotte, "you are very good to weep thus for me: it is a long time since I shed a tear for myself: my head and heart are both on fire, but these tears of your's seem to cool and refresh it. Oh now I remember you said you would send a letter to my poor father: do you think he ever received it? or perhaps you have brought me an answer: why don't you speak, Madam? Does he say I may go home? Well he is very good; I shall soon be ready."

She then made an effort to get out of bed; but being prevented, her frenzy again returned, and she raved with the greatest wildness and incoherence. Mrs. Beauchamp, finding it was impossible for her to be removed, contented herself with ordering the apartment to be made more comfortable, and procuring a proper nurse for both mother and child; and having learnt the particulars of Charlotte's fruitless application to Mrs. Crayton from honest John, she amply rewarded him for his benevolence, and returned home with a heart oppressed with many painful sensations, but yet rendered easy by the reflexion that she had performed her duty towards a distressed fellow-creature.

Early the next morning she again visited Charlotte, and found her tolerably composed; she called her by name, thanked her for her goodness, and when her child was brought to her, pressed it in her arms, wept over it, and called it the offspring of disobedience. Mrs. Beauchamp was delighted to see her so much amended, and begun to hope she might recover, and, spite of her former errors, become an useful and respectable member of society; but the arrival of the doctor put an end to these delusive hopes: he said nature was making her last effort, and a few hours would most probably consign the unhappy girl to her kindred dust.

Being asked how she found herself, she replied—"Why better, much better, doctor. I hope now I have but little more to suffer. I had last night a few hours sleep, and when I awoke recovered the full power of recollection. I am quite sensible of my weakness; I feel I have but little longer to combat with the shafts of affliction. I have an humble confidence in the mercy of him who died to save the world, and trust that my sufferings in this state of mortality, joined to my unfeigned repentance, through his mercy, have blotted my offences from the sight of my offended maker. I have but one care—my poor infant! Father of mercy," continued she, raising her eyes, "of thy infinite goodness, grant that the sins of the parent be not visited on the unoffending child. May those who taught me to despise thy laws be forgiven; lay not my offences to their charge, I beseech thee and oh! shower the choicest of thy blessings on those whose pity has soothed the afflicted heart, and made easy even the bed of pain and sickness."

She was exhausted by this fervent address to the throne of mercy, and though her lips still moved her voice became inarticulate: she lay for some time as it were in a dose, and then recovering, faintly pressed Mrs. Beauchamp's hand, and requested that a clergyman might be sent for.

On his arrival she joined fervently in the pious office, frequently mentioning her ingratitude to her parents as what lay most heavy at her heart. When she had performed the last solemn duty, and was preparing to lie down, a little bustle on the outside door occasioned Mrs. Beauchamp to open it, and enquire the cause. A man in appearance about forty, presented himself, and asked for Mrs. Beauchamp.

"That is my name, Sir," said she.

"Oh then, my dear Madam," cried he, "tell me where I may find my poor, ruined, but repentant child."

Mrs. Beauchamp was surprised and affected; she knew not what to say; she foresaw the agony this interview would occasion Mr. Temple, who had just arrived in search of his Charlotte, and yet was sensible that the pardon and blessing of her father would soften even the agonies of death to the daughter.

She hesitated. "Tell me, Madam," cried he wildly, "tell me, I beseech thee, does she live? shall I see my darling once again? Perhaps she is in this house. Lead, lead me to her, that I may bless her, and then lie down and die."

The ardent manner in which he uttered these words occasioned him to raise his voice. It caught the ear of Charlotte: she knew the beloved sound: and uttering a loud shriek, she sprang forward as Mr. Temple entered the room. "My adored father." "My long lost child." Nature could support no more, and they both sunk lifeless into the arms of the attendants.

Charlotte was again put into bed, and a few moments restored Mr. Temple: but to describe the agony of his sufferings is past the power of any one, who, though they may readily conceive, cannot delineate the dreadful scene. Every eye gave testimony of what each heart felt—but all were silent.

When Charlotte recovered, she found herself supported in her father's arms. She cast on him a most expressive look, but was unable to speak. A reviving cordial was administered. She then asked, in a low voice, for her child: it was brought to her: she put it in her father's arms. "Protect her," said she, "and bless your dying—"

Unable to finish the sentence, she sunk back on her pillow: her countenance was serenely composed; she regarded her father as he pressed the infant to his breast with a steadfast look; a sudden beam of joy passed across her languid features, she raised her eyes to heaven—and then closed them for ever.

CHAPTER XXXIV
Retribution.

In the mean time Montraville having received orders to return to New-York, arrived, and having still some remains of compassionate tenderness for the woman whom he regarded as brought to shame by himself, he went out in search of Belcour, to enquire whether she was safe, and whether the child lived. He found him immersed in dissipation, and could gain no other intelligence than that Charlotte had left him, and that he knew not what was become of her.

"I cannot believe it possible," said Montraville, "that a mind once so pure as Charlotte Temple's, should so suddenly become the mansion of vice. Beware, Belcour," continued he, "beware if you have dared to behave either unjustly or dishonourably to that poor girl, your life shall pay the forfeit:—I will revenge her cause."

He immediately went into the country, to the house where he had left Charlotte. It was desolate. After much enquiry he at length found the servant girl who had lived with her. From her he learnt the misery Charlotte had endured from the complicated evils of illness, poverty, and a broken heart, and that she had set out on foot for New-York, on a cold winter's evening; but she could inform him no further.

Tortured almost to madness by this shocking account, he returned to the city, but, before he reached it, the evening was drawing to a close. In entering the town he was obliged to pass several little huts, the residence of poor women who supported themselves by washing the cloaths of the officers and soldiers. It was nearly dark: he heard from a neighbouring steeple a solemn toll that seemed to say some poor mortal was going to their last mansion: the sound struck on the heart of Montraville, and he involuntarily stopped, when, from one of the houses, he saw the appearance of a funeral. Almost unknowing what he did, he followed at a small distance; and as they let the coffin into the grave, he enquired of a soldier, who stood by, and had just brushed off a tear that did honour to his heart, who it was that was just buried. "An please your honour," said the man, " 'tis a poor girl that was brought from her friends by a cruel man, who left her when she was big with child, and married another." Montraville stood motionless, and the man proceeded—"I met her myself not a fortnight since one night all wet and cold in the streets; she went to Madam Crayton's, but she would not take her in, and so the poor thing went raving mad." Montraville could bear no more; he struck his hands against his forehead with violence; and exclaiming "poor murdered Charlotte!" ran with precipitation towards the place where they were heaping the earth on her remains. "Hold, hold, one moment," said he. "Close not the grave of the injured Charlotte Temple till I have taken vengeance on her murderer."

"Rash young man," said Mr. Temple, "who art thou that thus disturbest the last mournful rites of the dead, and rudely breakest in upon the grief of an afflicted father."

"If thou art the father of Charlotte Temple," said he, gazing at him with mingled horror and amazement—"if thou art her father—I am Montraville." Then falling on his knees, he continued—"Here is my bosom. I bare it to receive the stroke I merit. Strike—strike now, and save me from the misery of reflexion."

"Alas!" said Mr. Temple, "if thou wert the seducer of my child, thy own reflexions be thy punishment. I wrest not the power from the hand of omnipotence. Look on that little heap of earth, there hast thou buried the only joy of a fond father. Look at it often; and may thy heart feel such true sorrow as shall merit the mercy of heaven." He turned from him; and Montraville starting up from the ground, where he had thrown himself, and at that instant remembering the perfidy of Belcour, flew like lightning to his lodgings. Belcour was intoxicated; Montraville impetuous: they fought, and the sword of the latter entered the heart of his adversary. He fell, and expired almost instantly. Montraville had received a slight wound; and overcome with the agitation of his mind and loss of blood, was carried in a state of insensibility to his distracted wife. A dangerous illness and obstinate delirium ensued, during which he raved incessantly for Charlotte: but a strong constitution, and the tender assiduities of Julia [his wife], in time overcome the disorder. He recovered; but to the end of his life was subject to severe fits of melancholy, and while he remained at New-York frequently retired to the churchyard, where he would weep over the grave, and regret the untimely fate of the lovely Charlotte Temple.

Hannah Webster Foster (1758–1840)

Hannah Foster led a life very different from Susanna Rowson's. While Rowson's career was unsettled but exciting, Foster's was stable and sedate. While Rowson produced a variety of books, Foster published only two. Nevertheless, one of them, *The Coquette; or, The History of Eliza Wharton* (1797), should assure Foster continued attention from critics and general readers of American literature.

Foster was born in Salisbury, Massachusetts, the eldest daughter of Hannah Wainwright and Grant Webster, a merchant. When her mother died in 1762, Foster was probably enrolled in an academy of the kind she describes in *The Boarding School; or, Lessons of a Preceptress to Her Pupils* (1798), a didactic commentary on female education in eighteenth-century America. Foster's education must have been excellent, as demonstrated by the wide range of historical and literary allusions included in her books.

By 1771 Foster had moved to Boston, where sometime later she began her literary career by contributing political articles to local newspapers. These articles attracted the attention of the Reverend John Foster of Cambridge, a graduate of Dartmouth College, whom she married in 1785. The couple settled in Brighton, Massachusetts, where John Foster ministered to the First Church. Between 1786 and 1796, Foster gave birth to six children. The year after the birth of her last child, she published *The Coquette*, and a year later, *The Boarding School*. Having published the two books, she returned to writing short newspaper articles. When her husband died, she moved to Montreal to live with two daughters, who also wrote.

Selected Bibliography

SECONDARY
Brown, Herbert Ross. *The Sentimental Novel in America, 1789–1860.* Durham, N.C.: Duke University Press, 1940.
Petter, Henri. *The Early American Novel.* Columbus: Ohio State University Press, 1971.
Shurter, Robert L. "Mrs. Hannah Webster Foster and the Early American Novel." *American Literature* 4 (November 1932): 306–308.
Wenska, Walter P., Jr. "*The Coquette* and the American Dream of Freedom." *Early American Literature* 12 (Winter 1977–1978): 243–255.

The Coquette (1797)

The Coquette was not as successful as Charlotte. Nevertheless, it went through thirteen editions and enjoyed great popularity in its time. Most critics find The Coquette artistically superior to its predecessors and the most readable of the early American novels. Following the custom of the era, it is "founded on truth." It fictionalizes the experience of Elizabeth Whitman of Hartford, who, after having rejected the Reverend Joseph Howe and the Reverend Joseph Buckminster, both of Yale, fell victim to seduction by either Aaron Burr or Pierrepont Edwards and died in childbirth in 1788. Foster came by the story naturally, as Elizabeth Whitman was a distant relation of John Foster. Probably because of the family connection, the original edition of The Coquette identified the author as "a Lady of Massachusetts," and not until 1866 did Foster's name appear on the title page.

At first glance The Coquette seems to be a typical seduction novel. The story is told in epistolary form, the letters being exchanged by the principal characters and their friends and confidants. The heroine, Eliza Wharton, falls prey to a rake, Peter Sanford. Sanford is called "a second Lovelace," a reference to the seducer in Samuel Richardson's Clarissa Harlowe (1747–1748). Eliza is punished, as were the heroines of countless volumes, by death in childbirth.*

Closer examination reveals some differences between The Coquette and the conventional novel of seduction. The breezy style of most of the letters undercuts the moralistic tone, and the subject matter of the letters focuses consistently on social customs, manners, and conventions, after the fashion of the novel of manners.

Character development is unusual. Generally, the heroine's innocence and virtue make seduction seem impossible; weakness and inexperience must somehow account for her fall. But Eliza Wharton is not a paragon; rather, she is a self-willed person who refuses to accept the strictures of her society. Eliza recognizes herself as a "coquette" and understands that her flirting can mislead potential suitors or ruin her reputation. Eliza simply does not want to marry. She considers marriage the "tomb of friendship," a "selfish state" that forces people into a "very limited sphere" in which they center all their concerns in one family and neglect their former associates.

Eliza's seducer is also atypical. An acknowledged rake, Major Sanford makes a study of seduction and seeks to thwart his rivals even though

---

*Death in childbirth occurs frequently in early American novels. Although there are no reliable statistics before 1915 covering the corresponding occurrence in real life, the following statement by Gerda Lerner in The Female Experience: An American Documentary (Indianapolis: Bobbs-Merrill, 1977) indicates that the high incidence was not merely the figment of authors' imaginations: "It is a rare family correspondence in nineteenth-century America that does not contain at least one account of the death of a mother in or after childbirth" (p. 160).

he himself has no intention of marrying the women he seduces. In Eliza's case, however, his goal also includes punishing her friends for rejecting him as a social equal. "It is this element of outraged pride," says Herbert Ross Brown, that distinguishes him "from many of his wicked contemporaries in English as well as American fiction" (*The Sentimental Novel in America, 1789–1860*, p. 46).

As the novel opens, Eliza has just escaped an unwanted marriage with an elderly clergyman, Mr. Haly, who died before her parents could get him to the altar. Delighted to be launched into "society" again, Eliza visits General and Mrs. Richman. Eliza soon receives the attentions of a minister named Boyer, but she cannot bring herself to marry him immediately. She flirts with Sanford against the advice of her friends.

LETTER I
To Miss Lucy Freeman.

New-Haven.
An unusual sensation possesses my breast; a sensation, which I once thought could never pervade it on any occasion whatever. It is *pleasure;* pleasure, my dear Lucy, on leaving my paternal roof! Could you have believed that the darling child of an indulgent and dearly beloved mother would feel a gleam of joy at leaving her? but so it is. The melancholy, the gloom, the condolence, which surrounded me for a month after the death of Mr. Haly, had depressed my spirits, and palled every enjoyment of life. Mr. Haly was a man of worth; a man of real and substantial merit. He is therefore deeply, and justly regreted by *his* friends; he was chosen to be a future guardian, and companion for me, and was, therefore, beloved by *mine.* As their choice; as a good man, and a faithful friend, I esteemed him. But no one acquainted with the disparity of our tempers and dispositions, our views and designs, can suppose my heart much engaged in the alliance. Both nature and education had instilled into my mind an implicit obedience to the will and desires of my parents. To them, of course, I sacrificed my fancy in this affair; determined that my reason should concur with theirs; and on that to risk my future happiness. I was the more encouraged, as I saw, from our first acquaintance, his declining health; and expected, that the event would prove as it has. Think not, however, that I rejoice in his death. No; far be it from me; for though I believe that I never felt the passion of love for Mr. Haly; yet a habit of conversing with him, of hearing daily the most virtuous, tender,

The Coquette; or, the History of Eliza Wharton; A Novel Founded on Fact (Boston: Printed by Samuel Ethridge for E. Larkin, 1797), 261 pp. Excerpts are taken from 5–9, 16–18, 25–26, 32–39, 48–50, 80–82, 211–214, 234–237, 247–256, 258–261.

and affectionate sentiments from his lips, inspired emotions of the sincerest friendship, and esteem.

He is gone. His fate is unalterably, and I trust, happily fixed. He lived the life, and died the death of the righteous. O that my last end may be like his! This event will, I hope, make a suitable and abiding impression upon my mind; teach me the fading nature of all sublunary enjoyments, and the little dependence which is to be placed on earthly felicity. . . .

.   .   .   .

The disposition of mind, which I now feel, I wish to cultivate. Calm, placid, and serene; thoughtful of my duty, and benevolent to all around me, I wish for no other connection than that of friendship.

This Letter is all egotism, I have even neglected to mention the respectable, and happy friends, with whom I reside; but will do it in my next. Write soon, and often; and believe me sincerely yours,

Eliza Wharton.

LETTER II
To The Same.

New-Haven.

Time, which effaces every occasional impression, I find gradually dispelling the pleasing pensiveness, which the melancholy event, the subject of my last, had diffused over my mind. Naturally cheerful, volatile, and unreflecting, the opposite disposition, I have found to contain sources of enjoyment, which I was before unconscious of possessing.

My friends, here, are the picture of conjugal felicity. The situation is delightful. The visiting parties perfectly agreeable. Every thing tends to facilitate the return of my accustomed vivacity. I have written to my mother, and received an answer. She praises my fortitude, and admires the philosophy which I have exerted, under, what she calls, my heavy bereavement. Poor woman! She little thinks that my heart was untouched; and when that is unaffected, other sentiments and passions make but a transient impression. I have been, for a month or two, excluded from the gay world; and, indeed, fancied myself soaring above it. It is now that I begin to descend, and find my natural propensity for mixing in the busy scenes and active pleasures of life returning. I have received your letter; your moral lecture rather; and be assured, my dear, your monitorial lessons and advice shall be attended to. I believe I shall never again resume those airs, which you term *coquettish*, but which I think deserve a softer appellation; as they proceed from an innocent heart, and are the effusions of a youthful, and cheerful mind. We are all invited to spend the day, to morrow, at Col. Farington's, who has an elegant seat in this neighbourhood. Both he and his Lady are strangers to me; but the friends, by whom I am introduced, will procure me a welcome reception. Adieu.

Eliza Wharton.

To Miss Lucy Freeman.

New-Haven.
These bewitching charms of mine have a tendency to keep my mind in a state of perturbation. I am so pestered with these admirers; not that I am so very handsome neither; but I don't know how it is, I am certainly very much the taste of the other sex. Followed, flattered, and caressed; I have cards and compliments in profusion. But I must try to be serious; for I have, alas! one serious lover. As I promised you to be particular in my writing, I suppose I must proceed methodically. Yesterday we had a party to dine. Mr. Boyer was of the number. His attention was immediately engrossed; and I soon perceived that every word, every action, and every look was studied to gain my approbation. As he sat next me at dinner, his assiduity and politeness were pleasing; and as we walked together afterwards, his conversation was improving. Mine was sentimental and sedate; perfectly adapted to the taste of my gallant. Nothing, however, was said particularly expressive of his apparent wishes. I studiously avoided every kind of discourse which might lead to this topic. I wish not for a declaration from any one, especially from one whom I could not repulse and do not intend to encourage at present. His conversation, so similar to what I had often heard from a similar character, brought a deceased friend to mind, and rendered me somewhat pensive. I retired directly after supper. Mr. Boyer had just taken leave.

Mrs. Richman came into my chamber as she was passing to her own. Excuse my intrusion, Eliza, said she; I thought I would just step in and ask you if you have passed a pleasant day?

Perfectly so, madam; and I have now retired to protract the enjoyment by recollection. What, my dear, is your opinion of our favorite Mr. Boyer? Declaring him your favorite, madam, is sufficient to render me partial to him. But to be frank, independent of that, I think him an agreeable man. Your heart, I presume, is now free? Yes, and I hope it will long remain so. Your friends, my dear, solicitous for your welfare, wish to see you suitably and agreeably connected. I hope my friends will never again interpose in my concerns of that nature. You, madam, who have ever known my heart, are sensible, that had the Almighty spared life, in a certain instance, I must have sacrificed my own happiness, or incurred their censure. I am young, gay, volatile. A melancholy event has lately extricated me from those shackles, which parental authority had imposed on my mind. Let me then enjoy that freedom which I so highly prize. Let me have opportunity, unbiassed by opinion, to gratify my natural disposition in a participation of those pleasures which youth and innocence afford. Of such pleasures, no one, my dear would wish to deprive you. But beware, Eliza!—Though strowed with flowers, when contemplated by your lively imagination, it is, after all, a slippery, thorny path. The round of fashionable dissipation is dangerous. A phantom is often pursued, which leaves its deluded votary the real form of wretchedness. She spoke with an emphasis, and taking up her candle, wished me a good night. I had not power to return the compliment. Something seemingly prophetic in her looks and expressions, cast a momentary gloom upon my mind! But I despise those contracted ideas which confine virtue to a cell. I have no notion of becoming a recluse. Mrs. Richman has ever been a beloved friend of mine; yet I always thought her rather prudish. Adieu,

Eliza Wharton.

LETTER VIII
To Mr. Charles Deighton.

New-Haven.

We had an elegant ball, last night, Charles; and what is still more to the taste of your old friend, I had an elegant partner; one exactly calculated to please my fancy; gay, volatile, apparently thoughtless of every thing but present enjoyment. It was Miss Eliza Wharton, a young lady, whose agreeable person, polished manners, and refined talents, have rendered her the toast of the country around for these two years; though for half that time she has had a clerical lover imposed on her by her friends; for I am told it was not agreeable to her inclination. . . . I fancy this young lady is a coquette; and if so, I shall avenge my sex, by retaliating the mischiefs, she meditates against us. Not that I have any ill designs; but only to play off her own artillery, by using a little unmeaning gallantry. And let her beware of the consequences. A young clergyman came in at Gen. Richman's yesterday, while I was waiting for Eliza, who was much more cordially received by the general and his lady, than was your humble servant; but I lay that up.

When she entered the room, an air of mutual embarrasment was evident. The lady recovered her assurance much more easily than the gentleman. I am just going to ride, and shall make it in my way to call and inquire after the health of my dulcinea.[1] Therefore, adieu for the present.

Peter Sanford.

LETTER XI
To Mr. Charles Deighton.

New-Haven.

Well, Charles, I have been manoeuvring today, a little revengefully. That, you will say, is out of character. So baleful a passion does not easily find admission among those softer ones, which you well know I cherish.

---

1. A reference to Dulcinea del Toboso, the hero's beloved in Cervantes's *Don Quixote*.

However, I am a mere Proteus,[2] and can assume any shape that will best answer my purpose.

I called this forenoon, as I told you I intended, at Gen. Richman's. . . . . . . I believe . . . that I have charmed the eye at least, of the amiable Eliza. Indeed, Charles, she is a fine girl. I think it would hurt my conscience to wound her mind or reputation. Were I disposed to marry, I am persuaded she would make an excellent wife; but that you know is no part of my plan, so long as I can keep out of the noose. Whenever I do submit to be shackled, it must be from a necessity of mending my fortune. This girl would be far from doing that. However, I am pleased with her acquaintance, and mean not to abuse her credulity and good nature, if I can help it.

Peter Sanford.

LETTER XII
To Miss Lucy Freeman.

New-Haven.

The heart of your friend is again besieged. Whether it will surrender to the assailants or not, I am unable at present to determine. Sometimes I think of becoming a predestinarian, and submitting implicitly to fate, without any exercise of free will; but, as mine seems to be a wayward one, I would counteract the operations of it, if possible.

Mrs. Richman told me this morning, that she hoped I should be as agreeably entertained this afternoon, as I had been the preceding; that she expected Mr. Boyer to dine, and take tea; and doubted not but he would be as attentive and sincere to me, if not as gay and polite as the gentleman who obtruded his civilities yesterday. I replied that I had no reason to doubt the sincerity of the one, or the other, having never put them to the test, nor did I imagine I ever should. Your friends, Eliza, said she, would be very happy to see you united to a man of Mr. Boyer's worth; and so agreeably settled, as he has a prospect of being. I hope, said I that my friends are not so weary of my company, as to wish to dispose of me. I am too happy in my present connections to quit them for new ones. Marriage is the tomb of friendship. It appears to me a very selfish state. Why do people, in general, so soon as they are married, centre all their cares, their concerns, and pleasures in their own families? former acquaintances are neglected or forgotten. The tenderest ties between friends are weakened, or dissolved; and benevolence itself moves in a very limited sphere. It is the glory of the marriage state, she rejoined, to refine, by circumscribing our enjoyments. Here we can repose in safety.

.   .   .   .

2. The Greek sea god, who could change his shape at will.

True, we cannot always pay that attention to former associates, which we may wish; but the little community which we superintend is quite as important an object; and certainly renders us more beneficial to the public. True benevolence, though it may change its objects, is not limited by time or place. Its effects are the same, and aided by a second self, are rendered more diffusive and salutary.

Some pleasantry passed, and we retired to dress. When summoned to dinner, I found Mr. Boyer below. If what is sometimes said be true, that love is diffident, reserved, and unassuming, this man must be tinctured with it. These symptoms were visible in his deportment when I entered the room. However, he soon recovered himself, and the conversation took a general turn. . . . After we rose from table, a walk in the garden was proposed, an amusement we are all peculiarly fond of. Mr. Boyer offered me his arm. When at a sufficient distance from our company, he begged leave to congratulate himself on having an opportunity which he had ardently desired for some time, of declaring to me his attachment; and of soliciting an interest in my favor; or, if he might be allowed the term, affection. I replied, that, Sir, is indeed laying claim to an important interest. I believe you must substitute some more indifferent epithet for the present. Well then, said he, if it must be so, let it be esteem, or friendship. Indeed, Sir, said I, you are intitled to them both. Merit has always a share in that bank; and I know of none, who has a larger claim on that score, than Mr. Boyer. I suppose my manner was hardly serious enough for what he considered a weighty cause. He was a little disconcerted; but soon regaining his presence of mind, entreated me, with an air of earnestness, to encourage his suit, to admit his addresses, and, if possible, to reward his love. I told him, that this was rather a sudden affair to me; and that I could not answer him without consideration. Well then, said he, take what time you think proper, only relieve my suspense, as soon as may be. Shall I visit you again to morrow? O, not so soon, said I. Next Monday, I believe will be early enough. I will endeavor to be at home. He thanked me even for that favor, recommended himself once more to my kindness; and we walked towards the company, returned with them to the house, and he soon took leave. I immediately retired to write this letter, which I shall close, without a single observation on the subject, until I know your opinion.

Eliza Wharton.

LETTER XIII
To Miss Eliza Wharton.

Hartford.

And so you wish to have my opinion before you know the result of your own. This is playing a little too much with my patience. But, however, I will gratify you this once, in hopes that my epistle may have a good effect. You will ask, perhaps, whether I would influence your judgment? I answer, no; provided you will exercise it yourself: but I am a little apprehensive that your fancy will mislead you. Methinks I can gather from your letters, a predilection for this Major Sanford. But he is a rake, my dear friend; and can a lady of your delicacy and refinement, think of forming a connection with a man of that character? I hope not. Nay, I am confident you do not. You mean only to exhibit a few more girlish airs, before you turn matron. But I am persuaded, if you wish to lead down the dance of life with regularity, you will not find a more excellent partner than Mr. Boyer. Whatever you can reasonably expect in a lover, husband, or friend, you may perceive to be united in this worthy man. His taste is undebauched, his manners not vitiated, his morals uncorrupted. His situation in life is, perhaps, as elevated as you have a right to claim. Forgive my plainness, Eliza. It is the task of friendship, sometimes to tell disagreeable truths. I know your ambition is to make a distinguished figure in the first class of polished society; to shine in the gay circle of fashionable amusements, and to bear off the palm amidst the votaries of pleasure. But these are fading honors, unsatisfactory enjoyments; incapable of gratifying those immortal principles of reason and religion, which have been implanted in your mind by nature; assiduously cultivated by the best of parents, and exerted, I trust, by yourself. Let me advise you then, in conducting this affair; an affair, big, perhaps, with your future fate, to lay aside those coquettish airs which you sometimes put on; and remember that you are not dealing with a fop, who will take advantage of every concession; but with a man of sense and honor, who will properly estimate your condescension, and frankness. Act then with that modest freedom, that dignified unreserve which bespeaks conscious rectitude and sincerity of heart.

I shall be extremely anxious to hear the process and progress of this business. Relieve my impatience, as soon as possible, and believe me yours, with undissembled affection.

Lucy Freeman.

LETTER XVIII

To Mr. Charles Deighton.

New-Haven.

Do you know, Charles, that I have commenced lover? I was always a general one; but now I am somewhat particular. I shall be the more interested, as I am likely to meet with difficulties; and it is the glory of a rake, as well as a christian to combat obstacles. This same Eliza, of whom I have told you, has really made more impression on my heart, than I was aware of; or than the sex, take them as they rise, are wont to do. But she is besieged by a priest (a likely lad though.) I know not how it is, but they are commonly successful with the girls, even the gayest of them. . . . O, I have another plan in my head; a plan of necessity, which, you know, is the mother of invention. It is this: I am very much courted and caressed by the family of Mr. Lawrence, a man of large property in this neighborhood. He has only one child; a daughter, with whom I imagine the old folks intend to shackle me in the bonds of matrimony. The girl looks very well. She has no soul though, that I can discover. She is heiress, nevertheless, to a great fortune; and that is all the soul I wish for in a wife. In truth, Charles, I know of no other way to mend my circumstances. But lisp not a word of my embarrassments for your life. Show and equipage are my hobby-horse; and if any female wish to share them with me, and will furnish me with the means of supporting them, I have no objection. Could I conform to the sober rules of wedded life, and renounce those dear enjoyments of dissipation, in which I have so long indulged, I know not the lady in the world with whom I would sooner form a connection of this sort than with Eliza Wharton. But it will never do. If my fortune, or hers were better, I would risk a union; but as they are, no idea of the kind can be admitted. I shall endeavor, notwithstanding, to enjoy her company as long as possible. Though I cannot possess her wholly myself, I will not tamely see her the property of another.

I am now going to call at General Richman's, in hopes of an opportunity to profess my devotion to her. I know I am not a welcome visitor to the family; but I am independent of their censure or esteem, and mean to act accordingly.

Peter Sanford.

LETTER XXVIII
To Mr. Charles Deighton.

New-Haven.

I go on finely with my amour. I have every encouragement that I could wish. Indeed my fair one does not verbally declare in my favor; but then, according to the vulgar proverb, *that actions speak louder than words,* I have no reason to complain; since she evidently approves my gallantry, is pleased with my company, and listens to my flattery. Her sagatious friends have undoubtedly given her a detail of my vices. If, therefore, my past conduct has been repugnant to her notions of propriety, why does she not act consistently, and refuse at once to associate with a man whose character she cannot esteem? But no; that, Charles, is no part of the female plan: our entrapping a few of their sex, only discovers the gaiety of our dispositions, the insinuating graces of our manners, and the irresistible charms of our persons and address. These qualifications are very alluring to the sprightly fancy of the fair. They think to enjoy the pleasures which result from this source; while their vanity and ignorance prompt each one to imagine herself superior to delusion; and to anticipate the honor of reclaiming the libertine, and reforming the rake! I dont know, however, but this girl will really have that merit with me;

for I am so much attached to her, that I begin to suspect I should sooner become a convert to sobriety than lose her. I cannot find that I have made much impression on her heart as yet. Want of success in this point mortifies me extremely, as it is the first time I ever failed. Besides, I am apprehensive that she is prepossessed in favor of the other swain, the clerical lover, whom I have mentioned to you before. The chord, therefore, upon which I play the most, is the dissimilarity of their dispositions and pleasures. I endeavor to detach her from him, and disaffect her towards him; knowing, that if I can separate them entirely, I shall be more likely to succeed in my plan. Not that I have any thoughts of marrying her myself; that will not do at present. But I love her too well to see her connected with another for life. I must own myself a little revengeful too in this affair. I wish to punish her friends, as she calls them, for their malice towards me; for their cold and negligent treatment of me whenever I go to the house. I know that to frustrate their designs of a connection between Mr. Boyer and Eliza would be a grievous disappointment. I have not yet determined to seduce her, though, with all her pretensions to virtue, I do not think it impossible. And if I should, she can blame none but herself, since she knows my character, and has no reason to wonder if I act consistently with it. If she will play with a lion, let her beware of his paw, I say. At present, I wish innocently to enjoy her society; it is a luxury which I never tasted before. She is the very soul of pleasure. The gayest circle is irradiated by her presence, and the highest entertainment receives its greatest charm from her smiles. Besides, I have purchased the seat of Capt. Pribble, about a mile from her mother's; and can I think of suffering her to leave the neighborhood, just as I enter it? I shall exert every nerve to prevent that, and hope to meet with the usual success of

Peter Sanford.

After returning home, Eliza becomes engaged to Boyer yet continues to see Sanford. Boyer warns Eliza of the risk she is taking with her reputation. Finally, Boyer, discovering Eliza in intimate conversation with Sanford in her family's garden, breaks off the engagement. Eliza's efforts to retrieve Boyer's good will fail completely. Meanwhile, Sanford marries a wealthy woman but resumes his pursuit of Eliza. Eventually he seduces her. When she becomes pregnant, Eliza leaves home secretly with Sanford.

LETTER LXV
To Mr. Charles Deighton.

Hartford.

Good news, Charles, good news! I have arrived to the utmost bounds of my wishes; the full possession of my adorable Eliza! . . .

I had a long and tedious siege. Every method which love could suggest, or art invent, was adopted. I was sometimes ready to despair, under an idea that her resolution was unconquerable, her virtue impregnable. Indeed, I should have given over the pursuit long ago, but for the hopes of success I entertained from her parlying with me, and in reliance upon her own strength, endeavoring to combat, and counteract my designs. Whenever this has been the case, Charles, I have never yet been defeated in my plan. If a lady will consent to enter the lists against the antagonist of her honor, she may be sure of loosing the prize. Besides, were her delicacy genuine, she would banish the man at once, who presumed to doubt, which he certainly does, who attempts to vanquish it!

But, far be it from me to criticise the pretensions of the sex. If I gain the rich reward of my dissimulation and gallantry, that you know is all I want.

To return then to the point. An unlucky, but not a miraculous accident, has taken place, which must soon expose our amour. What can be done? At the first discovery, absolute distraction seized the soul of Eliza, which has since terminated in a fixed melancholy. Her health too is much impaired. She thinks herself rapidly declining; and I tremble when I see her emaciated form!

My wife has been reduced very low, of late. She brought me a boy a few weeks past, a dead one though.

These circumstances give me neither pain nor pleasure. I am too much ingrossed by my divinity, to take an interest in any thing else. . . .

Julia Granby [one of Eliza's closest friends] is expected at Mrs. Wharton's every hour. I fear that her inquisitorial eye will soon detect our intrigue, and obstruct its continuation. Now there's a girl, Charles, I should never attempt to seduce; yet she is a most alluring object, I assure you. But the dignity of her manners forbid all assaults upon her virtue. Why, the very expression of her eye, blasts in the bud, every thought, derogatory to her honor; and tells you plainly, that the first insinuation of the kind, would be punished with eternal banishment and displeasure! Of her there is no danger! But I can write no more, except that I am &c.

Peter Sanford.

LETTER LXVIII
To Mrs. M. Wharton.

Tuesday.

My Honored and Dear Mamma,

In what words, in what language shall I address you? What shall I say on the subject which deprives me of the power of expression? Would to God I had been totally deprived of that power before so fatal a subject required its exertion! Repentance comes too late, when it cannot prevent the evil lamented. For your kindness, your more than maternal affection towards me, from my infancy to the present moment, a long life of filial duty and unerring rectitude could hardly compensate. How greatly deficient in gratitude must I appear then, while I confess, that precept and example, counsel and advice, instruction and admonition, have been all lost upon me!

. . . Yes, madam, your Eliza has fallen; fallen, indeed! She has become the victim of her own indiscretion, and of the intrigue and artifice of a designing libertine, who is the husband of another! She is polluted, and no more worthy of her parentage! She flies from you, not to conceal her guilt, that she humbly and penitently owns; but to avoid what she has never experienced, and feels herself unable to support, a mother's frown; to escape the heart-rending sight of a parent's grief, occasioned by the crimes of her guilty child!

.   .   .   .

I have no claim even upon your pity; but from my long experience of your tenderness, I presume to hope it will be extended to me. Oh, my mother, if you knew what the state of my mind is, and has been, for months past, you would surely compassionate my case! Could tears efface the stain, which I have brought upon my family, it would long since have been washed away! But, alas, tears are vain; and vain is my bitter repentance! It cannot obliterate my crime, nor restore me to innocence and peace! In this life I have no ideas of happiness. These I have wholly resigned! The only hope which affords me any solace, is that of your forgiveness. . . . Oh, let my sufferings be deemed a sufficient punishment; and add not the insupportable weight of a parent's wrath! At present, I cannot see you. The effect of my crime is too obvious to be longer concealed, to elude the invidious eye of curiosity. This night, therefore, I leave your hospitable mansion! This night I become a wretched wanderer from thy paternal roof! Oh, that the grave were this night to be my lodging! Then should I lie down and be at rest! Trusting in the mercy of God, through the mediation of his son; I think I could meet my heavenly father with more composure and confidence, than my earthly parent!

.   .   .   .

Farewell, my dear mamma! pity and pray for your ruined child; and be assured, that affection and gratitude will be the last sentiments, which expire in the breast of your repenting daughter,

Eliza Wharton.

Julia Granby, the friend who has been staying at the Whartons', reports Eliza's demise to Lucy Freeman, now Mrs. Sumner.

LETTER LXXI
To Mrs. Lucy Sumner.
Hartford.

The drama is now closed! A tragical one indeed it has proved!

How sincerely, my dear Mrs. Sumner, must the friends of our departed

Eliza, sympathize with each other; and with her afflicted, bereaved parent!

.   .   .   .

A few days after my last was written, we [Julia and Mrs. Wharton] heard that Major Sanford's property was attached, and he a prisoner in his own house. He was the last man, to whom we wished to apply for information respecting the forlorn wanderer; yet we had no other resource. And after waiting a fortnight in the most cruel suspense, we wrote a billet, entreating him, if possible, to give some intelligence concerning her. He replied, that he was unhappily deprived of all means of knowing himself; but hoped soon to relieve his own, and our anxiety about her.

In this situation we continued, till a neighbor (purposely, we since concluded) sent us a Boston paper. . . .

. . . I took it up, and soon found the fatal paragraph. I shall not attempt to paint our heartfelt grief and lamentation upon this occasion; for we had no doubt of Eliza's being the person described, as a stranger, who died at Danvers, last July. Her delivery of a child; her dejected state of mind; the marks upon her linen; indeed, every circumstance in the advertisement convinced us beyond dispute, that it could be no other. Mrs. Wharton retired immediately to her chamber, where she continued overwhelmed with sorrow that night and the following day. Such, in fact, has been her habitual frame ever since; though the endeavors of her friends, who have sought to console her, have rendered her somewhat more conversable. My testimony of Eliza's penitence, before her departure, is a source of comfort to this disconsolate parent. . . .

Eliza's brother has been to visit her last retreat; and to learn the particulars of her melancholy exit. He relates, that she was well accommodated, and had every attention and assistance, which her situation required. The people where she resided appear to have a lively sense of her merit and misfortunes. They testify [to] her modest deportment, her fortitude under the sufferings to which she was called, and the serenity and composure, with which she bid a last adieu to the world. Mr. Wharton has brought back several scraps of her writing, containing miscellaneous reflections on her situation, the death of her babe, and the absence of her friends. . . .

I am told that Major Sanford is quite frantic. Sure I am that he has reason to be. If the mischiefs he has brought upon others return upon his own head, dreadful indeed must be his portion! His wife has left him, and returned to her parents. His estate, which has been long mortgaged, is taken from him; and poverty and disgrace await him! Heaven seldom leaves injured innocence unavenged! Wretch, that he is, he ought for ever to be banished from human society! . . .

. . . Not only the life, but what was still dearer, the reputation and virtue of the unfortunate Eliza, have fallen victims at the shrine of *libertinism!* Detested be the epithet! Let it henceforth bear its true signature, and candor itself shall call it *lust* and *brutality!*

.

Execrable is the man, however arrayed in magnificence, crowned with wealth, or decorated with the external graces and accomplishments of fashionable life, who shall presume to display them, at the expense of virtue and innocence! Sacred names! attended with real blessings; blessings too useful and important to be trifled away! My resentment at the base arts, which must have been employed to complete the seduction of Eliza, I cannot suppress. I wish them to be exposed, and stamped with universal ignominy! Nor do I doubt but you will join with me in execrating the measures by which *we* have been robbed of so valuable a friend; and *society*, of so ornamental a member.

I am, &c.

Julia Granby.

LETTER LXXII
To Mr. Charles Deighton.

Hartford.

Confusion, horror and despair are the portion of your wretched, unhappy friend! Oh, Deighton, I am undone! Misery irremediable is my future lot! She is gone; yes, she is gone for ever! The darling of my soul, the centre of all my wishes and enjoyments is no more! Cruel fate has snatched her from me; and she is irretrievably lost! I rave, and then reflect: I reflect, and then rave! I have not patience to bear this calamity, nor power to remedy it! Where shall I fly from the upbraidings of my mind, which accuses me as the murderer of my Eliza? I would fly to death, and seek refuge in the grave; but the forebodings of a retribution to come, I cannot away with! Oh, that I had seen her; that I had once more asked her forgiveness! But even that privilege, that consolation was denied me! The day on which I meant to visit her, most of my property was attached, and to secure the rest, I was obliged to shut my doors, and become a prisoner in my own house! High living, and old debts, incurred by extravagance, had reduced the fortune of my wife to very little, and I could not satisfy the clamorous demands of my creditors.

I would have given millions, had I possessed them, to have been at liberty to see, and to have had the power to preserve Eliza from death! But in vain was my anxiety; it could not relieve; it could not liberate me! When I first heard the dreadful tidings of her exit, I believe I acted like a madman! Indeed, I am little else now!

.   .   .   .

While my being is prolonged, I must feel the disgraceful, and torturing effects of my guilt in seducing her! How madly have I deprived her of happiness, of reputation, of life! Her friends, could they know the pangs of contrition, and the horror of conscience which attend me, would be amply revenged!

It is said, she quitted the world with composure and peace. Well she might! She had not that insupportable weight of iniquity, which sinks me to despair! She found consolation in that religion, which I have ridiculed as priestcraft and hypocrisy! But whether it be true, or false, would to heaven I could now enjoy the comforts, which its votaries evidently feel!

.   .   .   .

Let it warn you, my friend, to shun the dangerous paths which I have trodden, that you may never be involved in the hopeless ignominy and wretchedness of

Peter Sanford.

LETTER LXXIII
To Miss Julia Granby.

Boston.

A melancholy tale have you unfolded, my dear Julia; and tragic indeed is the concluding scene!

Is she then gone! gone in this most distressing manner! Have I lost my once loved friend; lost her in a way which I could never have conceived to be possible.

Our days of childhood were spent together in the same pursuits, in the same amusements. Our riper years encreased our mutual affection, and maturer judgment most firmly cemented our friendship. Can I then calmly resign her to so severe a fate! Can I bear the idea of her being lost to honor, to fame, and to life! No; she shall still live in the heart of her faithful Lucy; whose experience of her numerous virtues and engaging qualities, has imprinted her image too deeply on the memory to be obliterated. However she may have erred, her sincere repentance is sufficient to restore her to charity.

.   .   .   .

Upon your reflecting and steady mind, my dear Julia, I need not inculcate the lessons which may be drawn from this woe-fraught tale; but for the sake of my sex in general, I wish it engraved upon every heart, that virtue alone, independent of the trappings of wealth, the parade of equipage, and the adulation of gallantry, can secure lasting felicity. From the melancholy story of Eliza Wharton, let the American fair learn to reject with disdain every insinuation derogatory to their true dignity and honor. Let them despise, and for ever banish the man, who can glory in the seduction of innocence and the ruin of reputation. To associate, is to approve; to approve, is to be betrayed!

I am, &c.

Lucy Sumner.

To Mrs. M. Wharton.

Boston.

Dear Madam,

We have paid the last tribute of respect to your beloved daughter. The day after my arrival, Mrs. Sumner proposed that we should visit the sad spot which contains the remains of our once amiable friend. The grave of Eliza Wharton, said she, shall not be unbedewed by the tears of friendship.

Yesterday we went accordingly, and were much pleased with the apparent sincerity of the people, in their assurances that every thing in their power had been done to render her situation comfortable. The minutest circumstances were faithfully related; and from the state of her mind, in her last hours, I think much comfort may be derived to her afflicted friends.

We spent a mournful hour, in the place where she is intered, and then returned to the inn, while Mrs. Sumner gave orders for a decent stone to be erected over her grave, with the following inscription:

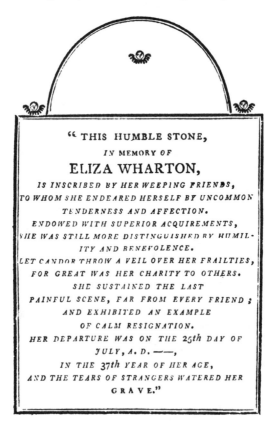

" THIS HUMBLE STONE,

IN MEMORY OF

ELIZA WHARTON,

IS INSCRIBED BY HER WEEPING FRIENDS,
TO WHOM SHE ENDEARED HERSELF BY UNCOMMON
TENDERNESS AND AFFECTION.
ENDOWED WITH SUPERIOR ACQUIREMENTS,
SHE WAS STILL MORE DISTINGUISHED BY HUMIL-
ITY AND BENEVOLENCE.
LET CANDOR THROW A VEIL OVER HER FRAILTIES,
FOR GREAT WAS HER CHARITY TO OTHERS.
SHE SUSTAINED THE LAST
PAINFUL SCENE, FAR FROM EVERY FRIEND ;
AND EXHIBITED AN EXAMPLE
OF CALM RESIGNATION.
HER DEPARTURE WAS ON THE 25th DAY OF
JULY, A. D. ——,
IN THE 37th YEAR OF HER AGE,
AND THE TEARS OF STRANGERS WATERED HER
GRAVE."

I hope, madam, that you will derive satisfaction from these exertions of friendship, and that, united to the many other sources of consolation with which you are furnished, they may alleviate your grief; and while they leave the pleasing remembrance of her virtues, add the supporting persuasion, that your Eliza is happy.

I am, &c.

Julia Granby.

Melodrama

Sally Barrell Wood

E.D.E.N. Southworth

Augusta Evans Wilson

IN 1788 SUSANNA ROWSON satirized the fashionable novels of her day in the following "recipe" for literary success: "Be sure you contrive a duel; and, if convenient, a suicide might not be amiss—lead your heroine through wonderful trials. . . . Manage your plot in such a manner as to have some surprising discovery made—wind up with two or three marriages; and the superlative felicity of all the 'dramatis personae.'" Eighty years later Harriet Beecher Stowe had one of her characters warn against the same type of book—"the sensational novel, the blood and murder and adultery story, of which modern literature is full." When novels were suspect as frivolous or immoral documents, it was typical for writers to put the works of others in the harmful category and exempt their own. Rowson's heroines, too, undergo "wonderful trials," and there is violence in Stowe. But to some extent Rowson and Stowe had a valid point; from Rowson's day to Stowe's, there were writers who indulged in extremes of plot. Naturally they had to declare a moral purpose, which perhaps was genuine, but their focus was on action and adventure. Their characters are usually pushed through a variety of exciting incidents; in addition to duels, suicides, and "blood and murder," there are kidnappings, acts of nature (storms, floods, fires, droughts), and accidents and wrecks (carriage, horse, ship, train). Wills and letters may be forged, lost, or stolen, separating relatives who are later reunited. Although adultery had to be suggested rather discreetly, near-incest was acceptable (after all, the characters could not know until the last chapter who their real parents and siblings were).

Most novels made use of some of these plot elements, but the melodramas are distinguished by the proliferation of incident and the authors' lack of interest in anything but plot. Many of the melodramatic novelists borrowed from the English gothic tradition and introduced touches of the strange and terrifying—crumbling castles, haunted graveyards, ghosts. Of the authors represented here, Sally Barrell Wood and E. D. E. N. Southworth liked to set their tales abroad or in wild landscapes, and Augusta Evans Wilson included exotic Oriental lore.

The three novelists treated the form very differently—Wood with high seriousness, Southworth with humor approaching self-parody, and Wilson with considerable intelligence as she wedded the melodramatic with the didactic and produced one of the most popular novels of the nineteenth century. The melodramas were not necessarily inferior to novels of other types; in fact, they can be more palatable to the modern reader because of the relative lack of preaching. And despite criticism of their sensationalism by moralists, critics, and other novelists, the melodramas were always popular.

Sally Barrell Wood (1759–1855)

Sally Sayward Barrell Keating Wood was the earliest writer of fiction
from the state of Maine and one of the first Americans to publish more
than a single novel. She was born in York, Maine, the eldest daughter of
Sarah Sayward and Nathaniel Barrell, a shipping merchant and lieutenant in the French and Indian Wars. Wood spent much of her childhood
living with her maternal grandfather, to whom she was very close. Judge
Jonathan Sayward, though a Tory during the Revolution, managed to retain most of his wealth and eminence. The Barrells leaned toward the
rebel side, and Nathaniel became a delegate to the Constitutional Convention. Wood later wrote an anti-war novel entitled *War, the Parent of
Domestic Calamity: A Tale of the Revolution* that was not published in
her lifetime.*

In 1778 Wood married Richard Keating, a clerk in her grandfather's office; they had three children before he died in 1783. During her widowhood Wood began to write. She did not lack money to support her children, as would be the case later with many of the widows who took up
writing, but she apparently needed some occupation. She states in the
preface to her first novel that her pen "soothed many *melancholy,* and
sweetened many *bitter* hours."

Wood's first efforts were stories published anonymously in journals.
Then, over a period of five years, she published four novels, again anonymously. The novels were melodramatic adventure stories, and all were
consistent with her conservative background. In *Julia and the Illuminated Baron* (1800) she attacks the French Revolution and makes the
villain a member of the secret society of the Illuminati, a supposed
hotbed of atheists and radicals.

After the publication of her fourth novel in 1804, she married General
Abiel Wood, a wealthy Tory who had been mobbed during the Revolution. They settled in Wiscasset, Maine, where Wood helped found the
Female Charitable Society of Wiscasset. When her husband died in 1811,
she moved to Portland and later to Kennebunk. "Madam Wood," as she
was known, was something of a celebrity in Maine but published very
little in her last fifty years—only *Tales of the Night* (1827) and a hymn
book for children. It is unclear whether Wood preferred an active social
life to writing or whether the rumor is true that she was so impressed by
the novels of Sir Walter Scott she destroyed most of her manuscripts and
gave up writing.

*First published in 1968 by the University of Maine Press.

Selected Bibliography

OTHER WORKS
Amelia; or the Influence of Virtue (1802); *Ferdinand and Elmira, a Russian Story* (1804).

SECONDARY
Goold, William. "Madam Wood, the First Maine Writer of Fiction." *Collections and Proceedings of the Maine Historical Society,* 2d ser., 1 (1890): 401– 408.
Marston, Doris R. "A Lady of Maine: Sally Sayward Barrell Keating Wood." Master's thesis, University of New Hampshire, 1970.

Dorval (1801)

Sally Barrell Wood's preface to *Dorval*, included in the selections below, is one of the earliest statements of American literary nationalism. Yet Wood's career illustrates the difficulty early novelists had in putting the nationalist impulse into practice. When she wrote her first novel, *Julia and the Illuminated Baron*, she was clearly uneasy about presenting "foreign fashions and foreign manners to a people . . . capable of fabricating their own." In her preface to *Julia*, she apologizes for the foreign setting (France and England), giving the weak explanation that she chose it to avoid introducing living characters who might be recognized. Wood's real problem was that her chosen form—the melodrama with gothic touches—could not easily be adapted to the American scene; after all, America had few barons, illuminated or not.

Dorval, Wood's second novel, is set entirely in America, as Wood proudly announces: "The following pages are wholly American; the characters are those of our own country." But apparently it did not occur to her (as it did not occur to other novelists of the time) to set the book in her native state. Instead, the action takes place in Boston, New York, and Philadelphia, the most prestigious American sites but places Wood hardly knew; they are named but not described or distinguished from one another. Nor did Wood succeed in her attempt to "catch the manners of her native land." The characters are stock characters of melodrama and behave like foul villains and fair heroines anywhere. Whatever American flavor the book has comes from references to the Revolution and actual financial practices in the new nation. Wood was a pioneer, but the difficulties in combining American manners and the melodramatic form proved too much for her. She set her subsequent novels, without apology, in France and Russia; the gothic element, prominent in *Julia* but missing from *Dorval*, reappeared. Not until her much later work, *Tales of the Night*, did Wood try another American setting, and this time she chose Maine. Later in life, Wood said she regretted having written so little about her own milieu.

Wood's intentions, as she states them in the preface to *Dorval*, and her actual practice conflict in other ways. She makes the standard claim that the story is based on fact and has a moral purpose. She assures the reader that women are really better off attending to domestic duties instead of writing novels. Whatever Wood's motivation, whether she wanted to disarm the potential critic or simply failed to translate her intentions, all her statements are misleading. The story is less than credible, and if, as Wood insists, the evil Dorval was "not the creature of imagination," America might not have survived him. Wood had an uncle who tried to increase his fortune through speculation and was swindled, but no real miscreant could equal Dorval's crimes: multiple murder, kidnapping and bigamy, in addition to fraud and theft. Although Wood expresses a desire to promote virtue and show by example "the evils that have arisen from speculation," it is hard to remember that the good characters' misfortunes stem from speculation and not simply the villainy of Dorval. Wood's focus on sensational events rather than moral lessons is clear in her treatment of Dorval's death. The didactic novelist would not have missed the chance to have Dorval repent at the last moment and be converted to Christianity by the heroine; instead Dorval brags about his crimes, tries to kill the heroine, and then shoots himself. The author gloats over his demise in a most un-Christian way. She does not allow Dorval a quick and painless exit but makes him linger in agony for a week.

It is hard to see how the creation of a character like Dorval could lead to an author's moral improvement, but such is Wood's excuse for writing. She maintains that domestic duties are the best occupation, but writing novels at least keeps women in the home and safe from "dissipation." In one of the excerpts below, Wood disassociates herself from any suggestion of feminism by attacking Mary Wollstonecraft's *Vindication of the Rights of Women*, published ten years earlier. Probably Wood's comments on woman's place were not simply attempts to protect herself from criticism but part and parcel of her general conservatism. Yet on the question of women, as well as in other respects, Wood was both traditionalist and pioneer. The major female character in *Dorval*, Aurelia, has more spirit than many heroines of the time. Although she understandably faints a lot, since she is confronted with murdered corpses and attempts on her own life, she is not weak or frail. She is capable of independent thought and action and is one of the few characters in the book with any sense; while the others become easy victims of Dorval, Aurelia suspects him from the beginning and triumphs in the end.

Preface to *Dorval*

While every library is filled with romances and novels, some apology is perhaps necessary for adding to the number, and introducing a similar work to the public. Wishing to avoid the imputation of arrogance, I will only say, that while society is so fond of literary amusements, some, and I believe, a large number, will be tempted to devote a part of their time to the perusal of the works of fancy and imagination; and while reading is so much in fashion, romantic tales will be read with avidity, and the works of the novelist will claim their station in almost every library. Hitherto we have been indebted to France, Germany, and Great Britain, for the majority of our literary pleasures. Why we should not aim at independence, with respect to our mental enjoyments, as well as for our more substantial gratifications, I know not. Why must the amusements of our leisure hours cross the Atlantic? and introduce foreign fashions

Dorval. or the Speculator (Portsmouth, N.H.: Printed at the Ledger Press by Nutting & Whitelock [For the Author], 1801), 285 pp. Excerpts are taken from iii–vi, 12–16, 17–18, 35–37, 43–44, 46–47, 108–109, 117–118, 239–241, 242–245, 254–257.

and foreign manners, to a people, certainly capable of fabricating their own. Surely we ought to make a return in the same way. I should indeed be vain, if I indulged for a moment an idea that any of my productions were worth transporting to another climate, or that they could be read with any satisfaction. . . . [Author's ellipsis]

But the attempt will be forgiven where the design is good; and it may possibly call forth the pens of some of my country women, better qualified to instruct and amuse. I hope no one will suppose that I entertain ideas so fallacious as to imagine it necessary for a female to be a writer: far from it. I am sure

"That Woman's noblest station is retreat;"[1]

and that a female is never half so lovely, half so engaging or amiable, as when performing her domestic duties, and cheering, with smiles of unaffected good humor, those about her. But there are some, who, forgetful of those sacred duties, or viewing them all in a circle very circumscribed, devote a large portion of time to dissipation, and such fashionable occupations, as waste many hours that might be devoted to better purposes. If a small share of that time were attached to the pen, I am certain no future author would agree with the Abbe Raynal,[2] "That America had produced but few persons of genius." Envy would be banished from society; and while a woman was drawing a picture of virtue and amiableness from imagination, she would imperceptibly follow the example and copy the portrait.

A small, a very small portion of praise, will, I am sure, be awarded to the Novelist. The philosopher will turn with disgust from the pages of Romance; and the prudent will think the time lost that is spent in perusing fictitious sorrow and fictitious joys; the gay and the giddy will prefer the ball room or the card table; and the idle cannot find time or inclination to read. But there are some, who retiring from domestic occupations, and whose time is not wholly spent in the city, will open, with pleasure a volume which is meant to convey a little instruction, while it amuses an idle or a leisure hour; who can enjoy the well meant fiction, and "shed a tear on sorrows not their own."

The following pages are wholly American; the characters are those of our own country. The author has endeavored to catch the manners of her native land: and it is hoped no one will find, upon perusal, a lesson, or even a sentence, that could authorize vice or sanction immorality. It has been her wish to show by example, the evils that have arisen from speculation, and which have fallen upon the virtuous and the good, as well as the wicked. She cannot help saying, in her own vindication, that the most vicious character is not the creature of imagination, "the vagrant fancy of a woman's brain." With regard to the other characters, it is left

1. George Lyttelton (First Baron), *Advice to a Lady* (London: Lawton Gulliver, 1733).
2. Guillaume Thomas François Raynal (1713–1796), French author who indicted royalty and praised American democracy. St. Jean de Crèvecoeur's *Letters from an American Farmer* (1782) is dedicated to Raynal.

to the world to determine whether they are visionary beings, or copied from real life. It is hoped, however, while they acknowledge the possibility of the existence of such a being as Dorval, they will believe it more than probable that an Aurelia, a Burlington, and many others, are full inhabitants of the world.

When the following pages were written, it was the warmest wish of the author's heart to dedicate them to a lady, whose goodness and virtues had deeply impressed her heart. But that lady's modesty has forbidden that public tribute. To admire in silence those qualities, which must create and rivet the esteem of all that know her, is all that is permitted.

The volume will of consequence appear without a patron to protect or acknowledge it. The author has only to beg that candor instead of criticism may be extended towards it. Not expecting that it will meet with applause, she only hopes it will not be too severely condemned.

The Author.

York, March 26, 1801.

After having served in the American army in the Revolution, Colonel Morely returns to his estate in New York. There he lives with his pleasure-loving wife, his young daughter Aurelia, and his sister-in-law, Miss Woodly, who takes charge of bringing up Aurelia. Morely indulges in his first bit of speculation, albeit from patriotic motives, and is successful.

CHAPTER II

.   .   .   .

The only disturbance to the felicity of this amiable family arose from the complaints and discontents of some of the late officers and soldiers of the disbanded army, who could not procure half the original value of the securities which they had received previously to their laying down their arms. The currency was discredited. Their complaints became every day louder calls for compensation; and murmurs and regret were more frequent and clamorous.

These complaints arose, in a great measure, from designing and avaricious men, who cried down the value of the soldiers' certificates and continental securities, more with a view to render them beneficial to themselves, by laying them up for a twentieth part of their original cost, than from any real doubts they entertained of the insufficiency of America to discharge her debts and make full compensation on a future day, which these speculators saw approaching.

The wants of the soldiers facilitated the success of their plans to supply those temporary wants. They spurned the advice of many persons of judgment and discernment, who wished them to take up some of those vast tracts of land, which are now a source of unfailing riches to America; to cultivate farms, and not part with their securities until Congress should be enabled to fulfil all her engagements, and call in every species of paper money; and in this way to secure to themselves not only a competency, but affluence. If this advice had been followed, many, who have ended their days in poverty, or are now struggling with various evils, had been enjoying a plentiful sufficiency of all the good things, which are procured by industry and economy.

The disbanding of the army had distributed, in every part of the United States, a number of vicious and idle men, who could not submit to return to the useful and honorable labors, from which they had been called by the voice of patriotism. They had become dissipated and profligate, and for a trifle parted with sums which, in a few years, would have placed them in very comfortable circumstances.

It was with heart felt regret, that Colonel Morely beheld these symptoms of civil dissension, and loss of public credit. Determined to do every thing in his power to support the sinking reputation of his country, he bought up, at their original value, as many certificates and securities, as his own finances would allow. For these he paid in silver and gold, and in the produce of his lands, which were at this time under high cultivation; and to some he sold farms.

It is true, Mrs. Morely who did not look into futurity, nor cast a glance beyond the veil that obscured the expected day, murmured a little at the disappearance of that affluence with which she had been surrounded; but while she was indulged in occasional visits to New-York, and entertained more company at home, and in a genteeler style than her neighbors, her regret was seldom the theme of conversation, and her complaints were generally hushed by a new gown, cap, or bonnet.

This was not the case with Miss Woodly, who entertained the most painful apprehensions. She had never felt so perfectly cordial to the cause of America, as its inhabitants in general. She thought that the light of liberty was extinguished by its own glare, and that the States would be finally obliged to return to their old bondage under Great Britain. Fearful that the family of her sister would by this indiscreet patriotism be reduced to poverty, she endeavoured to guard the heart of Aurelia from its worst effects; to fix upon her young mind a habit of industry, and to turn her active genius to some useful employment. . . .

.   .   .   .

. . . Miss Woodly managed with propriety, a majority of the servants were dismissed, and Aurelia became an assistant in the dairy, as well as a chamber maid. She was soon acknowledged a competent judge and mistress of all kinds of work, and capable of either directing or performing, as best suited her circumstances and situation. Her constant employment left no time for repining; and she arose with the sun to engage in the business or amusements of the day. Health had painted her cheek with its rosy hue, and good humor sparkled in her soft eye; her nerves were braced by exercise, and her countenance was animated and irradiated by a consciousness of her being useful to her family, pleasing to her aunt, and satisfied with her situation.

This continued till the new Constitution was formed, the old one having been found insufficient to secure that freedom and prosperity which had been so dearly purchased. Every state in the Union convened to decide upon its merits; and Col. Morely was chosen as a delegate for New-York.

It is unnecessary to say that the Federal Constitution was adopted by America; and that all but a few hot headed levellers were satisfied of its value. And may this Colossian fabric, which united fifteen[3] distinct and independent sovereignties into one great and solid union, and which, if adhered to, will support America against a world of opposing foes, truly answer the purposes for which it was erected!

CHAPTER III

. . . .

It was now that Colonel Morely beheld national prosperity once more dawn upon his country; his own followed of course; and while his generous and patriotic heart glowed with satisfaction at the happiness of the one; he could not but rejoice in the other.

Commerce flourished, trade and navigation were pursued with renewed vigor; agriculture was encouraged; our docks and ship yards resounded with the sound of the axe, adze, and hammer; teams laden with the produce of the land crowded to our markets; the vast Atlantic was covered with our sails; new and elegant buildings reared their magnificent heads in our cities, towns and villages; the industrious tradesman had full employ, the husbandman was well paid for his labor, and for the necessaries he furnished; public securities were all called in, and ample compensation made to every sufferer.

Mrs. Morely persuaded her husband to build a new house in the city upon a very tasty and elegant plan; and to gratify his own inclination he embellished and enlarged his estate in the country. His hospitable doors were opened with pleasure to the stranger; the poor were fed from his table; the naked were clothed by his bounty; the industrious employed, and the sick and the lame supported alike by his benevolence and judicious advice.

The Morelys visit Boston, and Aurelia, now grown up, writes to her best friend, Elizabeth Dunbar. Miss Woodly has died of smallpox, but her training helps Aurelia to question her father's plan to buy large amounts of Georgia land from a Mr. Dorval.

3. Wood apparently included in her calculation Vermont and Kentucky, which were admitted to statehood in 1791 and 1792 respectively.

CHAPTER VIII

.   .   .   .

Aurelia to Elizabeth.

July 13th.

Yesterday morning my father and Mr. Selkirk called upon Mr. Dorval; and upon their return I found they were much pleased with him. My father then gave us some intimation of the business which has brought him to Boston. I can't say that I am much pleased with it: I don't know any thing of the value of land; but it appears to me, there must be some deception when it is sold for a cent an acre. Only think, my dear, of purchasing a hundred acres of land for one dollar. Perhaps it is the observations, I have heard my aunt make upon the evils of speculation, and the impositions, that are often practiced, that give me this disgust to the most distant appearance of speculation.

As we were all engaged, I did not see Mr. Dorval yesterday; but he dined here to day. I do not remember that I was ever struck in a manner exactly similar, with any other person. His person is large; his figure is tall and commanding; and he loses not an inch by stooping. I think so erect a posture is less pleasing than a gentle inclination, which indicates humility of heart. His large black eyes are penetrating even to insolence. Though all his features are good, or rather handsome, when he is speaking; yet, if he is a moment silent, he knits his forehead and brows into a contracted frown, and seems to be turning in his eyes, as if to look upon himself.—Whether it is that the investigation does not give him pleasure, I do not pretend to determine; but of this I am certain, he does not look pleased; and if interrupted, his chagrin instantly disappears, and he assumes the smile of placid but commanding good humor. His manners are those of a gentleman, but do not seem to be the effect of education. Though all he said was sensible, and some of his remarks refined, yet his language was not elegant; and he expressed some sentiments, which were entirely dissonant to my feelings.

I am sorry to remark, that my father seems to have an ambition, to which I thought he was superior, that of possessing great wealth. He talks as if millions of acres were not large enough for a farm, and thousands too contracted for a garden. My mother is quite delighted with the idea that every dollar my father now pays away, will produce a hundred, twelve months hence. But every passion must have its reign; and I am inclined to say with the Preacher: "Surely man, in his best state, is altogether vanity."

Aurelia attends a Boston party where her hosts describe some of the guests.

CHAPTER IX

.   .   .   .

. . . "Behold, Miss Morely, that elegant woman now entering the room. You have seen her; but she will bear re-examination. See with what sweetness and dignity she advances. Were ever maiden modesty and matron chasteness so charmingly blended? She cannot be unconscious of the admiration she excites, whenever she is seen; and yet how affable, how engaging is every look and action!" . . .

.   .   .   .

"And here," cried Mr. Stewart, "is a subject at once for pity and aversion, a disciple of Mrs. Wolstoncraft, a masculine woman, a pupil and follower of that British female, who, in her rights of women, has endeavored to shake the foundation of female happiness; who wishes to rob them of their honor, probity, and integrity; who would teach them to trample upon duty and virtue, and dismiss those soft and feminine graces, which were given them as ornaments by their creator; who laughs at the institution of marriage, and would deprive the mother, as she has the wife, of her best and sweetest employment. The duties of the nursery must, according to her creed, devolve upon some creature of an inferior capacity; and the parent devote herself to the reform of the nation. The misery in which this system, if pursued, must involve her sex, fills my mind with the highest indignation. I know you will forgive me; but really I consider Mrs. Wolstoncraft's Rights of Women as injurious to female happiness, as Tom Paine's Age of Reason is to the cause of religion."

Back in New York, Aurelia's misfortunes begin. She falls in love with the virtuous Burlington, but he appears to run off with Elizabeth Dunbar. In reality, Dorval has tricked Burlington into going to Europe and has abducted Elizabeth, arranging their disappearances to look like an elopement. The Georgia land scheme turns out to be a fraud, and the Morelys are ruined.

CHAPTER XX

.   .   .   .

Mrs. Morley and Aurelia went out one forenoon in the chariot, which was very elegant, to call upon a lady of distinction . . . and as the day was very fine, they continued to ride till nearly one o'clock, when, as they were returning, and within a few streets of their house, the carriage was stopped, and an officer opening the door, levied a writ of arrest upon it. Mrs. Morely was quite ignorant of the meaning of this business, and though alarmed, desired the man to shut the door, and ordered the coachman to drive on. But Aurelia clearly understood this proceeding; and though pale and trembling, she begged the sheriff would permit them to be driven home, as in her present agitated state, she feared her mother could not walk.

The officer replied, with much civility, that they must then permit him to attend them, as his duty obliged him not to leave the carriage. He stepped in and seated himself in such a manner, as not to incommode them, and they were drove directly home.

Mrs. Morely was almost in fits; and Aurelia could with difficulty restrain her tears, when arrived at the door. The sheriff handed them into the house, whither he followed them, after leaving the carriage in the care of an assistant.

If they were surprised at this conduct, they were more so at finding several deputies in the hall. It was now evident that the house and furniture were attached. Mrs. Morely threw herself into a chair, and exclaimed, "what shall I do? What will become of me?" "My poor father!" said Aurelia, "what has become of him? Oh! my father." "Ah!" returned Mrs. Morely, "where is he? Why is he not here to support and comfort us?"

He has escaped to the country, where he greets his wife and daughter. Fortunately, Aurelia and Burlington had earlier persuaded Morely to put some property in his wife's name, so there is still a country estate.

CHAPTER XXI

.   .   .   .

Col. Morely received his wife and daughter with a calm and affectionate look of fixed and settled melancholy. He soon began to reproach his own folly and madness, that had thus driven them from society, from affluence, and from pleasures, that now appeared to him clothed with a thousand charms, which he had never found while possessed of them.

"Why, my dear father, why," said Aurelia, "will you thus damp the satisfaction which we ought to feel upon entering so comfortable and even delightful a retirement? A thousand sources of enjoyment, much more rational than those we have lost, are still open to us, still within our reach; they even court our approach, and solicit us to receive them. I have often heard you say, you meant, at some future period, to leave the city altogether, and reside here. Consider this as the period; and reflect upon it as a voluntary retirement. This place has been ornamented by your own taste. It has lost none of the beauties or elegancies that used to attract the eyes and arrest the admiration of every guest or even traveller. We have good neighbors, which is certainly a great favor; and your library is well stored." "Yes," replied the Colonel; "but I wish for no society, and am not fond of books." "Don't say so, my dear sir; in a few days your mind will become more calm, and you will be delighted to see Mr. and Mrs. Monsue. A love of reading will daily increase. Your enjoyments from this source, I am confident, will be greater than you at present imagine. Dr. Moore says, "Literature is preferable to all other accomplishments; and the men of rank, who possess it, have superiority over those, who do not, let their graces be what they will, which the latter feel and envy, while they affect to despise." You have been a soldier and a citizen. In these characters I am proud to know my father has shone with a lustre, that has always filled my bosom with rapture. You must now learn to be a philosopher."

Morely goes to jail, where Aurelia takes care of him until he dies. When Aurelia returns home, Mrs. Morely ignores her warnings and marries Dorval. On her twenty-first birthday Aurelia discovers that she is not a Morely but the daughter of a British major. Dorval throws Aurelia out, and she goes to Philadelphia to live with family friends. Here she finds Elizabeth, who had escaped from Dorval and been insane for a while, and meets a woman named Addela, who turns out to be Dorval's first and lawful wife. One day Mrs. Morely/Dorval shows up and tells her story.

CHAPTER XLIII

. . . .

Aurelia went immediately down; but what was her surprise, her astonishment, when she beheld—Mrs. Dorval! Embracing her with the warmth of an affectionate heart, "what, my dear mother," said she; "what has procured me so unexpected a favor?"

"A favor! Aurelia," returned the unhappy woman; "do you call my visit a favor? What will you say, when you know my folly has undone both myself and you? do you know that I have neither house nor home? that the wretch I married has stripped me of my property, as well as peace? and that I have not in the world a change of apparel, except what is contained in that small trunk?"

"I did not know it," replied Aurelia, "and am grieved to hear it. I always feared it would end in misery. But do not, my dear mother, do not give way to such violent emotions. Calm your spirits, dry up your tears, and say if I can be in any way serviceable to you."

"*You!* my dear," interrupted Mrs. Dorval, "what can you do? I thank you for your kindness; but I have ruined you, as well as myself: I have deprived you of the power of doing any good to any one. When I think how easy my circumstances were, and how happy I might have been, had I not been so easily duped, I am ready to die with vexation. But it was my fate, and I could not avoid it." Her tears prevented her proceeding. It was some time before Aurelia could compose her enough to understand, with any degree of precision, the extent of the evils she deplored. When she attempted to give any regular account, the narrative was so mingled with invectives against herself and Dorval, that it would be in vain to attempt transcribing it. The substance, however, was as follows.

"From the day of Mrs. Dorval's marriage, her husband had exerted all his eloquence to induce her to dispose of her estate in the country; but, advised . . . by Aurelia's letters, she had refused, though he held up the splendid bait, which he supposed would allure her—a removal to the city. Still she was determined to preserve that independence, which Col. Morely had secured to her, and remained so resolute, that he pretended to give up his design, and proposed to remove for a few months, to New-York, till he had settled some business, which would oblige him to be absent longer than he wished to leave Mrs. Dorval. She had accordingly accompanied him. They went into genteel ready furnished lodgings, with only two attendants; where they spent several weeks in balls, plays, assemblies, &c. Dorval appeared the fondest and most affection-ate of husbands; and she had been complimented, by all her acquaint-ance, as one of the happiest of women.

"It was now that her suspicions were lulled asleep. At a distance from her real friends, Dorval's specious wiles succeeded; and she consented to dispose of her estate, or rather to convey it to him by a deed of gift. From the very day he was secured in the possession of her property, he changed his former affectionate, and even servile behavior, and assumed one en-tirely opposite.

"This conduct continued for several weeks, when she saw him more elated than usual; and as her suspicions had been awakened, she got pos-session of a letter, which he had been careful to preserve from her. It was the letter of Addela, which she had written from Philadelphia, with an account of her safe arrival, and anxiety to see him.

"Shocked at his duplicity and her own disappointment, Mrs. Dorval did not reflect that her own credulity had been the occasion; but shift-ing the blame from herself upon fate and her husband, she was so weak as to vent her feelings in the most acrimonious terms of offended pride and insulted folly, even in the presence of the man whom she had so much reason to fear and despise. She reproached him with his infidelity and her ruin, and threatened to prosecute him for the open violation of every law sacred and divine, in having two wives at a time.

"Dorval only laughed at her menaces, and assured her that he had nothing to fear from her anger, as he only married her for the sake of her property, which he had the day before secured, and which he had dis-posed of to advantage, and received the money for it; that she need give herself no uneasiness respecting the furniture and clothing, as they were included in the bill of sale; that she had no pretentions to one article which she had left behind; and that he should leave her in a few days to take care of herself, as he now meant to rejoin his wife and reside in Philadelphia.

"Exasperated at conduct so vile, Mrs. Dorval applied to a lawyer: But, being entirely unacquainted with all kinds of business, she was surprised to find that she must go through the tedious process of a law suit, before justice could be obtained; and that even then it was probable the cause might be decided against her. Without friends to advise her, and destitute of money to see a council, she knew not what to do; but returned to her lodgings almost in a state of distraction, where she found that Dorval had dismissed her servants and left New-York without discharging her lodgings.

"The landlady refused to let her clothes be removed, till she received the pay for her board.—The whole stock of this once opulent, once happy woman, consisted of twenty dollars. Without consulting any person, she took a place in the stage, determined to see the almost forgotten Aurelia, whose prudence and amiable qualities were now viewed in a proper light; and to whom she resolved to apply for advice and consolation."

Aurelia was deeply affected with this account of Mrs. Dorval's sufferings; and though she could not help blaming her, she did not drop one reflection that could wound her already aching bosom. She assured her that she would consult some persons well acquainted with the law, and that she would do every thing in her power to make her happy.

Aurelia takes Mrs. Morely/Dorval in but soon finds her murdered.

CHAPTER XLIV

.   .   .   .

She [Aurelia] opened the door of Mrs. Dorval's chamber as softly as possible, and with a light in her hand advanced to the side of the bed. While drawing back the curtain, she observed that her features and countenance were pale and distorted. Advancing still nearer, she saw the clothes and the bed in a very disordered state, and with horror, glanced her eye upon—a naked sword!! which, together with the bed, was already crimsoned by the purple current of life, that still continued to flow from a wound in her side!!!
Aurelia became motionless with terror; her head grew dizzy; her eyes gazed as in death; she shrieked, staggered, and fell lifeless to the floor.

Dorval is arrested for the murder. He lures Aurelia to the jail and in the following excerpt commits suicide after having failed to kill her. Naturally Aurelia's rescuer turns out to be her half-brother, son of the British major. She is united with her long-lost father and marries Burlington, who has returned from Europe with a fortune.

CHAPTER XLVII

. . . .

. . . [Dorval said to Aurelia:] "I did not send for you . . . to preach and moralize. . . . I am soon to go hence: My opinions are fixed; and I now care but little for those of the world.—I will inform you how you became the object of my just resentment, then finish the business I am resolved upon, and prepare for my exit.

"In the first place, I loved you and it was in your power to make a virtuous man of me. Burlington was in my way; and Miss Dunbar loved me. To have removed the one without the other, would have been folly; for I knew your foolish prejudices would operate to prevent your connexion with me, when you saw *that* connexion would wound your friend. For this reason, I was determined to rid myself of both together. I had difficulties to encounter; but resolution and perseverance were competent to the business. I then courted your affections with assiduity: I was refused. From that moment I swore your ruin. Hitherto you have been preserved as a scourge to torment me; and though I had not forgotten my vengeance, yet like a fool, like a coward, I delayed the execution of it till your evil genius prompted you to meddle in my affairs, and inform my wife, my Addela, who was really my wife, of my marriage with that foolish woman whom you supposed your mother. When I arrived, upon the wings of expectation, at Philadelphia, I found your arts had prevailed, and she was gone.

"I now swore to delay my just revenge no longer. I conveyed myself to your chamber, and should have taken your life; but you awoke, and I escaped. A few nights after, I succeeded, as I thought; for with this hand I gave the fatal blow to your mother, supposing it to be you. For this blunder I am truly sorry; but I must stand acquited of her death. I attempted to leave the city that night; but was taken by a scoundrel of a sheriff, and confined for what is called a crime, of which I know I cannot clear myself. In a few days, I suffer death; but I do not go alone!"

After a pause, as if to recollect himself, he added; "This interview I have desired, in order to complete what I have long determined—and you must die. Aurelia—no power can save you—you must die—and this very hour; nay, this minute."

"What can you mean?" cried Aurelia. "You will not load your soul with such accumulated murders. Is it not enough that both Col. Morely and his wife have been your victims? Why can you wish for another?"

"To gratify the predominant passion of my soul; to satiate my revenge." returned Dorval. Aurelia sunk, trembling, upon her knees. "I do not implore your mercy," she cried; "'tis an attribute to which you have no pretensions. But I ask protection of him, who is all mercy, who is the father of orphans."

"Ah! Ah!" replied Dorval, "ask, and we shall see if you receive it. See you not this?" (presenting a pistol.) "What arm can save you? I should think it would suit your sentimental piety to die in the place which your foolish father's sufferings had made sacred. I should think you could call down blessings upon the head of him who had rejoined you. Half a minute I allow for the pious purpose of preparation; and when we meet in the shades, you shall thank me for my clemency."

While Aurelia was endeavoring to collect her confused and almost distracted thoughts, and resign herself to *His* will, without whose permission "not a sparrow falls to the ground," Dorval leveled the pistol at her bosom, crying, " 'Tis loaded with a faithful ball, and will find a passage through your obdurate heart." He applied his finger to the trigger; but at that eventful instant, his murderous arm was arrested by a person behind him; and the pistol, wrenched from his grasp, fell inoffensive upon the floor.

"Villain! murderous villain!" exclaimed a manly but trembling voice, "I thank heaven for having permitted me to be the instrument of saving innocence from thy diabolical purpose" . . .

At this moment, the bustle in the prisoner's apartment brought up the jailer and some attendants. They found Aurelia upon the floor deprived of sense and motion, and Dorval struggling with her deliverer. While they were carrying her to a distant apartment, the contest ended, and Dorval was put in irons. . . .

Scarcely was the door of the prison closed, when the report of a pistol called back the jailer and his attendants. Dorval had discharged it; himself was the victim. . . .

. . . But his hand trembling with rage, disappointed malice, and unexecuted revenge, had but half performed its office. Dorval had five days more to exist in extreme agony, both mental and corporeal.

E. D. E. N. Southworth (1819–1899)

In terms of overall sales of her works, E.D.E.N. Southworth may have been the most popular novelist of nineteenth-century America. By her own account, her life before literary success was "wretched." She was born in Washington, D.C. as Emma Dorothy Eliza Nevitte—hence the much-parodied initials (in *Little Women* she is referred to as Mrs. S. L. A. N. G. Northbury). Southworth's father, Charles Nevitte, who she felt rejected her in favor of her younger sister, died when she was three; and her mother Susanna Wailes, married a schoolteacher. Upon graduating from her stepfather's academy in 1835, Southworth taught school and pursued her interest in the Tidewater traditions and legends she would later use in her novels.

In 1840 she married Frederick Southworth, an inventor, and moved with him to Wisconsin, where she continued to teach and had a son. After a "stormy and disastrous" period she would never talk about, Southworth returned to Washington in 1844 without her husband and there gave birth to a daughter. As their titles indicate, her novels were to be full of evil or irresponsible husbands and fathers: *The Deserted Wife* (1849), *The Discarded Daughter* (1851), *The Fatal Marriage* (1869), *The Bride's Ordeal* (1877), *The Unloved Wife* (1882), *Why Did He Wed Her?* (1884).

For the next five years Southworth struggled to support her family by teaching in the Washington schools. During this period she began to write and in 1847 had her first novel, *Retribution*, serialized in the *National Era*. She was encouraged by John Greenleaf Whittier, to whom she later gave the story for his famous "Barbara Frietchie." Whittier approved the anti-slavery sentiment in *Retribution*; in spite of her southern background and prejudices (her books abound with racist stereotypes), Southworth supported the Union during the Civil War and became friendly with Harriet Beecher Stowe.

Southworth gave up teaching for writing and published several novels serially in the *National Era* and the *Saturday Evening Post* and then in book form. Still, she and the children were often ill, and she did not feel secure until Robert Bonner "saved her life" by offering her a royal sum to write for his *New York Ledger*. Southworth joined such popular writers as Fanny Fern and Sylvanus Cobb in writing for the enormously successful *Ledger*. Over the next thirty years the magazine featured thirty of her novels.

Southworth wrote at a punishing rate until the last few years of her life, producing from fifty to sixty novels, the exact number being difficult to fix because of the many title changes from serial to book. Her work remained popular into the twentieth century; in 1936 over half of her novels were still in print.

Selected Bibliography

OTHER WORKS
The Curse of Clifton (serialized 1852, published 1853), also known as
Fallen Pride; India: The Pearl of Pearl River (1855), serialized in
1853 as *Mark Sutherland* and also known as *The Pearl of Pearl Island; Self-Made, or Out of the Depths*, serialized 1863–1864 and
published in 1876 in 2 vols., *Ishmael, or In the Depths* and *Self-
Raised, or From the Depths*.

SECONDARY
Boyle, Regis Louise. *Mrs. E.D.E.N. Southworth, Novelist*. Washington,
    D.C.: Catholic University of America Press, 1939.
Habegger, Alfred. "A Well Hidden Hand." *Novel* 14 (Spring 1981):
    192–212.
Kenton, Edna. "Best Sellers of Yesterday: Mrs. E.D.E.N. Southworth."
    Bookman 44 (October 1916): 128–137.

The Hidden Hand (1859)

The Hidden Hand, which was published serially in the New York Ledger, became an instant success. It was Southworth's most popular novel and probably the most popular work ever printed in the Ledger. Women wore hats and suits named for the heroine, Capitola, just as men would later smoke "St. Elmo" cigars in honor of Augusta Evans Wilson's famous hero. The Hidden Hand was serialized three times before appearing in book form in 1888, and it inspired some forty different dramatizations. In one version John Wilkes Booth played the dashing robber, Black Donald.

The novel defies summary because of the sheer number of melodramatic incidents. Although there is only one murder, there are three kidnappings, three miraculous escapes from death, two duels, two prison outbreaks, two deathbed confessions, a carriage accident, and a shipwreck. The visible characters are supplemented by ghosts and lunatics imprisoned in secret rooms. Southworth herself sometimes lost track of the plot (a problem fairly common for writers of serials). For example, early in the novel the hidden hand of the title is established with some fanfare as a birthmark on Capitola's palm; Southworth apparently forgot it, however, since it is never mentioned again.

Southworth was clearly not the "domestic sentimentalist" she is classified as in many literary histories. She is not sentimental, seldom didactic or moralizing, and entirely uninterested in domesticity; a home to Southworth is as good as its trapdoors and secret passages. The Maryland and Virginia countryside that formed the setting for most of her works was often too tame by itself. Southworth had to import foreign noblemen with odd tastes in architecture or embellish the setting on her own with deep gorges and secret caverns. Varying the descriptions from novel to novel must have been a trial; in one work, Southworth wrote, "It was one of those fearful passes so frequently to be found in the Allegheny Mountains, and which I have described so often that I may be excused from describing this."

Southworth viewed her work with a certain detachment. She stated late in life that she had written to please the Ledger readers and might have done better if she had not needed money. She saw the absurdity of the conventions she used again and again and even makes fun of them so that her novels often parody themselves. What makes The Hidden Hand more readable than many other works of the time is Southworth's good humor. She seems to be saying, "Yes, reader, we know this is ridiculous, but isn't it fun?"

To Sarah Josepha Hale, editor of Godey's Lady's Book and arbiter of the refined and ladylike, it was "beyond the limits prescribed by correct taste or good judgment" (Woman's Record, p. 794). Southworth, as Nina Baym points out in Woman's Fiction, did not conform to the expected behavior of women writers. In her life she failed to hide her pleasure in becoming rich and famous, and in her novels she did not pretend to educate and uplift. Capitola, in The Hidden Hand, is the very opposite of

Hale's ideal of femininity. Southworth models Cap after Shakespeare's more spirited comic heroines; she is witty, disguises herself in male attire, and refuses to submit to authority. Instead of being punished and humiliated for her behavior, Cap is rewarded with all the heroic scenes. Cap, and not a male character, saves the passive heroine, foils the kidnappers, and captures the robber. She even fights a duel, an action Southworth accurately calls "the most astounding thing that ever a woman of the nineteenth or any former century attempted."

The story begins.

CHAPTER I
The Nocturnal Visit

.   .   .   .

Hurricane Hall is a large old family mansion, built of dark, red sandstone, in one of the loneliest and wildest of the mountain regions of Virginia.

The estate is surrounded on three sides by a range of steep, gray rocks, spiked with clumps of dark evergreens, and called, from its horseshoe form, the Devil's Hoof.

On the fourth side the ground gradually descends in broken rock and barren soil to the edge of the wild mountain stream known as the Devil's Run.

When storms and floods were high, the loud roaring of the wild mountain gorges, and the terrific raging of the torrent over its rocky course, gave to this savage locality its ill-omened names of Devil's Hoof, Devil's Run, and Hurricane Hall.

Major Ira Warfield, the lonely proprietor of the Hall, was a veteran officer, who, in disgust at what he supposed to be ill-requited services, had retired from public life to spend the evening of his vigorous age on this his patrimonial estate. Here he lived in seclusion, with his old-fashioned housekeeper, Mrs. Condiment, and his old family servants and his favorite dogs and horses. Here his mornings were usually spent in the chase, in which he excelled, and his afternoon and evenings were occupied in small convivial suppers among his few chosen companions of the chase or the bottle.

In character Major Warfield was arrogant, domineering and violent— equally loved and feared by his faithful old family servants at home— disliked and dreaded by his neighbors and acquaintances abroad, who,

The Hidden Hand appeared first in the *New York Ledger* in 1859. The excerpts used here are taken from *The Hidden Hand; or, Capitola, The Mad-Cap* (New York: G. W. Dillingham, 1888), 600 pp.: 9–10, 53–54, 57–59, 146–147, 155–156, 221–226, 439–440, 543–546, 574–575.

partly from his *house* and partly from his character, fixed upon him the appropriate Nickname of Old Hurricane.

Old Hurricane has long suspected without proof that his rival and the villain of the piece, Gabriel Le Noir, murdered his older brother Eugene Le Noir and spirited away his sister-in-law in order to gain control of the estate. Now Hurricane discovers from an old midwife's deathbed confession that Eugene's wife had had a child whom the midwife rescued from Gabriel and took to New York. Hurricane goes to New York, where he finds the fifteen-year-old Capitola being arrested for having disguised herself as a boy. She relates her adventures since "Granny," the midwife, left her.

CHAPTER VI
A Short, Sad Story

.   .   .   .

". . . I sold my clothes, piece by piece, to the old man, over the way, and bought corn meal, and picked up trash to make a fire, and cooked a little mush every day in an old tin can that had been left behind. And so I lived on for two or three weeks. And then when my clothes were all gone—except the suit I had upon my back—and my meal was almost out, instead of making *mush* every day I economized, and made *gruel.*"

"But my boy—*my good girl*, I mean—before you became so destitute, you should have found *something* or other to do," said the Recorder [of the court].

"Sir, I was trying to get jobs every hour in the day. I'd have done *any-*thing honest. I went around to all the houses Granny knew, but they didn't want a girl. Some of the good-natured landlords said, if I was a *boy*, now, they could keep me opening oysters, but as I was a *girl*, they had no work for me. I even went to the offices to get papers to sell, but they told me that crying papers was not proper work for a girl. I even went down to the ferry-boats and watched for the passengers coming ashore, and ran and offered to carry their carpet-bags or portmanteaus; but some growled at me, and others laughed at me, and one old gentleman asked me if I thought *he* was a North American Indian, to strut up Broadway with a female behind him carrying his pack. And so, sir, while all the ragged boys I knew could get little jobs to earn bread, I, because I was a girl, was not allowed to carry a gentleman's parcel, or black his boots, or shovel the snow off a shopkeeper's pavement, or put in coal, or do *any*thing that *I* could do just as well as *they*. And so because I was a girl, there seemed to be nothing but starvation or beggary before me." . . .

". . . [W]hen my last penny was spent for my last roll—and my last roll was eaten up—and I was dreading the gnawing hunger by day, and the horrid perils of the night, I thought to myself *if I were only a boy,* I might carry packages, and shovel in coal, and do lots of jobs by day, and sleep without terror by night! And then I felt bitter against fate for not making me a boy! And so thinking and thinking and thinking, I wandered on until I found myself in Rag Alley, where I used to live, standing right between the pile of broken bricks, plaster, and lumber, that used to be my home, and the old pawnbroker's shop where I sold my clothes for meal. And then, all of a sudden, a bright thought struck me: *and I made up my mind to be a boy!"*

"Made up your mind to be a boy!"

"Yes sir! for it was so easy! I wondered how I came to be so stupid as not to have thought of it before! I just ran across to the old shop, and offered to swap my suit of girl's clothes, that was good, though dirty, for *any,* even the raggedest suit of boy's clothes he had, whether they'd fit me or not, so they would only stay on me. The old fellow put his finger to his nose, as if he thought I'd been stealing and wanted to dodge the police. So he took down an old, not very ragged, suit that he said would fit me, and opened a door, and told me to go in his daughter's room and put 'em on."

"Well! not to tire your honors, I went into that little back parlor *a girl,* and I came out *a boy,* with a suit of pants and jacket, with my hair cut short and a cap on my head! The pawnbroker gave me a penny roll and a sixpence for my black ringlets."

"All seemed grist that came to his mill!" said Old Hurricane.

"Yes, Governor, he was a dealer in general. Well, the first thing I did was to hire myself to him, at a sixpence a day, and find myself, to shovel in his coal. That didn't take me but a day. So at night he paid me, and I slept in peace behind a stack of boxes. Next morning I was up before the sun, and down to the office of the little penny paper, the 'Morning Star.' I bought two dozen of 'em, and ran as fast as I could to the ferry-boats to sell to the early passengers. Well, sir, in an hour's time I had sold out, and pocketed just two shillings, and felt myself on the high road to fortune!"

"And so that was the way by which you came to put yourself in male attire?"

"Yes, sir! and the only thing that made me feel sorry, was to see what a fool I had been, not to turn to a boy before, when it was so easy! And from that day forth I was happy and prosperous! I found plenty to do? I carried carpet-bags, held horses, put in coal, cleaned sidewalks, blacked gentlemen's boots, and did everything an honest lad could turn his hand to! And so for more'n a year I was as happy as a king, and should have kept on so, only I forgot and let my hair grow, and instead of cutting it off, just tucked it up under my cap; and so this morning, on the ferry-boat, in a high breeze, the *wind blowed off my cap* and the *policeman blowed on me!"*

Capitola becomes Old Hurricane's ward and, back at Hurricane Hall, she begins the taming of her guardian. In the first part of the following

*excerpt, she returns home, having disobeyed his order not to go riding
alone. In the second part she turns the tables on Old Hurricane when
he arrives home late at night.*

CHAPTER XVII
Another Storm at Hurricane Hall

.   .   .   .

The old man stopped short in his furious strides, and glared upon her
with his terrible eyes.

Cap stood fire without blenching, merely remarking:

"Now I have no doubt that in the days when you went battleing, that
look used to strike terror into the heart of the enemy, but it doesn't into
mine, somehow!"

"Miss!" roared the old man, bringing down his cane with a resounding
thump upon the floor; "Miss! how *dare* you have the impudence to face
me, much less the—the—the assurance!—the effrontery!—the audac-
ity! the *brass* to speak to me!"

"Well, I declare," said Cap, calmly untying her hat, "this is the first
time I ever heard it was impudent in a little girl to give her uncle good
evening."

The old man trotted up and down the piazza two or three turns, then
stopping short before the delinquent, he struck his cane down upon the
floor with a ringing stroke, and thundered:

"Young woman! tell me instantly, and without prevarication, where
you have been?"

"Certainly, sir; 'going to and fro in the earth, and walking up and down
in it!'" said Cap, quietly.

"Flames and furies, that is no answer at all! Where have you been?"
roared Old Hurricane, shaking with excitement.

"Look here, uncle, if you go on that way you'll have a fit presently!"
said Cap, calmly.

"Where have you been!" thundered Old Hurricane.

"Well, since you will know—just across the river, and through the
woods and back again!"

"And didn't I *forbid* you to do that, minion? and how *dare* you disobey
me? *You,* the creature of my bounty! *you* the miserable little vagrant
that I picked up in the alleys of New York, and tried to make a young
lady of; but an old proverb says—'You can't make a silken purse out of a
pig's ear!' How dare *you,* you little beggar, disobey your benefactor!—a
man of my age, character and position?—I—I—" Old Hurricane turned
abruptly, and raged up and down the piazza.

All this time Capitola had been standing quietly, holding up her train
with one hand and her riding hat in the other. At this last insult she
raised her dark gray eyes to his face with one long, indignant, sorrowful

gaze, then turning silently away, and entering the house, she left Old Hurricane to storm up and down the piazza until he had raged himself to rest. . . .

. . . .

. . . The moon was shining brightly when he passed the gate and rode up the evergreen avenue to the horse-block in front of the house. There he dismounted and walked up into the piazza, where a novel vision met his surprised gaze.

It was Capitola, walking up and down the floor, with rapid, almost masculine strides, and apparently in a state of great excitement.

"Oh, is it you, my little Cap? Good evening, my dear," he said, very kindly.

Capitola "pulled up" in her striding walk, wheeled around, faced him, drew up her form, folded her arms, threw back her head, set her teeth, and glared at him.

"What the demon do you mean by *that!*" cried Old Hurricane.

"SIR!" she exclaimed, bringing down one foot with a sharp stamp— "SIR, how *dare* you have the impudence to *face* me, much less the— the—the—the brass! the *bronze*! the COPPER! to speak to me?"

"Why, what in the name of all the lunatics in Bedlam does the girl mean? Is she crazy?" exclaimed the old man, gazing upon her in astonishment.

Capitola turned and strode furiously up and down the piazza, and then, stopping suddenly and facing him, with a sharp stamp of her foot, exclaimed:

"OLD GENTLEMAN, tell me instantly, and without prevarication, where have you been?"

"To the demon with you! what do you mean? have you taken leave of your senses?" demanded Old Hurricane.

Capitola strode up and down the floor a few times, and stopping short and shaking her fist, exclaimed:

"DIDN'T you know, you headstrong, reckless, desperate, frantic veteran! *didn't* you know the jeopardy in which you placed yourself by riding out alone at this hour? Suppose three or four great runaway negresses had sprung out of the bushes—and—and—"

She broke off, apparently for want of breath, and strode up and down the floor; then, pausing suddenly before him, with a stern stamp of her foot and a fierce glare of her eye, she continued:

"You shouldn't have come back *here* any more! No dishonored old man should have entered the house of which *I* call myself the mistress!"

"Oh, I take! I take! ha! ha! ha! Good, Cap, good! You are holding up the glass before me; but your mirror is not quite large enough to reflect 'Old Hurricane,' my dear—'*I owe you one*,'" said the old man, as he passed into the house, followed by his capricious favorite.

Old Hurricane enlists the aid of the local minister.

CHAPTER XXIV
Capitola's Mother

.   .   .   .

[The minister said to Old Hurricane]: "This protegee of yours is a very
remarkable girl, as interesting to me in her character, as she is in her
history; her very spirit, courage and insubordination make her singularly hard to manage and apt to go astray. With your permission I will
make her acquaintance, with the view of seeing what good I can do her."
"Pray, do so, for then you will be better able to counsel me how to
manage the capricious little witch, who if I attempt to check her in her
wild and dangerous freedom of action, tells me plainly that liberty is too
precious a thing to be exchanged for food and clothing, and that rather
than live in bondage she would throw herself upon the protection of the
court!—if she does *that* the game is up! Le Noir, against whom we can
as yet prove nothing, would claim her as his niece and ward, and get her
into his power for the purpose of making away with *her*, as he did with
her father and mother." . . .

CHAPTER XXV
Cap's Tricks and Perils

.   .   .   .

The next day, according to agreement, the pastor came and dined at
Hurricane Hall. During the dinner he had ample opportunity of observing Capitola.
In the afternoon Major Warfield took an occasion of leaving him alone
with the contumacious young object of his visit.
Cap, with her quick perceptions, instantly discovered the drift and
purpose of this action, which immediately provoked all the mischievous
propensities of her elfish spirit.
"Uncle means that I shall be lectured by the good parson: if he preaches
to me, *won't* I humor him 'to the top of his bent?'—that's all!" was her
secret resolution, as she sat demurely, with pursed-up lips, bending over
her needle-work.
The honest and well-meaning old country clergyman hitched his
chair a little nearer to the perverse young rebel, and, *gingerly,*—for he
was half afraid of his questionable subject,—entered into conversation
with her.
To his surprise and pleasure, Capitola replied with the decorum of a
young nun.
Encouraged by her manner, the good minister went on to say how
much interested he felt in her welfare; how deeply he compassionated
her lot in never having possessed the advantage of a mother's teaching;
how anxious he was by his counsels to make up to her as much as possible such a deficiency.

Here Capitola put up both her hands and dropped her face upon them. Still farther encouraged by this exhibition of feeling, Mr. Goodwin went on. He told her that it behooved *her*, who was a motherless girl, to be even more circumspect than others, lest through very ignorance she might err; and in particular he warned her against riding or walking out alone, or indulging in any freedom of manners that might draw upon her the animadversions of their very strict community.

"Oh, sir, I know I have been very indiscreet, and I am very miserable!" said Capitola, in a heart-broken voice.

"My dear child, your errors have hitherto been those of ignorance only, and I am very much pleased to find how much your good uncle has been mistaken; and how ready you are to do strictly right when the way is pointed out!" said the minister, pleased to his honest heart's core that he had made this deep impression.

A heavy sigh burst from the bosom of Capitola.

"What is the matter, my dear child?" he said, kindly.

"Oh, sir, if I had only known you before!" exclaimed Capitola, bitterly.

"Why, my dear?—I can do you just as much good now."

"Oh, no, sir! it is too late! *it is too late!*"

"It is never too late to do well."

"Oh, yes, sir, it is for me! Oh, how I wish I had had your good counsel before! it would have saved me from so much trouble!"

"My dear child, you make me seriously uneasy! do explain yourself," said the old pastor, drawing his chair closer to hers, and trying to get a look at the distressed little face that was bowed down upon her hands, and vailed with her hair—"Do tell me, my dear, what is the matter?"

"Oh, sir, I'm afraid to tell you! you'd hate and despise me! you'd never speak to me again!" said Capitola, keeping her face concealed.

"My dear child," said the minister, very gravely and sorrowfully, "whatever your offense has been, and you make me fear that it has been a very serious one, I invite you to confide it to me, and having done so I promise however I may mourn the sin not to 'hate,' or 'despise,' or forsake the sinner. Come, confide in me."

"Oh, sir, I daren't! indeed I daren't!" moaned Capitola.

"My poor girl!" said the minister, "if I am to do you any good, it is absolutely necessary that you make me your confidant."

"Oh, sir, I have been a very wicked girl! I daren't tell you *how* wicked I have been!"

"Does your good uncle know or suspect this wrong-doing of yours?"

"Unclc! Oh, no sir! He'd turn me out of doors. He'd kill me! Indeed he would, sir. Please don't tell him!"

"You forget, my child, that *I* do not know the nature of your offence," said the minister, in a state of painful anxiety.

"But I'm going to inform you, sir! and, oh, I hope you will take pity on me and tell me what to do; for though I dread to speak, I can't keep it on my conscience any longer, it is such a heavy weight on my breast!"

"Sin always *is*, my poor girl!" said the pastor, with a deep groan.

"But, sir, you know I had no mother, as you said yourself."

"I know it, my poor girl, and am ready to make every allowance," said the old pastor, with a deep sigh, not knowing what next to expect.

"And—and—I hope you will forgive me, sir! but—*but he was so hand-some I couldn't help liking him!*"

"Miss Black!" cried the horrified pastor.

"There! I *knew* you'd just go and bite my head off the very first thing! Oh, dear, what shall I do!" sobbed Capitola.

The good pastor, who had started to his feet, remained gazing upon her in a panic of consternation, murmuring to himself:

"Good angels! I am fated to hear more great sins than if I were a prison chaplain!" Then going up to the sobbing delinquent, he said:

"Unhappy girl! who is this person of whom you speak?"

"H—h—h—him that I met when I went walking in the woods!" sobbed Capitola.

"Heaven of Heavens! this is worse than my very worst fears!—Wretched girl! tell me instantly the name of this base deceiver!"

"He—he—he's no base deceiver; he—he—he's very amiable and good-looking; and—and—and that's why I liked him so much; it was all my fault, not his, poor, dear fellow!"

"His name?" sternly demanded the pastor.

"Alf—Alf—Alfred," wept Capitola.

"Alfred *whom?*"

"Alfred Blen—Blen—Blenheim!"

"Miserable girl! how often have you met this miscreant in the forest?"

"I—don't—know!" sobbed Capitola.

"Where is the wretch to be found now?"

"Oh, please don't hurt him, sir! Please don't! He—he—he's *hid in the closet in my room.*"

A groan that seemed to have rent his heart in twain burst from the minister, as he repeated in deepest horror:

"In your room! (Well! I must prevent murder being done!) Did you not know, you poor child, the danger you ran by giving this young man private interviews; and, above all, admitting him to your apartment? Wretched girl! better you'd never been born than ever so to have received a man!"

"Man? man? MAN?—I'd like to know what you mean by *that*, Mr. Goodwin!" exclaimed Capitola, lifting her eyes flashing through their tears.

"I mean the man to whom you have given these private interviews."

"*I!—I* give private interviews to a man! Take care what you say, Mr. Goodwin! I won't be insulted! no not even by *you!*"

"Then if you are not talking of a man, who or what in the world *are* you talking about?" exclaimed the amazed minister.

"Why, Alfred, the Blenheim poodle that strayed away from some of the neighbor's houses, and that I found in the woods and brought home and hid in my closet, for fear he would be inquired after, or uncle would find it out, and make me give him up! I knew it was wrong, but then he was so pretty—"

Before Capitola had finished her speech, Mr. Goodwin had seized his hat, and rushed out of the house in indignation, nearly overturning Old Hurricane, whom he met on the lawn, and to whom he said:

"Thrash that girl as if she were a bad boy—for she richly deserves it!"

A sub-plot includes Cap's friend Herbert and his friend Traverse Rocke. Rocke gets engaged to Clara Day, the conventional heroine of the novel, and goes West to start a medical practice. Clara is abducted by Gabriel Le Noir, who tries to force her to marry his son, Craven. After Cap rescues Clara, Craven plots to marry Cap.

CHAPTER XLV
Cap Captivates a Craven

. . . .

Capitola looked up with surprise and interest; she had never in her life before heard an explicit declaration of love from anybody. She and Herbert somehow had always understood each other very well, without ever a word of technical love-making passing between them; so Capitola did not exactly know what was coming next.

Craven recovered his voice; and encouraged by the favorable manner in which she appeared to listen to him, actually threw himself at her feet and seizing one of her hands, with much ardor and earnestness and much more eloquence than any one would have credited him with, poured forth the history of his passion and his hopes.

"Well, I declare!" said Cap, when he had finished his speech and was waiting in breathless impatience for her answer, "this is what is called a declaration of love and a proposal for marriage, is it?—It is downright sentimental, I suppose, if I had only the sense to appreciate it! It is as good as a play! pity it is lost upon me!"

"Cruel girl! how you mock me!" cried Craven, rising from his knees and sitting beside her.

"No, I don't! I'm in solemn earnest! I say it is first rate! do it again! I like it!"

"Sarcastic and merciless one, you glory in the pain you give! But if you wish again to hear me say I love you, I will say it a dozen—yes, a hundred times over if you will only admit that you could love me a little in return!"

"Don't! that would be too tiresome! Two or three times is quite enough! Besides, what earthly good could my saying 'I love you,' do?"

"I might persuade you to become the wife of one who will adore you to the last hour of his life!"

"Meaning *you!*"

"Meaning *me*, the most devoted of your admirers!"

"That isn't saying much, since I haven't got any but you!"

"Thank fortune for it! Then I am to understand, charming Capitola, that at least your hand and your affections are free," said Craven, joyfully.

"Well, now, I don't know about that. Really, I can't positively say! but it strikes me, if I were to get married to anybody else, there's *somebody* would feel queerish!"

"No doubt there are many whose secret hopes would be blasted, for so charming a girl could not have passed through this world without having won many hearts, who would keenly feel the loss of hope, in her marriage! But what if they do, my enchanting Capitola? You are not responsible for any one having formed such hopes!"

"Fudge!" said Cap. "*I'm* no belle! never was! never can be! have neither wealth, beauty, nor coquetry enough to make me one! *I've* no lovers or admirers to break their hearts about me, one way or another; but there is one honest fellow—hem! never mind; I feel as if I belonged to somebody else; that's all."

Craven starts rumors that he seduced Cap. She challenges him to a duel and shoots him. For a time he is believed to be dying until Cap reveals that she shot him with split peas! Traverse Rocke returns from the West and takes a job as medical assistant in a New Orleans mental institution.

CHAPTER LVI

The Mysterious Maniac

.   .   .   .

Fatigued by his journey, Traverse slept soundly through the night; but early in the morning he was rudely awakened by the sounds of maniac voices from the cells. Some were crying, some laughing aloud, some groaning and howling, and some holding forth in fancied exhortations.

He dressed himself quickly and left his room, to walk down the length of the long hall and observe the cells on each side. The doors were at regular intervals, and each door had in its centre a small opening to enable the proprietor to look in upon the patients.

As these were all women, and some of them delicate and refined even in their insanity, Traverse felt shocked at this necessary, if it *were* necessary, exposure of their sanctuary.

The cells were in fact small bed rooms, that with their white-washed walls, and white curtained beds and windows, looked excessively neat, clean and cool, but also, it must be confessed, very bare, dreary and cheerless.

"Even a looking-glass would be a great benefit to those poor girls, for I remember that even Clara, in her violent grief, and mother in her life-long sorrow, never neglected their looking-glass, and personal appearance," said Traverse to himself, as he passed down the hall, and resolved that this little indulgence should be afforded the patients.

And except those first involuntary glances, he scrupulously avoided looking in through the gratings upon those helpless women who had no means of secluding themselves.

But as he turned to go down the stairs, his eyes went full into an opposite cell, and fell upon a vision of beauty and sorrow that immediately rivetted his gaze. . . .

.   .   .   .

After breakfast, Doctor St. Jean invited his young assistant to accompany him on a round of visits to the patients, and they went immediately up to the hall, at the end of which Traverse had slept.

"These are our incurables, but they are not violent; incurables never are. Poor Mademoiselle! she has just been conveyed to this ward," said the doctor, opening the door of the first cell on the right at the head of the stairs, and admitting Traverse at once into the presence of the beautiful, black-haired, snow-faced woman, who had so much interested him.

"This is my friend, Doctor Rocke, Mademoiselle; Doctor, this is my friend, Mademoiselle Mont De St. Pierre!"

Traverse bowed profoundly, and the lady arose, curtsied and resumed her seat, saying coldly:

"I have told you, Monsieur, never to address me as Mademoiselle; you persist in doing so; and I shall never notice the insult again."

"Ten thousand pardons, Madame! but if Madame will always look so young! so beautiful! can I ever remember that she is a widow?"

The classic lip of the woman curled in scorn, and she disdained a reply.

"I take an appeal to Monsieur Le Docteur—is not Madame young and beautiful?" asked the Frenchman, turning to Traverse, while the splendid black eyes of the stranger passed from one to the other.

Traverse caught the glance of the lady and bowed gravely. It was the most delicate, and proper reply.

She smiled almost as gravely, and with a much kinder expression than any she had bestowed upon the Frenchman.

"And how has Madame fared during my absence so long? The servants—have they been respectful? have they been observant? have they been obedient to the will of Madame? Madame has but to speak!" said the doctor, bowing politely.

"Why should I speak when every word I utter you believe, or affect to believe, to be the ravings of a maniac? I will speak no more," said the lady, turning away her superb dark eyes and looking out of the window.

"Ah, Madame will not so punish her friend, her servant! her slave!"

A gesture of fierce impatience and disgust was the only reply deigned by the lady.

"Come away; she is angry and may become dangerously excited," said the old doctor, leading the way from the cell.

"Did you tell me this lady is one of the incurables?" inquired Traverse, when they had left her apartment.

"Bah! yes, poor girl, vera incurable, as my sister would say."

"Yet, she appears to me to be perfectly sane, as well as exceedingly beautiful and interesting."

"Ah, bah! my excellent; my admirable; my inexperienced young friend, that is all you know of lunatics. With more or less violence of assertion, they every one insist upon their sanity; just as criminals protest their innocence! Ah, bah! you shall go into every cell in this ward, and not find one lunatic among them," sneered the old doctor, as he led the way into the next little room.

Of course the mental patient turns out to be Mrs. Eugene Le Noir, Capitola's mother, who had been imprisoned by her brother-in-law and then sent to the asylum. She is freed and reunited with Cap; Gabriel dies, confessing all his crimes; Traverse Rocke turns out to be Old Hurricane's long-lost son, and Hurricane and his estranged wife are reunited. Cap marries Herbert, and Traverse marries Clara. All end up married to the proper persons and receiving their proper inheritances. The only matter to be settled is the case of the robber, Black Donald. Cap had succeeded in capturing him, but he was falsely convicted of murder. Cap's final act of heroism, after the ensuing scene, is to help Black Donald escape from prison.

CHAPTER LX

Capitola a Capitalist

.   .   .   .

How glad I am to get back to my little Cap; for I know very well, reader, just as well as if you had told me, that you have been grumbling for two weeks for the want of Cap. But I could not help it, for, to tell the truth, I was pining after her myself, which was the reason that I could not do half justice to the scenes of the Mexican War.

Well, now let us see what Cap has been doing—what oppressors she has punished—what victims she has delivered—in a word, what new heroic adventures she has achieved.

Well, the trial of Donald Bayne, alias Black Donald, was over. Cap, of course, had been compelled to appear against him. During the whole course of the trial the court-room was crowded with a curious multitude, "from far and near," eager to get sight of the notorious outlaw.

Black Donald, through the whole ordeal, deported himself with a gallant and joyous dignity, that would have better become a triumph than a trial.

He was indicted upon several distinct counts, the most serious of which [murders] . . . were sustained only by circumstantial evidence. But the aggregate weight of all these, together with his very bad reputation, was sufficient to convict him, and Black Donald was sentenced to death.

This dreadful doom, most solemnly pronounced by the judge, was received by the prisoner with a loud laugh, and the words:

"You're out o' your reckoning now, cap'n! I never was a saint, the Lord knows, but my hands are free from blood-guiltiness! There's an honest little girl that believes me—don't you?" he said, turning laughingly to our little heroine.

"Yes, I do!" said Cap, bursting into tears; "and I am sorry for you as ever I can be, Donald Bayne."

"Bother! it is sure to come to this first or last, and I knew it! Now, to prove you do not think this rugged hand of mine stained with blood, give it a friendly shake!" said the condemned man. And before Old Hurricane could prevent her, Capitola had jumped over two or three intervening seats and climbed up to the side of the dock, and reached up her hand to the prisoner saying:

"God help you, Donald Bayne, in your great trouble, and I will do all I can to help you in this world. I will go to the Governor myself, and tell him I know you never did any murder."

Augusta Evans Wilson (1835–1909)

Like E. D. E. N. Southworth, Augusta Jane Evans Wilson was a southerner who gained fame and fortune with her enormously popular novels. She was born near Columbus, Georgia, the eldest daughter of Matt Evans, a well-descended merchant who went bankrupt when she was six. The family moved to Texas in search of prosperity and four years later to Mobile, Alabama. Wilson was educated by her mother, Sarah Skrine Howard, to whom she was very close and later attributed her success.

At the age of fifteen, Wilson began writing her first novel, *Inez: A Tale of the Alamo*, based on her experiences in Texas. A relative apparently paid Harper and Brothers to publish *Inez* in 1855, but the book did not sell. It was Wilson's second novel that brought her success. *Beulah* (1859) sold over 20,000 copies within the year and restored her family to economic security. Wilson is said to have made from $100,000 to $300,000 during her lifetime from the sales of her books.

Wilson wrote her next novel, *Macaria* (1863), to promote the Confederate cause. She was such a dedicated secessionist that she broke her engagement to a northern editor who supported Lincoln and devoted herself to organizing a hospital and writing propaganda for the Confederacy. After the war she published her most famous novel, *St. Elmo* (1866), and married Colonel Lorenzo Wilson, a wealthy man twenty-seven years her senior.

Even though she began her career very young, Wilson was not to become a prolific author in the manner of Southworth. She suffered from ill health and insomnia when writing, wrote slowly, and agreed with her husband that wives should put domestic duties first. She published only three more books before 1891, when he died, and two after his death. Wilson also differed from Southworth in her strong conservatism, which deepened with age. Her early novels show some ambivalence on social questions, but her later works attack women's suffrage, women's participation in public affairs, and labor unions. In *Devota* (1907), she describes Populists as "greedy, omnivorous, grudging 'Have Nots.'"

Selected Bibliography

OTHER WORKS
Vashti (1869); *Infelice* (1875); *At the Mercy of Tiberius* (1887); *A Speckled Bird* (1902).

SECONDARY
Calkins, Earnest Elmo. "St. Elmo: or, Named for a Best Seller." *Saturday Review of Literature*, December 16, 1939, 2–4, 14, 16–17.
Fidler, William. *Augusta Evans Wilson*. University: University of Alabama Press, 1951.

————. "Augusta Evans Wilson as Confederate Propagandist." *Alabama Review* 2 (January 1949): 32–44.
Jones, Anne Goodwyn. "Augusta Jane Evans: Paradise Regained." In *Tomorrow Is Another Day: The Woman Writer in the South, 1859–1936*, 51–91. Baton Rouge: Louisiana State University Press, 1981.
Webb, Charles. *St. Twel'mo, or the Cuneiform Cyclopedist of Chattanooga*. New York: C. H. Webb, Publisher, 1867.

St. Elmo (1866)

St. Elmo was not only Augusta Evans Wilson's most popular novel but one of the top sellers of the nineteenth century. It became more of a phenomenon than a novel, reminding one of today's advertising events. There were St. Elmo hotels, steamboats, plantations, and even towns; men smoked St. Elmo cigars and drank St. Elmo punch; hundreds of little Elmos were born to novel-reading parents. The story retained its popularity through the first quarter of the next century with numerous stage adaptations and two silent film versions.

Despite its popularity, St. Elmo was much ridiculed by critics of the time. They applied to St. Elmo a reviewer's comment on Wilson's first novel: "There is not a natural character, and scarcely a natural phrase in the whole volume" (Jay B. Hubbell, The South in American Literature, p. 610). Everyone noted Wilson's pedantry: the classical allusions and obscure quotations; the scholarly vocabulary used by all characters, regardless of class or education; the long conversations on such abstruse matters as the "Chaldee quandary" and the "Rabbinical Targum." The heroine, Edna Earl, publishes an article called "Keeping the Vigil of St. Martin Under the Pines of Grütli," in which she pays "eloquent tribute to the liberators of Helvetia, the Confederates of Schweitz, Uri, and Underwalden." In St. Twel'mo, a parody that appeared the year after St. Elmo, Edna is imagined to have swallowed an unabridged dictionary.

Why, then, was St. Elmo such a hit? For one thing, Wilson combined the most popular elements of different types of novels. St. Elmo follows the basic pattern of the didactic novel—orphan girl makes good—without actually being a didactic novel. Edna's childhood is dispensed with quickly so she can become a nubile seventeen; the reader does not have to endure the heroine's boring orphanhood or her boring education in piety and humility (Wilson thinks pride is a fine quality). Even Wilson's show of erudition seems designed less to educate than to awe her readers. Without the more ho-hum elements of the didactic novel, there is room for exciting incidents (duels, train wrecks, murders, etc.) and the main selling point of St. Elmo, the romance between Edna and St. Elmo.

This romance constitutes the major duel of the book. Pitted against the poor orphan is the ultimate "macho man," a man who, like Rochester in Charlotte Bronte's Jane Eyre (1847), radiates power and mystery. St. Elmo is rich and handsome; he is also murderer, seducer, atheist. Although the Victorian code banned seduction as a primary theme, St. Elmo is much more sexualized than the seduction novels popular in earlier years. Wilson skillfully sets up a highly charged atmosphere whenever Edna and St. Elmo meet, and St. Elmo's continual "crushing" Edna to him and "folding" her in his arms becomes more erotic than many explicit sex scenes. Through most of the novel Edna quivers with suppressed passion, but her will proves stronger than St. Elmo's. She resists even the temptation to reform him; he must reform himself, repenting his early crimes and renouncing his arrogance and cynicism. Not until St. Elmo becomes a minister does Edna accept him.

The conservative Wilson is careful not to make Edna's triumph into an explicit feminist argument. At the end of the novel when Edna marries St. Elmo, she must give up her career as a successful author, and she is made throughout the book to denounce women's suffrage and other rights. In *Woman's Fiction* Nina Baym suggests that because Wilson was stretching the limits with aggressive and intellectual heroines, she had to be more prescriptive than other writers about the proper place of women: "*St. Elmo* exists at the point of highest tension in a balance that cannot be maintained" (p. 279). Wilson's ambivalence is clear in the closing scene of the book, when Edna "loses consciousness" at the altar. Is it really exhaustion from her taxing career that causes her to faint? Perhaps she was animated all along by her struggle and not her "reward."

In the opening chapter Edna witnesses a duel.

CHAPTER I

·   ·   ·   ·   ·   ·   ·   ·   ·   ·   ·   ·   ·   ·   ·   ·

A slender girl of twelve years' growth steadied a pail of water on her head, with both dimpled arms thrown up, in ancient classic Caryatides[1] attitude; and, pausing a moment beside the spring, stood fronting the great golden dawn—watching for the first level ray of the coming sun, and chanting the prayer of Habakkuk.[2] Behind her in silent grandeur towered the huge outline of Lookout Mountain, shrouded at summit in gray mist; while centre and base showed dense masses of foliage, dim and purplish in the distance—a stern cowled monk of the Cumberland brotherhood. Low hills clustered on either side, but immediately in front stretched a wooded plain, and across this the child looked at the flushed sky, rapidly brightening into fiery and blinding radiance. Until her wild song waked echoes among the far-off rocks, the holy hush of early morning had rested like a benediction upon the scene, as though nature laid her broad finger over her great lips, and waited in reverent silence the advent of the sun. Morning among the mountains possessed witchery and glories which filled the heart of the girl with adoration, and called from her lips rude but exultant anthems of praise. The young face, lifted toward the cloudless east, might have served as a model for a

---

St. Elmo (New York: Carleton Publishers, 1866), 565 pp. Excerpts are taken from 7–10, 52–53, 85–87, 211–215, 325–328, 433–434, 444–446, 467–468, 568–569.
1. Sculptured female figures used as a column; for example, caryatides hold up the porch roof of the Erechtheum on the Acropolis in Athens.
2. A minor prophet of the seventh century B.C.

pictured Syriac priestess—one of Baalbec's vestals, ministering in the olden time in that wondrous and grand temple at Heliopolis.[3] . . .

. . . In the solemn beauty of that summer morning the girl seemed to have forgotten the mission upon which she came; but as she loitered, the sun flashed up, kindling diamond fringes on every dew-beaded chestnut leaf and oak-bough, and silvering the misty mantle which enveloped Lookout. A moment longer that pure-hearted Tennessee child stood watching the gorgeous spectacle, drinking draughts of joy, which mingled no drop of sin or selfishness in its crystal waves; for she had grown up alone with nature—utterly ignorant of the roar and strife, the burning hate and cunning intrigue of the great world of men and women, where "like an Egyptian pitcher of tamed vipers, each struggles to get its head above the other." To her, earth seemed very lovely; life stretched before her like the sun's path in that clear sky, and, as free from care or foreboding as the fair June day, she walked on, preceded by her dog—and the chant burst once more from her lips:

"He stood and measured the earth: and the everlasting mountains were scattered, the perpetual hills—"

The sudden, almost simultaneous report of two pistol-shots rang out sharply on the cool, calm air, and startled the child so violently that she sprang forward and dropped the bucket. The sound of voices reached her from the thick wood bordering the path, and, without reflection, she followed the dog, who bounded off toward the point whence it issued. Upon the verge of the forest she paused, and, looking down a dewy green glade where the rising sun darted the earliest arrowy rays, beheld a spectacle which burned itself indelibly upon her memory. A group of five gentlemen stood beneath the drippng chestnut and sweetgum arches; one leaned against the trunk of a tree, two were conversing eagerly in undertones, and two faced each other fifteen paces apart, with pistols in their hands. Ere she could comprehend the scene, the brief conference ended, the seconds resumed their places to witness another fire, and like the peal of a trumpet echoed the words:

"Fire! One!—two!—three!"

The flash and ringing report mingled with the command, and one of the principals threw up his arm and fell. When, with horror in her wide-strained eyes and pallor on her lips, the child staggered to the spot, and looked on the prostrate form, he was dead. The hazel eyes stared blankly at the sky, and the hue of life and exuberant health still glowed on the full cheek; but the ball had entered the heart, and the warm blood, bubbling from his breast, dripped on the glistening grass. The surgeon who knelt beside him took the pistol from his clenched fingers, and gently pressed the lids over his glazing eyes. Not a word was uttered, but while the seconds sadly regarded the stiffening form, the surviving principal coolly drew out a cigar, lighted and placed it between his lips. The

3. The ancient Greek name of Baalbec, a city (now in East Lebanon) where the Temple of the Sun was located.

child's eyes had wandered to the latter from the pool of blood, and now in a shuddering cry she broke the silence:
"Murderer!"

Soon after the duel Edna's only living relative, her grandfather, dies. She decides to travel from Tennessee to Georgia to work in a factory and earn money for her education. Upon being injured in a train accident, she is rescued by Ellen Murray, a wealthy widow. In the following passage Edna first meets the widow's son, St. Elmo, who has just returned from hunting.

CHAPTER IV

.   .   .   .

A painful thrill shot along Edna's nerves, and an indescribable sensation of dread, a presentiment of coming ill, overshadowed her heart. This was the son of her friend, and the first glimpse of him filled her with instantaneous repugnance; there was an innate and powerful repulsion which she could not analyze. He was a tall, athletic man, not exactly young, yet certainly not elderly; one of anomalous appearance, prematurely old, and, though not one white thread silvered his thick, waving, brown hair, the heavy and habitual scowl on his high full brow had plowed deep furrows such as age claims for its monogram. His features were bold but very regular; the piercing, steel-gray eyes were unusually large, and beautifully shaded with long, heavy, black lashes, but repelled by their cynical glare; and the finely-formed mouth, which might have imparted a wonderful charm to the countenance, wore a chronic, savage sneer, as if it only opened to utter jeers and curses. Evidently the face had once been singularly handsome, in the dawn of his earthly career, when his mother's good-night kiss rested like a blessing on his smooth, boyish forehead, and the prayer learned in the nursery still crept across his pure lips; but now the fair chiseled lineaments were blotted by dissipation, and blackened and distorted by the baleful fires of a fierce, passionate nature, and a restless, powerful, and unhallowed intellect. Symmetrical and grand as that temple of Juno, in shrouded Pompeii, whose polished shafts gleamed centuries ago in the morning sunshine of a day of woe, whose untimely night has endured for nineteen hundred years; so, in the glorious flush of his youth, this man had stood facing a noble and possibly a sanctified future; but the ungovernable flames of sin had reduced him, like that darkened and desecrated fane, to a melancholy mass of ashy arches and blackened columns, where ministering priests, all holy aspirations, slumbered in the dust. His dress was costly but negligent, and the red stain on his jacket told that his hunt had not been fruitless. He wore a straw hat, belted with broad black ribbon, and his spurred boots were damp and muddy.

Mrs. Murray determines to have Edna educated by the local minister, Mr. Hammond. Edna asks to study Greek as well as Latin.

CHAPTER VII

. . . Mrs. Murray said: "I think the child is as inveterate a book-worm as I ever knew; but for heaven's sake, Mr. Hammond, do not make her a blue-stocking."

"Ellen, did you ever see a genuine blue-stocking?"

"I am happy to be able to say that I never was so unfortunate!"

"You consider yourself lucky, then, in not having known De Staël, Hannah More, Charlotte Brontë, and Mrs. Browning?"[4]

"To be consistent of course I must answer yes; but you know we women are never supposed to understand that term, much less possess the jewel itself; and beside, sir, you take undue advantage of me, for the women you mention were truly great geniuses. I was not objecting to genius in women."

"Without those auxiliaries and adjuncts which you deprecate so earnestly, would their native genius ever have distinguished them, or charmed and benefited the world? Brilliant success makes blue-stockings autocratic, and the world flatters and crowns them; but unsuccessful aspirants are strangled with an offensive *sobriquet,* than which it were better that they had millstones tied about their necks. After all, Ellen, it is rather ludicrous, and seems very unfair that the whole class of literary ladies should be sneered at on account of the color of Stillingfleet's stockings eighty years ago."

"If you please, sir, I should like to know the meaning of 'blue stocking'?" said Edna.

"You are in a fair way to understand it if you study Greek," answered Mrs. Murray, laughing at the puzzled expression of the child's countenance.

Mr. Hammond smiled, and replied:

"A 'blue-stocking,' my dear, is generally supposed to be a lady, neither young, pleasant, nor pretty, (and in most instances unmarried;) who is unamiable, ungraceful, and untidy; ignorant of all domestic accomplishments and truly feminine acquirements, and ambitious of appearing very learned; a woman whose fingers are more frequently adorned with ink-spots than thimble; who holds housekeeping in detestation, and talks loudly about politics, science, and philosophy; who is ugly, and learned, and cross; whose hair is never smooth and whose ruffles are never fluted. Is that a correct likeness, Ellen?"

"As good as one of Brady's[5] photographs. Take warning, Edna."

4. Baronne Anne Germaine Nacher de Staël-Holstein (1766–1817), French critic, novelist, and literary patron; Hannah More (1745–1833), British religious writer and social reformer; Charlotte Brontë (1816–1855), British novelist; Elizabeth Barrett Browning (1806–1861), British poet.

5. Mathew B. Brady (1822?–1896), famous for his Civil War photographs.

"The title of 'blue-stocking,'" continued the pastor, "originated in a jest, many, many, many years ago, when a circle of very brilliant, witty, and elegant ladies in London, met at the house of Mrs. Vesey, to listen to and take part in the conversation of some of the most gifted and learned men England has ever produced. One of those gentlemen, Stillingfleet, who always wore blue stockings, was so exceedingly agreeable and instructive, that when he chanced to be absent the company declared the party was a failure without 'the blue stockings,' as he was familiarly called. A Frenchman, who heard of the circumstance, gave to these conversational gatherings the name of *'bas bleu,'* which means blue stocking; and hence, you see, that in popular acceptation, I mean in public opinion, the humorous title, which was given in compliment to a very charming gentleman, is now supposed to belong to very tiresome, pedantic, and disagreeable ladies. Do you understand the matter now?"

"I do not quite understand why ladies have not as good a right to be learned and wise as gentlemen."

"To satisfy you on that point would involve more historical discussion than we have time for this morning; some day we will look into the past and find a solution of the question. Meanwhile you may study as hard as you please, and remember, my dear, that where one woman is considered a blue-stocking, and tiresomely learned, twenty are more tiresome still because they know nothing."

Edna, now seventeen, recognizes a cousin of St. Elmo as the duelist of her childhood. She refuses to shake hands with him and is confronted by St. Elmo.

CHAPTER XVI

.   .   .   .

"Edna Earl! what apology have you to offer for insulting a relative and guest of mine under my roof?"

"None, sir."

"What! How dare you treat with unparalleled rudeness a visitor, whose claim upon the courtesy and hospitality of this household is certainly more legitimate and easily recognized than that of—"

He stopped and kicked out of his way a stool upon which Edna's feet had been resting. She had risen, and they stood face to face.

"I am waiting to hear the remainder of your sentence, Mr. Murray."

He uttered an oath and hurled his cigar through the window.

"Why the d—l did you refuse to shake hands with Allston? I intend to know the truth, and it may prove an economy of trouble for you to speak it at once."

"If you demand my reasons, you must not be offended at the plainness of my language. Your cousin is a murderer, and ought to be hung! I could not force myself to touch a hand all smeared with blood."

Mr. Murray leaned down and looked into her eyes.

"You are either delirious or utterly mistaken with reference to the identity of the man. Clinton is no more guilty of murder than you are, . . . too much learning hath made thee mad.'"

"No, sir, it is no hallucination; there can be no mistake; it is a horrible, awful fact, which I witnessed, which is burned on my memory, and which will haunt my brain as long as I live. I saw him shoot Mr. Dent, and heard all that passed on that dreadful morning. He is doubly criminal—is as much the murderer of Mrs. Dent as of her husband, for the shock killed her. Oh! that I could forget her look and scream of agony as she fainted over her husband's coffin!"

A puzzled expression crossed Mr. Murray's face; then he muttered:

"Dent? Dent? Ah! yes; that was the name of the man whom Clinton killed in a duel. Pshaw! you have whipped up a syllabub storm in a teacup! Allston only took 'satisfaction' for an insult offered publicly by Dent."

His tone was sneering and his lip curled, but a strange pallor crept from chin to temples; and a savage glare in his eyes, and a thickening scowl that bent his brows till they met, told of the brewing of no slight tempest of passion.

"I know, sir, that custom, public opinion, sanctions—at least tolerates that relic of barbarous ages—that blot upon Christian civilization which, under the name of 'dueling,' I recognize as a crime; a heinous crime which I abhor and detest above all other crimes! Sir, I call things by their proper names, stripped of the glozing[6] drapery of conventional usage. You say 'honorable satisfaction;' I say murder! aggravated, unpardonable murder; murder without even the poor palliation of the sudden heat of anger. Cool, deliberate, wilful murder, that stabs the happiness of wives and children, and for which it would seem that even the infinite mercy of Almighty God could scarcely accord forgiveness! Oh! save me from the presence of that man who can derive 'satisfaction' from the reflection that he has laid Henry and Helen Dent in one grave, under the quiet shadow of Lookout, and brought desolation and orphanage to their two innocent, tender darlings! Shake hands with Clinton Allston? I would sooner stretch out my fingers to clasp those of Gardiner, reeking with the blood of his victims, or those of Ravaillac![7] Ah! well might Dante shudder in painting the chilling horrors of Caïna."[8]

The room was dusky with the shadow of coming night; but the fading flush, low in the west, showed St. Elmo's face colorless, rigid, repulsive in its wrathful defiance.

6. Glossing, or flattering.

7. Francois Ravaillac (c. 1578–1610), the assassin of Henry IV of France. Gardiner is probably Stephen Gardiner (1483–1555), bishop of Winchester, who persecuted Protestants during the reign of Queen Mary.

8. One of the four divisions of Cocytus, the lowest part of Hell, where, in the *Inferno*, Dante places those who treacherously betray their kin.

He bent forward, seized her hands, folded them together, and grasping them in both his, crushed them against his breast.

"Ha! I knew that hell and heaven were leagued to poison your mind! That your childish conscience was frightened by tales of horror, and your imagination harrowed up, your heart lacerated by the cunning devices of that arch maudlin old hypocrite! [Mr. Hammond]. The seeds of clerical hate fell in good ground, and I see a bountiful harvest nodding for my sickle! Oh! you are more pliable than I had fancied! You have been thoroughly trained down yonder at the parsonage. But I will be—"

There was a trembling pant in his voice like that of some wild creature driven from its jungle, hopeless of escape, holding its hunters temporarily at bay, waiting for death.

The girl's hands ached in his unyielding grasp, and after two ineffectual efforts to free them, a sigh of pain passed her lips and she said proudly:

"No, sir; my detestation of that form of legalized murder, politely called 'dueling,' was not taught me at the parsonage. I learned it in my early childhood, before I ever saw Mr. Hammond; and though I doubt not he agrees with me in my abhorrence of the custom, I have never heard him mention the subject."

"Hypocrite! hypocrite! Meek little wolf in lamb's wool! Do you dream that you can deceive me? Do you think me an idiot, to be cajoled by your low-spoken denials of a fact which I know? A fact, to the truth of which I will swear till every star falls!"

"Mr. Murray, I never deceived you, and I know that however incensed you may be, however harsh and unjust, I know that in your heart you do not doubt my truthfulness. Why you invariably denounce Mr. Hammond when you happen to be displeased with me, I can not conjecture; but I tell you solemnly that he has never even indirectly alluded to the question of 'dueling' since I have known him. Mr. Murray, I know you do entirely believe me when I utter these words."

A tinge of red leaped into his cheek, something that would have been called hope in any other man's eyes looked out shyly from under his heavy black lashes, and a tremor shook off the sneering curl of his bloodless lips.

Drawing her so close to him that his hair touched her forehead, he whispered:

"If I believe in you my—it is in defiance of judgment, will, and experience, and some day you will make me pay a most humiliating penalty for my momentary weakness. To-night I trust you as implicitly as Samson did the smooth-lipped Delilah; to-morrow I shall realize that, like him, I richly deserve to be shorn for my silly credulity."

He threw her hands rudely from him, turned hastily and left the library.

Edna sat down and covered her face with her bruised and benumbed fingers, but she could not shut out the sight of something that astonished and frightened her—of something that made her shudder from head to foot, and crouch down in her chair cowed and humiliated. Hitherto she had fancied that she thoroughly understood and sternly governed her heart—that conscience and reason ruled it; but within the past hour it had suddenly risen in dangerous rebellion, thrown off its allegiance to all things else, and insolently proclaimed St. Elmo Murray its king. She could not analyze her new feelings, they would not obey the summons to the tribunal of her outraged self-respect; and with bitter shame and reproach and abject contrition, she realized that she had begun to love the sinful, blasphemous man. . . .

This danger had never once occurred to her, for she had always believed that love could only exist where high esteem and unbounded reverence prepared the soil; and she was well aware that this man's character had from the first hour of their acquaintance excited her aversion and dread. Ten days before she had positively disliked and feared him; now, to her amazement, she found him throned in her heart, defying ejection. The sudden revulsion bewildered and mortified her, and she resolved to crush out the feeling at once, cost what it might.

In the biggest "love scene" of the novel, St. Elmo reveals his youthful crimes to Edna. He had discovered that his best friend, Mr. Hammond's son, was the secret lover of Agnes, his fiancée. The two had mocked him, confessing that they were after his money, and St. Elmo killed Hammond in a duel. Seeking further revenge, he seduced and abandoned Mr. Hammond's daughter Annie, who then killed herself. More recently St. Elmo has made overtures to Agnes's daughter, Gertrude, in order to hurt Agnes and pique Edna's jealousy.

CHAPTER XXII

.   .   .   .

The orphan's face was concealed, and after a moment St. Elmo Murray opened his arms, and said in that low winning tone which so many women had found it impossible to resist: "Come to me now, my pure, noble Edna. You whom I love, as only such a man as I have shown myself to be can love."

"No, Mr. Murray; Gertrude stands between us."

"Gertrude! Do not make me swear here, in your presence—do not madden me by repeating her name! I tell you she is a silly child, who cares no more for me than her mother did before her. Nothing shall stand between us. I love you; the God above us is my witness that I love you as I never loved any human being, and I will not—I swear I will not live without you! You are mine, and all the legions in hell shall not part us!"

He stooped, snatched her from the chair as if she had been an infant, and folded her in his strong arms.

"Mr. Murray, I know she loves you. My poor little trusting friend! You trifled with her warm heart, as you hope to trifle with mine; but I know you; you have shown me how utterly heartless, remorseless, unprincipled you are. You had no right to punish Gertrude for her mother's sins; and if you had one spark of honor in your nature, you would marry her, and try to atone for the injury you have already done."

"By pretending to give her a heart which belongs entirely to you? If I wished to deceive you now, think you I would have told all that hideous past, which you can not abhor one half as much as I do?"

"Your heart is not mine! It belongs to sin, or you could not have so maliciously deceived poor Gertrude. You love nothing but your ignoble revenge and the gratification of your self-love! You—"

"Take care, do not rouse me. Be reasonable, little darling. You doubt my love? Well, I ought not to wonder at your scepticism after all you have heard. But you can feel how my heart throbs against your cheek, and if you will look into my eyes, you will be convinced that I am fearfully in earnest, when I beg you to be my wife to-morrow—to-day—now! if you will only let me send for a minister or a magistrate! You are—"

"You asked Annie to be your wife, and—"

"Hush! hush! Look at me. Edna, raise your head and look at me."

She tried to break away, and finding it impossible, pressed both hands over her face and hid it against his shoulder.

He laughed and whispered:

"My darling, I know what that means. You dare not look up because you can not trust your own eyes! Because you dread for me to see something there, which you want to hide, which you think it your duty to conceal."

He felt a long shudder creep over her, and she answered resolutely:

"Do you think, sir, that I could love a murderer? A man whose hands are red with the blood of the son of my best friend?"

"Look at me then."

He raised her head, drew down her hands, took them firmly in one of his, and placing the other under her chin, lifted the burning face close to his own.

She dreaded the power of his lustrous, mesmeric eyes, and instantly her long silky lashes swept her flushed cheeks.

"Ah! you dare not! You can not look me steadily in the eye and say, 'St. Elmo, I never have loved—do not—and never can love you!' You are too truthful; your lips can not dissemble. I know you do not want to love me. Your reason, your conscience forbid it; you are struggling to crush your heart. You think it your duty to despise and hate me. But, my own Edna—my darling! my darling! you do love me! You know you do love me, though you will not confess it! My proud darling!"

He drew the face tenderly to his own, and kissed her quivering lips repeatedly; and at last a moan of anguish told how she was wrestling with her heart.

"Do you think you can hide your love from my eager eyes? Oh! I know that I am unworthy of you! I feel it more and more every day, every hour. It is because you seem so noble—so holy—to my eyes, that I reverence while I love you. You are so far above all other women—so glorified in your pure consistent piety—that you only have the power to make my future life—redeem the wretched and sinful past. I tempted and tried you, and when you proved so true and honest and womanly, you kindled a faint beam of hope that, after all, there might be truth and saving, purifying power in religion. . . . O my darling! I know I have been sinful and cruel and blasphemous; but it is not too late for me to atone! It is not too late for me to do some good in the world; and if you will only love me, and trust me, and help me—"

His voice faltered, his tears fell upon her forehead, and stooping he kissed her lips softly, reverently, as if he realized the presence of something sacred.

"My precious Edna, no oath shall ever soil my lips again; the touch of yours has purified them. I have been mad—I think, for many, many years, and I loathe my past life; but remember how sorely I was tried, and be merciful when you judge me. With your dear little hand in mine, to lead me, I will make amends for the ruin and suffering I have wrought, and my Edna—my own wife shall save me!"

Before the orphan's mental vision rose the picture of Gertrude, the trembling coral mouth, the childish wistful eyes, the lovely head nestled down so often and so lovingly on her shoulder; and she saw too the bent figure and white locks of her beloved pastor, as he sat in his old age, in his childless desolate home, facing the graves of his murdered children.

"O Mr. Murray! You can not atone! You can not call your victims from their tombs. You can not undo what you have done! What amends can you make to Mr. Hammond, and to my poor little confiding Gertrude? I can not help you! I can not save you!"

Refusing to marry St. Elmo or be adopted by Mrs. Murray or Mr. Hammond, Edna goes to New York in search of literary success. She has already published some erudite articles and now works on a novel while supporting herself as a governess. The following passages concern her completion of the novel, the critics' reaction, and her use of her new influence as successful author.

CHAPTER XXIX

.   .   .   .

The night was almost spent when Edna laid down her pen, and raised her clasped hands over the MS., which she had just completed.

For many weary months she had toiled to render it worthy of its noble theme, had spared neither time nor severe trains of thought; by day and by night she had searched and pondered; she had prayed fervently and ceaselessly, and worked arduously, unflaggingly, to accomplish this darling hope of her heart, to embody successfully this ambitious dream, and at last the book was finished.

The manuscript was a mental tapestry, into which she had woven exquisite shades of thought, and curious and quaint devices and rich, glowing imagery that flecked the groundwork with purple and amber and gold.

But would the design be duly understood and appreciated by the great, busy, bustling world, for whose amusement and improvement she had labored so assiduously at the spinning-wheels of fancy—the loom of thought? Would her fellow-creatures accept it in the earnest, loving spirit in which it had been manufactured? Would they hang this Gobelin[9] of her brain along the walls of memory, and turn to it tenderly, reading reverently its ciphers and its illuminations; or would it be rent and ridiculed, and trampled under foot? This book was a shrine to which her purest thoughts, her holiest aspirations travelled like pilgrims, offering the best of which her nature was capable. Would those for whom she had patiently chiselled and built it guard and prize and keep it; or smite and overturn and defile it?

Looking down at the mass of MS. now ready for the printer, a sad, tender, yearning expression filled the author's eyes; and her little white hands passed caressingly over its closely-written pages, as a mother's soft fingers might lovingly stroke the face of a child about to be thrust out into a hurrying crowd of cold, indifferent strangers, who perhaps would rudely jeer at and brow-beat her darling.

For several days past Edna had labored assiduously to complete the book, and now at last she could fold her tired hands, and rest her weary brain.

. . . .

Newspapers pronounced her book a failure. Some sneered in a gentlemanly manner, employing polite phraseology; others coarsely caricatured it. Many were insulted by its incomprehensible erudition; a few growled at its shallowness. To-day there was a hint at plagiarism; to-morrow an outright, wholesale theft was asserted. Now she was a pedant; and then a sciolist.[10] Reviews poured in upon her thick and fast; all found grievous faults, but no two reviewers settled on the same error. What one seemed disposed to consider almost laudable the other denounced violently. One eminently shrewd, lynx-eyed editor discovered that two of her characters were stolen from a book which Edna had never seen; and another, equally ingenious and penetrating, found her entire plot in a work of which she had never heard; while a third, shocked at her pedantry, indignantly assured her readers that they had been imposed upon, that the learning was all "picked up from encyclopædias;"

9. A tapestry, the name of which refers to a tapestry factory of the Gobelins in Paris.
10. A superficial pretender to knowledge.

whereat the young author could not help laughing heartily, and wondered why, if her learning had been so easily gleaned, her irate and insulted critics did not follow her example.

The book was for many days snubbed, buffeted, brow-beaten; and the
carefully-woven tapestry was torn into shreds and trampled upon; and it
seemed that the patiently sculptured shrine was overturned and despised and desecrated.

Edna was astonished. She knew that her work was not perfect, but she
was equally sure that it was not contemptible. She was surprised rather
than mortified, and was convinced, from the universal howling, that she
had wounded more people than she dreamed were vulnerable.

She felt that the impetuosity and savageness of the attack must neces-
sitate a recoil; and though it was difficult to be patient under such circumstances, she waited quietly, undismayed by the clamor.

.   .   .   .

While the critics snarled, the mass of readers warmly approved; and
many who did not fully appreciate all her arguments and illustrations,
were at least clear-eyed enough to perceive that it was their misfortune,
not her fault.

Gradually the book took firm hold on the affections of the people; and
a few editors came boldly to the rescue, and nobly and ably cham-
pioned it.

During these days of trial, Edna could not avoid observing one humiliating fact, that saddened without embittering her nature. She found that
instead of sympathizing with her, she received no mercy from authors,
who, as a class, out-Heroded Herod in their denunciations, and left her
little room to doubt that—

> "Envy's a sharper spur than pay,
> And unprovoked 'twill court the fray;
> No author ever spared a brother;
> Wits are gamecocks to one another."[11]

CHAPTER XXXI

.   .   .   .

Each day brought her noble fruitage, as letters came from all regions
of the country, asking for advice and assistance in little trials of which
the world knew nothing. Over the young of her own sex she held a singular sway; and orphan girls of all ranks and ages wrote of their respective sorrows and difficulties, and requested her kind counsel. To these
her womanly heart turned yearningly; and she accepted their affectionate confidence as an indication of her proper circle of useful labor.

---

11. John Gay, "The Elephant and the Bookseller," *Fables* (1727–1738).

Believing that the intelligent, refined, modest Christian women of the United States were the real custodians of national purity, and the sole agents who could successfully arrest the tide of demoralization breaking over the land, she addressed herself to the wives, mothers, and daughters of America; calling upon them to smite their false gods, and purify the shrines at which they worshipped. Jealously she contended for every woman's right which God and nature had decreed the sex. The right to be learned, wise, noble, useful, in woman's divinely limited sphere; the right to influence and exalt the circle in which she moved; the right to mount the sanctified bema[12] of her own quiet hearthstone; the right to modify and direct her husband's opinions, if he considered her worthy and competent to guide him; the right to make her children ornaments to their nation, and a crown of glory to their race; the right to advise, to plead, to pray; the right to make her desk a Delphi,[13] if God so permitted; the right to be all that the phrase "noble, Christian woman" means. But not the right to vote; to harangue from the hustings; to trail her heaven-born purity through the dust and mire of political strife; to ascend the rostra of statesmen, whither she may send a worthy husband, son, or brother, but whither she can never go, without disgracing all womanhood.

Edna was conscious of the influence she exerted, and ceaselessly she prayed that she might wield it aright. While aware of the prejudice that exists against literary women, she endeavored to avoid the *outré*[14] idiosyncrasies that justly render so many of that class unpopular and ridiculous.

She felt that she was a target at which all observers aimed random shafts; and while devoting herself to study, she endeavored to give due attention to the rules of etiquette, and the harmonious laws of the toilette.

Edna turns down numerous proposals of marriage from wealthy and charming men but still refuses to see St. Elmo, even when he reforms and becomes reconciled with Mr. Hammond. After he becomes a minister, she accepts him and in the following passage is married.

CHAPTER XXXVII

·   ·   ·   ·   ·   ·   ·   ·   ·   ·   ·   ·   ·   ·

The orphan's eyes were bent to the floor, and never once lifted, even when the trembling voice of her beloved pastor pronounced her St. Elmo Murray's wife. The intense pallor of her face frightened Mrs. Andrews, who watched her with suspended breath, and once moved eagerly toward her. Mr. Murray felt her lean more heavily against him during the cere-

12. A rostrum, or platform for speakers; the apse or chancel of a basilica.
13. The shrine where Apollo spoke through his priestess-oracle.
14. Outrageous.

mony; and, now turning to take her in his arms, he saw that her eye-lashes had fallen on her cheeks—she had lost all consciousness of what was passing.

Two hours elapsed before she recovered fully from the attack; and when the blood showed itself again in lips that were kissed so repeatedly, Mr. Murray lifted her from the sofa in the study, and passing his arm around her, said:

"To-day I snap the fetters of your literary bondage. There shall be no more books written! No more study, no more toil, no more anxiety, no more heart-aches! And that dear public you love so well, must even help itself, and whistle for a new pet. You belong solely to me now, and I shall take care of the life you have nearly destroyed, in your inordinate ambition. Come, the fresh air will revive you."

They stood a moment under the honeysuckle arch over the parsonage gate, where the carriage was waiting to take them to Le Bocage, and Mr. Murray asked:

"Are you strong enough to go to the church?"

"Yes, sir; the pain has all passed away. I am perfectly well again."

They crossed the street, and he took her in his arms and carried her up the steps, and into the grand, solemn church, where the soft, holy violet light from the richly-tinted glass streamed over gilded organ-pipes and sculptured columns.

Neither Edna nor St. Elmo spoke as they walked down the aisle; and in perfect silence both knelt before the shining altar, and only God heard their prayers of gratitude.

After some moments Mr. Murray put out his hand, took Edna's, and, holding it in his on the top of the balustrade, he prayed aloud, asking God's blessing on their marriage, and fervently dedicating all their future to his work.

And the hectic flush of the dying day was reflected on the window high above the altar, and burning through the red mantle of the Christ, fell down upon the marble shrine like sacred, sacrificial fire.

Edna felt as if her heart could not hold all its measureless joy. It seemed a delightful dream to see Mr. Murray kneeling at her side; to hear his voice earnestly consecrating their lives to the service of Jesus Christ.

She knew from the tremor in his tone, and the tears in his eyes, that his dedication was complete; and now to be his companion through all the remaining years of their earthly pilgrimage, to be allowed to help him and love him, to walk heavenward with her hand in his; this—this was the crowning glory and richest blessing of her life.

When his prayer ended, she laid her head down on the altar-railing, and sobbed like a child.

Frontier Romance

Ann Eliza Schuyler Bleecker

Lydia Maria Francis Child

Catharine Maria Sedgwick

THE FRONTIER ROMANCE has been loosely defined as a novel "containing Indian characters and written between 1790 and 1860." In *The Ignoble Savage*, from which this definition is taken (p. 17), Louise K. Barnett lists over seventy such works. Eleven are by James Fenimore Cooper, the most famous practitioner of the frontier romance, and nine-tenths are by men authors. Women, however, played an important role in the development of the form and authored one-quarter of the examples published before 1828, when the frontier romance had become a clearly recognizable genre.

The frontier romance had two obvious sources, one indigenous to America and one borrowed from England. The American antecedent, the captivity narrative, described the abduction of white settlers by Indians, the experiences of the whites in captivity, and their eventual escape. Enormously popular, captivity narratives were reprinted into the nineteenth century; *The Narrative of the Captivity and Restauration of Mrs. Mary Rowlandson*, first published in 1682, had a fifteenth edition in 1800. Captivity narratives were true (or supposedly true) stories. Not until the late 1700s, with Ann Eliza Schuyler Bleecker's *The History of Maria Kittle* (1791), did fictional captivity narratives begin to appear.

Captivity narratives were limited in scope, and it took the impetus of Sir Walter Scott to develop the full-fledged frontier romance. After the war of 1812, when Scott's Waverly novels were in vogue, fiction by Americans on native themes was at an ebb. Critics demanded local scenes, just as they had in the 1780s at the time of Sally Wood, only now they had a model. Why could not Americans write historical romances á la Scott about the Pilgrims, the Revolution, the Indians? Native writers took up the challenge. Cooper in *The Pioneers* (1823), Lydia Maria Child in *Hobomok* (1824), and the novelists who followed them adopted the Scott plot; as Barnett describes it, "Against the backdrop of a significant historical moment, a genteel hero and heroine experience adventures which temporarily separate them" (p. 49). The novelists placed the action on the American frontier, where the captivity narratives were set—on the border between the wilderness, populated by Indians, and "civilization," populated by white colonists.

An innovation of the women writers, which was unfortunately not adopted by the men, was their willingness to portray intermarriage between whites and Indians. Although the women presented miscegenation in a rather negative light, as the selections from Child and Catharine Maria Sedgwick show, they at least did not avoid the subject. The women also tended, more than the men, to replace the "bad" Indian, the faceless enemy in the captivity narratives, with the "good" Indian, the noble savage. Yet it was always clear that, no matter how noble, the Indian was doomed to destruction. Many critics have noted the cathartic emotional function of the frontier romance. Roy Harvey Pearce describes it succinctly in *The Savages of America*. The task of writers, he says, was "at once publicly to admit that the Indian had been cruelly destroyed and to satisfy themselves and their readers that that destruction was part of a universal moral progress which it was the special destiny of America to manifest" (p. 212).

The frontier romance thus served as a form of expiation. In the ensuing selections from Ann Eliza Schuyler Bleecker, Lydia Maria Child, and Catharine Maria Sedgwick, dramatic differences emerge that illustrate the development of the frontier romance. Yet the controlling point of view, the assumption of Manifest Destiny, remains the same: it is a staple of the genre.

Ann Eliza Schuyler Bleecker (1752–1783)

Although Ann Eliza Schuyler Bleecker was never captured by Indians, like the protagonist of her best known work, she lived a dramatic life. The youngest daughter of Margareta Van Wyck and Brandt Schuyler of New York City, she was born into an aristocratic family. Her father died before her birth, but she grew up amidst wealth and culture and was encouraged in her predilection for reading and writing verse. At sixteen she married John Bleecker and moved with him to Tomhanick, New York, a frontier village where he owned property.

The Bleeckers lived in material comfort but were constantly threatened by raids of hostile Indians and Tories. John spent much time away on militia duty while Ann read the classics and wrote sentimental verse far removed from her real situation. With the approach of General Burgoyne's army in 1777, John went to nearby Albany to find safer accommodations for the family. During his absence Ann heard that a band of Indians was about to attack the village and fled with her baby and four-year-old daughter; they had trouble finding shelter and the baby eventually died.

Ann Eliza Bleecker was obliged to flee Tomhanick on other occasions during the war years, and in 1781 she set out to rescue her husband, who had been captured by Tories. Although he was soon delivered, the strain of her experiences had affected her health. She wrote her cousin, "I am charmed with the lovely scene the spring opens around me. —Alas! the wilderness is within: I muse so long on the dead until I am unfit for the company of the living. . . . Affliction has broken my spirit and constitution." She became increasingly ill and melancholic and died at the age of thirty-one.

Bleecker never published any of her writings during her lifetime. According to her daughter, Margaretta Bleecker Faugeres, she destroyed many of her manuscripts in periods of depression. Bleecker's surviving works were published several years after her death in the *New-York Magazine*, undoubtedly through the efforts of her daughter, who also contributed her own poems to the magazine. In 1793 *The Posthumous Works of Ann Eliza Bleecker* appeared; the volume contains the poems and prose works published earlier in the *New-York Magazine*, letters from Bleecker to her family, and writings by Magaretta Bleecker Faugeres.

Selected Bibliography

SECONDARY
Faugeres, Margaretta Bleecker. "Memoirs of Mrs. Ann Eliza Bleecker." In *The Posthumous Works of Ann Eliza Bleecker*. New York: T. and J. Swords, 1793.
Hendrickson, James. "Ann Eliza Bleecker: Her Life and Works." Master's thesis, Columbia University, 1935.

The History of Maria Kittle (1791)

The History of Maria Kittle is the earliest known frontier romance. Although written by Ann Eliza Schuyler Bleecker in 1779, it was not published until after her death; it appeared in *New-York Magazine* in 1791, was collected with her *Posthumous Works* in 1793, and came out alone in book form in 1797. In form *The History* lies somewhere between short story and novel, what we would today call a "novelette." It is presented as one long letter from the author to her cousin, Susan Ten Eyck.

Literary historians have put more emphasis on Bleecker's unrealistic use of the popular epistolary form than they have on her subject matter. Herbert Ross Brown complains in *The Sentimental Novel in America 1789–1860* that Bleecker destroyed any illusion of reality by trying to "pack the entire narrative into a single, long-winded letter." He continues: "The author was not unmindful of the difficulty of preserving the atmosphere of actual correspondence in a letter containing upwards of seventeen thousand words! After a breathless spurt of forty-two hundred words, the correspondent announced, 'I am sorry, dear Susan, to quit Maria in this interesting part of her history; but order requires that we should now return to her spouse, whom we left on his way through the wood'" (p. 64).

Bleecker was not really as artless as such passages make her seem. She had greater success in adapting her major model, the captivity narrative, than she did with the epistolary novel form. Although she makes the conventional claim that her story is true—she heard it from an honest neighbor—she imposes the type of careful pattern that belongs to fiction. For instance, the typical captivity narrative begins immediately with the Indian attack and capture of the author; Bleecker devotes the first part of her book to setting the scene and creating suspense through forebodings that the idyllic existence of the Kittles will soon be shattered. When the Indian attack comes; it is presented in more gruesome detail than in the captivity narratives. Bleecker can justly be accused of blood-and-guts sensationalism. Maria Kittle's soliloquy ("O barbarians!") after the murder of her child seems more a rhetorical device than a realistic response.

The attitude toward Indians in *The History of Maria Kittle* is less complicated that it would be in later frontier romances. To Bleecker, the Indians are simply barbarians—cruel savages with nothing of the noble, or indeed the human, about them. Maria expects better treatment from the Indian women, because they are women; but they are (inexplicably) hostile, and Maria is attacked by an "old hag frantic, and insatiable of blood." The Indians belong with wolves and earthquakes and violent eruptions of nature that form an extreme contrast to the beauty of a sunset or the pastoral Eden of the Kittle home. There seems to be no middle ground in Bleecker's imagination between paradise and hell. All her writings except *Maria Kittle* emphasize one side of the split above the other. In her poems and *The Story of Henry and Anne*, which are imitative and polite, America appears as the stereotyped land of peace and plenty; in her more vivid letters, it is a country wracked by the brutalities of war. In *Maria Kittle* the two attitudes are placed in uneasy juxtaposition. The tension gives the book an interest beyond its status as our earliest fictional treatment of the frontier.

The book begins with the marriage of the Kittles.

Tomhanick, December 1779

Dear Susan,

.   .   .   .

Maria was fifteen when married. They removed to his farm, on which he had built a small neat house, surrounded by tall cedars, which gave it a contemplative air. It was situated on an eminence, with a green inclosure in the front, graced by a well cultivated garden on one side, and on the other by a clear stream, which, rushing over a bed of white pebble, gave them a high polish, that cast a soft gleam through the water.

Here they resided in the tranquil enjoyment of that happiness which so much merit and innocence deserved: the indigent, the sorrowful, the unfortunate were always sure of consolation when they entered those peaceful doors. They were almost adored by their neighbors, and even the wild savages themselves, who often resorted thither for refreshments when hunting, expressed the greatest regard for them, and admiration of their virtues.

In little more than a year they were blessed with a daughter, the lovelier resemblance of her lovely mother: as she grew up, her graces increasing, promised a bloom and understanding equal to her's; the Indians, in particular, were extremely fond of the smiling Anna; whenever they found a young fawn, or caught a brood of wood-ducks, or surprised the young beaver in their daily excursions through the forest, they presented them with pleasure to her; they brought her the earliest strawberries, the scarlet plumb, and other delicate wild fruits in painted baskets.

How did the fond parents' hearts delight to see their beloved one so universally caressed! When they sauntered over the vernal fields with the little prattler wantoning before them collecting flowers and pursuing the velvet elusive butterfly, Maria's cheek suffusing with rapture, "Oh my dear," she would say, "we are happier than human beings can expect to be; how trivial are the evils annexed to our situation! may God avert that our heaven be limited to this life!"

Eleven years now elapsed before Mrs. Kittle discovered any signs of pregnancy: her spouse silently wished for a son, and his desires were at

The History of Maria Kittle, taken from pp. 19–87, *The Posthumous Works of Ann Eliza Bleecker in Prose and Verse* (New York: Printed by T. & J. Swords, 1793). Excerpts are taken from 21–25, 33–42, 48–49, 54–61.

length gratified; she was delivered of a charming boy, who was named, after him, William.

A French and Indian war had commenced sometime before; but about eight months after her delivery, the savages began to commit the most horrid depredations on the English frontiers. Mr. Kittle, alarmed at the danger of his brothers, who dwelt near Fort-Edward, (the eldest being just married to a very agreeable young woman) invited them to reside with him during the war.

They were scarce arrived when the enemy made further incursions in the country, burning the villages and scalping the inhabitants, neither respecting age or sex. This terribly alarmed Mrs. Kittle; she began to prepare for flight, and the next evening after receiving this intelligence, as she and Mr. Kittle were busily employed in packing up china and other things, they were accosted by several Indians, whose wigwams were contiguous to the village of Schochticook, and who always seemed well affected to the English. An elderly savage undertook to be pro-locutor, and desired the family to compose themselves, assuring them they should be cautioned against any approaching danger. To inforce his argument, he presented Maria with a belt interwoven with silk and beads, saying, "There, receive my token of friendship: we go to dig up the hatchet, to sink it in the heads of your enemies; we shall guard this wood with a wall of fire—you shall be safe." A warm glow of hope deep-ened in Maria's cheek at this—Then ordering wine to be brought to the friendly savages, with a smile of diffidence, "I am afraid," said she, "ne-cessity may oblige you to abandon us, or neglect of your promise may deprive us of your protection."—"Neglect of my promise!" retorted he with some acrimony: "No, Maria, I am a true man; I shoot the arrow up to the Great Captain every new moon: depend upon it, I will trample down the briars round your dwelling, that you do not hurt your feet." Maria now retired, bowing a grateful acknowledgment, and leaving the savages to indulge their festivity, who passed the night in the most vo-ciferous mirth.

One of Mr. Kittle's brothers is shot by an Indian while hunting in the woods. Mr. Kittle decides, over his wife's protests, to go alone to get wagons so the family can flee to safety. He leaves his wife and two children, his remaining brother, Henry, and his sister-in-law, Comelia.

Mrs. Kittle now approached with her playful infant in her arms; but its winning actions extorted nothing but groans from her pained bosom, which was more stormy than Ontario-Lake, when agitated by fierce winds. Mr. Kittle percieving this uncommon emotion, gently took the child from her, and repeatedly kissed it, while new smiles dimpled its lovely aspect. "Oh!" said he to himself, "this gloom that darkens Maria's soul is supernatural!—it seems dreadfully portentous!—Shall I yet stay?" But here a servant informing him that his horse was ready, he blushed at his want of fortitude; and having conquered his irresolution, after the most affecting and solemn parting, he quitted his house, never to review it more!

Maria then walked sadly back again, and having assembled the family in a little hall, they closed and barred the doors. Mrs. Comelia Kittle, Maria's sister-in-law, was far advanced in her pregnancy, which increased her husband's uneasiness for her; and they were debating in what manner to accommodate her at Albany, when the trampling of feet about the house, and a yell of complicated voices, announced the Indians arrival. Struck with horror and consternation, the little family crouded together in the center of the hall, while the servants at this alarm, being in a kitchen distant from the house, saved themselves by a precipitate flight. The little Billy, frightened at such dreadful sounds, clung fast to his mother's throbbing breast, while Anna, in a silent agony of amazement, clasped her trembling knees. The echo of their yells yet rung in long vibrations through the forest, when, with a thundering peal of strokes at the door, they demanded entrance. Distraction and despair sat upon every face. Maria and her companions gazed wildly at each other, till, upon repeated menaces and efforts to break open the door, Comelia's husband, giving all for lost, leisurely advanced to the door. Comelia seeing this, uttered a great shriek, and cried out, "O God! what are you doing, my rash, rash, unfortunate husband! you will be sacrificed!" Then falling on her knees, she caught hold of his hand and sobbed out, "O pity me! have mercy on yourself, on me, on my child!"—"Alas! my love," said he, half turning with a look of distraction, "what can we do? let us be resigned to the will of God." So saying he unbarred the door, and that instant received a fatal bullet in his bosom, and fell backward writhing in agonies of death; the rest recoiled at this horrible spectacle, and huddled in a corner, sending forth the most piercing cries: in the interim the savages rushing in with great shouts, proceeded to mangle the corpse, and having made an incision round his head with a crooked knife, they tugged off his bloody scalp with barbarous triumph. While this was perpetrating, an Indian, hideously painted, strode ferociously up to Comelia, (who sunk away at the sight, and fainted on a chair) and cleft her white forehead deeply with his tomahack. Her fine azure eyes just opened, and then suddenly closing for ever, she tumbled lifeless at his feet. His sanguinary soul was not yet satisfied with blood; he deformed her lovely body with deep gashes; and, tearing her unborn babe away, dashed it to pieces against the stone wall; with many additional circumstances of infernal cruelty.

During this horrid carnage, the dead were stripped, and dragged from the house, when one of the hellish band advanced to Maria, who circling her babes with her white arms, was sending hopeless petitions to heaven, and bemoaning their cruelly lost situation: as he approached, expecting the fatal stroke, she endeavoured to guard her children, and with supplicating looks, implored for mercy. The savage attempted not to strike; but the astonished Anna sheltered herself behind her mamma, while her blooming suckling quitting her breast, gazed with a pleasing wonder on the painted stranger.—Maria soon recognized her old friend that presented her with the belt, through the loads of shells and feathers that disguised him. This was no time, however, to irritate him, by reminding him of his promise; yet, guessing her thoughts, he anticipated her remonstrance. "Maria," said he, "be not afraid, I have promised to protect you; you shall live and dance with us around the fire at Canada: but you have one small incumbrance, which, if not removed, will much impede your progress thither." So saying he seized her laughing babe by the wrists, and forcibly endeavoured to draw him from her arms. At this, terrified beyond conception, she exclaimed, "O God! leave me, leave me my child! he shall not go, though a legion of devils should try to separate us!" Holding him still fast, while the Indian applied his strength to tear him away, gnashing his teeth at her opposition; "Help! God of heaven!" screamed she, "help! have pity, have mercy on this infant! O God! O Christ! can you bear to see this? O mercy! mercy! mercy! let a little spark of compassion save this inoffending, this lovely angel!" By this time the breathless babe dropt its head on its bosom; the wrists were nigh pinched off, and seeing him just expiring, with a dreadful shriek she resigned him to the merciless hands of the savage, who instantly dashed his little forehead against the stones, and casting his bleeding body at some distance from the house, left him to make his exit in feeble and unheard groans.—Then indeed, in the unutterable anguish of her soul, she fell prostrate, and rending away her hair, she roared out her sorrows with a voice louder than natural, and rendered awfully hollow by too great an exertion. "O barbarians!" she exclaimed, "surpassing devils in wickedness! so may a tenfold night of misery enwrap your black souls, as you have deprived the babe of my bosom, the comfort of my cares, my blessed cherub, of light and life—O hell! are not thy flames impatient to cleave the center and engulph these wretches in thy ever burning waves? are there no thunders in Heaven—no avenging Angel—no God to take notice of such heaven defying cruelties?" Then rushing to her dead infant with redoubled cries, and clapping her hands, she laid herself over his mangled body; again softened in tears and moans, she wiped the blood from his ghastly countenance, and prest him to her heaving bosom, alternately caressing him and her trembling Anna, who, clinging to her with bitter wailings, and kissing her hands and face, entreated her to implore the savages for mercy. "Do, my angel mamma," she urged, "do beg them yet to pity—beg them yet to save you for my poor, poor papa's sake!—Alas! if we are all killed, his heart will break!— Oh! they can't be rocks and stones!—Don't cry mamma, they will spare us!"—Thus the little orator endeavoured to console her afflicted mother; but their melancholy endearments were soon interrupted by the relentless savages, who having plundered the house of every valuable thing that was portable, returned to Maria, and rudely catching her arm, commanded her to follow them; but repulsing them with the boldness of despair, "Leave me, leave me," she said, "I cannot go—I never will quit my murdered child! Too cruel in your mercies; you have given me life

only to prolong my miseries!"—Meanwhile the lovely Anna, terrified at
the hostile appearance of the enemy, left her mamma struggling to dis-
engage herself from the Indians, and fled precipitately to the house. She
had already concealed herself in a closet, when Mrs. Kittle pursuing her,
was intercepted by flames, the savages having fired the house. The
wretched child soon discovered her deplorable situation, and almost suffocated by the smoke, with piercing cries called for help to her dear,
dear mother.—Alas! what could the unhappy parent do? whole sheets of
flames rolled between them, while in a phrenzy of grief she screamed
out, "O my last treasure! my beloved Anna! try to escape the devouring
fire—come to me my sweet child—the Indians will not kill us—O my
perishing babe! have pity on your mother—do not leave me quite destitute!" Then turning to the calm villains who attended her, she cried,
"Why do you not attempt to rescue my sweet innocent? can your unfeeling hearts not bear to leave me one—a solitary single one?" Again calling to her Anna, she received no answer, which being a presumption of
her death, the Indians obliged Maria and her brother Henry to quit the
house, which they effected with some difficulty, the glowing beams falling around them and thick volumes of smoke obscuring their passage.
The flames now struck a long splendor through the humid atmosphere,
and blushed to open the tragical scene on the face of heaven. They had
scarce advanced two hundred yards with their reluctant captives, when
the flaming structure tumbled to the earth with a dreadful crash. Our
travellers by instinct turned their eyes to the mournful blaze; and Maria, bursting afresh into grievous lamentations, cried, "There, there my
brother, my children are wrapt in arching sheets of flames, that used to
be circled in my arms! they are entombed in ruins that breathed their
slumbers on my bosom! yet, oh! their spotless souls even now rise from
this chaos of blood and fire, and are pleading our injured cause before our
God, my brother!" He replied only in sighs and groans; he scarcely heard
her; horror had froze up the avenues of his soul; and all amazed and
trembling, he followed his leaders like a person in a troublesome dream.

The distant flames now cast a fainter light, and the northern breeze
bent the columns of smoke over the south horizon. Sad and benighted
they wandered through almost impenetrable swamps, forded the broad
stream of Tomhanick and the rapid river of Hosack; they passed through
deserted settlements, where the yelling of solitary dogs increased the
solemnity of midnight, nor halted till the stars, emitting a feebler lustre, presaged the approach of day. Maria, overcome by sorrow and fatigue,
immediately sunk helpless at the foot of the tree, while the savages
(who were six in number) kindled a fire, and prepared their meal, (in a
calabash) which consisted only of some parched maize pulverized and
enriched with the fat of bears flesh. Observing Maria had fallen asleep,
they offered not to disturb her, but invited Henry Kittle to partake of
their repast. He durst not refuse them; and having swallowed a few
mouthfuls of their unpalatable food, and accepted a pipe of tobacco, he
desired leave to repose himself, which being readily granted, they soon

followed his example, and sunk asleep, leaving two centinels to guard against surprise, which precaution they always make use of.

I am sorry, dear Susan, to quit Maria in this interesting part of her history; but order requires that we should now return to her spouse, whom we left on his way through the wood.

Returning home and concluding that his entire family perished, Mr. Kittle is delirious for six weeks. Upon his recovery he joins the British army to get revenge on the Indians. The scene shifts to Mrs. Kittle.

But doubtless, my dear, your generous sensibility is alarmed at my silence about Mrs. Kittle; I think we left her reposing under a tree: she was the first that awaked as the sun began to exhale the crystal globules of morning, when half rising, and reclining on her elbow, she surveyed the lovely landscape around her with a deep sigh; they were on an eminence that commanded an unlimited prospect of the country every way. The birds were cheerful; the deer bounded fearless over the hills; the meadows blushed with the enamel of Flora: but grief had saddened every object in her sight; the whole creation seemed a dark blank to the fair mourner. Again recollection unlocked the sluices of her eyes, and her soft complaints disturbed her savage companions, who, rising and kindling up the dying embers, began to prepare their victuals, which they invited her to partake of. This she declined with visible detestation; and turning to her brother, with the dignity of conscious merit in distress, "No," said she, "I never will receive a morsel from those bloody hands yet dropping with recent murder!—let me perish—let the iron hand of famine first pinch out my vitals and send me after my children!"

Henry persuades Maria to eat, and they travel with their captors. After the following passage describing the journey, the party reaches Montreal. The Indians deliver Maria and Henry to the French governor, who treats them very well. (During the French and Indian War, when the action is supposed to be taking place, the French were enemies. During the period Bleecker was writing the book, however, the French were allies and it was politic to praise them.) Maria lives in Montreal for two years with French and English women, many of whom have had similar experiences. Finally Henry encounters Mr. Kittle and the family is reunited.

. . . In the evening they crossed the river somewhat below Fort-Edward, in a canoe left hid under some bushes for that purpose. They observed the most profound silence until they entered the woods again; but it was very late before they halted, which they did in a deep hollow, surrounded by pines whose tops seemed to be lost in the clouds. It was necessary here to light a fire, for the wolves howled most dreadfully, and the whole forest rung with the cries of wild beasts of various sorts. The confines of hell could not have given Maria more dismal ideas than her present situation: the horrid gloom of the place, the scowling looks of her murderous companions, the shrill shrieks of owls, the loud cries of the wolf, and mournful screams of panthers, which were redoubled by distant echoes as the terrible sounds seemed dying away, shook her frame with cold tremors—she sunk under the oppression of terror, and almost fainted in Henry's arms; however, on perceiving the beasts durst not approach the light, but began to retire, she became a little more assured, and helped Henry to erect a booth of pine branches, making a bed of the same materials in it while he prepared their supper: having eaten, and kindled a large fire in the front of her arbour, she laid down and soon fell in a deep sleep. She felt herself refreshed by this unexpected repose, and the next morning, with some alacrity, continued her journey, hoping at last to arrive at some Christian settlement. Arriving at Lake-Champlain, they raised a wigwam on the bank, expecting the coming of Indians from the opposite shore to carry them over.

Here our unfortunate captives were stript of their habits, already rent to pieces by briers, and attired each with remnants of old blankets. In this new dress Mrs. Kittle ventured to expostulate with the savages, but it was talking to the stormy ocean; her complaints served only to divert them; so retiring among the bushes, she adjusted her coarse dress somewhat decently, and then seating herself silently under a spreading tree, indulged herself in the luxury of sorrow. Henry, sensible that they expected more fortitude from him, and that if he sunk under his adverse fortune he should be worse treated, affected to be cheerful; he assisted them in catching salmon, with which the lake abounds; an incredible quantity of wild fowl frequenting the lake also, he laid snares for those of the lesser sort, (not being allowed fire-arms) and succeeded so well, that his dexterity was highly commended, and night coming on, they regaled themselves on the fruits of their industry. The night was exceedingly dark, but calm; a thick mist hovered over the woods, and the small ridgy waves softly rolled to the shore, when suddenly a large meteor, or fiery exhalation, passed by them with surprising velocity, casting on every side showers of brilliant sparkles. At sight of this phænomenon the Indians put their heads between their knees, crying out in a lamentable voice, "Do not! do not! do not!" continuing in the same attitude until the vapour disappeared. Henry, with some surprise, demanded the reason of this exclamation; to which they replied, "What he had seen was a fiery dragon on his passage to his den, who was of so malevolent a temper, that he never failed, on his arrival there, to inflict some peculiar calamity on mankind." In about five minutes after the earth was violently agitated, the waves of the lake tumbled about in a strange manner, seeming to emit flashes of fire, all the while attended with most tremendous roarings, intermixed with loud noises, not unlike the explosion of heavy cannon. Soon as the Indians perceived it was an earthquake, they cried out, "Now he comes home!" and casting themselves in their former posture, filled the air with dismal howlings. This was a terrible scene to Maria, who had never been witness to so dreadful a convulsion of Nature before; she started up and fled from her savage companions towards an eminence at some distance, where, dropping on her knees, she emphatically implored the protection of Heaven: however, she was followed by an Indian and Henry; the latter, highly affected with her distresses, taking hold of her trembling hand, "But why, my sister!" said he, "have you fled from us? is the gloom of a forest more cheering than the sympathising looks of a friend?" "No, my brother!" replied Maria; "but the thought was suggested to me, that the supreme God perhaps was preparing to avenge himself of these murderers by some awful and uncommon judgment, and I fled from them as Lot did from Sodom, lest I might be involved in the punishment of their guilt." They conversed in English, which displeasing the Indian, he ordered them to return to the wigwam, threatening to bind Maria fast if she offered to elope again. The shock being over, silence again spread through the realms of darkness, when a high wind arose from the north and chilled our half-naked travellers with excessive cold. The savages (whose callous skins were proof against the inclement weather) not caring to continue their fires, lest they should be discovered and surprised by some English party, they passed here a very uncomfortable night; but the wind subsiding, and the sky growing clear, the sun rose peculiarly warm and pleasant, streaming ten thousand rays of gold across the lake. Maria had scarcely performed her oraisons, when the savages, forming a circle round her and Henry, began to dance in a most extravagant manner, and with antic gestures that at another time would have afforded mirth to our travellers. Having continued their exercise some time, they incontinently drew out boxes of paint, and began to ornament their captives with a variety of colours; one having crossed their faces with a stroke of vermillion, another would intersect it with a line of black, and so on until the whole company had given a specimen of their skill or fancy.

Soon after two canoes arrived, in which they passed over the lake, which was uncommonly serene and pleasant. They proceeded not far on their way before they were obliged to halt for two days, on account of Maria's inability to travel, her feet being greatly swoln and lacerated by the flinty path. At length, by easy stages, they came in view of an Indian settlement, when Maria's long unbent features relaxed into a half smile, and turning to Henry, "Here, my brother!" said she, "I shall find some of my own sex, to whom simple Nature, no doubt, has taught humanity; this is the first precept she inculcates in the female mind, and this they generally retain through life, in spite of every evil propensity." As she uttered this elogium[1] in favour of the fair, the tawny villagers, perceiving their approach, rushed promiscuously from their huts with an execrable din, and fell upon the weary captives with clubs and a shower of stones, accompanying their strokes with the most virulent language; among the rest an old deformed squaw, with the rage of a Tisiphone,[2]

1. Eulogy.
2. One of the Greek Erinyes (Furies).

flew to Maria, aiming a pine-knot at her head, and would certainly have given the wretched mourner her quietus had she not been opposed by the savage that guarded Mrs. Kittle: he at first mildly expostulated with his passionate countrywoman; but finding the old hag frantic, and insatiable of blood, he twisted the pine-knot from her hand and whirled it away to some distance, then seizing her arm roughly and tripping up her heels, he laid her prostrate, leaving her to howl and yell at leisure, which she performed without a prompter.—Maria was all in a tremor, and hastily followed her deliverer, not caring to risk another encounter with the exasperated virago. By this time the rage and tumult of the savages subsiding, the new-comers were admitted into a large wigwam, in the center of which blazed a fire. After they were seated, several young Indians entered with baskets of green maize in the ear, which, having roasted before the fire, they distributed among the company.

Lydia Maria Francis Child (1802–1880)

The frontier romance, which first brought her fame, was finally only a minor achievement for Lydia Maria Child. She made her greatest contribution as an abolitionist writer and activist. Child was born in Medford, Massachusetts, the youngest child of Susannah Rand and Convers Francis, a baker. Although she received some formal education at a local seminary, she studied most profitably with her brother, a Unitarian minister and later a professor at the Harvard Divinity School. During the 1820s Child conducted a private school and began to write, publishing two novels and editing *Juvenile Miscellany*, America's first periodical for children. Against her family's advice she married David Child, an improvident lawyer.

To this point, Child's career resembles those of many literary women in the early 1800s. Like Sarah Josepha Hale, for example, she had become a successful editor and accepted member of the literary establishment; her own writings were popular and broad in scope, ranging from fiction (*The Rebels; or, Boston Before the Revolution*, 1825) to poetry (*The Coronal*, 1831) to advice books (*The Frugal Housewife*, 1829). But, unlike Hale, Child went on to become a radical. The Childs were converted by William Lloyd Garrison to the abolitionist cause, and Lydia Maria promptly wrote the first anti-slavery work published in book form in America, *Appeal in Favor of That Class of Americans Called Africans* (1833). This influential book caused Child to be ostracized and killed the *Juvenile Miscellany* and the sales of her other writings.

While the conservative Hale was complaining that Child's "fine genius, her soul's wealth has been wasted" (*Woman's Record*, p. 620), Child wrote more anti-slavery pamphlets and worked all the harder for abolition. From 1840 to 1843 she edited the *National Anti-Slavery Standard* in New York, and in the early 1850s she and her husband moved to a small farm in Wayland, Massachusetts, which became a station in the Underground Railroad. After the Civil War, Child lived a relatively quiet existence on the farm; she did, however, publish *The Freedmen's Book* (1865), a handbook for freed slaves that included selections by black writers.

Although she was best known as an abolitionist, Child also became the champion of other oppressed groups. She wrote on behalf of Indians and women. Child associated with Margaret Fuller, the feminist and Transcendentalist writer, and participated in Fuller's famous "conversations," or seminars, for women. While she never became active in women's rights organizations, Child advocated suffrage for women. She was also interested in women's history and biography; for a series called *Ladies' Family Library*, she wrote several biographies of famous women and *History of the Condition of Women in Various Ages and Nations* (2 vols., 1835).

Selected Bibliography

OTHER WORKS
Philothea (1836); *Letters from New York* (2 vols., 1843, 1845); *Progress of Religious Ideas through Successive Ages* (3 vols., 1855); *Correspondence between Lydia Maria Child and Governor Wise and Mrs. Mason of Virginia* (1860); *Aspirations of the World* (1878).

SECONDARY
Baer, Helene G. *The Heart Is Like Heaven: The Life of Lydia Maria Child.* Philadelphia: University of Pennsylvania Press, 1964.
Conrad, Susan Phinney. "Lydia Maria Child: The Many Worlds of Women and an Intellectual's Dilemma." Chap. 3 in *Perish the Thought: Intellectual Women in Romantic America, 1830–1860,* *104–116.* New York: Oxford University Press, 1976.
Jeffrey, Kirk. "Marriage, Career, and Feminine Ideology in the Nineteenth Century: Reconstructing the Marital Experience of Lydia Maria Child, 1828–1874." *Feminist Studies* 2 (1975): 113–130.
Meltzer, Milton. *Tongue of Flame: The Life of Lydia Maria Child.* New York: Thomas Y. Crowell Co., 1965.
Osborne, William S. *Lydia Maria Child.* Boston: Twayne Publishers, 1980.
[Review of *Hobomok*]. *North American Review,* 10th ser., 19 (July 1824): 266.
Taylor, Lloyd C., Jr. "Lydia Maria Child and the Indians." *Boston Public Library Quarterly* 12 (1960): 51– 56.

Hobomok (1824)

Lydia Maria Child began her writing career at age twenty-two with *Hobomok*. She was motivated by reading in *North American Review* a notice of a celebrated narrative poem, *Yamoyden, A Tale of the Wars of King Philip* (1820). The reviewer's assertion that the early history of New England was a promising field for novelists gave Child a subject. She had some reservations about fiction—she thought novels like *Charlotte Temple* were harmful ("The morality should be *in* the book, not tacked upon the *end* of it")—but an historical novel would allow her to indulge her interest in Puritan Massachusetts and find useful lessons in the past. Child also took the reviewer's advice about the potential of Indian characters and customs. Her hero would be a gallant Indian chief, like Yamoyden in the popular poem, only he would be defeated in love rather than war.

When it was *Hobomok*'s turn to be reviewed in *North American Review* (July 1824), the reaction was mixed. The subject matter and setting received unqualified praise. The reviewer appreciated the portrayal of Salem and Plymouth and the introduction of real characters from history, such as Governor Endicott. Child's storytelling had definite appeal. A "speak for yourself, John" sub-plot anticipates Longfellow, and the self-sacrifice of Hobomok looks forward to Tennyson's *Enoch Arden*. But the "morality" of the book was another question. While it was acceptable for Child to criticize the excesses of Puritanism and even to introduce an ultra-noble Indian, it was not acceptable for her to let the Indian marry the Puritan's daughter. Said the *North American Review* (see Selected Bibliography): "Now this is a train of events not only unnatural, but revolting, we conceive, to every feeling of delicacy in man or woman" (p. 266). No wonder most frontier romancers scrupulously avoided miscegenation.

To the modern reader, the marriage of Hobomok and the heroine, Mary Conant, is indelicate for another reason. Whatever humanitarian effect Child intended is severely compromised by her assumption of white superiority. Hobomok views the appropriately named Mary as a sort of goddess. In the beginning of the novel he can only "reverence" and "adore"; apparently it would be blasphemy to love her, to say nothing of marry her. Child takes pains to show that the marriage comes about only when Mary hears the news that her white fiancé, Charles, has been killed and her father's harshness pushes her into a fit of insanity. Ultimately the marriage must be dissolved. When Charles returns alive, Hobomok has to fade off nobly into the woods, losing his son as well as his wife. Hobomok's low status is clear in that he plays the role usually reserved for women. He is the one who must sacrifice himself, like the heroines in the author's other novels, and has to see his identity erased in his child. The son, aptly named Charles Hobomok Conant, is stripped of his Indian heritage and eventually becomes a "distinguished graduate" of Cambridge, an honor presumably great enough to compensate for his mixed blood. At least Charles H. is spared the fate of the son in Ann Stephens's *Malaeska* (1860). In this later frontier romance, the son of a white man and an Indian woman grows up with Indian-hating grandparents and commits suicide when he discovers his parentage.

It may be difficult for the modern reader of *Hobomok* to imagine the author a champion of Indians, but in the nineteenth century Lydia Maria Child was certainly that. She wrote two books defending Indian rights, both works in response to specific events. President Andrew Jackson's complicity in exiling the Cherokees from their land stirred her to write *The First Settlers of New England* (1828), drawing on early histories of Pequod and Narraganset Indians. After the Civil War she responded to the report of a peace commission appointed to recommend ways of ending the Indian wars in the West. In *An Appeal for the Indians* (1868), she discussed the "curse of white superiority" and criticized the commission's obvious desire to wipe out Indian tradition and culture. She objected, for instance, to the commission's insistence that Indian children be taught only in English and suggested that instruction be bilingual.

In her non-fiction works, Child showed more sensitivity to Indian life and culture than she did in *Hobomok.* Of course, both her knowledge of Indians and her understanding of oppressed groups had increased since she wrote *Hobomok* in her extreme youth. Hobomok seems to be a white man (or perhaps a white woman) disguised as an Indian—in double drag, as it were. While Cooper's Indians are none too realistic, Hobomok is even less convincing. In *The Early American Novel* Lillie Loshe provides an apt description: "Hobomok is a gentle youth of domestic tastes who walks with a heavy tread and when hunting bounds through the forest, whistling and singing, in a manner that one feels would have been displeasing to Chingachgook" (p. 101).

Mary Conant is in love with Charles Brown, an Oxford graduate and lawyer, but her Puritan father disapproves because Charles is loyal to the Church of England. When Charles and his brother hold an Episcopal meeting, Governor Endicott banishes them from the colony. In the following passage Charles visits Mary and her mother to bid farewell. Mrs. Conant criticizes patriarchal religion.

CHAPTER X

.   .   .   .

. . . When Brown entered, he received a cordial grasp both from the mother and daughter, as they anxiously inquired,
"What have they done?"

Hobomok, A Tale of Early Times (Boston: Cummings, Hilliard & Co., 1824), 188 pp. Excerpts are taken from 91–96, 104–111, 150–151.

"A vessel sails for England in a week," replied Brown; "and Samuel and I depart from America, perhaps forever."

Whenever Mary thought of the possibility of separation, and of late she had frequently feared that the time would soon come, she had felt that the youth was still dearer and dearer to her heart. And now when she heard him announce the speedy certainty of this, her pale lip quivered, and in the silent unreserve of hearts long wedded to each other, she threw herself sobbing on his neck, her slender arms clinging around him, in all the energy of grief.

"I know not," said Mrs. Conant, dashing the tears from her cheek, "I know not that I ought to allow this. Remember, dear Mary, what I owe to your father."

"Madam Conant," replied Brown, "we have loved each other too long, and too purely, to stand upon idle ceremonies at this painful moment. Had I been treated with more moderation, perhaps I might never have been so hasty as to declare my religious opinions. Then these unhappy differences had never arisen, and with my Mary, I could happily have shared a log hut in the wilderness. But I have been spurned, goaded, trampled on, as a heretic—and worse than all, I have been doomed to hear every thing blasphemed which I held most sacred. As it is, you cannot deny us this sorrowful alleviation of our lot."

"It is the duty of woman to love and obey her husband," answered Mrs. Conant; "but had you known whereunto my heart has been inclined in this matter—" she would have said more, but something unbidden rose and prevented her utterance.

"I do know it," rejoined the young man; "and wherever I go, you will be in my pleasantest and most grateful thoughts. But, Mary, it will not be always thus—You will come to England and be my wife."

Mary looked at her mother and sighed.

"It may as well be said as not, my child," observed Mrs. Conant. "I shall not long hang a dead weight upon your young life. Nay, do not weep, Mary; I know that you are willing to bear the burden, and that you have been kind and cheerful beneath it; but the shadows of life are fleeting more dimly before me, and I feel that I must soon be gathered to my fathers."

The expression brought with it a flash of painful recollection.

"No," she continued, "like the wife of Abraham, I must be buried far from my kindred. If my grey-haired father could but shed one tear upon my grave, methinks it would furnish wherewithal to cheer my drooping heart. I loved my husband,—nor have I ever repented that I followed him hither; but oh, Mary, I would not have you suffer as I have suffered, when I have thought of that solitary old man. . . .

"Dear mother," replied Mary, "you know that grandfather loves you, and has long since forgiven you [for having married a Puritan]."

.   .   .   .

["I am sorry," observed Brown] "that my unruly tongue led me far beyond my reason in this matter. . . . I believe some [Puritans] are conscientious; though the arch enemy of souls hath led them far from the true path of safety."

"I cannot think with you and Mary," observed Mrs. Conant, "about forms and ceremonies. But it appears to me that an error in judgment is nothing, if the life be right with God. I have lately thought that a humble heart was more than a strong mind, in perceiving the things appertaining to divine truth. Matters of dispute appear more and more like a vapor which passeth away. I have seldom joined in them; for it appears to me there is little good in being convinced, if we are not humbled; to know every thing about religion, and yet to feel little of its power—yea, even to feel burdened with a sense of sin and misery, and yet be content to remain in it."

"Why, I must say," replied Brown, "that I think the Bible is clear enough, as explained by our holy bishops. But to my mind, the view of God's works brings more devotion than any thing relating to controversy."

"Ah, Mr. Brown, the Bible is an inspired book; but I sometimes think the Almighty suffers it to be a flaming cherubim, turning every way, and guarding the tree of life from the touch of man. But in creation, one may read to their fill. It is God's library—the first Bible he ever wrote."

"Bless me," exclaimed Mary, "here is father at the very doors."

Her lover hastily relinquished her hand, and she sprang from his side; but there was no chance for him to retreat. Mrs. Conant's pulse throbbed high, for she saw that her husband was already in no pleasant humor. The old gentleman hung up his hat, and drew his chair forward, without being aware of the presence of any one but his own family, till Brown rose and stood before him. The countenance of Mr. Conant was flushed with anger, when he saw the bold intruder.

"Mr. Brown," said he, stamping his foot violently, "how came you hither?"

"*Why*, I came hither, you already know," replied the youth calmly; "and most gladly would I have had my last visit here, a peaceable one."

The tyrannical man opened the door, and pointed to it, as he said, "A man may not touch pitch, and remain undefiled. I marvel if you bring not a curse on the whole house."

"I was about to depart," answered his guest; "but there is one thing I would say before I go. In my anger I spoke disrespectfully to men older and better than myself. It is a matter of choice as well as of necessity to leave New England, and be no more among you; and now, Mr. Conant, for the sake of those who are dear to me, I would fain have our parting, not that of churchman and non-conformist, but of christians."

"Out with you, and your damnable doctrines, you hypocritical son of a strange woman," exclaimed Mr. Conant.

Pride was struggling hard for utterance, as Brown moved towards the door; but for Mary's sake it was repressed—and before the old man was aware of his purpose, he stept back and took the hand of the mother and daughter, as he said,

"God bless you both. To me you have been all kindness."

He then made a formal, stately bow to Mr. Conant, who muttered, "Take my curse with you," and slammed the door after him.

Mary rushed into her apartment, and hiding her face in the bed clothes, gave free vent to her tears.

But the poor may not long indulge their grief. Her father's supper must be prepared, and her mother's wants must not be neglected; and, with as much serenity as she could assume, she again appeared in his presence. The tears of his sickly wife had allayed the first gust of passion, and perhaps even the heart of that rigid man reproached him for its violence. However that might be, pride would suffer no symptoms of remorse to appear before his family. Every thing went wrong through the whole evening. The cake was burned,—and the milk was not sweet,—and there had been too much fire to prepare their little repast; till wearied out with his continual fretfulness, they both retired to their beds at an early hour, and Mary sobbed herself into an uneasy slumber.

Charles leaves for England. Mary's friend Sally receives a marriage proposal by proxy and ends up marrying the messenger, Mr. Collier. Left alone, Mary becomes more friendly with Hobomok, an Indian chief; she often remembers the "mystic circle" game she played at Sally's suggestion (whoever first appeared in a chosen clearing in the woods would be her husband; Hobomok stepped into the circle first). In the following passage Hobomok takes the Conants on a hunt by moonlight. The dispute over the deer is reminiscent of the opening scene of Cooper's The Pioneers.

CHAPTER XII

During the long and dreary winter which followed, there was nothing to break the monotony of the scene, except the occasional visits of Hobomok, who used frequently to come up from Plymouth and join the hunters in their excursions. At such seasons, he was all vigor and elasticity; and none returned more heavily laden with furs and venison, than the tawny chieftan. The best of these spoils were always presented to the "child of the Good Spirit," as he used to call Mary; and never to Squantam or Abbamocho had he paid such unlimited reverence.

A woman's heart loves the flattery of devoted attention, let it come from what source it may. Perhaps Mary smiled too complacently on such offerings; perhaps she listened with too much interest, to descriptions of the Indian nations, glowing as they were in the brief, figurative language of nature. Be that as it may, love for Conant's daughter, love deep and intense, had sunk far into the bosom of the savage. In minds of a light and thoughtless cast, love spreads its thin, fibrous roots upon the surface, and withers when laid open to the scorching trials of life; but in souls of sterner mould, it takes a slower and deeper root. The untutored chief knew not the strange visitant which had usurped such empire in his heart; if he found himself gazing upon her face in silent eagerness, 'twas but adoration for so bright an emanation from the Good Spirit; if something within taught him to copy, with promptitude, all the kind attentions of the white man, 'twas gratitude for the life of his mother which she had preserved. However, female penetration knew the plant, though thriving in so wild a soil; and female vanity sinfully indulged its growth. Sometimes a shuddering superstition would come over her, when she thought of his sudden appearance in the mystic circle, and she would sigh at the vast distance which separated her from her lover; but the probability of Brown's return, would speedily chase away such thoughts.

Hobomok seldom spoke in Mr. Conant's presence, save in reply to his questions. He understood little of the dark divinity which he attempted to teach, and could not comprehend wherein the traditions of his fathers were heathenish and sinful; but with Mary and her mother, he felt no such restraint, and there he was all eloquence.

It was in the middle of the "cold moon," by which name he used to designate January, that he arrived in Salem, on one of his numerous visits, bringing with him some skins of the beautiful grey fox of the Mississippi.

"Hobomok brought you fur for moccasins," said he, as he handed them to Mary.

"How very soft it is," said she, showing it to her mother. "It seems like the handsome fur, which grandfather had from Russia. You did not kill it yourself, Hobomok?"

The Indian shook his head. "His tracks are toward the setting sun," replied he. "Hobomok give beaver skins like sand to a warrior come in from the west. He say they call it Muzaham Shungush. . . .

. . . .

"Well," rejoined Mary, "I hope they'll bring more such handsome fur hither. . . . I am going to make you a wampum belt of the shells you brought, and I want you to tell me how to put them together."

"Hobomok glad," replied the Indian, his eyes sparkling with joy at such a proof of gratitude. "You see that shell, the color of the sky when the sun goes down? Put him in the big moose there," pointing to the middle of the belt. "Him like the rainbow, put on the back of the deer; and him like the heaped snow, put on the big snake. That's like Tatobam's wampum. Tatobam kill snakes—make the great spirit snake very angry—That's reason the Indian from the west call him Tongoomlishcah."

"And who is he?" asked Mary.

"The grass has now grown on Tatobam's grave, and trees are planted thereon," answered the savage. "He was the father of Sassacus, great Sachem[1] of the Pequods. In council, cunning as the beaver, and quick-

1. North American Indian chief.

sighted as the eagle. His tribe were like swallows before a storm, and his wrath like the rising of a thunder cloud. Furious as a wounded buffalo in the fight, but true to his love as the star of the north."

. . . .

"Hobomok," interrupted Mr. Conant, who entered at this moment, "it is a pity you were not out with your bow, forasmuch as a fine deer just ran through the settlement."

"There's a tribe of 'em, out on the plains to night," answered the Indian. "Their tracks are thick as flies in the Sturgeon moon.[2] Sagamore John's men are coming out with—with—" and unable to think of the English word, he pointed to the candle.

"Oh, they are coming out by torch-light," exclaimed Mary, "as Hobomok says the western Indians do. How I do wish I could see them hunt by torch-light."

"I shall go out with you," said Mr. Conant, "to see what success the Lord giveth us in this matter. I have heard wonderful stories appertaining to the taking of deer after this fashion. They say that in the lightest night that ever was made, the creatures are so bewitched, that they'll not move a jot, after they once get sight of the fire."

"And wherefore shouldn't I go, father?" asked Mary.

"A pretty sight truly," replied the old man, "to see you out at midnight with twenty hunters."

"But," rejoined his wife, "two or three horses can be procured; and if a few of the young folks will go, assuredly I see no harm therein; more especially as you will accompany Mary. You must remember," continued she, in an insinuating tone, "that there are few such like gratifications in this wilderness."

"No doubt there is enough of them; wherewithal to entice their wandering hearts," answered her husband; "but if you think it fitting the girl should go, verily I have no objection thereto."

Preparations were accordingly made. The widow Willet agreed to come up and stay with Mrs. Conant; and a few young women readily consented to accompany Mary, on such horses as the settlement could afford. As for Hobomok, he was all eagerness to display his skill. His arrows were carefully selected, and the strength of his bow was tried again and again, as he occasionally turned to Mary, and boasted of the service it had always done him, in field and forest.

Winter seldom presents a night of such glittering beauty, as the one they chose for their expedition. The mellow light of moon and star looked down upon the woods, and as the trees danced to the shrill music of the winds, their light was reflected by ten thousand undulating motions, in all the rich varieties of frost work. It seemed as if the sylphs and fairies, with which imagination of old, peopled the mountain and the stream, had all assembled to lay their diamond offerings on the great al-

2. August [Child's footnote].

tar of nature. Silently Mary gazed on the going down of that bright planet, and tree and shrub bowed low their spangled plumes in homage to her retiring majesty, till her oblique rays were only to be seen in faint and scattered radiance, on the cold, smooth surface of the earth.

At length the party were in motion, proceeding through the woods by the twinkling lustre of the stars. Mr. Conant held the rein of Mary's horse, and guided his footsteps along the rough and narrow path. Hobomok walked by her side, as silent and thoughtful as he usually was in the presence of her father. They soon came out upon the open plain; and a few moments after, six neighboring Indians were seen winding along from the opposite woods, with their torches carried upon poles high above their heads, casting their lurid glare on the mild, tranquil light of the evening. As they drew up, a few inquiries were made by Hobomok in his native tongue, and answered by his companions in scarcely an audible tone, as they significantly placed their fingers upon their lips. Mr. Conant and his ten associates formed a line and fell into the rear, while the Indians who carried the poles, did the same, and placed themselves forward. It was indeed a strange, romantic scene. The torches sent up columns of dense, black smoke, which vainly endeavoured to rise in the clear, cold atmosphere. Hobomok stood among his brethren, gracefully leaning on his bow, and his figure might well have been mistaken for the fabled deity of the chase. The wild, fitful light shone full upon the unmoved countenance of the savage, and streamed back unbroken upon the rigid features of the Calvinist, rendered even more dark in their expression by the beaver cap which deeply shaded his care-worn brow. The pale loveliness of Mary's face, amid the intense cold of the night, seemed almost as blooming as her ruddy companions; and the frozen beauty of the surrounding woods again flashed brightly beneath the unwonted glow of those artificial rays.

There, in that little group, standing in the loneliness and solitude of nature, was the contrast of heathen and christian, social and savage, elegance and strength, fierceness and timidity. Every eye bent forward, and no sound broke in upon the stillness, excepting now and then, the low, dismal growl of the wolf was heard in the distance. Whenever this fearful sound came upon the ear, the girls would involuntarily move nearer to their protectors, who repeatedly assured them that wolves would never approach a fire. Presently a quick, light step was heard, and a deer glided before them. The beautiful animal, with rapid and graceful motion, was fast hurrying to the woods, when his eye seemed caught by the singular light which gleamed around him. He paused, and looking back, turned his pert, inquiring gaze full upon the hunters. He saw the forms of men, and knew they were his enemies; but so powerful was the fascination of the torches, that his majestic antlers seemed motionless as the adjacent shrubbery.

The arrow of Hobomok was already drawn to the head, when Mary touched his shoulder, as she said, "Don't kill it, Hobomok—don't;" but the weapon was already on the wing, and from his hand it seldom missed its mark. The deer sprung high into the air, its beautiful white breast was displayed for an instant, a faint, mournful sound was heard—and Hobomok stept forward to seize the victim he had wounded. As he brought it up to Mary, the glossy brown of its slender sides was heaving with the last agonies of life, and she turned away from the painful sight.

But a short space ensued, ere another was seen sweeping across the plain. He too noticed the unnatural brightness, and stood bound by the same bewitching spell. One of the Indians gave his torch to Hobomok, and placing his eye on a level with his bow, took steady and deliberate aim. However, it seemed he had not effected his purpose entirely; for the creature uttered a piercing cry, and bounded forward with incredible swiftness. The next Indian handed his torch to one of the white men, and rushing before his companion, he buried his knife deep in the bosom of the wounded deer. A loud laugh of derision followed.

"It's mine," exclaimed he, in Indian language. "It's mine, for I killed it."

"'Tisn't yours," retorted the other, furiously; "the deer hadn't run ten rods; and a hunter never gave up a beast under that."

The girls could not understand what was spoken by the contending savages; but they saw that a quarrel was likely to ensue, and Mary whispered to her father to guide them homeward. The route they had taken was a short one, and the difficulties in retracing it were few. The maidens gladly welcomed their own quiet apartments, and Mr. Conant returned to the plain. The Indian who had first wounded the animal, had proudly relinquished his claim, and stood by, in sullen, offended majesty. The others were preparing a new set of flambeaux for a fresh attack.

Mrs. Conant dies after making Mr. Conant promise to accept Charles if he returns. But Charles is reported killed in a shipwreck. In her grief, Mary decides to marry Hobomok.

CHAPTER XVII

.   .   .   .

. . . [T]here was a partial derangement of Mary's faculties. A bewilderment of despair that almost amounted to insanity. She sat down by her mother's grave, and wished to weep. The sorrow that can be exhausted, however keen it may be, has something of luxury in it, compared with grief when her fountains are all sealed, and her stormy waters are dashing and foaming within the soul. Mary's heart refused to overflow, and she laid down her head on the cold sod, in hopes it would cool the burning agony of her brain. As she sat thus, insensible of the autumnal chilliness, she felt something lightly thrown over her. She looked up, and perceived that it was Hobomok, who had covered her with his blanket, and silently removed a short distance from her. He approached when he saw her rise.

"It's a cold night for Mary to be on the graves," said he.

"Ah, Hobomok," she replied, "I shall soon be in my own grave."

The savage turned away his head for some time, as if struggling with some violent emotion.

"How Hobomok wish he could make you happy," at length said he.

There was a chaos in Mary's mind;—a dim twilight, which had at first made all objects shadowy, and which was rapidly darkening into misery, almost insensible of its source. The sudden stroke which had dashed from her lips the long promised cup of joy, had almost hurled reason from his throne. What now had life to offer? If she went to England, those for whom she most wished to return, were dead. If she remained in America, what communion could she have with those around her? Even Hobomok, whose language was brief, figurative, and poetic, and whose nature was unwarped by the artifices of civilized life, was far preferable to them. She remembered the idolatry he had always paid her, and in the desolation of the moment, she felt as if he was the only being in the wide world who was left to love her. With this, came the recollection of his appearance in the mystic circle. A broken and confused mass followed; in which a sense of sudden bereavement, deep and bitter reproaches against her father, and a blind belief in fatality were alone conspicuous. In the midst of this whirlwind of thoughts and passions, she turned suddenly towards the Indian, as she said,

"I will be your wife, Hobomok, if you love me."

"Hobomok has loved you many long moons," replied he; "but he loved like as he loves the Great Spirit."

"Then meet me at my window an hour hence," said she, "and be ready to convey me to Plymouth."

Mary is welcomed by Hobomok's mother, and Mary and Hobomok are married in an Indian ceremony. The following selection is the next-to-the-last chapter of the novel. In the last chapter Mary and Charles are reunited.

CHAPTER XIX

. . . .

For several weeks Mary remained in the same stupified state in which she had been at the time of her marriage. She would lie through the live-long day, unless she was requested to rise; and once risen, nothing could induce her to change her posture. Language has no power to shadow forth her feelings as she gradually awoke to a sense of her situation. But there is a happy propensity in the human mind to step as lightly as possible on the thorns which infest a path we are compelled to tread. It is only when there is room for hope, that evils are impatiently borne. Desolate as Mary's lot might seem, it was not without its alleviations. All the kind attentions which could suggest themselves to the mind of a savage, were paid by her Indian mother. Hobomok continued the same tender reverence, he had always evinced, and he soon understood the changing expression of her countenance, till her very looks were a law. So much love could not but awaken gratitude; and Mary by degrees gave way to its influence, until she welcomed his return with something like affection. True, in her solitary hours there were reflections enough to make her wretched. Kind as Hobomok was, and rich as she found his uncultivated mind in native imagination, still the contrast between him and her departed lover, would often be remembered with sufficient bitterness. Beside this, she knew that her own nation looked upon her as lost and degraded; and, what was far worse, her own heart echoed back the charge. Hobomok's connexion with her was considered the effect of witchcraft on his part, and even he was generally avoided by his former friends. However, this evil brought its own cure. Every wound of this kind, every insult which her husband courageously endured for her sake, added romantic fervor to her increasing affection, and thus made life something more than endurable. While all her English acquaintances more or less neglected her, her old associate, Mrs. Collier, firmly and boldly stemmed the tide, and seemed resolved to do all in her power to relieve the hardships of her friend. For a long time her overtures were proudly refused; for Mary could not endure that the visits of one, who had been so vastly her inferior, should now be considered an honor and obligation. However, persevering kindness did in time overcome this feeling, and in less than a year, Sally became a frequent inmate of her wigwam. To this, was soon likely to be added another source of enjoyment. Before two years passed away, she became the mother of a hopeful son. Under such circumstances, his birth was no doubt entwined with many mournful associations; still the smiles of her infant brought more of pleasure than of pain. As Mary looked on the little being, which was "bone of her bone, and flesh of her flesh," she felt more love for the innocent object, than she thought she should ever again experience.

During the period before his birth, nothing occurred of any importance to our story, excepting that Mr. Conant had written two letters to his daughter. The first conjured her not to consider a marriage lawful, which had been performed in a moment of derangement, and invited her to return to the arms of a parent who tenderly loved her. The second informed her of a considerable legacy left to her by the Earl of Rivers, and again offered her a welcome home and oblivion of all the past. Mary's heart was melted at these proofs of affection, when she had so little expected them; but she well knew she should only be considered an outcast among her brethren, and she could not persuade herself that her marriage vow to the Indian was any less sacred, than any other voluntary promise. So she wrote to her father, implored his forgiveness, hinted at the deplorable state of mind which had led her to this extremity, stated many reasons which now rendered it impossible for her to return, even if she were so disposed, and concluded by urging him to appropriate her property to his own comfort, as she should probably never be in a situation to enjoy it.

After this general view of things, we must now pass over to the 16th of September, 1633, and leave the interim to the reader's imagination. The old squaw had lately died of a fever, and symptoms of the same disorder began to appear in her little grandson, now nearly two years old. On the morning we have mentioned, Mrs. Collier took her own little blooming daughter in her arms, and went into the wigwam to inquire concerning the health of the boy. No sooner was she seated, than the children, accustomed to see each other, began to peep in each other's faces, and look up to their mothers, their bright, laughing eyes beaming with cherub love. Hobomok entered, and for a moment stood watching with delighted attention, the bewitching sports of childhood. He caught up the infant, and placing his little feet in the centre of his hand, held him high above his head.

"My boy, my brave hunter's boy," said he, and pressing him in his arms he half suffocated him with caresses. He placed him in his mother's lap, and took down his quiver, as he said, "Hobomok must be out hunting the deer." The child jumped down upon the floor, and tottling up to him, took hold of his blanket and looked in his face, as he lisped, "Fader come back gin to see 'ittle Hobomok."

Again the father stooped and kissed him, as he answered

"Hobomok very much bad, if he didn't come back always to see little Hobomok, and his good Mary."

He went out, but soon returned and lifting the blanket, which served for a door, he again looked at his boy, who would alternately hide his head, and then reach forward to catch another glimpse of his father.

"Good bye, Hobomok—Good bye, Mary"—said the Indian. "Before the sun hides his face, I shall come home loaded with deer."

"Take care of yourself," said his wife, affectionately; "and see that Corbitant[3] be not in your path."

"Sally, you have never said one word about my marrying Hobomok," continued she; "and I have no doubt you think I must be very miserable; but I speak truly when I say that every day I live with that kind, noble-hearted creature, the better I love him."

"I always thought he was the best Indian I ever knew," answered Sally; "and within these three years he has altered so much, that he seems almost like an Englishman. After all, I believe matches are foreordained."

"I don't know concerning that," rejoined Mary. "I am sure I am happier than I ever expected to be after Charles' death, which is more than I deserve, considering I broke my promise to my dying mother, and deserted my father in his old age."

While conversation of this nature was going on at home, Hobomok was pursuing his way through the woods, whistling and singing as he went, in the joyfulness of his heart. He had proceeded near half a mile in

3. A rival of Hobomok's from another tribe.

this way, when he espied an eagle, soaring with a flight so lofty, that he seemed almost like a speck in the blue abyss above. The Indian fixed his keen eye upon him, and as he gradually lowered his flight, he made ready his arrow, and a moment after the noble bird lay fluttering at his feet.

"A true aim that, Hobomok," said a voice which sounded familiar to his ears. He raised his head to see from whence it proceeded. Charles Brown stood by his side! The countenance of the savage assumed at once the terrible, ashen hue of Indian paleness. His wounded victim was left untouched, and he hastily retreated into the thicket, casting back a fearful glance on what he supposed to be the ghost of his rival. Brown attempted to follow; but the farther he advanced, the farther the Indian retreated, his face growing paler and paler, and his knees trembling against each other in excessive terror.

"Hobomok," said the intruder, "I am a man like yourself. I suppose three years agone you heard I was dead, but it has pleased the Lord to spare me in captivity until this time, and to lead me once more to New England. The vessel which brought me hither, lieth down a mile below, but I chose the rather to be put on shore, being impatient to inquire concerning the friends I left behind. You used to be my good friend, Hobomok, and many a piece of service have you done for me. I beseech you feel of my hand, that you may know I am flesh and blood even as yourself."

After repeated assurances, the Indian timidly approached—and the certainty that Brown was indeed alive, was more dreadful to him than all the ghosts that could have been summoned from another world.

"You look as if you were sorry your old friend had returned," said the Englishman; "but do speak and tell me one thing—Is Mary Conant yet alive?"

Hobomok fixed his eyes upon him with such a strange mixture of sorrow and fierceness, that Brown laid his hand upon his rifle, half fearful his intentions were evil. At length, the Indian answered with deliberate emphasis,

"She is both alive and well."

"I thank God," rejoined his rival. "I need not ask whether she is married?"

The savage looked earnestly and mournfully upon him, and sighed deeply, as he said,

"The handsome English bird hath for three years lain in my bosom; and her milk hath nourished the son of Hobomok."

The Englishman cast a glance of mingled doubt and despair towards the Indian, who again repeated the distressing truth. Disappointed love, a sense of degradation, perhaps something of resentment, were all mingled in a dreadful chaos of agony, within the mind of the unfortunate young man; and at that moment it was difficult to tell to which of the two, anguish had presented her most unmingled cup. The Indian gazed upon his rival, as he stood leaning his aching head against a tree; and once and again he indulged in the design of taking his life.

"No," thought he, "She was first his. Mary loves him better than she does me; for even now she prays for him in her sleep. The sacrifice must be made to her."

For a long time, however, it seemed doubtful whether he could collect sufficient fortitude to fulfil his resolution. The remembrance of the smiling wife and the little prattling boy, whom he had that morning left, came too vividly before him. It recks not now what was the mighty struggle in the mind of that dark man. He arose and touched Brown's arm, as he said,

"'Tis all true which I have told you. It is three snows since the bird came to my nest; and the Great Spirit only knows how much I have loved her. Good and kind she has been; but the heart of Mary is not with the Indian. In her sleep she talks with the Great Spirit, and the name of the white man is on her lips. Hobomok will go far off among some of the red men in the west. They will dig him a grave, and Mary may sing the marriage song in the wigwam of the Englishman."

"No," answered his astonished companion. "She is your wife. Keep her, and cherish her with tenderness. A moment ago, I expected your arrow would rid me of the life which has now become a burden. I will be as generous as you have been. I will return from whence I came, and bear my sorrows as I may. Let Mary never know that I am alive. Love her, and be happy."

"The purpose of an Indian is seldom changed," replied Hobomok. "My tracks will soon be seen far beyond the back-bone of the Great Spirit. For Mary's sake I have borne the hatred of the Yengees, the scorn of my tribe, and the insults of my enemy. And now, I will be buried among strangers, and none shall black their faces for the unknown chief. When the light sinks behind the hills, see that Corbitant be not near my wigwam; for that hawk has often been flying round my nest. Be kind to my boy."—His voice choked, and the tears fell bright and fast. He hastily wiped them away as he added, "You have seen the first and last tears that Hobomok will ever shed. Ask Mary to pray for me—that when I die, I may go to the Englishman's God, where I may hunt beaver with little Hobomok, and count my beavers for Mary."

Before Brown had time to reply, he plunged into the thicket and disappeared. He moved on with astonishing speed, till he was aware he must be beyond the reach of pursuit; then throwing himself upon the grass, most earnestly did he hope that the arrow of Corbitant would do the office it had long sought, and wreck upon his head deep and certain vengeance. But the weapon of his enemy came not. He was reserved for a fate that had more of wretchedness. He lay thus inactive for several hours, musing on all he had enjoyed and lost. At last, he sprung upon his feet, as if stung with torture he could longer endure, and seizing his bow, he pursued with delirious eagerness every animal which came within his view.

The sun was verging towards the western horizon, when he collected his game in one spot, and selecting the largest deer, and several of the handsomest smaller animals, he fastened them upon a pole and proceeded towards Plymouth.

It was dark and the tapers were lighted throughout the village, when he entered Governor Winslow's dwelling. Whatever was the purpose of his visit, it was not long continued; and soon after, the deer was noiselessly deposited by the side of Mr. Collier's house, with a slip of paper fastened on his branching horns. Hobomok paused before the door of his wigwam, looked in at a small hole which admitted the light, saw Mary feeding her Indian boy from his little wooden bowl, and heard her beloved voice, as she said to her child, "Father will come home and see little Hobomok presently."

How much would that high-souled child of the forest have given for one parting embrace—one kind assurance that he should not be forgotten. Affection was tugging hard at his heart strings, and once his foot was almost on the threshold.

"No," said he; "it will distress her. The Great Spirit bless 'em both."

Without trusting another look, he hurried forward. He paused on a neighboring hill, looked toward his wigwam till his strained vision could hardly discern the object, with a bursting heart again murmured his farewell and blessing, and forever passed away from New England.

Catharine Maria Sedgwick (1789–1867)

At the height of her career, Catharine Maria Sedgwick was considered a major American author. Critics ranked her with Washington Irving, James Fenimore Cooper, and William Cullen Bryant, and she enjoyed Nathaniel Hawthorne's praise as "our most truthful writer."

Sedgwick was born in Stockbridge, Massachusetts, the ninth of ten children of Pamela Dwight, who came from wealthy New England aristocracy, and Theodore Sedgwick, who rose from humble beginnings to serve in both houses of Congress. The contrast in her parents' origins shows up repeatedly in Sedgwick's life and work. Although she attended "finishing schools" and developed aristocratic manners, she espoused democratic principles, shared her father's abolitionist sympathies, and turned from Calvinistic Congregationalism to Unitarianism. In her later writings she tries to teach the poor how to rise by improving their habits and manners.

Sedgwick's mother died in 1804, having suffered throughout her married life from mental and physical illnesses brought on, according to Sedgwick, by "the medical treatment of the times, and the terrible weight of domestic cares." After her father's remarriage, Sedgwick initiated a lifelong practice of wintering in New York at the homes of her married brothers, to whom she was very close. Her brothers encouraged her to write and acted as her agents.

Sedgwick began her first literary venture, *A New-England Tale* (1822), as a Unitarian tract but increasingly employed realistic detail and local color. Her next two novels, *Redwood* (1824) and *Hope Leslie* (1827), continued this trend and were enthusiastically received here and abroad. After two more critical successes, *Clarence* (1830) and *The Linwoods* (1835), Sedgwick turned to writing didactic fiction intended for laborers and children. Works like *The Poor Rich Man and the Rich Poor Man* (1836) were Sedgwick's most popular, but they received less critical attention and helped contribute to the decline of her literary reputation in the 1850s.

Although writing made Sedgwick a celebrity and helped her through recurrent periods of depression, she always doubted her talents and felt ambivalent about her career. At one point she noted, "I hardly know any treasure I would not exchange to be where I was before my crow-tracks passed into the hands of printers' devils." On a better day she wrote, "My books have been a pleasant occupation and excitement in my life. The notice, and friends, or acquaintance they have procured me, have relieved me from the danger of ennui and blue devils, that are most apt to infest a single person. But they constitute no portion of my happiness—that is, of such as I derive from the dearest relations of life."

Selected Bibliography

OTHER WORKS
Home (1835); *Tales and Sketches* (1835); *Live and Let Live* (1837); *A Love-token for Children* (1838); *Tales and Sketches, Second Series* (1844); *The Morals of Manners* (1846); *The Boy of Mount Rhigi* (1848); *Married or Single?* (1857); *Life and Letters* (1871).

SECONDARY
Bell, Michael D. "History and Romance Convention in Catharine Sedgwick's *Hope Leslie.*" *American Quarterly* 22 (Summer 1970): 213–221.
Birdsall, Richard D. "William Cullen Bryant and Catharine Sedgwick—Their Debt to Berkshire." *New England Quarterly* 28 (September 1955): 349–371.
Foster, Edward Halsey. *Catharine Maria Sedgwick.* New York: Twayne Publishers, 1974.
———. Foreword to *Hope Leslie; or Early Times in the Massachusetts,* by Catharine Maria Sedgwick, iii–x. New York: Garrett Press, 1969.
Kelley, Mary. *Private Woman, Public Stage: Literary Domesticity in Nineteenth-Century America.* New York: Oxford University Press, 1984.
Welsh, Sister Mary Michael. *Catharine Maria Sedgwick: Her Position in the Literature and Thought of Her Time up to 1860.* Washington, D.C.: Catholic University of America, 1937.

Hope Leslie (1827)

Hope Leslie resembles *Hobomok* in several ways. Like Lydia Maria Child, Catharine Sedgwick set her novel in Puritan New England, drawing closely upon her reading of early colonial history. She too included historical personages—John Winthrop, governor of the Massachusetts Bay Colony, is an important character—and she went further than Child in using actual incidents from her sources. Thus the colonists' attack on the Pequod Indians really took place, in May of 1637, and John Winthrop's journal account of the battle mentions an escaped warrior named "Mononottoh."

The Unitarian Sedgwick's attitude toward her material is much the same as Child's. She presents the Puritans as admirably brave and enterprising but too harsh and inflexible in their religion to be truly "Christian"; she calls John Eliot, the famous Puritan minister, a "fanatical incendiary." Sedgwick portrays the Indians sympathetically, introducing a savage just as noble as Hobomok. Magawisca also sacrifices herself on behalf of the white colonists, literally giving her right arm, and ends like Hobomok disappearing westward into the wilderness. The character of Magawisca is so idealized that it called forth one of the few contemporary criticisms of *Hope Leslie* amidst a torrent of praise: one reviewer sarcastically labeled Magawisca "the first genuine Indian angel." Magawisca does not, like Hobomok, marry a white, but Sedgwick follows Child in depicting an intermarriage in the novel. Hope Leslie's sister Faith marries one of her Indian captors and refuses to leave him for "civilization" when she has the opportunity. Her choice is clearly seen as inferior; either because she was moronic enough to marry an Indian in the first place or because savage life erodes her intellect, Faith comes to wear a "vacant" look. Nevertheless, Sedgwick has the marriage endure.

In his book on Sedgwick (see Selected Bibliography), Edward Halsey Foster suggests that she may have considered her novel an "answer" to James Fenimore Cooper's *The Last of the Mohicans,* which appeared the year before *Hope Leslie.* Foster observes that both novels contain a set of sisters, one fair and passive, the other dark and self-reliant; but while Cooper must kill off the self-reliant sister and prevent miscegenation, Sedgwick both permits the strong sister to triumph and allows an intermarriage. One might also note that Sedgwick's Magawisca, self-sacrificing as she appears, is less accommodating to whites than either Child's Hobomok or Cooper's Chingachgook. She never acts against her own people, refusing, for instance, to give warning of the Indian attack, and never adopts colonial attitudes. Interestingly, Sedgwick provides considerable narrative support for Magawisca's point of view; thus, the description of the Indian attack on the English (in itself very different from Ann Eliza Schuyler Bleecker's version) is balanced by Magawisca's account of the prior violence of the English.

Comparing Sedgwick and Cooper, Foster judges Sedgwick not guilty of the stylistic "offenses" Mark Twain found in Cooper's works. Indeed,

Sedgwick's style is relatively simple and straightforward, and although she concentrates on adventure, furnishing plenty of exciting chases through the woods, she attends more than Cooper or Child to character development. Hope Leslie is more realistic than Cooper's heroes and more interesting than his faceless "females." Of course, as an early-nineteenth-century heroine, Hope has to be "naturally virtuous," with a strong Christian character and a readiness to place the welfare of others above her own. But Sedgwick makes Hope's friend Esther Downing a repository for the duller virtues—Esther is "humble," "reserved," and "timid"—and allows Hope some "flaws," such as impulsiveness and a tendency to resist authority. So, unlike Child's passive Mary Conant, Hope can act throughout the novel, in one instance defying the Winthrops to meet her sister, and in others bravely escaping from her Indian captors and playing the crucial role in freeing Magawisca from prison. The lively Hope was popular with Sedgwick's contemporaries and seems to a modern critic like Foster "entirely a three-dimensional person" and "one of the most convincing women in American fiction before the Civil War" (Foreword to *Hope Leslie*, p. viii; see Selected Bibliography).

William and Martha Fletcher, Puritans who live in frontier Springfield, Massachusetts, with their fourteen-year-old son Everell and four younger children, receive several additions to their household. First, Governor Winthrop asks them to take in as servants Oneco and Magawisca, teen-aged son and daughter of a Pequod warrior recently defeated in battle. Then William becomes the guardian of a deceased friend's daughters, Alice and Mary Leslie, soon rechristened Hope and Faith.

Everell Fletcher shows special kindness to Magawisca, and she confides the story of the English attack on the Pequods. Everell says he heard the English "had all the honour of the fight."

CHAPTER IV

.   .   .   .

"Honour! was it, Everell—ye shall hear. Our warriors rushed forth to meet the foe; they surrounded the huts of their mothers, wives, sisters, children; they fought as if each man had a hundred lives, and would give each, and all, to redeem their homes. Oh! the dreadful fray, even now, rings in my ears! Those fearful guns that we had never heard before—the shouts of your people—our own battle yell—the piteous cries of the little children—the groans of our mothers, and, oh! worse—worse than

Hope Leslie; or, Early Times in the Massachusetts (New York: White, Gallaher, and White, 1827), 296 pp. Excerpts are taken from 1: 83−84, 86−87, 106−110, 154−158, 270−271; 2: 89−95, 260−264, 290, 292.

all—the silence of those that could not speak——the English fell back; they were driven to the palisade; some beyond it, when their leader gave the cry to fire our huts, and led the way to my mother's. Samoset [her brother], the noble boy, defended the entrance with a prince-like courage, till they struck him down; prostrate and bleeding he again bent his bow, and had taken deadly aim at the English leader, when a sabre-blow severed his bowstring. Then was taken from our hearth-stone, where the English had been so often warmed and cherished, the brand to consume our dwellings. They were covered with mats, and burnt like dried straw. The enemy retreated without the palisade. In vain did our warriors fight for a path by which we might escape from the consuming fire; they were beaten back; the fierce element gained on us; the Narragansetts[1] pressed on the English, howling like wolves for their prey. Some of our people threw themselves into the midst of the crackling flames, and their courageous souls parted with one shout of triumph; others mounted the palisade, but they were shot and dropped like a flock of birds smitten by the hunter's arrows. Thus did the strangers destroy, in our own homes, hundreds of our tribe."

.   .   .   .

"You did not tell me, Magawisca," said Everell, "How Samoset perished; was he consumed in the flames, or shot from the palisade?"

"Neither—neither. He was reserved to whet my father's revenge to a still keener edge. He had forced a passage through the English, and hastily collecting a few warriors, they pursued the enemy, sprung upon them from a covert, and did so annoy them that the English turned and gave them battle. All fled save my brother, and him they took prisoner. They told him they would spare his life if he would guide them to our strong holds; he refused. He had, Everell, lived but sixteen summers; he loved the light of the sun even as we love it; his manly spirit was tamed by wounds and weariness; his limbs were like a bending reed, and his heart beat like a woman's; but the fire of his soul burnt clear. Again they pressed him with offers of life and reward; he faithfully refused, and with one sabre-stroke they severed his head from his body."

Magawisca paused—she looked at Everell and said with a bitter smile—"You English tell us, Everell, that the book of your law is better than that written on our hearts, for ye say it teaches mercy, compassion, forgiveness—if ye had such a law and believed it, would ye thus have treated a captive boy?"

Magawisca's reflecting mind suggested the most serious obstacle to the progress of the christian religion, in all ages and under all circumstances; the contrariety between its divine principles and the conduct of its professors; which, instead of always being a medium for the light that emanates from our holy law, is too often the darkest cloud that ob-

1. Allies of the English against the Pequods.

structs the passage of its rays to the hearts of heathen men. Everell had been carefully instructed in the principles of his religion, and he felt Magawisca's relation to be an awkward comment on them. . . .

Mr. Fletcher and Hope Leslie are away in Boston when Magawisca learns that her father, Mononotto, plans to revenge himself on the English by attacking the Fletcher home. Magawisca resists the temptation to warn Everell, but she begs her father for mercy when he arrives with his warriors.

CHAPTER V

.   .   .   .

Mononotto was silent and motionless, his eye glanced wildly from Magawisca to Oneco. Magawisca replied to the glance of fire—"yes, they have sheltered us—they have spread the wing of love over us—save them—save them—oh it will be too late," she cried, springing from her father, whose silence and fixedness showed that if his better nature rebelled against the work of revenge, there was no relenting of purpose. Magawisca darted before the Indian who was advancing towards Mrs. Fletcher with an uplifted hatchet. "You shall hew me to pieces ere you touch her," she said, and planted herself as a shield before her benefactress.

The warrior's obdurate heart untouched by the sight of the helpless mother and her little ones, was thrilled by the courage of the heroic girl—he paused and grimly smiled on her when his companion, crying, "hasten, the dogs will be on us!" levelled a deadly blow at Mrs. Fletcher—but his uplifted arm was penetrated by a musket shot and the hatchet fell harmless to the floor.

"Courage, mother!" cried Everell, reloading the piece, but neither courage nor celerity could avail—the second Indian sprang upon him, threw him on the floor, wrested his musket from him, and brandishing his tomahawk over his head, he would have aimed the fatal stroke, when a cry from Mononotto arrested his arm.

.   .   .   .

. . . Mrs. Fletcher's senses had been stunned with terror. She had neither spoken nor moved after she grasped her infant. Everell's gallant interposition, restored a momentary consciousness; she screamed to him— "Fly, Everell, my son, fly; for your father's sake, fly."

"Never," he replied, springing to his mother's side.

The savages, always rapid in their movements, were now aware that their safety depended on despatch. "Finish your work, warriors," cried Mononotto. Obedient to the command, and infuriated by his bleeding wound, the Indian, who on receiving the shot, had staggered back, and leant against the wall, now sprang forward, and tore the infant from its mother's breast. She shrieked, and in that shriek, passed the agony of death. She was unconscious that her son, putting forth a strength beyond nature, for a moment kept the Indian at bay; she neither saw nor felt the knife struck at her own heart. She felt not the arms of her defenders, Everell and Magawisca, as they met around her neck. She fainted, and fell to the floor, dragging her impotent protectors with her.

The savage, in his struggle with Everell, had tossed the infant boy to the ground; he fell quite unharmed on the turf at Mononotto's feet. There raising his head, and looking up into the chieftain's face, he probably perceived a gleam of mercy, for with the quick instinct of infancy, that with unerring sagacity directs its appeal, he clasped the naked leg of the savage with one arm, and stretched the other towards him with a piteous supplication, that no words could have expressed.

Mononotto's heart melted within him; he stooped to raise the sweet suppliant, when one of the Mohawks fiercely seized him, tossed him wildly around his head, and dashed him on the doorstone. But the silent prayer—perhaps the celestial inspiration of the innocent creature, was not lost. "We have had blood enough," cried Mononotto, "you have well avenged me, brothers."

Then looking at Oneco, who had remained in one corner of the portico, clasping Faith Leslie in his arms, he commanded him to follow him with the child. Everell was torn from the lifeless bodies of his mother and sisters, and dragged into the forest. Magawisca uttered one cry of agony and despair, as she looked, for the last time, on the bloody scene, and then followed her father.

As they passed the boundary of the cleared ground, Mononotto tore from Oneco his English dress, and casting it from him—"Thus perish," he said, "every mark of the captivity of my children. Thou shalt return to our forests," he continued, wrapping a skin around him, "with the badge of thy people."

In the scene most popular with Sedgwick's contemporaries, Magawisca sacrifices her arm to save Everell's life. Mononotto has taken his captives into the forest and placed Magawisca under guard, thwarting her attempts to free Everell. Magawisca finally manages to drug her guard, and while she waits impatiently for him to show the effects, Mononotto and his warriors prepare to kill Everell.

CHAPTER VII

.   .   .   .

Seated around their sacrifice-rock—their holy of holies—they listened to the sad story of the Pequod chief, with dejected countenances and downcast eyes, save when an involuntary glance turned on Everell, who stood awaiting his fate, cruelly aggravated by every moment's delay, with a quiet dignity and calm resignation, that would have become a hero, or a saint. Surrounded by this dark cloud of savages, his fair countenance kindled by holy inspiration, he looked scarcely like a creature of earth.

There might have been among the spectators, some who felt the silent appeal of the helpless courageous boy; some whose hearts moved them to interpose to save the selected victim; but they were restrained by their interpretation of natural justice, as controlling to them as our artificial codes of laws to us.

Others of a more cruel, or more irritable disposition, when the Pequod described his wrongs, and depicted his sufferings, brandished their tomahawks, and would have hurled them at the boy, but the chief said—"Nay, brothers—the work is mine—he dies by my hand—for my first-born—life for life—he dies by a single stroke, for thus was my boy cut off. The blood of sachems[2] is in his veins. He has the skin, but not the soul of that mixed race, whose gratitude is like that vanishing mist," and he pointed to the vapour that was melting from the mountain tops into the transparent ether; "and their promises are like this," and he snapped a dead branch from the pine beside which he stood, and broke it in fragments. "Boy, as he is, he fought for his mother, as the eagle fights for its young. I watched him in the mountain-path, when the blood gushed from his torn feet; not a word from his smooth lip, betrayed his pain."

Mononotto embellished his victim with praises, as the ancients wreathed theirs with flowers. He brandished his hatchet over Everell's head, and cried, exultingly, "See, he flinches not. Thus stood my boy, when they flashed their sabres before his eyes, and bade him betray his father. Brothers—My people have told me I bore a woman's heart towards the enemy. Ye shall see. I will pour out this English boy's blood to the last drop, and give his flesh and bones to the dogs and wolves."

He then motioned to Everell to prostrate himself on the rock, his face downward. In this position the boy would not see the descending stroke. Even at this moment of dire vengeance, the instincts of a merciful nature asserted their rights.

Everell sunk calmly on his knees, not to supplicate life, but to commend his soul to God. . . .

At this moment a sun-beam penetrated the trees that enclosed the area, and fell athwart his brow and hair, kindling it with an almost supernatural brightness. To the savages, this was a token that the victim was accepted, and they sent forth a shout that rent the air. Everell bent forward, and pressed his forehead to the rock. The chief raised the deadly weapon, when Magawisca, springing from the precipitous side of the rock, screamed—"Forbear!" and interposed her arm. It was too late. The blow was levelled—force and direction given—the stroke aimed at Everell's neck, severed his defender's arm, and left him unharmed. The

2. North American Indian chiefs.

lopped quivering member dropped over the precipice. Mononotto staggered and fell senseless, and all the savages, uttering horrible yells, rushed toward the fatal spot.

"Stand back!" cried Magawisca. "I have bought his life with my own. Fly, Everell—nay, speak not, but fly—thither—to the east!" she cried, more vehemently.

Everell's faculties were paralyzed by a rapid succession of violent emotions. He was conscious only of a feeling of mingled gratitude and admiration for his preserver. He stood motionless, gazing on her. "I die in vain then," she cried, in an accent of such despair, that he was roused. He threw his arms around her, and pressed her to his heart, as he would a sister that had redeemed his life with her own, and then tearing himself from her, he disappeared. No one offered to follow him. The voice of nature rose from every heart, and responding to the justice of Magawisca's claim, bade him "God speed!" To all it seemed that his deliverance had been achieved by miraculous aid. All—the dullest and coldest, paid involuntary homage to the heroic girl, as if she were a superior being, guided and upheld by supernatural power.

Every thing short of miracle she had achieved. The moment the opiate dulled the senses of her keeper, she escaped from the hut; and aware that, if she attempted to penetrate to her father through the semicircular line of spectators that enclosed him, she should be repulsed, and probably borne off the ground, she had taken the desperate resolution of mounting the rock, where only her approach would be unperceived. She did not stop to ask herself if it were possible, but impelled by a determined spirit, or rather, we would believe, by that inspiration that teaches the bird its unknown path, and leads the goat, with its young, safely over the mountain crags, she ascended the rock. There were crevices in it, but they seemed scarcely sufficient to support the eagle with his grappling talon, and twigs issuing from the fissures, but so slender, that they waved like a blade of grass under the weight of the young birds that made a rest on them, and yet, such is the power of love, stronger than death, that with these inadequate helps, Magawisca scaled the rock, and achieved her generous purpose.

Seven years pass, during which Everell is in England and Hope in Springfield; she hears that Magawisca, Oneco, and her sister Faith are living among the Mohawks. Mr. Fletcher sends Hope to Boston to receive "pious instruction" from Mrs. Winthrop and her "godly niece," Esther Downing. Hope and Esther become friends, and Everell returns. Both women love Everell; Everell loves Hope; but through a series of misunderstandings where each character tries to be noble, he and Esther end up engaged.

Magawisca secretly contacts Hope and arranges for her to meet her sister. Hope finds it hard to endure a long church service before the meeting.

CHAPTER XI

. . . .

[Hope said], "I wish the service were over. Do you think it will be long?"

"It may be long, but I trust not tedious," replied Esther, with a gravity which was the harshest rebuke she could ever command.

"Oh, it will be both!" said Hope, in a despairing tone; "for there is Mr. Wheeler in the pulpit, and he always talks of eternity till he forgets time."

"My dear Hope!" said Esther, in a voice of mingled surprise and reproof.

The service presently began, and Hope endeavoured dutifully to assume a decorous demeanour, and join Esther in singing the psalm; but her mind was soon abstracted, and her voice died away.

The preacher had not proceeded far in his discourse, before all her patience was exhausted. Even those who are the most strenuous advocates for the passive duties of the sanctuary, might have bestowed their pity on our heroine, who had really serious cause for her feverish impatience; obliged to sit, while a young man, accounted a 'universal scholar,' seemed determined, like many unfledged preachers, to tell all he knew in that one discourse. . . .

"Do, Esther, look at the candles," she whispered; "don't you think it must be nine o'clock?"

"Oh, hush!—no, not yet eight."

Hope sighed audibly, and once more resumed a listening attitude. All human labours have their end, and therefore had the preacher's.

Hope sneaks off to the appointed meeting place, on a nearby island, and awaits Faith.

VOL. II

CHAPTER V

. . . .

. . . She gazed and listened till her senses ached; and at last, when anticipation had nearly yielded to despair, her ear caught the dash of oars; and at the next moment, a canoe glanced around the headland into the cove; she darted to the brink of the water—she gazed intently on the little bark—her whole soul was in that look. Her sister was there. At this first assurance, that she really beheld this loved, lost sister, Hope uttered a scream of joy; but when, at a second glance, she saw her in her savage attire, fondly leaning on Oneco's shoulder, her heart died within her; a sickening feeling came over her, an unthought of revolting of nature; and instead of obeying the first impulse, and springing forward to clasp her in her arms, she retreated to the cliff, leaned her head against it, averted her eyes, and pressed her hands on her heart, as if she would have bound down her rebel feelings.

Magawisca's voice aroused her. "Hope Leslie," she said, "take thy sister's hand."

Hope stretched out her hand, without lifting her eyes; but when she felt her sister's touch, the energies of nature awoke, she threw her arms around her, folded her to her bosom, laid her cheek on hers, and wept as if her heart would burst in every sob.

Mary (we use the appellative by which Hope had known her sister,) remained passive in her arms. Her eye was moistened, but she seemed rather abashed and confounded, than excited; and when Hope released her, she turned towards Oneco with a look of simple wonder. Hope again threw her arm around her sister, and intently explored her face for some trace of those infantine features that were impressed on her memory. "It is—it is my sister!" she exclaimed, and kissed her cheek again and again. "Oh! Mary, do you not remember when we sat together on mother's knee? Do you not remember, when with her own burning hand, the very day she died, she put those chains on our necks? Do you not remember when they held us up to kiss her cold lips?" Mary looked toward Magawisca for an explanation of her sister's words. "Look at *me*, Mary—speak to *me*," continued Hope.

"No speak Yengees," replied Mary, exhausting in this brief sentence, all the English she could command.

Hope, in the impetuosity of her feelings, had forgotten that Magawisca had forewarned her not to indulge the expectation that her sister could speak to her; and the melancholy truth, announced by her own lips, seemed to Hope to open a new and impassable gulf between them. She wrung her hands; "Oh what shall I do! what shall I say?" she exclaimed.

. . . Hope knew not how to address one so near to her by nature, so far removed by habit and education. She thought that if Mary's dress, which was singularly and gaudily decorated, had a less savage aspect, she might look more natural to her; and she signed to her to remove the mantle she wore, made of bird's feathers, woven together with threads of the wild nettle. Mary threw it aside, and disclosed her person, light and agile as a fawn's, clothed with skins, neatly fitted to her waist and arms, and ambitiously embellished with bead work. The removal of the mantle, instead of the effect designed, only served to make more striking the aboriginal peculiarities; and Hope, shuddering and heart-sick, made one more effort to disguise them by taking off her silk cloak and wrapping it close around her sister. Mary seemed instantly to comprehend the language of the action, she shook her head, gently disengaged herself from the cloak, and resumed her mantle. An involuntary exclamation of triumph burst from Oneco's lips. "Oh tell her," said Hope to Magawisca, "that I want once more to see her in the dress of her own people—of her own family—from whose arms she was torn to be dragged into captivity."

A faint smile curled Magawisca's lip, but she interpreted faithfully Hope's communication, and Mary's reply, "'she does not like the English dress,' she says."

"Ask her," said Hope, "if she remembers the day when the wild Indians sprung upon the family . . . like wolves upon a fold of lambs?—If she remembers when Mrs. Fletcher and her innocent little ones were murdered, and she was stolen away?"

"She says, 'she remembers it well, for then it was Oneco saved her life.'"

Hope groaned aloud. "Ask her," she continued with unabated eagerness, "if she remembers when we played together, and read together, and knelt together at our mother's feet; when she told us of the God that made us, and the Saviour that redeemed us?"

"She remembers something of all this, but she says, 'it is faint and distant, like the vanishing vapour on the far-off mountain.'"

"Oh, tell her, Magawisca, if she will come home and live with me, I will devote my life to her. I will watch over her in sickness and health. I will be mother, sister, friend to her—tell her, that our mother, now a saint in heaven, stoops from her happy place to entreat her to return to our God, and our father's God."

Mary shook her head in a manner indicative of a more determined feeling than she had before manifested, and took from her bosom a crucifix, which she fervently pressed to her lips.

Every motive Hope offered was powerless, every mode of entreaty useless, and she leaned her head despondently on Mary's shoulder. The contrast between the two faces thus brought together, was most striking. Hope's hat had slipped back, and her rich brown tresses fell about her neck and face; her full eye was intently fixed on Mary, and her cheek glowing with impassioned feeling. She looked like an angel touched with some mortal misery; while Mary's face, pale and spiritless, was only redeemed from absolute vacancy by an expression of gentleness and modesty.

The reunion is interrupted by the English, who were informed of the meeting by Sir Philip Gardiner, a villain who has been trying unsuccessfully to seduce Hope. Magawisca and Faith are captured, while Oneco and Mononotto grab Hope and escape by canoe. Mononotto is struck by lightning and killed, whereby Hope flees from Oneco and makes her way back to Boston.

Governor Winthrop imprisons Magawisca as an enemy of the colony, and Hope and Everell help her escape. In the following excerpts they beg her to return once they get her pardoned. Magawisca also advises Hope regarding her sister and responds passionately when Hope expresses the fear that Magawisca's "noble mind" will be "wasted in those hideous solitudes."

CHAPTER XIV

.   .   .   .

[Hope said], "Promise us that you will return and dwell with us—as you would say, Magawisca, we will walk in the same path, the same joys shall shine on us, and, if need be that sorrows come over us, why, we will all sit under their shadow together."

"It cannot be—it cannot be," replied Magawisca, the persuasions of those she loved, not, for a moment, overcoming her deep invincible sense of the wrongs her injured race had sustained. "My people have been spoiled—we cannot take as a gift that which is our own—the law of vengeance is written on our hearts—you say you have a written rule of forgiveness—it may be better—if ye would be guided by it—it is not for us—the Indian and the white man can no more mingle, and become one, than day and night."

.   .   .   .

. . . "Both virtue and duty . . . bind your sister to Oneco. She hath been married according to our simple modes, and persuaded by a Romish father, as she came from Christian blood, to observe the rites of their law. When she flies from you, as she will, mourn not over her, Hope Leslie—the wild flower would perish in your gardens—the forest is like a native home to her—and she will sing as gaily again as the bird that hath found its mate."

.   .   .   .

"Solitudes!" echoed Magawisca, in a voice in which some pride mingled with her parting sadness. "Hope Leslie, there is no solitude to me; the Great Spirit, and his ministers, are every where present and visible to the eye of the soul that loves him; nature is but his interpreter; her forms are but bodies for his spirit. I hear him in the rushing winds—in the summer breeze—in the gushing fountains—in the softly running streams. I see him in the bursting life of spring—in the ripening maize—in the falling leaf. Those beautiful lights," and she pointed upward, "that shine alike on your stately domes and our forest homes, speak to me of his love to all,—think you I go to a solitude, Hope Leslie?"

"No, Magawisca; there is no solitude, nor privation, nor sorrow, to a soul that thus feels the presence of God," replied Hope. She paused—it was not a time for calm reflection or protracted solicitation; but the thought that a mind so disposed to religious impressions and affections, might enjoy the brighter light of Christian revelation—a revelation so much higher, nobler, and fuller, than that which proceeds from the voice of nature—made Hope feel a more intense desire than ever to retain Magawisca; but this was a motive Magawisca could not now appreciate, and she could not, therefore, urge [it].

Hope's sister Faith eventually runs away with Oneco, just as Maga-wisca predicted. Esther Downing comes to realize that Hope and Ever-ell love each other and goes to England, leaving them to marry. In the last chapter of the novel, Sedgwick disposes of the minor characters and includes one short paragraph on Hope and Everell, reserving the end of the novel for Esther. ·

CHAPTER XV

.   .   .   .

We leave it to that large, and most indulgent class of our readers, the misses in their teens, to adjust, according to their own fancy, the cere-monial of our heroine's wedding, which took place in due time, to the joy of her immediate friends, and the entire approbation of all the in-habitants of Boston. . . .

.   .   .   .

After the passage of two or three years, Miss Downing returned to New-England, and renewed her intercourse with Everell and Hope, with-out any other emotions, on either side, than those which belong to warm and tender friendship. Her personal loveliness, Christian graces, and the high rank she held in the colony, rendered her an object of very general attraction.

Her hand was often and eagerly sought, but she appears never to have felt a second engrossing attachment. The current of her purposes and af-fections had set another way. She illustrated a truth, which, if more gen-erally received by her sex, might save a vast deal of misery: that mar-riage is not *essential* to the contentment, the dignity, or the happiness of woman. Indeed, those who saw on how wide a sphere her kindness shone, how many were made better and happier by her disinterested de-votion, might have rejoiced that she did not

"Give to a party what was meant for mankind."[3]

3. Oliver Goldsmith, *Retaliation* (1774), line 29.

Satire and Humor

BY THE BEGINNING of the nineteenth century, America had acquired a confidence that encouraged writers to assume a comic stance. Economic and political stability, westward expansion, and a general air of security allowed people to breathe more easily and laugh more readily. As Walter Blair demonstrates in *Native American Humor*, increased mobility, as well as almanacs, newspapers, dramas, and travel books intensified awareness of national and regional differences and prompted humorous comparisons.

This shift in cultural perception influenced the tone and direction of the novel and women's writing in general. The puritanic public that winced at the sensational novels published under a didactic guise gave way to another public that winked at the ridiculousness of such works. By 1801, as Helen Papashvily points out in *All the Happy Endings*, readers could enjoy Tabitha Tenney's satire *Female Quixotism* "and even laughed at her novel-reading Dorcas who changed her name to Dorcasina, romanticized every scoundrel she met, and longed to elope in a chaise" (p. 31). Even so, the satiric mode did not lose its moralistic strain, and Tenney's novel, whatever her intent, carried repeated reminders of the evils of indiscriminate novel-reading.

By the 1830s, American humor had come into its own. Down East and frontier humor were everywhere. Alongside Seba Smith's Jack Downing and Benjamin P. Shillaber's Mrs. Parkington, Frances Miriam Whitcher's Widow Spriggins, Widow Bedott, and Aunt Maguire more than held their own. In her initial sketches, narrated by Permilly Ruggles Spriggins, Whitcher used colloquial dialect sprinkled with misspellings and malapropisms to burlesque the English sentimental novel. Although Whitcher's humor is less pretentious than Tenney's satire, Whitcher nods to Tenney's influence by borrowing the name and mimicking the characterization of Philander, a roguish schoolteacher. In her most famous series, the Widow Bedott sketches, Whitcher focuses her comic attention on people in realistic settings, thereby broadening her appeal.

Tenney and Whitcher, and Ann Stephens in her *New York High Life* (1843), made satire and humor their primary interest. Caroline Lee Hentz, Sara Parton ("Fanny Fern"), Harriet Beecher Stowe, Stephens, and the many other authors mentioned by Kate Sanborn in *The Wit of Women* inserted comic characters and incidents into their more general works. The comic element, whether coded or overt, was so pervasive in women's works as to justify Alice Wellington Robbins's comment (*Critic*, March 29, 1884) that contrary to popular opinion, the rarest of things is not a woman with a sense of humor but a woman without one.

Tabitha Gilman Tenney (1762–1837)

Nothing in Tabitha Tenney's heritage or environment could have foretold that Tenney would become the author of a satire that would earn her a permanent place in American letters. Descended from New Hampshire pioneers distinguished for civil and military service, she was born in Exeter, New Hampshire, to Samuel Gilman and his second wife, Lydia Robinson.

Tenney received the education considered appropriate for a young woman of her social status: a general knowledge of the arts, classics, social practices, and household accomplishments. Her own education may well have been reflected in *The New Pleasing Instructor,* an anthology of poetry and classical pieces she designed for the education of young women. Unfortunately, there is no extant copy of the book; but an advertisement in the *Newburyport Herald and Country Gazette* of May 7, 1799 recommended it for "Female Academies" and described it as blending instruction with rational amusement "to inform the mind, correct the manners, or to regulate the conduct."

In 1788 she married Samuel Tenney, a native of Byfield, Massachusetts, who had been a surgeon during the Revolutionary War. From 1800 to 1807 Samuel Tenney served in the U.S. House of Representatives, and the couple lived in Washington. During this period Tenney wrote *Female Quixotism: Exhibited in the Romantic Opinions and Extravagant Adventures of Dorcasina Sheldon* (1801), the two-volume satire that made her famous. After her husband's death in 1816, Tenney returned to Exeter, where she spent her remaining years engaged in charitable works and the production of intricate needlework.

Selected Bibliography

SECONDARY
Brown, Herbert Ross. *The Sentimental Novel in America, 1789–1860.* Durham, N.C.: Duke University Press, 1940.
Loshe, Lillie Deming. *The Early American Novel.* New York: Columbia University Press, 1907.
Petter, Henri. *The Early American Novel.* Columbus: Ohio State University Press, 1971.

Female Quixotism (1801)

As the title of Tabitha Tenney's *Female Quixotism: Exhibited in the Romantic Opinions and Extravagant Adventures of Dorcasina Sheldon* (1801) suggests, the novel follows Cervantes's *Don Quixote* (1605–1615) in satirizing romantic fiction and its readers. Tenney also found a model in *The Female Quixote* (1752), published in England by Charlotte Ramsay Lennox, reportedly an American by birth. Like Lennox, Tenney recognized that she could not send her heroine out on worldly adventures, so she brought the world to her. Also like Lennox, she carried her novel-reading heroine through numerous experiences calculated to counteract her misconceptions of reality.

Although she followed the general pattern set by Lennox, Tenney wrote a very different novel. Lennox's Arabella, young and beautiful, lives in the genteel surroundings of the English countryside. Her romantic reading corrupts her, but after a series of unfortunate experiences, she is cured of her addiction early in life through the wise counsel of a pious minister. Tenney's Dorcasina, on the other hand, grows up in the rugged American countryside, succumbs repeatedly to romantic delusions, which bring on physical and social indignities, and only in old age, after many trials, recognizes on her own the difference between fiction and reality.

The American wilderness setting allows for rollicking satire, and Tenney takes every opportunity to develop the comic possibilities. The harsh physical treatment to which she submits Dorcasina shows the obvious influence of Tobias Smollett's *Humphrey Clinker* (1771). The broad comedy that results often dominates the novel. Tenney introduces beatings and kidnappings, disguise and transvestism. One of her contemporaries observed in the *Monthly Anthology and Boston Review* (September 1808): "Many of us have doubtless dwelt with great sympathy on the pathetick story of the unfortunate Dorcasina Sheldon, and have been inclined to believe that the ingenious author had almost outquixoted Don Quixote" (p. 498).

Tenney dedicates the book to "All Columbian Young Ladies Who Read Novels and Romances" and works her way into her readers' confidence as slyly as Susanna Rowson or Hannah Foster:

> I am sensible you will find it a very singular and extraordinary piece of biography, and that you may suspect it to be a mere romance, an Hogarthian caricatura, instead of a true picture of real life. But, when you compare it with the most extravagant parts of the authentic history of the celebrated hero of La Mancha, the renowned Don Quixote, I presume you will no longer doubt its being a true uncoloured history of a romantic country girl, whose head had been turned by the unrestrained perusal of Novels and Romances. That, by observing their baneful effects on Miss Sheldon, who was in every other respect a sensible, judicious, and amiable

girl, you may avoid the disgraces and disasters that so long rendered her despicable and miserable is the wish,
    My dear young ladies,
        Of your Friend and Admirer,
            The Compiler

The fun Tenney subsequently enjoys at her heroine's expense—plunging
her into increasingly more unpleasant situations—may seem cruel. Tenney, however, continually shows readers Dorcasina's good qualities,
thereby reminding them that it is the evil of novel-reading, not the person, that is being attacked.

*Tenney sets her story on "the beautiful banks of the Delaware," where
Mr. Sheldon had settled with his wife—"a necessary ingredient in
man's domestic happiness." After his wife's death, Mr. Sheldon takes
over the guidance of his three-year-old daughter Dorcas. Dorcas develops into a cheerful and affectionate person but is also excessively romantic, obstinate, and vain. The narrator introduces her in the following passage.*

CHAPTER I

.   .   .   .

Now I suppose it will be expected that, in imitation of sister novel
writers (for the ladies of late seem to have almost appropriated this department of writing) I should describe her as distinguished by the elegant form, delicately turned limbs, auburn hair, alabaster skin, heavenly
languishing eyes, silken eyelashes, rosy cheeks, aquiline nose, ruby lips,
dimpled chin, and azure veins, with which almost all our heroines of
romance are indiscriminately decorated. In truth she possessed few of
these beauties, in any great degree. She was of a middling stature, a little
embonpoint,[1] but neither elegant nor clumsy. Her complexion was rather
dark; her skin somewhat rough; and features remarkable neither for
beauty nor deformity. Her eyes were grey and full of expression, and her
whole countenance rather pleasing than otherwise. In short, she was a
middling kind of person, like the greater part of her countrywomen;
such as no man would be smitten with at first sight, but such as any
man might love upon intimate acquaintance.

*Female Quixotism: Exhibited in the Romantic Opinions and Extravagant Adven-
tures of Dorcasina Sheldon*, in 2 vols. (Boston: Printed by I. Thomas and E. T. Andrews,
1801), 293 pp. Excerpts are taken from 1: iii–iv, 6–7, 12, 15–16, 31–33, 135–138,
172, 175–177; 2: 51–52, 201, 210–213.
1. Plump.

Like her father, Dorcas loves books, but while he studies history and reads novels for recreation, Dorcas makes novels her study and "history only her amusement." At the age of eighteen she changes her name to the more romantic Dorcasina. At the age of twenty she looks forward to the visit of her first potential suitor, Lysander, the son of her father's best friend. The meeting shatters her hopes, but Lysander gradually recognizes her good features and writes, asking permission to court her.

CHAPTER II

. . . .

. . . Mr. Sheldon then introducing his daughter to the father and son, the latter complimented her in the same style of easy politeness in which he had done her father; no trembling, no emotion, no hesitation in speaking to her. What a thunder-stroke for poor Dorcasina, who had calculated upon piercing him through and through at the very first glance! So great was her chagrin and disappointment, that she appeared to great disadvantage, sitting silent and thoughtful through the tedious hours of evening, which to her had never before appeared so long. Lysander, several times, politely endeavored to engage her in conversation; but all his attempts proving fruitless, he listened the remainder of the evening to the two old gentlemen, who were talking over the adventures of their youth.

. . . .

Upon the perusal of this letter [asking permission to court her], Dorcasina experienced but one sentiment, and that was mortification. She read it over and over again; and was, to the last degree, chagrined at its coldness. She compared it with various letters in her favorite authors; and found it so widely different in style and sentiment, that she abhorred the idea of a connexion with a person who could be the author of it. What added greatly to her disgust was, that he said not a word of her personal charms, upon which she so much valued herself. Not even the slightest compliment to her person; nothing of angel or goddess, raptures or flames, in the whole letter. She determined, therefore, without much deliberation, to answer it in plain terms, and to give him a flat refusal; and accordingly wrote as follows:

"Sir,

I received your letter safe by the post, and will answer you with the same sincerity by which it appears to have been dictated. I know not the man who possesses a larger share of my esteem. I have noticed your good qualities, and acknowledge your merit; and your friendship I should think it an honour to deserve. But my heart is untouched; and I experienced not that violent emotion, at first sight of you, which always accompanies genuine love; nor do I think the passion with which I have inspired you, sufficiently ardent to ensure my happiness; as your letter was such as I suppose your grandfather might write, were he, at the age of eighty, to take it into his head to marry. I hope you will not take amiss the freedom with which I speak my sentiments, or suppose it the effect of levity; but be assured that it is from a firm conviction, that we are not destined by Heaven to make each other happy.

With sentiments of the highest esteem,

I wish to remain your friend,
Dorcasina Sheldon"

Upon the receipt of this curious epistle, Lysander was lost in astonishment. He could hardly credit the evidence of his own senses, or believe that the agreeable Miss Sheldon could think and write in so whimsical and romantic a manner, when, upon every other subject, she conversed with the greatest good sense and propriety. He at length concluded that to be her weak side; and endeavored to console himself by reflecting that he was fortunate in escaping a connexion with a woman whose ideas of matrimonial happiness were too exalted ever to be realized; convinced that violent raptures are never lasting, and that the greatest connubial happiness is enjoyed, where the passion on both sides is founded on the solid basis of esteem, and heightened by a knowledge of the good qualities of the beloved object.

Isolated in the country, Dorcasina cannot attract other young men. When she has reached the age of thirty-four, a twenty-one-year-old gambler, Patrick O'Connor, hears her story and sets out to woo her according to the book. Meeting her "by chance" in the grove behind her home, and claiming to have learned about her from Lysander, O'Connor creates exactly the kind of first meeting of which Dorcasina had dreamed.

CHAPTER IV

.   .   .   .

After this, they entered into a conversation of a more general nature; Dorcasina imagining, that if he were the friend of Lysander, she ran no risque in his acquaintance, as she was very sure that none but men of honour and character would be admitted to a place in his friendship. They, therefore, conversed together in an easy and agreeable manner. O'Connor entertained her with an account of the customs and manners of Europe, and of all the British modern authors of the greatest celebrity; but dwelt with peculiar pleasure on the writers of novels, and asserted that they alone described the passion of love in its true and genuine colours. While he was thus haranguing, he would cast such languishing glances upon Dorcasina, from his fine black eyes, and heave such amorous sighs from his apparently enraptured bosom, that she was pierced through and through. In this pleasing delirium she continued chatting with our adventurer, till at length the setting sun admonished her that it was time to retire, though she was surprised when she observed that luminary sinking into the lap of Thetis;[2] so agreeably and imperceptibly had the moments passed. She, however, retained prudence and resolution sufficient to make a motion to rise, saying, it was time for her to be gone. O'Connor, upon this, sprang lightly from his seat, and offered her his hand, to aid her in rising. She did not decline his proffered assistance, at which he appeared penetrated with joy, and stood for sometime, silently and ardently gazing at her, while he pressed her hand in both his. At length, his words, as it were finding utterance, "Must I then lose you?" he said; "must I thus part with you, and never, perhaps, be again favored with your presence? Oh! forbid it Heaven, I cannot support the idea!" Then dropping her hand, and pretending a degree of confusion for the liberty he had taken, he fell on one knee and exclaimed, "Forgive me, Miss Sheldon! divine excellence, forgive a man so enraptured with your charms that he hardly has the full exercise of his reason." "Rise, sir," said Dorcasina, "I beg of you to rise. I cannot bear to see you in this humble posture." "I never will, I never can rise," replied O'Connor, "till Miss Sheldon will promise that she will not drive me to despair, till she gives me some encouragement that she will, as usual, frequent her favorite grove, where I shall daily and nightly wander, like a restless ghost, in expectation of the supreme felicity of again beholding her." Dorcasina, with a gracious smile, replied, that the appearance of a real ghost would hardly deter her from taking her agreeable and accustomed walk. O'Connor, overjoyed with his success, having poured out his thanks for her goodness, arose from his humble posture; and they slowly took their way together out of the grove. Having arrived at the spot where Betty was stationed, who, by this time, had begun to be alarmed for the health of her mistress, on account of the heavy dew which was beginning to fall, they bid each other good night. Dorcasina leaning on the arm of her faithful maid, directed her steps homeward. Not so, our artful adventurer. He fixed himself against the body of a tree, and stood straining his eyes till Dorcasina was out of sight; while she, pleased with this proof of his love, moved slowly onward, and every few steps, desired Betty to look behind and see if he still kept his post. Nor could she avoid frequently turning her own head to have a last look of her charming enamarato.

O'Connor continues wooing Dorcasina, and forging a letter of recommendation from Mr. W. of Philadelphia, he gains access to the Sheldon home. When Mr. Sheldon becomes suspicious, O'Connor flees, but Dorcasina refuses to acknowledge his dishonesty and con-

2. A sea nymph, the mother of Achilles.

tinues to dream of him. While Mr. Sheldon is in Philadelphia on busi-
ness, Philander, a local schoolteacher about to leave town, decides to
have a lark at Dorcasina's expense. He requests a rendezvous with her
and then turns up disguised as a woman.

CHAPTER XV

.   .   .   .

Being arrived at the arbour they [Dorcasina and her maid Betty] seated
themselves on the turf. They had not sat long, when, instead of the expected lover, a female entered, and placing herself by the side of Dorcasina, accosted her in the following manner. "You will, perhaps, be surprised," said she, "when I inform you that I know you did not come here
with the expectation of meeting a woman. Philander was the person,
whom you expected to see; but know, abhorred rival, that I have effectually prevented his meeting you this night, and am now come to enjoy
your disappointment. I would have you to know, you witch! you sor-
ceress! that you have robbed me of the heart of my lover; and I am determined to be revenged."
Dorcasina, as might naturally be expected, was astonished at this
address; and remained, for some moments, in a profound silence. At
length, she attempted to justify herself, by saying, that she was sorry to
be the cause of pain to any one; that, from her own experience, she
knew too well the power of love, not to commiserate any person who
nourished a hopeless passion; that she had never yet seen Philander, to
her knowledge; that this interview was none of her seeking; and that
she had consented to it, at his earnest entreaty, on the express condition
that it should never be repeated. She concluded by declaring that, as she
now found he had been false to another, she would immediately retire,
and hold no further intercourse with him.
This mildness served, in appearance, but to irritate the supposed female. "I know your arts too well," cried she, raising her voice, "to believe a syllable of what you say. It is all mere pretence, and you will consent to meet him again the very first opportunity. But you shall not go
on thus practicing your devilish arts, with impunity. Your basilisk glance
shall not thus rob every man of his heart, and every woman of her lover
or husband. Those bewitching eyes, that cause mischief, wherever they
are seen, I will tear them from their orbits. Thus saying, she laid violent
hands on the terrified Dorcasina; tore off her hat; pulled her hair; and
was proceeding to tear off her handkerchief, when Betty, seeing her mistress so roughly handled, started up in her defence, and attacking the
stranger with great fury, compelled her to quit Dorcasina in order to defend herself. Dorcasina, thus liberated, darted out of the grove and fled
towards the house with all speed, leaving Betty to sustain the combat
alone. Finding herself deserted, and her antagonist much her superior in

strength, Betty endeavoured likewise to make her escape; but her attempt was unsuccessful. She was held, cuffed, pulled by the hair, twirled round and round like a top, shaken, and pushed up against the trees, without mercy; the person, who thus roughly handled her, exclaiming, all the time, "you ugly old witch, I'll teach you to carry letters, and contrive meetings between your mistress and my lover; you pander, you go-between, you s--t! Poor Betty begged for mercy, in the most moving terms, professing that she had said everything to dissuade her mistress from this meeting; but the enraged virago would not suffer her to go, till she had stripped off her upper garments (her gown being a short one, and of no great value) torn them to rags, and scattered them about the arbour. She then suffered her to depart, telling her, at the same time, that, if ever she caught her engaged in the same business again, she would not only divest her of her clothes, but strip off her old wrinkled hide.

·   ·   ·   ·   ·   ·   ·   ·   ·   ·   ·   ·   ·

On her arrival at the house, Betty went immediately and presented herself before her mistress, in the same forlorn plight, in which she had left the grove. "I hope you are satisfied now ma'am," said she, "and won't think of visiting that confounded arbour, to meet any more of them impudent, ill-manner'd, low-liv'd fellers, who make such a fuss, and pretend to be dying for love, and are only brewing mischief all the time." "Why you surely cannot suppose, Betty, that Philander had any hand in this mischief, any further than leaving the woman he had once pretended to love: pretended, I say; for if it had been a real passion, he could not so soon have forgotten her."

"Well, I knows what I knows. That was no woman, that handled me so. It was either a very strong man, or the old nick himself. I knows I am none of the weakest; but heaven help me! I was no more in his hands than an infant. Why, I was thump'd, and cuff'd, and bounc'd, and shook, and twirl'd, and had my clothes stripped off, and tore to tatters, as if I had been nothing at all. Besides, what I shall not soon forget, in a grum and angry voice, that was no woman's, he call'd me old, and ugly; go between, and strum, and a great many other hard names, which in my fright, I forgot; Oh! I expect that vile Philander is at the bottom of it all, a good-for-nothing cur, with his pretentions, of love and hanging; I declare I shou'dn't desire any better sport than to see him strung up."

"Hush! Betty; you are in a passion and know not what you say: I am extremely sorry that you were so rudely treated; but it is unjust to impute it to Philander. I dare say the poor youth is well nigh distracted at his disappointment.

Mr. Sheldon, realizing that Dorcasina still believes in O'Connor's innocence, takes her to Philadelphia, where he intends that she witness O'Connor's public beating for robbery.

CHAPTER XVIII

.   .   .   .

The next morning at ten o'clock, was the hour appointed for O'Connor to receive his punishment. After breakfast, therefore, Mr. Sheldon proposed to his daughter to get into a chaise, and ride with him round the city, in order to observe the alterations that had taken place since her last visit. She consented, with great cheerfulness, and he contrived to be on the spot at the moment they were tying up the criminal. Naturally of a compassionate nature, and averse from exhibitions of cruelty of any kind, Dorcasina turned away her head, and begged her father to hasten from the scene. This was the moment for the exertion of all his fortitude. The remedy was painful even to himself, but he hoped it would be effectual to his daughter. Instead, therefore, of hastening, as Dorcasina had requested, he stopped the chaise, and desired her to look out for a moment, and tell him whether that was not one of their acquaintance, or whether he was deceived. She did as she was desired, and beheld O'Connor. They gave him the first stroke and she went into a strong hysteric fit.

.   .   .   .

Mr. Sheldon, observing Dorcasina's dejection, was extremely desirous of knowing what impression the recent transaction had made upon her, and whether it had not altered her opinion of O'Connor. An unwillingness to begin with her, upon so delicate a subject, for some time prevented his entering upon it. But finding that she kept a profound and melancholy silence, he at length interrupted it, by observing that he thought her happening to be a witness to the punishment of O'Connor a very fortunate circumstance, as he was sure it must convince her that his aversion to him was not without foundation. The mention of this name roused Dorcasina from the profound reverie in which she had been absorbed; her eyes overflowed with tears, and she thus replied. "You are deceived, sir, in thinking I have changed my opinion of O'Connor. Appearances, I acknowledge are at present against him, and the malice of his enemies is unwearied in persecuting him. Be kind enough to inform me, sir, who were the authors of the barbarous treatment he has so recently received." Mr. Sheldon rejoiced at the request, related every particular of the robbery, which he said, he himself heard so incontestibly proved in court, that it was impossible not to believe it, the things being found in his possession. "Besides," added he, "for my own satisfaction, and to be certain that I did not condemn him unjustly, I have conversed with Mr. W. a man as well noted for integrity as any in the city, and with the master of the vessel, for whose veracity, Mr. W. pledged himself, and they both persist in the former declaration; Mr. W. that he never knew any such person as O'Connor, and that the letter in his name (which I had with me and produced) was a vile forgery; and the captain that he brought him over, (to his shame he confesses it) and that he knew him to be, in England, an abandoned villain, a gambler, and highway robber."

Conviction, now for the first time, flashed in the mind of Dorcasina. She could no longer resist the concurring testimony of so many witnesses. "Alas! Sir," said she, "who could have thought there was so much deceit in mankind!" Mr. Sheldon, more rejoiced at this one short sentence, than at any he had ever before heard her utter, as he was thereby convinced that her eyes were at length opened to the worthlessness of O'Connor, mildly replied, "I have before, my dear, had occasion to observe to you, that your retired manner of life, and almost total ignorance of the world, led you to judge other people by your own virtuous and unsuspecting heart. You have now learnt a lesson, which I hope you will ever remember, and in future put less confidence in external appearances and empty professions." Dorcasina, extremely hurt and mortified at having been the dupe of such an arrant imposter, answered not a word; and her father perfectly satisfied with the complete success of his little plan, was content to drop the subject. Nor did he think fit to interrupt her meditations, till they arrived, towards sunset, in safety and silence, at their mansion on the banks of the Delaware.

Betty's joy at the return of her mistress was unfeigned, nor was that of the latter, at seeing again her faithful confidant, less sincere. She no sooner entered the house, than retiring to her chamber and desiring the attendance of one who participated in all her afflictions, she poured into her faithful bosom her griefs, her trials, her mortifications; relating, in a minute manner, everything which had happened in her absence.

When she had made an end of her relation, "could you have thought Betty," said she, "that so much deceit and falsehood could be concealed under so fair an exterior?" "Why ma'am, you knows I never liked him from the first. I always thought he look'd cross and proud; he never, to my notion, was half as handsome as Lysander. I thought all the time what he was after; and that he cared more about your father's money than he did about you. But I was afraid to tell you so. I rejoice to think you found out the creature before it was too late: what a dreadful thing it would have been ma'am, if you had married him first, and found him out afterwards, to be a gambler, a thief, and a robber!" "I desire Betty, to be grateful to a kind providence, who knows much better what is best for us than we do ourselves, for saving me from the snare so artfully spread for me, but still it is a mortifying thing to find the object upon whom we set our first and warmest affections, so totally unworthy of them."

"So I should think ma'am," replied Betty; "and I should think too that, the next time you intend to fall in love with a stranger, you wou'd first find out what sort of man he is." Dorcasina, notwithstanding her melancholy, could not help smiling at Betty's simplicity and total ignorance of the operations of the mischievous little deity. "Why, surely," said she, "you do not think people can fall in love by design, or when and with whom they please?" "Why, I don't know ma'am what I thinks; but I

desire to be thankful that I don't know what this love is that you have
read so much about: and I hope ma'am, you have done with it as to
O'Connor; and don't intend for to worry, and cry, and make yourself sick
any more about him." "Alas, Betty!" replied Dorcasina, "you speak the
truth, when you say you are unacquainted with the tender passion. You
know not the struggles, and the time it will cost me to erase, from my
heart, an image so deeply engraved there; but as it is now impossible
that I should ever be his, I am determined to set about it and endeavour
to accomplish it."

Having learned her lesson only partially, Dorcasina resumes her cus-
tomary habits. At the age of forty-one, she falls for Captain Barry, a
twenty-four-year-old soldier recuperating at the Sheldon home. Barry,
a modest, retiring person, cannot extricate himself from Dorcasina's
grasp. His servant, James, disguises himself as Barry and persuades
Dorcasina to elope.

VOL. II

CHAPTER V

.   .   .   .

   As soon as they thought they had fairly made their escape, the tongues
of this happy couple were loosed, and they gave way to the most rapturous expressions of love and exultation. But, alas, how transitory is
every earthly joy! and how is every cup of pleasure, ere we have tasted it,
infused with some alloy of bitterness! After travelling, with the utmost
steadiness five or six miles, the horse, which carried these enraptured
lovers, suddenly took fright at something which lay in his way, and set
out upon a full run. James used all his address to coax him, and all his
strength to stop his career, but in vain. On he went as if lashed by a
thousand furies. Dorcasina was terrified and would have jumped out of
the sleigh; but James entreated her to be quiet; assuring her that as the
road was good they had nothing to fear. But, while he was endeavouring
to encourage his affrighted companion, he was not himself free from
apprehension.
   At length, what he feared, actually happened. One side of the sleigh
rising upon a rock, it was fairly overset, and the lovers thrown out. The
horse, however, still kept on, and was out of sight in a moment, leaving
them half buried in a deep snow bank. Luckily they were neither of
them hurt, but their situation was truly pitiable. There was no house in
sight, and they did not recollect having passed one for two or three
miles. What was now to be done? If they staid where they were they perished; if they turned back it was doubtful whether Dorcasina could hold
out to walk to the nearest house; and if they went forward it was uncertain at what distance they would find one. After deliberating for a few

minutes, James thought it most advisable, upon the whole, to go on. "Possibly," he said, "the horse may tire, and stop of his own accord, and we may overtake him; or at any rate it is probable we shall reach a house sooner than by turning back." Dorcasina, shivering with the cold, assented to this proposal, and on they trudged, with spirits as much depressed as they had been elated at their first starting.

As the pair trudges toward shelter, James reveals his identity. He flees and the alarmed Dorcasina returns home. After her father's death, Dorcasina decides that her servant John Brown is a gentleman in disguise and prepares to marry him. The Stanlys, in whose care her father has left her, endeavor to prevent the marriage. The Stanlys' daughter, Harriot, disguising herself as "Captain Montague" and pretending to be a rival for Dorcasina's affections, arranges to have her carried off to one of the Stanly farms. During her exile, Dorcasina is once again "courted," this time by a Mr. Seymore, a supposed widower. When his true identity as imposter, swindler, and attempted bigamist is revealed, Seymore tells Dorcasina the truth about herself.

CHAPTER XVIII

.   .   .   .

"So, madam," said Seymore, as soon as he saw her, "what has procured me the honor of this visit?" Dorcasina could not refrain her tears at beholding him. "I come," said she, "to ask how you could so basely deceive me; how you could invent so many falsehoods; and pretend so much affection?" "I can very easily answer your questions," replied the shameless wretch; and, adding insult to injury, "it was your money, and my necessities that induced me to deceive you; and you, credulous old fool, so greedily swallowed the grossest flattery, that it would have been difficult to avoid imposing on you. Ridiculous vanity, at your age, with those grey locks, to set out to make conquests! I have really so much regard for you, as to advise you to give up all thoughts of that kind, and to assure you that any man would be distracted to think of marrying you except for your money."

Dorcasina was thunderstruck at this rudeness, and, hastening out of the apartment, hurried to her own, where throwing herself upon the bed, she lay a long time without speaking; while Betty sat patiently by her side, waiting to see what would be the effect of the disagreeable truths, which Seymore had uttered.

Dorcasina, once again brought to her senses, spends some time with Harriot Stanly, who is now married to Captain Barry. Returning home, she learns from Betty of the care the Stanlys had taken to protect her and of "Captain Montague's" identity. Dorcas writes to Harriot full of gratitude and duly sobered by reflecting on her life.

CHAPTER XVIII, CONTINUED

.   .   .   .

"My Dear Mrs. Barry,
    " 'Till very lately, I was ignorant of the extent of my obligations to you and Mrs. Stanly. Betty has informed me to whom I am indebted for my preservation from a connection, on which I cannot reflect without extreme mortification. What exertions did you not make to save me from rendering myself despicable and miserable! Heaven be praised that they were successful.
    "My fate is singular; and I sincerely wish it may serve as a beacon to assist others, of similar dispositions, to avoid the rock on which I have been wrecked.
    "My dear father—But I will cast no reflections on his memory. Attached to novels himself, as a source of amusement, from which he had received no injury, he did not foresee, or suspect the mischiefs they might produce, in a young girl like me, ignorant of the world, and of a turn of mind naturally romantic. I was therefore left to gratify my taste for this kind of reading, without restraint; and this imprudent indulgence has been the cause of my ruin. I now find that I have passed my life in a dream, or rather a delirium; and have grown grey in chasing a shadow, which has always been fleeing from me, in pursuit of an imaginary happiness, which, in this life, can never be realized. The spell is now broken; the pleasing illusion has vanished. Having long been a dupe no less to my own vanity and credulity, than to the artifices of those, who chose to seek their interest or their amusement, in playing upon them, I now find, and most sensibly feel the consequences of my ridiculously romantic and absurd conduct.
    "However unjust and indelicate may be the opinion, that matrimony is essential to happiness, it is perhaps the first that a romantic girl forms. For myself, I candidly acknowledge that it has governed all the actions of my life. My parentage, my fortune, and I may add, my moral character, gave me the fairest prospect of forming an advantageous connubial connection; and such a connection was once in my power. Heaven forgive me if I am sometimes half tempted to wish its curse on the authors of the writings, which had so far perverted my judgment, and depraved my taste, as to induce me to reject it. To their fascinating influence on my young and unexperienced mind it is owing that, instead of being a matron, rendering a worthy man happy, surrounded by a train of amiable children, educated in virtuous principles, and formed by our mutual cares and examples to virtuous habits, and of promoting and participating [in] the happiness of the social circle, in which we might be placed, I am now, in the midst of the wide world, solitary, neglected, and despised.
    "In this situation, in order to avoid becoming a female cynic, or sinking into a state of total apathy, I have sketched out for myself a plan, from which I expect to derive happiness, sufficient to prevent life from

being a burden. My income is considerable, and my expenses comparatively small. Having no dependants nor needy relations, that accumula-
tion of property, which in most cases is prudent and commendable,
would in me be ridiculous. It is, therefore, my intention to seek out
proper objects of charity, principally among those who, by misfortunes,
and without any blameable misconduct of their own, have been reduced
from opulent or easy circumstances to indigence; and to bestow on
them what I have no occasion to use myself. . . .

.   .   .   .

"And now, my dear Mrs. Barry, if you should ever be blessed with
daughters, let me urge you, by all the regard you must feel for their best
interest and happiness, to copy in their education, the plan pursued by
your excellent mother. Withhold from their eye the pernicious volumes,
which, while they convey false ideas of life, and inspire illusory expectations, will tend to keep them ignorant of every thing really worth
knowing; and which, if they do not eventually render them miserable,
may at least prevent their becoming respectable. Suffer not their imaginations to be filled with ideas of happiness, particularly in the connubial state, which can never be realized. Describe life to them as it
really is, and as you have yourself found it, chequered with good and evil.
Teach them that a considerable proportion of human misery proceeds
from human imprudence; and that, although the most exemplary virtue
will not secure its possessors from the common calamities of life, it will
enable them to bear, with equanimity and resignation, the portion of
evil which the wisdom of providence shall see fit to allot them.

"With a high sense of the obligations I am under to you, and the most
cordial wishes for the happiness of yourself and family, I am, my dear
Mrs. Barry, most sincerely, and affectionately yours,

Dorcas Sheldon."

L-----, July 8th, 1800.

Frances Miriam Berry Whitcher (1811[?]–1852)

Near the end of her career Frances Miriam Berry Whitcher wrote that it is a "very serious thing to be a funny woman." Her perception of that fact had begun years earlier. The eleventh of fifteen children, Miriam, as she was called, was born to Elizabeth Wells and Lewis Berry, an innkeeper, in Whitesboro, New York. She was a precocious child who reportedly recited long poems at two and made rhymes shortly thereafter. Instructed at home and at the local academy, Whitcher did not receive the education her intelligence and artistic ability deserved; nevertheless, she developed her gifts to a remarkable extent.

Early in life she discovered her talent for making visual and verbal caricatures of classmates and neighbors, a talent that would bring both literary success and lifelong loneliness. Writing to a literary acquaintance, she described her experience: "I received at my birth, the undesirable gift of a remarkably strong sense of the ridiculous. I can scarcely remember the time when the neighbors were not afraid that I would 'make fun of them.' . . . I became a lonely child, almost without companionship; wandering alone, for hours, in the woods and fields, creating for myself an ideal world, and in that ideal world I lived for many years. At times I was melancholy almost to despair" (Alice B. Neal, Introduction to *The Widow Bedott Papers*, p. xiii–xiv; see Selected Bibliography).

Neither melancholy nor despair show through Whitcher's work. She wrote her first sketches, monologues by the Widow Spriggins, to entertain a local literary group. The sketches, printed in a Rome, New York, weekly, received immediate recognition. Encouraged by this initial success, Whitcher in 1846 sent copies of a second series, the Widow Bedott sketches, to Joseph C. Neal for his *Saturday Gazette and Lady's Literary Museum*. The sketches, published as "Widow Bedott's Table Talk," under the pseudonym Frank, won widespread attention. As a result, Whitcher was invited to write for *Godey's Lady's Book*. She answered the request with "Aunt Maguire's Experiences" and "Letters from Timberville," which appeared between 1847 and 1849. The Widow Bedott and Aunt Maguire series were collected and published as *The Widow Bedott Papers* in 1856. Whitcher also contributed hymns and devotional poems to Neal's *Gazette* and to the *Gospel Messenger*.

Brought up a staunch Calvinist, Whitcher joined the First Presbyterian church after Charles G. Finney's revival meeting in 1832. Later she turned to the more liberal Episcopal church. In 1847 she married the Reverend Benjamin W. Whitcher, an Episcopal clergyman, and moved with him to Elmira, New York. Whitcher's husband urged her to continue writing for the magazines, but when his parishioners learned that their minister's wife was "Aunt Maguire" and suspected that they were the objects of her humor, they forced him to resign. The Whitchers returned to Whitesboro, where, in 1849, their daughter was born. Whitcher developed tuberculosis shortly thereafter and died in 1852.

Selected Bibliography

OTHER WORKS
The Widow Spriggins, Mary Elmer and Other Sketches (1867).

SECONDARY
Finton, Linda A. "Women Vernacular Humorists in Nineteenth-Century America: Ann Stephens, Frances Whitcher, and Marietta Holley." Ph.D. diss., University of California, 1978.
Neal, Alice B. Introduction to *The Widow Bedott Papers*, ix–xix. New York: J. C. Derby, 1856.
O'Donnell, Thomas F. "The Return of the Widow Bedott: Mrs. F. M. Whitcher of Whitesboro and Elmira." *New York History* 55 (January 1974): 5–34.
Patter, Kate Berry. "Passages in the Life of the Author of Aunt Maguire's Letters, Bedott Papers, etc." *Godey's Lady's Book*, July 1853, 49–55; August 1853, 109–115.
Whitcher, Mrs. M. L. Ward. A Biographical Introduction to *The Widow Spriggins, Mary Elmer, and Other Sketches*, 9–35. New York: George W. Carleton and Co., Publisher, 1867.

The Widow Bedott Papers (1856)

Like many humorists, once she saw her work in print and tasted some success, Frances Miriam Whitcher began to have misgivings about herself and the value of her gift. When sending a set of Widow Bedott manuscripts to Neal for the *Saturday Gazette,* she wrote: "I fear criticism; I fear 'the world's dread laugh.' I fear a repulse, a failure; there are a thousand things to make me shrink from taking a step which may look like courting publicity; and I assure you, nothing but the hope of one day reaping some pecuniary benefit, induces me to offer myself as a contributor to your paper" (M. L. W. Whitcher, Introduction to *The Widow Spriggins,* p. 23; see Selected Bibliography).

Neal, himself a humorist of some note, understood her feelings. In his response, he urged Whitcher to continue writing the Widow's comments, assuring her that "all the world is full of Bedott. Our readers talk of nothing else, and almost despise 'Neal' if the Widow be not there" (Alice Neal, p. x; see Selected Bibliography). Neal was accurate in his judgment of the Widow's popularity. Once collected in *The Widow Bedott Papers* (1856), the sketches went through twenty-three editions by 1864, selling over 100,000 copies within the decade. And in 1879 David Ross Locke (Petroleum V. Nasby) adapted the monologues for the stage, where they brought actor Neil Burgess great success.

The Widow Bedott Papers brings together the twenty-one Widow Bedott monologues from the *Gazette* and the nine Aunt Maguire monologues from *Godey's Lady's Book.* Although neither series forms a novel per se, the Widow's series has a minimal narrative, and each series is unified by its respective persona. The Widow Bedott series follows Priscilla Bedott's thoughts and adventures from the death of her first husband, Hezekiah Bedott, through her attempts to find his replacement. The Widow uses the rough dialect of frontier humor augmented by malapropisms, misspellings, and mispronunciations. She is a crude, opinionated character who fancies herself a practicing poet and an authority on all subjects. The Widow herself is usually the butt of Whitcher's humor. Aunt Maguire, the persona of the latter part of the volume, is a wiser and more compassionate person than the Widow. Through Aunt Maguire's comments, Whitcher satirizes the genteel pretensions of small-town people.

Good humorist that she was, Whitcher not only perceived the weaknesses of individual characters and types but also understood the temper of the times. Many of the objects of her satire are people just emerging from frontier life and attempting to ape the manners of genteel society. One of the issues about which her characters as well as her readers were divided was women's rights. Whitcher, who had developed a career of her own, was apparently in favor of sexual equality, but to keep the good will of her general readership, she kept her references to women's rights ambiguous. In the first chapter of the Widow Spriggins series, Whitcher inserts her most straightforward remark. Permilly Ruggles (later, the

Widow Spriggins) describes her mother's attitude toward work quite forthrightly: "my mother eddicated all her children jest alike. She didn't aprove of havin' the boys do all the out-door work and the gearls all the housework, so in the arternoon the gearls went out and helpt the boys chop wood and hoe taturs, &c., and in the evenin' the boys cum in and helpt the gearls do up the chores." Later, in the Aunt Maguire series, Whitcher treats the topic of equality in a more ambivalent manner.

In the first chapter of The Widow Bedott Papers, *the Widow describes her husband and unwittingly characterizes herself.*

CHAPTER I
Hezekiah Bedott

He was a wonderful hand to moralize, husband was, 'specially after he begun to enjoy poor health. He made an observation once when he was in one of his poor turns, that I never shall forget the longest day I live. He says to me one winter evenin' as we was a settin' by the fire, I was a knittin' (I was always a wonderful great knitter) and he was a smokin' (he was a master hand to smoke, though the doctor used to tell him he'd be better off to let tobacker alone; when he was well, used to take his pipe and smoke a spell after he'd got the chores done up, and when he wa'n't well, used to smoke the biggest part o' the time). Well, he took his pipe out of his mouth and turned toward me, and I knowed something was comin', for he had a pertikkeler way of lookin' round when he was gwine to say any thing oncommon. Well, he says to me, says he, "Silly," (my name was Prissilly naterally, but he ginerally called me "Silly," cause 'twas handier, you know.) Well, he says to me, says he, "Silly," and he looked pretty sollem, I tell you, he had a sollem countenance naterally—and after he got to be deacon 'twas more so, but since he'd lost his health he looked sollemer than ever, and certingly you wouldent wonder at it if you knowed how much he underwent. He was troubled with a wonderful pain in his chest, and amazin' weakness in the spine of his back, besides the pleurissy in the side, and having the ager a considerable part of the time, and bein' broke of his rest o' nights 'cause he was so put to't for breath when he laid down. Why its an onaccountable fact that when that man died he hadent seen a well day in fifteen year, though when he was married and for five or six year after I shouldent desire to see a ruggeder man than what he was. But the time I'm speakin' of he'd been out o' health nigh upon ten year, and O dear sakes! how he had altered since the first time I even see him! That was to a quiltin' to Squire Smith's a spell afore Sally was married. I'd no idee

The Widow Bedott Papers, with introduction by Alice B. Neal (New York: J. C. Derby, 1856), 403 pp. Excerpts are from 21–25, 175–183, 273–274, 288–293, 295, 297–302, 309–312.

then that Sal Smith was a gwine to be married to Sam Pendergrass. She'd ben keepin' company with Mose Hewlitt, for better'n a year, and every body said *that* was a settled thing, and lo and behold! all of a sudding she up and took Sam Pendergrass. Well, that was the first time I ever see my husband, and if any body'd a told me then that I should ever marry him, I should a said—but lawful sakes! I most forgot, I was gwine to tell you what he said to me that evenin', and when a body begins to tell a thing I believe in finishin' on't some time or other. Some folks have a way of talkin' round and round and round for evermore, and never comin' to the pint. Now there's Miss Jinkins, she was that Poll Bingham afore she was married, she is the tejusest individooal to tell a story that ever I see in all my born days. But I was a gwine to tell you what husband said. He says to me says he, "Silly," says I, "What?" I dident say "What, Hezekier?" for I dident like his name. The first time I ever heard it I near killed myself a laffin. "Hezekier Bedott," says I, "well, I would give up if I had sich a name," but then you know I had no more idee o' marryin' the feller than you have this minnit o' marryin' the governor. I s'pose you think it's curus we should a named our oldest son Hezekier. Well, we done it to please father and mother Bedott, it's father Bedott's name, and he and mother Bedott both used to think that names had ought to go down from gineration to gineration. But we always called him Kier, you know. Speakin' o' Kier, he *is* a blessin', ain't he? and I ain't the only one that thinks so, I guess. Now don't you ever tell nobody that I said so, but between you and me I rather guess that if Kezier Winkle thinks she is a gwine to ketch Kier Bedott she is a *leetle* out of her reckonin'. But I was going to tell what husband said. He says to me, says he, "Silly," I says, says I, "What?" If I dident say "what" when he said "Silly," he'd a kept on saying "Silly," from time to eternity. He always did, because, you know, he wanted me to pay pertikkeler attention, and I ginerally did; no woman was ever more attentive to her husband than what I was. Well, he says to me, says he, "Silly." Says I, "What?" though I'd no idee what he was gwine to say, dident know but what 'twas something about his sufferings, though he wa'n't apt to complain, but he frequently used to remark that he wouldent wish his worst enemy to suffer one minnit as he did all the time, but that can't be called grumblin'—think it can? Why, I've seen him in sitivations when you'd a thought no mortal could a helped grumblin', but *he* dident. He and me went once in the dead o' winter in a one hoss slay out to Boonville to see a sister o' hisen. You know the snow is amazin' deep in that section o' the kentry. Well, the hoss got stuck in one o' them are flambergasted snow-banks, and there we sot, onable to stir, and to cap all, while we was a sittin' there, husband was took with a dretful crick in his back. Now *that* was what I call a *perdickerment*, don't you? Most men would a swore, but husband dident. He only said, says he, "Consarn it." How did we get out, did you ask? Why we might a been sittin' there to this day fur as *I* know, if there hadent a happened to come along a mess o' men in a double team and they hysted us out. But I was gwine to tell you that observation o' hisen.

Says he to me, says he, "Silly," (I could see by the light o' the fire, there
dident happen to be no candle burnin', if I don't disremember, though
my memory is sometimes ruther forgitful, but I know we wa'n't apt to
burn candles exceptin' when we had company) I could see by the light of
the fire that his mind was oncommon solemnized. Says he to me, says
he, "Silly." I says to him, says I, "What?" He says to me, says he, "*We're
all poor critters!*"

*After the Widow loses her first prospect of a replacement for Heze-
kiah, she leaves her native Wiggletown to spend the winter with "Sister Maguire" in Scrabble Hill. There she "sets her cap" for Elder
Shadrack Sniffles of the Baptist church. Learning that she has a rival
for the Elder's affections in Sally Hugle, a local poet who signs herself
"Hugelina," the Widow publishes a "poim" celebrating the Elder's
preaching. A subsequent composition reveals her growing emotional
attachment to the Elder, as the following excerpt shows. The Elder is
less interested in the Widow than in her reputed wealth (*Bedott *is a
derivative of the French word for "endowed").*

CHAPTER XVII
The Widow Retires to a Grove
in the Rear of Elder Sniffles's House

She sits down on a log and sings in a plaintive voice,

> Ere love had teached my tears to flow,
> I was oncommon cherful,
> But now such misery I dew know
> I'm always sad and ferful.

> What peaceful hours I once enjoyed,
> All on a summer's day!
> But O, my comforts was destroyed,
> When Shadrack crossed my way!

> I heerd him preach—I heerd him pray—
> I heerd him sweetly sing,
> Dear suz! how I did feel that day!
> It was a dretful thing!

> Full forty dollars would I give,
> If we'd continnerd apart—
> For though he's made my sperrit live,
> He's surely bust my heart!

(She sighs profoundly—and the elder advances *unexpectedly.*)
"Good gracious! is that you, Elder Sniffles! how you *did* scare me!
Never was so flustrated in all the days o' my life! hadent the most re-

motest idee o' meetin *you* here—wouldent a come for forty dollars if I'd a s'posed you ever meander'd here. I never was here afore—but I was a settin' by my winder and I cast my eyes over here, and as I obsarved the lofty trees a wavin' in the gentle blast, and heerd the feathered singsters a wobblin' their mellancolly music, I felt quite a call to come over, it's so retired and morantic—such an appropriate place to marvel round in, ye know, when a body feels low sperrited and unconsolable, as I dew to-night. O, d-e-a-r!"

"Most worthy Mrs. Bedott, your evident depression fills me with un-mitigated sympathy. Your feelings, (if I may be permitted to judge from the language of your song, which I overheard")—

"You dident though, elder! the dretful suz! what *shall* I dew! I would-ent a had you heerd that song for no money! I wish I hadent a come! I wish to gracious I hadent a come!"

"I assure you, Mrs. Bedott, it was unintentional on my part, entirely unintentional, but my contiguity to yourself, and your proximity to me, were such as rendered it impossible for me to avoid hearing you—"

"Well, it can't be helped now, it's no use cryin' for spilt milk, but I wouldent hev you to think I know'd *you* ever come here."

"On the contrary, this grove is a favorite resort of mine; it affords a congenial retreat after the exterminating and tremendous mental labors of the day. I not unfrequently spend the declining hours of the evening here, buried in the most profound meditation. On your entrance, I was occupying my customary seat beneath that umbrageous mounting ash which you perceive a few feet from you: indeed, had not your mind been much pre-occupied, you could scarcely have avoided discovering me."

"O, granf'ther grievous! I wish I'd a stayed to hum! I was born for mis-fortin' and nothin' else! I wish to massy I'd a stayed to hum to-night! but I felt as if I'd like to come here once afore I leave the place." (She weeps.)

"Ah! indeed! do you preject leaving Scrabble Hill?"

"Yes, I dew, I calklate to go next week. I *must* hear you preach once more—*once* more, elder, and then I'm agwine—somewher—I don't care where, nor I don't care what becomes o' me when I git there." (She sobs violently.)

"O, Mrs. Bedott, you distress me beyond limitation—permit me to in-quire the cause of this uncontrollable agony?"

"O, Elder Sniffles, you're the last indiwiddiwal that ought to ax such a question. O, I *shall* die! I *shall* give it up!"

"Madam my interest in your welfare is intense, allow me to entreat you still more vehemently to unburden your mind, perhaps it is in my power to relieve you."

"Relieve me! what an idee! O, elder, you *will* be the death o' me if you make me revulge my feelins so. An hour ago, I felt as if I'd a' died afore I'd a said what I hev said now, but you've draw'd it out o' me."

"Respected madam, you have as yet promulged nothing satisfactory, permit me—"

"O, granf'ther grievous! must I come to't! well then, if I must, I must, so to begin at the beginnin'. When I fust heern you preach, your sarmons onsettled my faith; but after a spell I was convinced by yer argefyin', and gin up my 'roneus notions, and my mind got considerable carm. But how could I set Sabberday after Sabberday under the droppin's o' yer voice, and not begin to feel a mor'n ordinary interest in the speaker? I indevored not tew, but I couldent help it; 'twas in vain to struggle against the feelins that prepossest my buzzom. But it's all over with me now! my felicitude is at an eend! my sittiwation is hopeless! I shall go back to Wiggletown next week and never trouble you no more."

"Ah, Mrs. Bedott, you alarm—"

"Yes, you never 'll see no more trouble with Prissilly. I'm agwine back to Wiggleton. Can't bear to go back there nother, on account o' the indi-widdiwals that I come away to git rid of. There's Cappen Canoot, he's always been after me ever since my husband died, though I hain't never gin him no incurridgement—but he won't take no for an answer. I dread the critter's attentions. And Squire Bailey—he's wonderful rich—but that ain't no recommendation to me, and I've told him so time and agin, but I s'pose he thinks I'll come round bumby. And Deacon Crosby, he lost his pardner a spell afore I come away, he was very much pleased with me, he's a wonderful fine man—make a fust rate husband. I kind o' hesi-tated when he promulgated his sentiments tew me, told him I'd think on't till I come back—s'pose he'll be at me as soon as I git there. I hate to disappoint Deacon Crosby, he's such a fine man, and my dezeased com-panion sot so much by him, but then I don't feel for him, as I dew for——. He's a Presbyterian tew, and I don't think 'twould be right to unite my destination to hisen."

"Undoubtedly in your present state of feeling, the uncongeniality would render a union—"

"O, dear, dear, dear! I can't bear to go back there and indure their at-tentions, but thank fortune, they won't bother me long—I shall go into a decline, I know I shall, as well as I want to know it. My troubles'll soon be over—ondoubtedly they'll put up a monnyment to my memory—I've got the discription all ready for't—it says,

> Here sleeps Prissilly P. Bedott,
> Late relic of Hezekier,
> How mellancolly was her lot!
> How soon she did expire!
>
> She did n't commit self-suicide,
> 'Twas tribbilation killed her,
> O, what a pity she had n't a'died
> Afore she saw the elder!—

And O, elder, you 'll visit my grave, won't ye, and shed tew or three tears over it? 'Twould be a consolation tew me to think you would."

"In case I should ever have occasion to journey thro' that section of country, and could consistently with my arrangements make it convenient to tarry for a short time at Wiggletown, I assure you it would afford me much pleasure to visit your grave agreeably to your request."

"O, elder, how onfeelin'!"

"Unfeeling! did I not understand you correctly when I understood you to request me to visit your grave?"

"Yes, but I don't see how you can be so carm, when I'm a talkin' about dyin'."

"I assure you, Mrs. Bedott, I had not the slightest intention of manifesting a want of feeling in my remark. I should regard your demise as a most deplorable event, and it would afford me no small degree of satisfaction to prevent so melancholy a catastrophe were it in my power."

"Well, I guess I'll go hum. If Sally should know you was here a talkin' with me, she'd make an awful fuss."

"Indeed, I see no reason to fear that my domestic should interfere in any of my proceedings."

"O, lawful sakes! how numb you be, elder! I dident illude to Sal Blake—I meant Sal Hugle, she't you're ingaged tew."

"Engaged to Miss Hugle! you alarm me, Mrs. Be—"

"Now don't undertake to deny it, elder; every body says it's a fact."

"Well then, it only remains for me to assert that every body is laboring under an entire and unmitigated mistake."

"You don't say so, elder! well, I declare I dew feel relieved. I couldent indure the idee o' stayin' here to see that match go off. She's so onworthy—so different from what your companion had ought to be—and so lazy—and makes such awful poitry; and then she hain't worth a cent in the world. But I don't want to say a word aginst her; for if you ain't ingaged now, mabby you will be. O, elder! promise me, dew promise me how 't you won't marry that critter. 'Twould be a consolation tew me when I'm fur away on my dyin' bed, to know—" [she weeps with renewed energy.] "O, elder, I'm afreard I'm a gwine to hev the highsterics. I'm subjick to spasmatic affections when I'm excited and over come."

"You alarm me, Mrs. Bedott! I will hasten to the house, and bring the sal volatile, which may restore you."

"For the land's sake, elder, don't go after Sal; she can't dew nothing for me. It'll only make talk, for she'll tell it all round the village. Jest take that are newspaper that sticks out o' yer pocket, and fan me with it a leetle. There—I feel quite resusticated. I'm obleeged tew ye; guess I can manage to git hum now." [She rises.]

"Farewell, Elder Sniffles! adoo! we part to meet no more!"

"Ah, Mrs. Bedott! do not speak in that mournful strain; you distress me beyond all mitigation"—[he takes her hand] "pray reseat yourself, and allow me to prolong the conversation for a short period. As I before observed, your language distresses me beyond all duration."

"Dew you actilly feel distressed at the idee o' partin' with me?"

"Most indubitably, Mrs. Bedott."

"Well, then, what's the use o' partin' at all? O, what *hev* I said! what *hev* I said!"

"Ahem—ahaw! allow me to inquire—are you in easy circumstancez, Mrs. Bedott?"

"Well, not intirely, yet; though I feel considerable easier'n what I did an hour ago."

"Ahem! I imagine that you do not fully apprehend my meaning. I am a clergyman—a laborer in the vineyard of the Lord—as such you will readily understand I can not be supposed to abound in the filthy lucre of this world my remuneration is small—hence—"

"O, elder, how can you s'pose I'd hesitate on account o' your bein' poor? Don't think on't—it only increases my opinion of you; money ain't no objick to me."

"I naturally infer from your indifference respecting the amount of *my* worldy possessions, that you yourself have—"

"Don't be oneasy, elder, dear—don't illude tew it again; depend on't you 're jest as dear to me, every bit and grain, as you would be if you owned all the mines of Ingy."

"I will say no more about it."

"So I s'pose we're engaged."

"Undoubtedly."

"We're ingaged, and my tribbilation is at an end." [Her head droops on his shoulder.] "O, Shadrack! what will Hugelina say when she hears on't?"

The most interesting monologues of Aunt Maguire, the persona of the latter part of the volume, describe the organization of the Scrabble Hill Sewing Society.

CHAPTER XXIV

Aunt Maguire Treats of the Contemplated Sewing Society at Scrabble Hill

We're a gwine to have a Sewin' Society at Scrabble Hill. Miss Birsley, lawyer Birsley's wife, was the first one that proposed it. She hain't lived here but about a year, and she's always ben used to such societies where she come from, so she felt as if she'd like to have one here. Miss Birsley's jest the woman to take hold o' any such thing. She's a wonderful active little body, and a real good woman tew. But, above all, she's got a way o' sayin' jest what she pleases to every body without even givin' any offense. I've often wondered how it was that Miss Birsley could speak her mind so freely and never make no enemies by it. Why, if I should venter to talk half so plain as she does I should be univarsally hated. But she comes right out with every thing she thinks, and yet she's more popilar than any other woman in the place. I guess it must be because folks has found out that she never says no wuss about 'em to their backs than she says to their faces. Well, she come into our house one day last week (she

and I's very good friends); she come in and axed me how I'd like to jine a
Sewin' Society for benevolent purposes? I told her that not knowin' I
couldent say, for I hadent never belonged to none. So she went into an
explanation; and after I understood the natur of 'em I liked the idee, and
said I'd go in for it. So she wanted me to go round with her and talk it up
to the folks; and as I dident see no reason why I shouldent, I put on my
things and off we started. . . .

.   .   .   .

    Well, . . . we went over to Professor Stubbleses to present the case to
Miss Stubbles and Jerushy. Miss Stubbles is quite a clever woman, and a
good member o' society as fur as she dares to be; but she's dretfully
under the Professor's thumb, and he's a wonderful curus man; he's got
some o' the oddest notions in his head that ever you heerd of—thinks
that property ought to be equilly divided—calls all rich men oppressors,
and all the laborin' class abused and deprived o' their rights—holds that
men and wimmin ought to be eddicated jest alike. He's always a whalin'
away about the dignity o' labor—has jest ben deliverin' a course o' lec-
ters on the subjict, and he calls all men that don't take hold and dew
kitchen work, domestic tyrants; but he has such a blind, twistical way o'
talkin', that a body can't tell what he means half the time—husband
says he don't know himself what he's a drivin' at. When we got there,
Miss Stubbles was in the side yard a splittin' wood; she come round and
went in with us. They hadent no fire only in the kitchen, so she took us
in there. The professor was a churnin'—I thought I should go off when I
see him. He's a great, tall, lank, ongainly man, and there he stood with a
check apron on, a churnin' away like fury—he *did* look like old Time.
Their overgrown gawkey son, Nathan, was a settin' the tea-table. There 's
somethin' wonderful quizzical about the boy's looks. His clus is a great
deal tew small for him, and he looks as if he was jest a gwine to bust out
of 'em like a chicken out o' the shell. He looked wonderful sober a settin' the table; but they say he's up to all sorts o' tricks away from home.
We inquired for Jerushy, and they said she'd gone to milk. Well, we told
our bizness, and axed Miss Stubbles if she'd jine the society? She looked
at the Professor to see how he took it afore she answered us—so I says,
says I, "What do *you* think o' the plan, Professor Stubbles?" The Professor giv three or four awful *hams* to clear out his throat, and then says
he, "Did I believe that an organization of this description would be a
labor-promotin' association, I would give it my heart-willing approval."
"No doubt it will be so," says Miss Birsley. "Ladies," says he, "it is high
time that the dignity of labor was appreciated world-wide." (We see he
was in for a speech, so we let him go on.) "It's high time that the purse-
proud and vice-bloated aristocracy o' the land was compelled to toil like
the hard-handed sons and daughters of honest poverty;—it's high time
that the artificial arrangements of society was done away, and this sin-
distracted, folly-bewildered, hag-ridden world was governed by such
laws as the Great Heart of the universe originally intended. Ladies, the

earth-mission of mundane souls is twofold; first, to discharge with self-interest-sacrificing zeal our duty toward down-trodden humanity; second, to perform with soul-earnest, wife-assisting, daughter-helping, labor-loving fidelity, such domestic services as shall be to be performed at home; and I pronounce that soul who refuses to acknowledge the dignity of household labor, a pride-be-sotted, contempt-deserving, heaven-provoking churl." Here the churn-dasher come down with such a vengeance, that the cream spirted up and splattered all round, and some on 't went onto Miss Birsley's shawl. "The land alive!" says she, "that was dignified, any how." Miss Stubbles jumped up to clean it off. "Set still, Miss Stubbles," says Miss Birsley, "it's the Professor's bizness to repair the mischief. Come, Professor, git a wet cloth and wipe off my shawl afore the grease soaks in." The Professor looked mad and dident stir. "Well," says she, "accordin' to what you jest advanced, you must own yerself to be a pride-besotted wretch. Now, Professor, I should like to know if it would n't be ruther more dignified for you to go out and split wood, than 'tis to make yer wife do it while you stay in the kitchen and churn? Would n't it be quite as dignified to send that great able-bodied boy to the pastur' to milk, as 'tis to make Jerushy go? It kind o' seems to me as if labor wa'n't dignified only when it's done by the right persons, and in the right time and place. It seems to me as if it's the best way for every body to dew ther duty in the station where Providence has placed 'em—mabby it's an *artificial arrangement*, but it strikes me as ruther a good one." The Professor looked quite beat, and begun to *ham* and clear his throat, and I see he was a preparin' to let off another speech, so I says to Miss Birsley, "Come, it's time we was a gwine." So we riz to come away, and Miss Birsley says she, "Well, Professor Stubbles, I s'pose you'll be offended if I don't invite you and Nathan to come to the Sewin' Society and help us, but as my idees respectin' the dignity o' labor differ from yourn, I think I'd a leetle ruther have Miss Stubbles and Jerushy come." The Professor looked real wrathy, but dident say nothing, and we left him a churnin' away for dear life.

CHAPTER XXV
Aunt Maguire Continues Her Account of the Sewing Society

I wish to gracious you could attend one of our Sewin' Society meetin's. You never see nothin' to beat 'em, I'll be bound for't. We've had tew now. At the first one, at Squire Birsley's, ther was twenty-five present. Miss Birsley had got some shirts cut out o' Cappen Smalley's cloth, and as fast as they come in she sot 'em to work—at least she gin 'em some work, but there was so much talkin' to dew ther was precious little sewin' done. Ther tongues went a good deal faster'n their fingers did, and the worst on't was, they was all a runnin' at once. Ther was an everlastin' sight o' talkin', but it did seem as if they wouldent never come to no decision in creation. 'Twa'n't expected we should dew much at the first meetin' more'n to elect the managers, and make up our minds how often we should meet—and I begun to think we shouldent dew even that much, there was such o' sight o' discussin' and disputin' about every thing. . . .

. . . .

Well, at the next meetin' ther was about the same number present, and we talked up what we'd dew with the money. The difficulty was, the members couldent agree upon nothin'—some wanted to work for *this* objict, and some wanted to work for *that*. . . .

. . . At last I went to Miss Birsley and told her my idee, and axed her what she though on't. She said she liked the notion. "Well, then, you propose it," says I, "for I can't git 'em to listen to me if I try till Doomsday." So she spoke out, and says she, "Ladies!" but ther was such a racket nobody dident hear her. So she tried agin: "Ladies, I say!" but still they dident pay no attention. Then she took the tongs and knockt on the stove as loud as ever she could. "Order!" says she. They stoppt talkin' then, and lookt round to see what she wanted. "Ladies," says she, "Miss Magwire has proposed an object to work for that strikes me as an excellent one. She thinks we'd better raise enough to repair the meetin'-house, and for my part, I think we couldent dew better: the meetin'-house is in a miserable condition; the plasterin's a comin' off in ever so many places, and the pulpit's a forlorn old thing, away up in the air; it's enough to break a body's neck to look at the minister, and shakes like an old egg shell. Mr. Tuttle says he's a'most afeard to go into it. Don't you think 'twould be a good plan to tear it down and build another? Now don't all speak at once. We never shall dew nothing in creation if we don't have some sort o' order. Miss Skinner, what's *your* opinion?"

Well, Miss Skinner was delighted with the idee, and so was the Grimeses, and the Fosters, and the Peabodys. Miss Peabody said the Baptists and the Episcopals was all a pintin' at us for lettin' our house o' worship be in such a condition. Miss John Brewster said she'd long thought our meetin'-house was a disgrace to the village; she'd no doubt but what 'twould be an advantage to the cause o' religion to repair it, for the Widder Pettibone told her how't if we'd had a decent meetin'-house *she* wouldent a went off and jined the Episcopals, but she got so disgusted with the old nasty house and so tired a stretchin' her neck to see the minister, that she couldent stan' it no longer.

"The dear me!" says Charity Grimes, "I want to know if she gives *that* as a reason! Why, every body knows she went there 'cause Curnel Dykeman's an Episcopal."

"Yes," says Polly Mariar Stillman, "I guess it's ginerally known what took *her* there."

"She's a wonderful oneasy critter," says Miss Peabody; "she's ben a

Baptist and a Presbyterian, and now she's an Episcopal. I wonder what she'll be next."

"Well, it's cause she's a widder," says Glory Ann Billins. "I never know'd a widder yet but what was as oneasy as a fish out o' water. I raly believe it's nat'ral tew 'em."

"Jest so," says Liddy Ann Buill, "widders will be widders."

"Not if they can help it," says I. I was sorry as soon as I said it, Sister Bedott lookt so mad. I tell ye she gin me an awful blowin-up when we got hum—said every body in the room thought I meant her, and she dident mean to go to the meetin' no more. I don't know whether she will or not.

Well, they'd got hold o' the Widder Pettibone, and they dident let her drop right off: if her ears dident burn that afternoon, I'm mistaken. Some on 'em got so engaged talkin' about her they stopt sewin' intirely. Bymeby Miss Birsley got out o' patience, and knockt on the stove. "Order!" says she. When they got still, says she—"When the ladies have got the Widder Pettibone sufficiently done up, I'd like to have 'em take hold and dew up ther shirts." "Law me," says old Aunt Betsy Crocker, "they ain't a dewin' her up; they're a pickin' on her tew pieces." Aunt Betsy ain't no great talker, but when she does speak she always says somethin' to the pint. . . .

"Well, ladies," says Miss Birsley, "if it's a possible thing, I'd like to have it decided whether we shall repair the meetin'-house or not. I think we'd better put it to vote. Them that's in favor on't will please to signify it by holdin' up their right hand." Well, all o' the members held up their right hand exceptin' Miss Ben Stillman and Polly Mariar. "Miss Stillman," says Miss Birsley, "I see that you and Polly Mariar don't hold up yer hands. Don't you approve of appropriatin' the money for that purpose?"

"Well, I can't say as I disapprove on't," says Miss Stillman, "but I should think we'd better not be in a hurry about makin' up our minds what we'll dew with the money."

"What's the use o' waitin'?" says Miss Birsley. "For my part, I think we should go ahead with more sperrit if we had an object fixed on to work for." "I think so tew," says Miss Stillman; "but, you know, we'd ought to be unanimous." "Then why don't you agree with us?" says Miss Birsley; "that's the way to be unanimous."

"I mean," says Miss Stillman, says she, "that we'd ought to wait till ther's a full meetin' afore we vote."

"The land alive!" says Miss Birsley, "I don't know what you call a full meetin' if this ain't one."

"The fact is," says Polly Mariar, stretchin' her great mouth from ear to ear and displayin' all her big teeth—(Jeff says her mouth looks like an open sepulcher full o' dead men's bone)—"the fact is," says she, "mar and me's of opinion that we hadent ought to vote till Miss Samson Savage is consulted."

"Miss Samson Savage ain't a member o' the Society," says Miss Birsley, "and she don't go to meetin' once in six months. I don't know what we should want to consult her for, I'm sure."

"But you know," says Miss Stillman, "her means is such that she's able to contribbit a great deal to any object she approves of."

"And we'd ought to be careful about offendin' her," says Polly Mariar, "for, you know, she withdraw'd herself from the Baptists because their Sewin' Society dident dew as she wanted to have 'em."

"Did the Baptists break down after it?" says Miss Birsley. Jest then the door opened, and in marched Miss Samson Savage. But afore I go on, I'd ought to tell you something about her. She's one o' the *big bugs* here— that is, she's got more money than a'most any body else in town. She was a tailoress when she was a gal, and they say she used to make a dretful sight o' mischief among the folks where she sewed. But that was when she lived in Varmount. When Mr. Savage married her, he was one o' these ere specilators. Wonderful fellers to make money, them Varmounters. Husband says they come over the Green Mountains with a spellin'-book in one hand and a halter in t'other, and if they can't git a school to teach, they can steal a hoss. . . .

.   .   .   .

. . . Miss Gipson come to the door and axed us to walk out to tea— she'd ben out all the afternoon a gittin' it reddy—so we put up our work and went out. We don't have the tea handed round at our meetin's as a gineral thing; we have the things sot on a long table; the woman o' the house pours tea at one eend, and we all stan' round and help ourselves. It's very convenient, especially where they don't keep no help. Well, we all took hold, and for a while Parson Tuttle and his wife and every body else had a restin' spell, for even Miss Samson Savage had other use for her tongue. She believes in dewin' one thing to once. When *she* eats she *eats*—and when she talks she talks.

And we had a real nice tea, I tell ye—biscuit and butter, and crackers and cheese, and cold meat and pickles, and custard and whipt cream, and three kinds o' presarves, and four kinds o' cake, and what not! I couldent help o' thinkin' that the money laid out on that tea would a went a good way toward the new pulpit.

"What delightful biscuit," says Miss Grimes. "They are *so*," says Miss Skinner; "but Miss Gipson never has poor biscuit." "O shaw!" says Miss Gipson, "you ain't in arnest: my biscuits is miserable—not nigh so good as common. I don't think the flour's first rate." "Miss Gipson, how *dew* you make crackers?" says Miss Stillman; "I never tasted none so good." "Now you don't *mean* so," says Miss Gipson. "I *can* make good crackers, but them's very poor; the oven wasn't jest right when I put 'em in." "I *must* have another piece o' this cheese, it's *so* good," says Miss Lippincott. "Where *did* you git it?" "Well, I got it of old Daddy Sharp: he ginerally makes excellent cheese, but I tell Mr. Gipson old Sharp's failed for once—that's what I call *poor* cheese." "Dew taste o' this plum sass,

Miss Peabody," says Miss Brewster; "I never see the beat on't." "I'd ruther have these peaches," says Miss Peabody; "they're *derlicious*. It is a mystery to me how Miss Gipson always has such luck with her presarves. I never dew, and I always take pound for pound tew." "This appel-jel's the clearest I ever see," says old Miss Parker. "How *did* you make it, Miss Gipson? Dident you dew it in the sun? I'm sure it don't look as if it ever was nigh the fire." "Now don't speak o' that jel," says Miss Gipson. "I told Carline I was ashamed o' my jel after seein' Miss Parker's, and I was a'most sorry I'd made any preserves since I'd eat some o' Miss Peabody's and Miss Skinner's, theirn was so much nicer." So they went on. . . .

Well, every thing arthly comes to an eend, and so did that tea after a spell, and purty soon after we went hum. Miss Stillman invited us to meet to their house next time. She urged Miss Sampson Savage to come, and I don't doubt but what she will if she thinks ther's any chance for kickin' up a muss. I was in to Miss Birsley's the next day, and she and I talked it over. She says we hain't accomplished much yit, for some o' the work's done so miserable 'twon't never sell in creation without it's picked out and done over better. The rest is put together wrong, and has got to be took to pieces whether or no. For my part, I feel any most discouraged about the Sewin' Society.

Early Realism

Sarah Josepha Buell Hale　　　*Caroline Stansbury Kirkland*

JOSEPH KIRKLAND, the son of one of the writers included in this section and a self-professed realist, stated as his literary creed, "Let only truth be told." In "Realism Versus Other Isms" (*Dial*, February 16, 1893), Kirkland criticized romance as trivial and remote from the concerns of ordinary life. In his view literature had progressed from infantile romance to adult realism: "We now have flesh and blood to laugh and cry over, and the puppets, with all their sawdust, are laid away—or dandled by those eager to live in past times."

Critics have since pointed out that literary realism is less distinguishable from other isms than Kirkland and its other advocates assumed, for all writers attempt to present a view of the truth; all use details from actual life; and all create "puppet" characters. But even though the late-nineteenth-century realists did not have a monopoly on "truth," they unquestionably formed a literary movement with definite characteristics. In their choice of subject, the realists avoided the exotic and remote; they exalted the ordinary and average, which they could observe personally, and thus their characters tended to represent a lower social level. In matters of technique, where the realists were most innovative, they eschewed coincidence and neat denouements. Seeking objectivity, they disdained chatting with the reader as Fielding and Thackeray had done and tried instead to suppress the authorial voice. They paid strict attention to details of the physical scene and characters' dress and speech. They used the vernacular, introduced dialect, and made frequent use of humor and satire. Many of the realists shared a common philosophy as well. Their world view tended to be scientific as opposed to religious or mystical, but as Harold Kolb notes in *The Illusion of Life: American Realism as a Literary Form*, they had a "fundamental moral orientation" (p. 49), as for instance in "their condemnation of American materialism" (p. 15).

Realism did not become a literary movement in America until the 1880s, nor was the term *realism* in use during the period represented by this collection. But the late-nineteenth-century realist movement did not spring abruptly into being. There were transitional writers. Most literary historians mention John De Forest, author of *Miss Ravenel's Conversion* (1867), and a number of women: Harriet Beecher Stowe (for her New England novels), Rose Terry Cooke, Rebecca Harding Davis, and Elizabeth Stuart Phelps Ward. In the years before these pioneer realists, who were active in the 1860s and 1870s, other writers were consciously striving for realistic effects. In the 1820s Sarah Josepha Hale wrote *Northwood* (1827), a novel dedicated, in her words, to "the delineation of scenes faithful to nature." In it, she mixed the typical moralism and melodrama of the period with description of daily life in New England. Twelve years later Caroline Kirkland was employing in *A New Home— Who'll Follow?* (1839) and in her other works about the West almost all the techniques mentioned above as characteristic of realism. She influenced not only her son Joseph but also the later realists who were familiar with her work: Harriet Beecher Stowe and Rose Terry Cooke.

Sarah Josepha Buell Hale (1788–1879)

As editor for many years of *Godey's Lady's Book*, one of the leading periodicals of the nineteenth century, Sarah Josepha Hale was perhaps the most widely known and influential woman of her time. She was born Sarah Buell, daughter of Gordon and Martha Whittlesey Buell, in Newport, New Hampshire, where she lived a quiet rural life until age forty. She received a better-than-average education from her mother and older brother and conducted a private school for children until 1813, when she married David Hale. By her own account, Hale's married life was idyllic; in 1822, however, just before the birth of their fifth child, her husband died, leaving her in financial distress. She soon turned to writing, publishing *The Genius of Oblivion* (1823), a thin volume of poetry, and the novel *Northwood*.

The success of *Northwood* brought Hale an offer to edit a new Boston periodical, *Ladies' Magazine*. She dedicated the magazine to "female improvement," promising to "cherish the effusions of female intellect" and educate women in domestic skills. Each issue contained poems, essays, household hints, and sketches of American life, the latter often written by Hale herself. In 1827 the Philadelphia publisher Louis Godey bought out the *Ladies' Magazine* and united it with his inferior *Lady's Book* under Hale's editorship. She edited *Godey's Lady's Book* until 1877, when she was in her ninetieth year.

Because Godey could finance the novel practice of paying contributors, Hale could attract better writers, and she also expanded the number of domestic departments begun in *Ladies' Magazine*. In *Godey's* can be found the forerunners of most departments existing in today's home magazines: cooking and recipes, sewing and patterns, domestic architecture, interior decoration, etiquette, health advice, gardening, child psychology, beauty, and fashion. *Godey's* gained fame for its hand-colored fashion plates and steel engravings. The magazine became enormously successful, as circulation climbed from 10,000 in 1837 to 150,000 by 1860. *Godey's* was the arbiter of American taste and manners, and Hale's name literally a household word.

During her career as editor Hale continued to produce her own work. She published poems, novels, and collections of her sketches; she compiled recipe books and household handbooks; she edited gift books, anthologies of verse and letters by women, and works for children. In her *Poems for Our Children* (1830) is "Mary Had a Little Lamb," the poem for which she is best known today, although her authorship of the first stanza has been disputed. Hale's major work is *Woman's Record, or Sketches of All Distinguished Women from 'The Beginning' till A. D. 1850* (1853; 1869; 1876). This monumental biographical encyclopedia, containing some 2,500 entries, took her several years to write.

Selected Bibliography

OTHER WORKS
Sketches of American Character (1829); *Traits of American Life* (1835); *The Ladies' Wreath* (1837; rev. ed. 1839); *Keeping House and House Keeping* (1845); *The New Household Receipt Book* (1853; rev. ed. 1857); *Manners, or, Happy Homes and Good Society All the Year Round* (1868).

SECONDARY
Entrikin, Isabelle Webb. *Sarah Josepha Hale and Godey's Lady's Book.* Philadelphia: Lancaster Press, 1946.
Finley, Ruth E. *The Lady of Godey's.* Philadelphia and London: J. B. Lippincott Co., 1931.
Fryatt, Norma R. *Sarah Josepha Hale.* New York: Hawthorn Books, 1975.
Martin, Lawrence. "The Genesis of *Godey's Lady's Book.*" *New England Quarterly* 1 (January 1928): 41–70.
Riley, Glenda G. "The Subtle Subversion: Changes in the Traditionalist Image of the American Woman." *Historian* 32 (February 1970): 210–227.
Taylor, William. *Cavalier and Yankee,* 115–141 [discussion of *Northwood*]. New York: George Braziller, 1961.

Northwood (1827)

Northwood is not realistic in the late-nineteenth-century sense. Although Sarah Josepha Hale claims to be describing New England life as it is, she concentrates on presenting Northwood, New Hampshire, as a model town for the new American republic. The book was undoubtedly influenced by a passage in Jeremy Belknap's *The History of New Hampshire* (1784–1792) in which the noted historian pictures the ideal rural community. Hale is heavily didactic, preaching about the superiority of New England character, promoting her favorite causes, and including moral homilies on subjects ranging from the proper education of children to the sins of greed and vanity.

There is no doubt, however, that she intended to write a realistic novel. In the beginning pages of her book, she says she would like its success to rest on the "delineation of scenes faithful to nature." She inveighs against "those restless readers who can find gratification only in constant excitement—who will not allow a writer one moment for description." In her *Godey's* reviews, Hale always scorned melodrama and over-elaborate plots. She pays little attention to plot in *Northwood*, except for a frenzied effort at the end to satisfy those "restless readers" who have survived the long, detailed descriptions of New England architecture, food, clothing, and customs. Nor does she make any attempt to develop character. The real hero of the novel is Northwood; Hale succeeds in conveying a sense of place that is atypical for the time. For all her moralizing and idealizing, in this novel (though not in her succeeding works) she describes things rather than sentiments.

Ironically, *Northwood* has been awarded a place in American literary history for the wrong reason. It is usually represented as the earliest, or one of the earliest, novels to discuss slavery and contrast life in the North and South. The subtitle of the book, *A Tale of New England*, more accurately reflects Hale's intent. Southern scenes and characters are introduced, like British ones, to heighten by contrast the description of Yankee life. It was not until 1852, after the appearance of *Uncle Tom's Cabin*, that Hale revised the novel, changing the subtitle to *Life North and South: Showing the True Character of Both* and adding lengthy discussions of slavery. In the original version she mentions slavery as a temporary evil that should not disturb the harmony of North and South. In the later version Hale advances the view that slaves should be taught Christianity, whereupon they might be freed and sent to Africa "to plant Free States and organize Christian civilization." This theory is further developed in her didactic novel *Liberia* (1853).

Hale made other revisions in the 1852 edition of *Northwood*, most of them based on causes she was currently promoting in her *Godey's* editorials. The two most obvious changes in the chapter printed below are her promotion of Thanksgiving as a festival to be held on the same day throughout the country and her campaign to abolish the use of *female* as a noun. She was finally successful in persuading President Lincoln to declare Thanksgiving a national holiday and in convincing her friend Matthew Vassar to remove the "animal epithet" *female* from the name of his college.

It may seem odd that a person who considered herself a reformer and wielded tremendous influence should labor for such trivial causes. Interpretation of Hale has always varied widely: *Northwood* and *Liberia* have been called anti-slavery and pro-slavery; Hale has been labeled both a "militant feminist" and a "true conservative." Her philosophy, expressed repeatedly in her works, explains some of the contradictions. She believed that God created women morally superior to men, but women's punishment for Eve's sin is to be subordinate to men. A woman must work through her husband, elevating him and transforming his nature in order to save humanity. Woman's sphere is restricted. She can use her influence only in the domestic realm because participation in public affairs might contaminate her. Thus Hale spoke against women's rights and attacked those leaders who wanted the vote; but because women had to be educated for effective use of their moral powers, she campaigned vigorously for higher education for women. Similarly, although Hale believed slavery was wrong, she thought the slaves should not be freed until their "moral sense" was developed (by female teachers, of course); nor could women properly support abolition because in their role as spiritual guardians they should cultivate only peace and harmony.

Hale discusses abolition in her preface to the 1852 edition of *Northwood*. In this preface, printed below, she also presents the image of herself as author that, as skillful advertiser of herself and her work, she promoted throughout her long career. She claimed repeatedly that she had never sought a literary life, that she had turned to writing and editing, not for personal financial gain, fame, or ego-satisfaction, but only for funds to educate her children.

The preface to the 1852 edition follows.

A WORD WITH THE READER

Twenty-five years ago the book you are about to read was written; and thus commenced my literary life. To those who know me, it is also known that this was not entered upon to win fame, but a support for my little children. Northwood was written literally with my baby in my arms—the "youngling of the flock," whose eyes did not open on the world till his father's were closed in death!

Northwood; A Tale of New England (Boston: Bowles & Dearborn, 1827), 500 pp. Excerpts are taken from 1: 70–86 and from *Northwood, or Life North and South: Showing the Truth of Both* (New York: H. Long & Brother, [1852]): iii–iv, 58, 64, 67–69.

The Reader who has suffered, or who is struggling to perform sacred duties, will rejoice that this work not only succeeded, but that the mode of its success proved it was not unworthy of public favor.

Northwood was published in Boston, where I was not then personally known to a single individual. The MS. was sent to a stranger; in less than a month after the book appeared I had received many letters of congratulation and promises of friendly aid. Among these letters was one from a publishing firm in that city, proposing to establish a periodical for Ladies, and offering me the editorship, if I would remove to Boston. This proposal was accepted, and the "Ladies' Magazine" established, the first literary work exclusively devoted to women ever published in America. Its success led to others of a similar spirit. Among these was Godey's "Lady's Book," published at Philadelphia. With this work my Magazine was united in 1837, and ever since I have continued editor of the "Ladies' Book."

Furthermore, the success of my literary life has enabled me to educate my children liberally, as their father would have done—and I hope the influence of the various productions I have sent forth has been in some degree beneficial to my own sex, and to the cause of sound literature and of pure morality.

Thus the kind Reader will see why this, my first novel, should be referred to as an era in my life.

Moreover, Northwood received commendations where no personal motives could have held sway. Under the title of "A New England Tale," it was republished in London—at that time a very remarkable compliment to an American book,—and honored with favorable notices in some of the leading Metropolitan Journals. In short, the author had no reason to feel dissatisfied with the success of her book. The portraitures of American character were pronounced excellent—particularly that phase generally known as *the Yankee*. The habits and tone of feeling characterizing the real yeomanry of this class are nowhere so clearly marked as in New Hampshire. There, the Farmers are really lords of the soil,—loving their country next to their God, and holding talents and learning in higher estimation than wealth or rank. And from the glorious old Granite State, where the scenes of this novel begin, have come forth those great men, "Defenders of the Constitution,"—who "know no North and no South,"—but wherever the sacred Charter of Union stretches its cordon of brotherhood, and the Eagle and the Stars keep guard, is their country. In the same spirit our book goes forth. Northwood was written when what is now known as "Abolitionism" first began seriously to disturb the harmony between the South and the North. In the retirement of my mountain home, no motives save the search for truth and obedience to duty prompted the sentiments expressed in this work; nor has a wider sphere of observation, nor the long time for examination and reflection changed, materially, the views I had then adopted. These views, based on the conditions of the compact the framers of the Constitution recognized as lawful, and the people of the United States solemnly promised to observe, have been confirmed by a careful study of the word of God, as well as of human history.

It is, therefore, a proud satisfaction to know that my own "Granite State," during all the fury of a sectional strife, has stood firm for the Constitution and the Union, like the pine on her hills, gathering strength of root from the storm that shakes its strong arms and even rends some of the noble branches from the parent tree.

One cheering proof of the world's progress is the earnestness of those who are now working in the cause of humanity. Men and women, too, are seeking for light to guide them in the way of duty. That it is easier to burn a temple than to build one, and that two wrongs never make one right, are points conceded by all; yet all seem not to have considered what is quite as sure, that fraud and falsehood never promote the cause of goodness, nor can physical force make or keep men free. The chain may be broken in one direction, only to be more firmly riveted in another, unless Love and Truth act as solvents, and destroy the fetters altogether. The great error of those who would sever the Union rather than see a slave within its borders, is, that they forget the *master* is their brother, as well as the *servant;* and that the spirit which seeks to do good to all and evil to none is the only true Christian philanthropy. Hoping that Northwood might, in some degree, aid in diffusing this true spirit, I have consented to its republication at this time. The few additions made to the original work are only to show more plainly how the principles advocated may be effectually carried out. Fiction derives its chief worth from the truths it teaches. I have aimed to set forth some important truths—their worth I leave to be estimated by the Reader.

Philadelphia, September 9th, 1852

In Chapter VI of Northwood, *which appears below in its entirety, Hale's hero Sidney Romelee, who has been brought up by his wealthy aunt and uncle on a southern plantation, returns to his family in Northwood. With him is his friend Frankford, an Englishman, who is contemptuous of Yankees. Most of the remainder of the book is devoted to detailed description of Northwood; Frankford is, of course, converted. At the end of the novel, Sidney inherits his uncle's estate and, after some intrigue, marries a Northwood woman and brings her to the plantation. In the 1852 edition Hale adds a long lecture on slavery and abolition. Sidney does not free his slaves because of his duty to "support and protect" them. His wife is to provide the slaves with religious instruction in order to fit them for eventual freedom in Liberia. The text of Chapter VI follows the first (1827) edition. Significant changes in the revised edition of 1852 are added in brackets.*

CHAPTER VI
[Home as Found]

"All hail, ye tender feelings, dear!
The smile of love, the friendly tear,
The sympathetic glow." [Burns.

The house, before which our travellers now stood, was a two story building in front, with a range of low buildings behind; the whole painted red, with white window sashes and green doors, and every thing around looked snug and finished. The house stood about five rods from the highway, and this fact deserves to be recorded, as a genuine, old school Yankee seldom leaves so many feet before his habitation. Indeed, they usually appear to grudge every inch of ground devoted merely to ornament, the mowing lot, cow pasture and cornfield being all the park and lawn and garden they desire. A neat railing, formed of slips of pine boards, painted white, and inserted in cross pieces, which were supported by wooden posts, ran from the highway to the house, on each side, and stretched across the front, enclosing an oblong square, to which was given the name of the "front door yard." Around this square were set Lombardy poplars, an exotic, which has been cherished in New England to the exclusion of far more beautiful indigenous trees, as foreign articles are considered more valuable in proportion to the distance from whence they must be imported. It appeared, however, that the Romelees had already discovered their error, and were endeavoring to correct it; this was evinced by the young elms and maples planted between the poplars, evidently with the design to have them for the guard and ornament of their scene, whenever their size would permit their tall, strait neighbors to be displaced. A gravelled walk led up to the front door steps, which were formed of hewn granite, and wrought to appear nearly as beautiful as marble. Clumps of rose bushes, lilacs, and honeysuckles were scattered over this lawn, as it should be called, and it was evident the forming hand of taste had been busy in disposing all to the best advantage; and had it been the season of sweets, the senses and imagination of even the most refined, might have found full gratification. On the east side of the railing, a gate opened into the back yard; and there was a carriage-way to drive round to the kitchen door, beyond which the barns, sheds, corn house, and all the various offices of a thriving and industrious farmer's establishment were scattered about, like a young colony rising around a family mansion. The last gleams of the setting sun yet lingered on the distant mountains, the village lights were beginning to appear, and a strong gleam, as of the blaze from a fire, illuminated the windows of one of the front apartments in the house of Mr. Romelee.

"What if this worshipful father of yours should not acknowledge you?" said Frankford, half laughing, "we seem to be thrown entirely on his mercy."

"He will, at least, entertain us for the night," replied Sidney, opening the gate and going forward, "as we have money sufficient to clear our score."

"Yes," replied the Englishman, "I have been told a Yankee will sell any civility for cash; and it is usually on that alone we must depend for favors in our intercourse with them."

The last remark was uttered in a low tone, and did not reach the ear of Sidney, who was just rapping at the door for admittance. A masculine voice was heard, bidding him "walk in"; and immediately obeying, they entered what in Europe is called the hall, here the front entry. It was about ten feet wide, and ran through the building, and at its termination was a door leading to the kitchen. A flight of stairs, painted to imitate marble, conducted to the chambers above; and doors, opening on either side below, led to apartments called the parlor and sitting room. As they entered the hall, the door of the sitting room was thrown open by a little girl, with her knitting work in her hand, who, in a soft tone, said, "walk in here, if you please." They followed her, and entered an apartment about eighteen feet square and eight feet in height, finished in the style of the country. The floor, which was formed of pine boards, was white as a table, and a ceiling of the same appearance rose about three feet from the floor and extended around the room. Above this and overhead, it was plastered and whitewashed. There were no paper hangings, nor tapestry, nor pictures; but some itinerant painter had exerted his skill, probably to the no small admiration of the wondering community, to ornament the room by drawing around on the plaster wall, a grove of trees, all looking as uniform in appearance as Quakers at a meeting, or soldiers on a parade, excepting that here and there one would tower his head above his fellows like a commander. Over the mantel piece, the eagle spread his ample pinions, his head powdered with stars, his body streaked with white and red alternately, his crooked talons grasping an olive branch and a bundle of arrows, thus significantly declaring, that, although he loved peace he was prepared for war; and in his beak he held a scroll, on which was inscribed the talisman of American liberty—*E pluribus unum*. A bed occupied one corner of the apartment; its high and square form, white pillows and ample quilt promising a comfortable refuge from the cares and fatigues of the day. A desk, surmounted by a bookcase, whose open door showed it nearly filled with well worn volumes; a large cherry table, a small work table, a wooden clock and about a dozen chairs, completed the furniture of the apartment. There was no candle burning; perhaps the precise time to light it had not arrived, but a large wood fire sent forth a bright blaze from the hearth, and before it, in an arm chair, was seated a serious but happy looking man. In one hand he held a newspaper which he had, probably, been perusing, and with the other he was pressing to his bosom a rosy-cheeked girl of three or four years, who sat on his knee.

Rising at the approach of the strangers, he set down his child, and offered them his hand with a "how d'y do!"—and then bidding Mary set some chairs, he resumed his own, while his little daughter immediately regained her station on his knee.

Sidney at once recognised his father, and his heart beat violently.

"A fine evening for the season!" said Squire Romelee—so I must call him to avoid confusion, though I do hate titles.

"It is quite cold, I think," replied Frankford, moving his chair towards the fire.

"You have been riding, I suppose," returned the Squire, "and that makes you feel the cold more sensibly. I have been at work all day, and thought it very moderate."

While he spoke he gave the fire a rousing stir, and threw on some wood that was standing in the corner of the fire-place. He then looked several times from one to the other, as if endeavoring to recollect them, and bidding Mary draw a mug of cider, again addressed himself to entertain them.

"Do you find the roads pretty good the way you travel?"

"Not the best," replied Sidney, who determined to speak, though the effort was a painful one.

"There ought to be better regulations respecting the highways, I think," said the Squire.—"Where every man is permitted to work out his own tax, the public are but little benefitted. I was telling Deacon Jones the other day—he is our surveyor this year—that I would take half the money and hire workmen, who should repair the roads better than they are now done by collecting the whole in the manner it is now managed."

"Then Deacon Jones is living yet?" said Sidney, glad to hear a familiar name.

"Yes, he is living," answered the Squire, surveying Sidney attentively, "are you acquainted with him?"

"I have seen him many times, but it is now some years since," replied Sidney.

"I expect he will call here this evening," observed the Squire.

"He would not probably recollect me now," answered the other, "yet I have been at his house often."

"Then you once lived in this neighborhood?"

"I have."

"And how long since?" said the Squire, whose curiosity seemed powerfully awakened.

"It is nearly thirteen years," replied Sidney, raising his hat from his head and turning his fine eyes full on his father's face.

The truth flashed on his mind—"My son!" exclaimed he, starting from his seat.

"Sidney Romelee!" replied his son, and they were locked in each others' arms.

Just then Mary entered with her pitcher of cider; she caught the last words, and setting down her pitcher, darted out of the room, and "Sidney has come! Sidney has come!" resounded through the house in a moment. In the next, the room was filled. Mother, brothers and sisters crowded around the long absent but never forgotten Sidney. Oh! it was a meeting of unalloyed joy—one of those sunlit points of existence, when the heart lives an age of rapture in a moment of time.

Mr. Frankford, who often described the scene thus far, always declared it would be in vain for him to attempt more. And I must follow his example, leaving it to the reader's imagination, and those who have the best hearts will best portray it. When the first burst of affectionate exclamations and interrogatories was over, Sidney introduced Mr. Frankford, as an Englishman, and his particular friend, with whom he had travelled from the south, and made a tour to Saratoga Springs, and north as far as Montreal. At the latter place Mr. Frankford had been confined nearly three months, with the typhous fever, from which he was now recovering, and Sidney wished them to consider him with particular attention.

Mr. Frankford had hitherto sat entirely unnoticed, though not unnoticing; for he there learned a lesson from the exhibition of natural feelings, which made him ever after disgusted with the heartlessness and frivolity of the fashionable world. And whenever he wished to dwell on a holy and touching picture of nature, he always recalled that scene to his remembrance. He was not, however, suffered to be any longer a stranger or a spectator. The friend of Sidney was the friend of the family, and every one seemed anxious to render him attentions. Mr. Romelee immediately resigned his arm chair, in which one of the little girls officiously placed a cushion; and having persuaded Frankford to seat himself in it, Mrs. Romelee brought from her closet a cordial of her own preparation, which she recommended as "the best thing in the world to prevent a cold after riding;" and bidding the girls hasten supper, she told him, after the repast she should [that before going to bed, he must] bathe his feet in warm water, and then a good night's rest would restore his spirits at once; adding, "you must, sir, endeavor to be at home and enjoy yourself, for I cannot bear to think any one is sad while I am so happy."

She was a goodly looking woman of five and forty, perhaps dressed as if she had been engaged in domestic affairs but still neatly. She had on a black flannel gown, a silk handkerchief pinned carefully over her bosom, and a very white muslin cap, trimmed with black ribbon—her mother had been dead more than a year, but she still wore her mourning. Her apron she would doubtless have thrown off before entering the room, had she thought of any thing save her son; for when she returned after leaving the apartment to assist her daughters in their culinary preparations, it was laid aside. The dress of the daughters, which their mother observed was "according to their work," it may perhaps be interesting to describe, and then, a century hence, when our country boasts its tens of millions of inhabitants, all ladies and gentlemen, arrayed in satins and sinchaws, muslins and mecklin laces, chains of gold and combs of pearl, this unpretending book may be a reference, describing faithfully the age when to be industrious was to be respectable, and to be neatly dressed fashionable. Both sisters, who were of the ages of seventeen and fifteen, were habited precisely alike, in striped cotton gowns, in which deep blue was the prevailing color. The gowns were fitted closely to the form, fastened behind with blue glass buttons, and displaying the finely rounded symmetry of the shape to the greatest advantage. The gowns were cut high in front, concealing all the bosom but the white neck, which was uncovered and ornamented—when does a female [girl] forget her ornaments?—with several strings of glass beads, braided to imitate a chain; and no eye that rested on those lovely necks would deem they needed richer adornments. They, also, like their mother, wore aprons; but theirs was of calico and ruffled across the bottom. The only difference in their costume was in the manner they dressed their hair. Sophia, the eldest, confined hers on the top of the head with a comb, and Lucy let hers flow in curls around the neck. Both fashions were graceful and becoming, as not a lock on either head seemed displaced; both were combed till the dark brown hair resembled fine glossy silk. Around their foreheads the curls were laid thickly and confined with pins; probably a little more carefully than usual, as the morrow would require a display of dress, which would render all their curls necessary; and these children of nature never had recourse to artificial decorations, or displayed borrowed finery. But those who gazed on their sweet faces, glowing with health and happiness, where the soul seemed beaming forth its innocence and intelligence, and the smile of serenity playing on lips that had never spoken save in accents of gladness and love, would feel no regret that they were uninitiated in the fashionable mysteries of the toilet. Frankford often declared he never, before seeing them, felt the justness of Thompson's assertion, that

> —   —   —   —   "Loveliness
> Needs not the foreign aid of ornament,
> But is, when unadorned, adorned the most."

They were, indeed, beautiful girls—the Romelees were a comely race—and every fair reader who honors these pages with a perusal, and does not think them, at least, as handsome as herself, may be certain she possesses either a vain head or an envious heart.

The supper was now in active preparation. The large table was set forth, and covered with a cloth as white as snow. Lucy placed all in order, while Sophia assisted her mother to bring in the various dishes. No domestics appeared, and none seemed necessary. Love, warm hearted love, supplied the place of cold duty; and the labor of preparing the entertainment was, to Mrs. Romelee, a pleasure which she would not have relinquished to have been made an empress, so proud was she to show Sidney her cookery; and she tried to recollect the savory dishes he used to like, and had prepared them now in the same manner. At length all was pronounced ready, and after Squire Romelee had fervently besought a blessing, they took their seats.

The supper consisted of every luxury the season afforded. First came fried chicken, floating in gravy; then broiled lamb, toast and butter, wheat bread, as white as snow, and butter so yellow and sweet, that it drew encomiums from the Englishman, till Mrs. Romelee colored with pleasure while she told him she made it herself. Two or three kinds of pies, all excellent, as many of cake, with pickles and preserves, custards and cheese, and cranberry sauce—the last particularly for Sidney—furnished forth the feast. The best of young hyson,[1] with cream and loaf sugar, was dispensed around by the fair hand of Sophia, who presided over the department of the tea pot; her mother being fully employed in helping her guests to the viands, and urging them to eat and make out a supper if they could.

Sidney's feelings were too much occupied to allow any great appetite for mere corporeal food. He wanted every moment to gaze on the loved faces smiling around him, or listen to voices whose soft tones, when calling him *son* or *brother*, made every fibre of his heart thrill with rapture. But Frankford was as hungry as fasting and fever could make him. He was just in that stage of returning health when the appetite demands its arrearages with such imperious calls, that the whole mind is absorbed in the desire of satisfying its cravings. He did honor to every dish on the table; till Sidney, fearing he would injure himself by eating to excess, was obliged to beg he would defer finishing his meal till the next morning; "for you know, Mr. Frankford," added he laughing, "the physician forbade your making a full meal till you could walk a mile before taking it."

"If that be the case," said Squire Romelee, "I hope you will exert yourself tomorrow. It is our Thanksgiving, and I should be loath to have the supper of any one at my table abridged. It will, indeed, be a day of joy to us, and Sidney could not have come home at a more welcome season."

While he spoke he directed a glance towards Silas, whose cheeks, fresh as they were, showed a heightened color, and his black eyes were involuntarily cast down. Sidney observed it, and asked his father if there were to be any peculiarity in the approaching festival. "Do you," said he, "still have your plum pudding and pumpkin pies, as in former times?"

"O yes," replied his father, "our supper will be the same; but our evening's entertainment will be different."

A wink from Mrs. Romelee, who evidently pitied the embarrassment of Silas, prevented further inquiries or explanations, and they soon obeyed her example of rising from the table.

Mr. Frankford, who they feared would exert himself too much, [was now installed on the wide sofa, (or *settle*) drawn up to the fire, and all the pillows to be found in the house, as he thought, were gathered for him to nestle in. When he was fairly arranged, like a Turk on his divan, half sitting, half reclining, he addressed Squire Romilly, and inquired the cause of the Thanksgiving he had heard mentioned.

"Is it a festival of your church?" said he.

"No; it is a festival of the people, and appointed by the Governor of the State."

---

1. A Chinese green tea made from thinly rolled and twisted leaves.

"But there is some reason for the custom—is there not?" inquired the Englishman.

"Certainly; our Yankees seldom do what they cannot justify by reasons of some sort," replied the Squire. "This custom of a public Thanksgiving is, however, said to have originated in a providential manner."

Mr. Frankford smiled rather incredulously.

The Squire saw the smile, but took no heed, while he went on.

"Soon after the settlement of Boston, the colony was reduced to a state of destitution, and nearly without food. In this strait the pious leaders of the pilgrim band appointed a solemn and general fast."

"If they had no food they must have fasted without that formality," said Frankford.

"True; but to convert the necessity into a voluntary and religious act of homage to the Supreme Ruler they worshiped and trusted, shows their sagacity as well as piety. The faith that could thus turn to God in the extremity of physical want, must have been of the most glowing kind, and such enthusiasm actually sustains nature. It is the hidden manna."

"I hope it strengthened them: pray, how long did the fast continue?"

"It never began."

"Indeed! Why not?"

"On the very morning of the appointed day, a vessel from London arrived laden with provisions, and so the fast was changed into a Thanksgiving."

"Well, that was wise; and so the festival has been continued to the present day?"

"Not with any purpose of celebrating that event," replied the Squire. "It is considered as an appropriate tribute of gratitude to God to set apart one day of Thanksgiving in each year; and autumn is the time when the overflowing garners of America call for this expression of joyful gratitude."

"Is Thanksgiving Day universally observed in America?" inquired Mr. Frankford.

"Not yet; but I trust it will become so. We have too few holidays. Thanksgiving, like the Fourth of July, should be considered a national festival, and observed by all our people."

"I see no particular reason for such an observance," remarked Frankford.

"I do," returned the Squire. "We want it as the exponent of our Republican institutions, which are based on the acknowledgment that God is our Lord, and that, as a nation, we derive our privileges and blessings from Him. You will hear this doctrine set forth in the sermon tomorrow."

"I thought you had no national religion."

"No established religion, you mean. Our people do not need compulsion to support the gospel. But to return to our Thanksgiving festival. When it shall be observed, on the same day, throughout all the states and territories, it will be a grand spectacle of moral power and human happiness, such as the world has never yet witnessed."

Here Mrs. Romilly interrupted her husband, to ask, in a whisper, which was rather loud,—

"Was that basket of things carried to old Mrs. Long?"

"Certainly; I sent Sam with it."

"She will have a good Thanksgiving then; for Mrs. Jones has sent her a pair of chickens and a loaf of cake," said Lucy.

"Every one ought to have a good dinner to-morrow," said Sophia.

"Is the day one of good gifts as well as good dinner?" inquired Mr. Frankford.

"So far as food is concerned," replied the Squire. "Everybody in our State will be provided with the means of enjoying a good dinner to-morrow: paupers, prisoners, all, will be feasted."

Mr. Frankford now confessing he felt wearied,] was persuaded to retire, after bathing his feet and taking another glass of cordial, Mrs. Romelee all the time lamenting he had not reached Northwood before his sickness, and repeatedly saying, "If you and Sidney had only come here instead of going on to Montreal, how much better it would have been! I would have nursed you, and we have the best doctor in the country. I don't believe you would have been half as sick here."

"Nor do I," replied he, gratefully smiling. "And to have been a witness and partaker of so much goodness and benevolence, would have made disease not only tolerable but pleasant; the sympathy and interest I should have awakened in such a kind heart as yours, would have more than indemnified me for my sufferings."

Squire Romelee attended him to his chamber. It was directly over the sitting room, and finished nearly in the same style. The ornament of the eagle, however, was wanting; but its place over the mantel piece was supplied, and in Frankford's estimation, its beauty excelled, by a "Family Record," painted and lettered by Sophia Romelee.

There were two excellent looking beds in the chamber, with white curtains and counterpanes; a mahogany bureau, half a dozen handsome chairs, a mirror, and a dressing table, covered with white muslin and ornamented with fringe and balls. Every thing was arranged with perfect neatness, order and taste—yes, taste; nor let the fashionable belle flatter herself that she monopolizes the sentiment. The mind of a rural lass may be possessed of as just conceptions of the sublime and beautiful; and less trammelled by fashion; she consults nature in selecting the appropriate, which is sure to please all who have good sense, whatever may be their refinement or station.

Squire Romelee set down the light, and was about leaving the chamber, when Mr. Frankford, laying his hand on the door, remarked there was no lock nor fastening.

"We don't make use of any," said the Squire. "I never in my life fastened a door or window; you will be perfectly safe, sir."

"Why, have you no rogues in this country?" asked Frankford.

"None here that will enter your dwelling in the night with felonious intentions," replied the other. "I suppose you might find some in the cities, but they are mostly imported ones," he added, smiling.

"And can you really retire to rest," reiterated Frankford, with a look of incredulity, "and sleep soundly and securely with your doors unbarred?"

"I tell you, sir," replied the Squire, "I have lived here twenty five years, and never had a fastening on a door or window, and never was my sleep disturbed except when some neighbor was sick and needed assistance."

"And what makes your community so honestly disposed?" asked Frankford.

"The fear of God," returned the Squire, "and the pride of character infused by our education and cherished by our free institutions."

"But I should think there might be some strolling vagrants," said Frankford, "against whom it might be prudence to guard."

"We seldom think of a shield when we never hear of an enemy," answered the Squire. "However, if you feel insecure, I will tell Sidney—he too will sleep in this chamber—to place his knife or some fastening over the door, before going to bed."

"I hope," said Sidney to his mother, after his father and the Englishman had withdrawn, "that Mr. Frankford will have a good bed. He complains bitterly of his lodgings since he came to America."

The matron drew herself up with a look of exultation. "He will find no fault here, I'll warrant him," said she. "My beds are as soft as down; indeed, those two in the chamber where you and he will sleep are nearly all down, for I made them for the girls, though I keep them now for spare beds; and I told your father I could afford to give each of the girls a down bed when they were married, as I have always had such capital luck with my geese."

Sidney, laughing, bestowed a kiss on the blushing cheeks of each of his fair sisters, telling his mother he thought it much easier to provide beds for such sweet girls, than find husbands worthy to share them. The idea of matrimony, however, awakened a desire in Mrs. Romelee's mind to communicate the intelligence her significant looks had prevented her husband from relating while at supper. With true feminine delicacy, she did not wish to have Sidney first apprised of it in the presence of Silas; nor did she feel willing a stranger should hear the remarks and interrogations which Sidney might make. These objections were now removed, as Silas had gone out and Mr. Frankford retired to bed; and so she ventured to say that "tomorrow evening Silas is to be married to Priscilla Jones; and," said she, "it is an excellent match for him. Deacon Jones is very rich, and has only three daughters; the other two have already married and moved away, and so your brother will go there to live and have the *homestead*."

Squire Romelee now returning to the room, they drew their chairs around the fire and entered into a confidential, family conversation. And the *conversationes* of Italy offer no entertainment like that which the Romelee's enjoyed—the interchange of reciprocal and holy affection.

A thousand mutual inquiries were made, and Sidney listened, delighted, to many an anecdote of his boyish acquaintance, or the history of many an improvement in his native village. The clock struck twelve before they thought the evening half spent, and then, with repeated wishes for his good night's rest, Sidney was suffered to retire, to dream over the happiness he had just enjoyed.

Caroline Stansbury Kirkland (1801–1864)

The first author to write realistic fiction about the American frontier was born in New York City, the eldest of eleven children of Eliza Alexander and Samuel Stansbury. The strongest influence in Caroline Kirkland's childhood was her Quaker aunt, Lydia Stansbury Mott, who conducted several schools for girls in Manhattan and upstate New York. After being educated by her aunt, Caroline taught in one of the upstate schools and met William Kirkland, a tutor at nearby Hamilton College.

After their marriage in 1828 the Kirklands opened a girls' school in Geneva, New York. In 1835 they moved to Michigan, where Caroline taught at the Detroit Female Seminary and cared for their six children. William served as the first principal of the seminary while he pursued his dream of investing in land and establishing a settlement. When he had amassed some 1,300 acres west of Detroit, the Kirklands moved to a log cabin in Pinckney, a clearing in the woods where they intended to build a town. The Kirklands spent six years in Pinckney under primitive conditions. Kirkland began describing her frontier experiences in letters to eastern friends and eventually cast them in fictional form as *A New Home—Who'll Follow? or, Glimpses of Western Life* (1839). *A New Home* was greeted so enthusiastically in the East that she followed it with *Forest Life* (1842).

In 1843 the Kirklands returned to New York, disillusioned with their frontier venture. They had missed intellectual stimulation and been victims of the sharp financial practices (swindling land agents, wildcat banks, various types of graft) Kirkland describes in her western books. The Kirklands left Michigan poorer than when they arrived. Back in New York City, Kirkland had just completed another book about Michigan, *Western Clearings* (1845), when her husband accidentally drowned. With four children to support, Kirkland alternated between teaching and writing. Her subsequent literary career was highly conventional. She abandoned her western subjects and realistic technique and wrote sentimental fiction for periodicals. Kirkland became, in Edgar Allen Poe's view, a leader among the literati of New York City. She edited the *Union Magazine of Literature and Art* and compiled gift annuals and anthologies.

In her later years Kirkland also engaged in charitable and social reform works. Most notably, she served as an officer of the Female Department of the New York Prison Association, which opened a home for female ex-convicts. Kirkland wrote *The Helping Hand* (1853), an appeal for support of the home. During the Civil War she organized programs and benefits on behalf of the Union cause; she died suddenly after a period of overwork in preparing a fair for the U.S. Sanitary Commission.

Selected Bibliography

OTHER WORKS
Holidays Abroad (1849); *A Book for the Home Circle* (1853); *Autumn Hours, and Fireside Reading* (1854); *Personal Memoirs of George Washington* (1857); *The School-Girl's Garland* (1864).

SECONDARY
Bray, Robert. "The Art of Caroline Kirkland: The Structure of *A New Home: Who'll Follow?*" *Midwestern Miscellany* 3 (1975): 11–17.
Hill, Douglas. Foreword to *A New Home—Who'll Follow?* New York: Garrett Press, 1969.
McCloskey, John. "Back-Country Folkways in Mrs. Kirkland's *A New Home—Who'll Follow?*" *Michigan History* 40 (September 1956): 97–308.
———. "Jacksonian Democracy and Mrs. Kirkland's *A New Home—Who'll Follow?*" *Michigan History* 45 (December 1961): 347–352.
———. "Land Speculation in Michigan in 1835–36 as Described in Mrs. Kirkland's *A New Home—Who'll Follow?*" *Michigan History* 42 (March 1958): 26–34.
Nerber, John. Introduction to *A New Home—Who'll Follow?* New York: G. P. Putnam's Sons, 1953.
Osborne, William. *Caroline M. Kirkland.* New York: Twayne Publishers, 1972.
Twamley, Edna M. "The Western Sketches of Caroline Mathilda (Stansbury) Kirkland." *Michigan Historical Collections* 39 (1915): 89–124.

A New Home—Who'll Follow? (1839)

In the first chapter of *A New Home* Caroline Kirkland mentions her previous reading about the West: "All I knew of the wilds was from Hoffman's tour or Captain Hall's 'graphic' delineations. . . . These pictures, touched by the glowing pencil of fancy, gave me but incorrect notions of a real journey through Michigan." Charles Fenno Hoffman's *A Winter in the West* (1835) and James Hall's *Legends of the West* (1832) typify early idealized treatments of the frontier that presented the West in terms of romance and adventure. Kirkland sought instead to write an account that, though fictional, would be solidly based on her own observations and would have, in her words, "general truth of outline." The characters would be "every-day people" and the incidents "commonplace occurrences."

Kirkland's prefatory remarks resemble Sarah Josepha Hale's in *Northwood*, but Kirkland far surpasses Hale in conforming her practice to her intention. She describes realities like Michigan mudholes, the ague or fever, and crude table manners, all of which Hale would have thought too low to be mentioned. Kirkland also pays close attention to the speech of her characters, claiming that she is providing "an impartial record of every-day forms of speech." Unlike Hale, Kirkland shows a strong sense of humor. She pokes fun not only at western manners but also at eastern expectations. Kirkland's persona, "Mrs. Mary Clavers," arrives at her log cabin in Montacute (as Kirkland calls Pinckney), Michigan, with such essentials as "a nest of delicate japanned tables," a china soup tureen, and an elegant cupboard. Her neighbors soon point out that the tables would make good kindling, the tureen a chamber pot, and the cupboard a corn crib.

In the beginning of the book, Mary Clavers is the superior outsider shocked by the poor accommodations and amused by the oddities of the natives. Gradually, as shown in the first two selections below, she becomes a participant in the life of Montacute. Kirkland's adjustment to western ways was clearly eased by her ability to identify with women of all types and classes. *The Helping Hand*, the appeal she later wrote on behalf of female ex-convicts, expresses an unusual attitude: "We are obliged to own that the faults of these degraded ones are our own, carried out to their legitimate consequences, and that of what we consider our superior virtues, they are found to retain . . . in a number and amount which could hardly be expected under the circumstances." In *A New Home* Kirkland presents two female characters who are unconventional but obviously to be admired by the reader. Mrs. Danforth and Cleory Jenkins, an outspoken schoolteacher who smokes a pipe, are strong, independent women. In *New England Local Color Literature*, Josephine Donovan sees them as "literary foremothers of the great female characters created by the local colorists: (Stowe's) Grandmother Badger in *Oldtown Folks* and (Jewett's) Mrs. Todd in *The Country of the Pointed Firs*" (p. 36).

Kirkland makes fun of some of her female characters, such as the romantic Eloise Fidler, whose fashionable clothing confines her indoors; but she reserves her strongest satire for men. It is not that she shared Hale's belief in women's inherent superiority; rather, she believed that men in their control of the economic sphere were responsible for an unjust and inhumane economic system. Kirkland condemns not only the abuses of the system—the swindling and cheating flagrant in the West—but also its very basis. In *Western Clearings* she notes that men were obsessed with buying land "not to clear and plough, but as men buy a lottery-ticket or dig for gold—in the hope of unreasonable and unearned profits." In her vocal opposition to capitalist exploitation, Kirkland brought into focus a tendency that had always been present in fiction by American women. Sally Wood had denounced land speculation in *Dorval* (1801); even Hale in her eulogy of New England conceded one flaw—"an inordinate thirst for riches." Later in the century anti-capitalism would become a staple of women's literary realism.

Despite, or perhaps because of, its unconventional technique and sentiments, *A New Home* delighted the eastern critics. Everyone praised the characterization, the humor, and especially the lack of "romantic coloring." Edgar Allen Poe concluded an enthusiastic review by calling Kirkland one of America's best writers. But back in Pinckney, Michigan the neighbors were indignant. According to contemporary accounts, they felt slandered and were "exasperated almost to frenzy. One woman threatened to have her put under bonds, and the life of the Kirkland family in Pinckney thereafter was the reverse of agreeable." Kirkland's biographer William Osborne (see Selected Bibliography) suggests that the hostile reception of her books in Michigan, combined with her need to support her children, may have led Kirkland to abandon realism in favor of sentimental magazine pieces. Whatever the case, *A New Home* was written against the prevailing traditions of the day; at the time of her death, Kirkland was lauded not for her pioneering realism but for her more conventional writings.

On their way to Montacute, Mrs. Clavers and her husband stay at an "inn," a small log cabin owned by Mr. and Mrs. Danforth; their "room" is a six-foot strip in the attic.

CHAPTER V

> Such soon speeding geer
> As will dispense itself through all the veins.
> —Shakespeare.

A New Home—Who'll Follow? or, Glimpses of Western Life (New York: C. S. Francis and Boston: J. H. Francis, 1839), 317 pp. Excerpts are taken from 29–39, 107–113, 209–214.

By her help I also now
Make this churlish place allow
Some things that may sweeten gladness
In the very heart of sadness.

—Withers.

The next day I was to spend in the society of my hostess; and I felt in no haste to quit my eyrie,[1] although it was terribly close, but waited a call from one of the little maidens [Mrs. Danforth's daughters] before I attempted my twilight toilet. When I descended the ladder, nobody was visible but the womankind.

After breakfast Mrs. Danforth mentioned that she was going about a mile into the woods to visit a neighbor whose son had been bitten by a Massisauga, (I spell the word by ear), and was not expected to live.

I inquired of course—"Why, law! it's a rattlesnake; the Indians call them Massisaugas and so *folks* calls 'em so too."

"Are they often seen here?"

"Why, no, not very; as far from the *mash* as this. I han't seen but two this spring, and them was here in the garden, and I killed 'em both."

"*You* killed them!"

"Why, law, yes!—Betsey come in one night after tea and told me on 'em, and we went out, and she held the candle while I killed them. But I tell you we had a real chase after them!"

My desire for a long walk through the woods was somewhat cooled by this conversation; nevertheless upon the good dame's reiterated assurance that there was no danger, and that she would "as lief meet forty on 'em as not," I consented to accompany her, and our path through the dim forest was as enchanting as one of poor Shelley's gemmed and leafy dreams. The distance seemed nothing and I scarcely remembered the rattlesnakes.

We found the poor boy in not quite so sad a case as had been expected. A physician had arrived from——, about fourteen miles off, and had brought with him a quantity of spirits of Hartshorn, with which the poisoned limb had now been constantly bathed for some hours, while frequent small doses of the same specific had been administered. This course had produced a change, and the pale and weary mother had begun to hope.

This boy had been fishing in the stream which was to make the fortune of Montacute, and in kneeling to search for bait, had roused the snake which bit him just above the knee. The entire limb was frightfully swollen and covered with large livid spots "exactly like the snake," as the woman stated with an air of mysterious meaning.

When I saw the body of the snake, which the father had found without difficulty, and killed very near the scene of the accident, so slow are

1. A highly placed nest, as of an eagle.

these creatures generally—I found it difficult to trace the resemblance between its brilliant colors, and the purplish brown blotches on the poor boy's leg. But the superstition once received, imagination supplies all deficiencies. A firm belief in some inscrutable connexion between the spots on the snake and the spots on the wounded person is universal in this region, as I have since frequently heard.

During our walk homeward, sauntering as we did to prolong the enjoyment, my hostess gave a little sketch of her own early history, and she had interested me so strongly by her unaffected kindliness, and withal a certain dash of espièglerie,[2] that I listened to the homely recital with a good deal of pleasure.

"I was always pretty lucky" she began—and as I looked at her benevolent countenance with its broad expansive brow and gentle eyes, I thought such people are apt to be "lucky" even in this world of disappointments.

"My mother did'n't live to bring me up," she continued, "but a man by the name of Spangler that had no children took me and did for me as if I had been his own; sent me to school and all. His wife was a real mother to me. She was a weakly woman, hardly ever able to sit up all day. I don't believe she ever spun a hank of yarn in her life; but she was a proper nice woman, and Spangler loved her just as well as if she had been ever so smart."

Mrs. Danforth seemed to dwell on this point in her friend's character with peculiar respect,—that he should love a wife who could not do her own work. I could not help telling her she reminded me of a man weeping for the loss of his partner—his neighbors trying to comfort him, by urging the usual topics; he cut them short, looking up at the same time with an inconsolable air—"Ah! but she was such a dreadful good creature to work!"

Mrs. Danforth said gravely, "Well, I suppose the poor feller had a family of children to do for;" and after a reflective pause continued—"Well *Miss* Spangler had a little one after all, when I was quite a big girl, and you never see folks so pleased as they! Mr. Spangler seemed as if he could not find folks enough to be good to, that winter. He had the prayers of the poor, I tell ye. There wasn't a baby born anywheres in our neighborhood, that whole blessed winter, but what he found out whether the mother had what would make her comfortable, and sent whatever was wanted.

"He little thought that baby that he thought so much on was going to cost him so dear. His wife was never well again! She only lived through the summer and died when the frost came, just like the flowers; and he never held up his head afterwards. He had been a professor for a good many years, but he didn't seem then to have neither faith nor hope. He wouldn't hear reason from nobody. I always thought that was the reason

2. Mischievousness.

the baby died. It only lived about a year. Well, I had the baby to bring up by hand, and so I was living there yet when Mr. Spangler took sick. He seemed always like a broken-hearted man, but still he took comfort with the baby, and by and bye the little dear took the croup and died all in a minute like. It began to be bad after tea and it was dead before sunrise. Then I saw plain enough nothing could be done for the father. He wasted away just like an April snow. I took as good care on him as I could, and when it came towards the last, he wouldn't have any body else give him even so much as a cup of tea. He set his house in order if ever any man did. He settled up his business and gave receipts to many poor folks that owed him small debts, besides giving away a great many things, and paying all those that had helped take care of him. I think he knew what kind of a feller his nephew was, that was to have all when he was gone.

"Well, all this is neither here nor there. George Danforth and I had been keeping company then a good while, and Mr. Spangler knew we'd been only waiting till I could be spared, so he sent for George one day and told him that he had long intended to give me a small house and lot jist back of where he lived, but, seein things stood jist as they did, he advised George to buy a farm of his that was for sale on the edge of the village, and he would credit him for as much as the house and lot would have been worth, and he could pay the rest by his labor in the course of two or three years. Sure enough, he gave him a deed and took a mortgage, and it was so worded, that he could not be hurried to pay, and every body said it was the greatest bargain that ever was. And Mr. Spangler gave me a nice settin out besides.—But if there is n't the boys comin in to dinner, and I bet there's nothin ready for 'em!" So saying, the good woman quickened her pace, and for the next hour her whole attention was absorbed by the "savory cates," fried pork and parsnips.

CHAPTER VI

> A trickling stream from high rock tumbling down,
> And ever drizzling rain upon the loft,
> Mixt with a murmuring wind, much like the sound
> Of swarming bees.
> > —Spencer.—*House of Sleep.*

> While pensive memory traces back the round
> Which fills the varied interval between;
> Much pleasure, more of sorrow, marks the scene.
> > —Warton.

When we were quietly seated after dinner, I requested some further insight into Mrs. Danforth's early history, the prosy flow of which was just in keeping with the long dreamy course of the afternoon, unbroken as it was by any sound more awakening than the ceaseless click of knitting-needles, or an occasional yawn from the town lady, who found the *far-niente*[3] rather burdensome.

She smiled complacently and took up the broken thread at the right place, evidently quite pleased to find she had excited so much interest.

"When Mr. Spangler's nephew came after he was dead and gone, he was very close in asking all about the business, and seein' after the mortgages and such like. Now, George had never got his deed recorded. He felt as if it wasn't worth while to lose a day's work, as he could send it any time by one of his neighbors. But when we found what sort of a man Mr. Wilkins was, we tho't it was high time to set about it. He had talked a good deal about the place, and said the old man must have been crazy to let us have it so cheap, and once went so far as to offer my husband a hundred dollars for his bargain. So John Green, a good neighbor of ours, sent us word one morning that he was going, and would call and get the deed, as he knew we wanted to send it up, and I got it out and laid it ready on the stand and put the big Bible on it to keep it safe. But he did not come, something happened that he could not go that day: and I had jist took up the deed to put it back in the chest, when in came Wilkins. He had an eye like a hawk; and I was afraid he would see that it was a deed, and ask to look at it, and then I couldn't refuse to hand it to him, you know, so I jist slipped it back under the Bible before I turned to ask him what was his will.

"'Did n't John Saunderson leave my bridle here?' says he. So I stepped into the other room and got it, and he took it and walked off without speaking a word; and when I went to put away the deed, it was gone!

"My husband came in while I sat crying fit to break my heart; but all I could do I could not make him believe that Wilkins had got it. He said I had put it somewhere else without thinking, that people often felt just as sure as I did, and found themselves mistaken after all. But I knew better, and though I hunted high and low to please him, I knew well enough where it was. When he found we must give it up he never gave me a word of blame, but charged me not to say anything about the loss, for, wherever the deed was, Wilkins was just the man to take advantage if he knew we had lost it.

"Well, things went on in this way for a while, and I had many a good cryin' spell, I tell ye! and one evening when George was away, in comes Wilkins, I was sittin' alone at my knittin', heavy hearted enough, and the schoolmaster was in the little room; for that was his week to board with us.

"'Is your man at home?' says he; I said—No; but I expect him soon, so he sat down and began the old story about the place, and at last he says,

"'I'd like to look at that deed if you've no objection, Mrs. Danforth.' I was so mad, I forgot what George had told me, and spoke right out.

"I should think, says I, you'd had it long enough to know it all by heart.

3. Idleness.

"'What does the woman mean?' says he.

"You know well enough what I mean, says I, you know you took it from off this table, and from under this blessed book, the very last time you was in this house.

"If I had not known it before, I should have been certain then, for his face was as white as the wall, and he trembled when he spoke in spite of his impudence. But I could have bit off my own tongue when I tho't how imprudent I had been, and what my husband would say. He talked very angry as you may think.

"'Only say that where anybody else can hear you,' says he, 'and I'll make it cost your husband all he is worth in the world.'

"He spoke so loud that Mr. Peeler, the master, came out of the room to see what was the matter, and Wilkins bullied away and told Peeler what I had said, and dared me to say it over again. The master looked as if he knew something about it but did not speak. Just then the door opened, and in came George Danforth, led between two men, as pale as death, and dripping wet from head to foot. You may think how I felt! Well, they wouldn't give no answer about what was the matter till they got George into bed—only one of 'em said he had been in the canal. Wilkins pretended to be too angry to notice my husband, but kept talking away to himself—and was jist a beginning at me again, when one of the men said, 'Squire, I guess Henry'll want some looking after; for Mr. Danforth has just got him out of the water.'

"If I live to be a hundred years old I shall never forget how Wilkins looked. There was every thing in his face at once. He seemed as if he would pitch head-foremost out of the door when he started to go home—for Henry was his only child.

"When he was gone, and my husband had got warm and recovered himself a little, he told us, that he had seen Henry fall into the lock, and soused right in after him, and they had come very near drowning together, and so stayed in so long that they were about senseless when they got into the air again. Then I told him all that had happened—and then Peeler, he up, and told that he saw Wilkins take a paper off the stand the time I opened the bed-room door, to get the bridle, for he was at our house then.

"I was very glad to hear it to be sure; but the very next morning came a new deed and the mortgage with a few lines from Mr. Wilkins, saying how thankful he was, and that he hoped George would oblige him by accepting some compensation. George sent back the mortgage, saying he would rather not take it, but thanked him kindly for the deed. So then I was glad Peeler hadn't spoke, 'cause it would have set Wilkins against him. After that we thought it was best to sell out and come away, for such feelings, you know, a'n't pleasant among neighbors, and we had talked some of coming to Michigan afore.

"We had most awful hard times at first. Many's the day I've worked from sunrise till dark in the fields gathering brush heaps and burning stumps. But that's all over now; and we've got four times as much land as we ever should have owned in York State."

I have since had occasion to observe that this forms a prominent and frequent theme of self-gratulation among the settlers in Michigan. The possession of a large number of acres is esteemed a great good, though it makes but little difference in the owner's mode of living. Comforts do not seem to abound in proportion to landed increase, but often on the contrary, are really diminished for the sake of it; and the habit of selling out so frequently, makes that *home*-feeling, which is so large an ingredient in happiness elsewhere, almost a nonentity in Michigan. The man who holds himself ready to accept the first advantageous offer, will not be very solicitous to provide those minor accommodations, which, though essential to domestic comfort, will not add to the moneyed value of his farm, which he considers merely an article of trade, and which he knows his successor will look upon in the same light. I have sometimes thought that our neighbors forget that "the days of man's life are three score years and ten," since they spend all their lives in getting ready to begin.

After she is settled in a log cabin in Montacute, Mrs. Clavers gains a neighbor.

CHAPTER XVII

> The house's form within was rude and strong,
>   Like an huge cave hewn out of rocky clift;
> From whose rough vault the ragged breaches hung:—
> And over them Arachne high did lift
>   Her cunning web, and spread her subtle net,
> Enwrapped in foul smoke, and clouds more black than jet.
> —Spencer.—*Faery Queene.*

> It were good that men, in their innovations, would follow the example of time itself, which indeed, innovateth greatly, but quietly, and by degrees scarce to be perceived.—Bacon.

It was on one of our superlatively doleful ague days, when a cold drizzling rain had sent mildew into our unfortunate bones; and I lay in bed, burning with fever, while my stronger half sat by the fire, taking his chill with his great-coat, hat, and boots on, that Mr. Rivers came to introduce his young daughter-in-law. I shall never forget the utterly disconsolate air, which, in spite of the fair lady's politeness, would make itself visible in the pauses of our conversation. She *did* try not to cast a curious glance round the room. She fixed her eyes on the fire-place—but there were the clay-filled sticks, instead of a chimney-piece—the half-consumed wooden *crane*, which had, more than once let our dinner fall—the Rocky-Mountain hearth, and the reflector, baking biscuits for tea—so she thought it hardly polite to appear to dwell too long there. She turned towards the window: there were the shelves, with our remaining crockery, a grotesque assortment! and, just beneath, the unnameable in tin affairs, that are reckoned among the indispensables, even of the half-civilized state. She tried the other side, but there was the ladder, the flour-barrel, and a host of other things—rather odd parlor furniture—and she cast her eyes on the floor, with its gaping cracks, wide enough to admit a massasauga from below, and its inequalities, which might trip any but a sylph. The poor thing looked absolutely confounded, and I exerted all the energy my fever had left me, to try to say something a little encouraging.

"Come to-morrow morning, Mrs. Rivers," said I, "and you shall see the aspect of things quite changed; and I shall be able to tell you a great deal in favor of this wild life."

She smiled faintly, and tried not to look miserable, but I saw plainly that she was sadly depressed, and I could not feel surprised that she should be so. Mr. Rivers spoke very kindly to her, and filled up all the pauses in our forced talk with such cheering observations as he could muster.

He had found lodgings, he said, in a farm-house, not far from us, and his son's house would, ere long, be completed, when we should be quite near neighbors.

I saw tears swelling in the poor girl's eyes, as she took leave, and I longed to be well for her sake. In this newly-formed world, the earlier settler has a feeling of hostess-ship toward the new comer. I speak only of women—men look upon each one, newly arrived, merely as an additional business-automaton—a somebody more with whom to try the race of enterprise, i. e. money-making.

The next day Mrs. Rivers came again, and this time her husband was with her. Then I saw at a glance why it was that life in the wilderness looked so peculiarly gloomy to her. Her husband's face shewed but too plainly the marks of early excess; and there was at intervals, in spite of an evident effort to play the agreeable, an appearance of absence, of indifference, which spoke volumes of domestic history. He made innumerable inquiries, touching the hunting and fishing facilities of the country around us, expressed himself enthusiastically fond of those sports, and said the country was a living death without them, regretting much that Mr. Clavers was not of the same mind.

Meanwhile I had begun to take quite an interest in his little wife. I found that she was as fond of novels and poetry, as her husband was of field-sports. Some of her flights of sentiment went quite beyond my sobered-down views. But I saw we should get on admirably, and so we have done ever since. I did not mistake that pleasant smile, and that soft sweet voice. They are even now as attractive as ever. And I had a neighbor.

Before the winter had quite set in, our little nest was finished, or as nearly finished as any thing in Michigan; and Mr. and Mrs. Rivers took possession of their new dwelling, on the very same day that we smiled our adieux to the loggery.

Our new house was merely the beginning of a house, intended for the reception of a front-building, Yankee fashion, whenever the owner should be able to enlarge his borders. But the contrast with our sometime dwelling, made even this humble cot seem absolutely sumptuous. The children could do nothing but admire the conveniences it afforded. Robinson Crusoe exulted not more warmly in his successive acquisitions than did Alice in "a kitchen, a real kitchen! and a pantry to put the dishes!" while Arthur found much to praise in the wee bed-room which was allotted as his sanctum in the "hic, hæc, hoc," hours. Mrs. Rivers, who was fresh from the "settlements," often curled her pretty lip at the deficiencies in her little mansion, but we had learned to prize any thing which was even a shade above the wigwam, and dreamed not of two parlors or a piazza.

Other families removed to Montacute in the course of the winter. Our visiting list was considerably enlarged, and I used all my influence with Mrs. Rivers to persuade her that her true happiness lay in making friends of her neighbors. She was very shy, easily shocked by those sins against Chesterfield,[4] which one encounters here at every turn, did not conceal her fatigue when a neighbor happened in after breakfast to make a three hours' call, forgot to ask those who came at one o'clock to take off their things and stay to tea, even though the knitting needles might peep out beneath the shawl. For these and similar omissions I lectured her continually but with little effect. It was with the greatest difficulty I could persuade her to enter any house but ours, although I took especial care to be impartial in my own visiting habits, determined at all sacrifice to live down the impression that I felt *above* my neighbors. In fact, however we may justify certain exclusive habits in populous places, they are strikingly and confessedly ridiculous in the wilderness. What can be more absurd than a feeling of proud distinction, where a stray spark of fire, a sudden illness, or a day's contre-temps, may throw you entirely upon the kindness of your humblest neighbor? If I treat Mrs. Timson with neglect to-day, can I with any face borrow her broom to-morrow? And what would become of me, if in revenge for my declining her invitation to tea this afternoon, she should decline coming to do my washing on Monday?

It was as a practical corollary to these my lectures, that I persuaded Mrs. Rivers to accept an invitation that we received for the wedding of a young girl, the sister of our cooper, Mr. Whitefield. I attired myself in

---

4. Reference to Philip Stanhope, earl of Chesterfield (1694–1773), whose extracts from his letters to his son on etiquette were well known.

white, considered here as the extreme of festal elegance, to do honor to the occasion; and called for Mrs. Rivers in the ox-cart at two o'clock.

I found her in her ordinary neat home-dress; and it required some argument on my part to induce her to exchange it for a gay chally with appropriate ornaments.

"It really seemed ridiculous," she said, "to *dress* for such a place! and besides, my dear Mrs. Clavers, I am afraid we shall be suspected of a desire to outshine."

I assured her we were in more danger of that other and far more dangerous suspicion of under-valuing our rustic neighbors.

"I s'pose they didn't think it worth while to put on their best gowns for country-folks!"

I assumed the part of Mentor on this and many similar occasions; considering myself by this time quite an old resident, and of right entitled to speak for the natives.

Mrs. Rivers was a little disposed to laugh at the ox-cart; but I soon convinced her that, with its cushion of straw overspread with a buffalo robe, it was far preferable to a more ambitious carriage.

"No letting down of steps, no ruining one's dress against a muddy wheel! no gay horses tipping one into the gutter!" . . .

The pretty bride was in white cambric, worn over pink glazed muslin. The prodigiously stiff under-dress with its large cords, (not more than three or four years behind the fashion,) gave additional slenderness to her taper waist, bound straitly with a sky-blue zone. The fair hair was decorated, not covered, with a cap, the universal adjunct of full dress in the country, placed far behind the ears, and displaying the largest puffs, set off by sundry gilt combs. The unfailing high-heeled prunelle shoe gave the finishing-touch, and the whole was scented, *à l'outrance*,[5] with essence of lemon.

After the ceremony, which occupied perhaps three minutes, fully twice as long as is required by our State laws, tea was served, absolutely handed on a salver, and by the master of the house, a respectable farmer. Mountains of cake followed. I think either pile might have measured a foot in height, and each piece would have furnished a meal for a hungry school-boy. Other things were equally abundant, and much pleasant talk followed the refreshments. I returned home highly delighted, and tried to persuade my companion to look on the rational side of the thing, which she scarcely seemed disposed to do, so *outré*[6] did the whole appear to her. I, who had begun to claim for myself the dignified character of a cosmopolite, a philosophical observer of men and things, consoled myself for this derogatory view of Montacute gentility, by thinking, "All city people are so cockneyish!"

5. To excess.
6. Outrageous.

Harley Rivers, husband of Mrs. Clavers's friend, becomes president of a new bank in the nearby settlement of Tinkerville. Bank commissioners investigate rumors that the Tinkerville Bank is a "wildcat," or paper, bank, in other words, that it issues paper banknotes that are not backed up with specie. The bank passes the first inspection, but the commissioners soon return.

CHAPTER XXXII

And whare is your honors gaun the day wi' a' your picks
and shules?—*Antiquary.*
On peut ètre plus fin qu' un autre, mais non pas plus fin que tous les autres.—Rochefoucault.[7]

All too soon came the period when I must part with my pleasant neighbor Mrs. Rivers, the opening brilliancy of whose lot seemed to threaten a lasting separation. . . .

Mr. Rivers had for some time found abundant leisure for his favorite occupations of hunting and fishing. The signing of bills took up but little time, and an occasional ride to the scene of future glories, for the purpose of superintending the various improvements, was all that had necessarily called him away. But now, final preparations for a removal were absolutely in progress; and I had begun to feel really sad at the thought of losing the gentle Anna, when the Bank Commissioners again paced in official dignity up Main-street, and, this time, alighted at Mr. Rivers' door.

The President and Greenhorn[8] had trotted to Tinkerville that morning . . . so our men of power gravely wended their way towards the newly-painted and pine-pillared honors of the Merchants' and Manufacturers' Banking-house, not without leaving behind them many a surmise as to the probable object of this new visitation.

It was Mr. Skinner's opinion, and Mr. Skinner is a long-headed Yankee, that the Bank had issued too many bills; and for the sincerity of his judgment, he referred his hearers to the fact, that he had for some time been turning the splendid notes of the Merchants' and Manufacturers' Bank of Tinkerville into wheat and corn as fast as he conveniently could.

A sly old farmer, who had sold several hundred bushels of wheat to Mr. Skinner, at one dollar twenty-five cents a bushel, winked knowingly as the merchant mentioned this proof of his own far-seeing astuteness; and informed the company that he had paid out the last dollar long ago on certain outstanding debts.

---

7. "You may be more subtle than another, but not more subtle than all others."
Rochefoucault, *Maxims*, no. 294.
8. His horse.

Mr. Porter knew that the Tinkerville blacksmith had run up a most unconscionable bill for the iron doors, &c. &c., which were necessary to secure the immense vaults of the Bank; that would give, as he presumed, some hint of the probable object of the Commissioners.

Mr. Simeon Jenkins, if not the greatest, certainly the most grandiloquent man in Montacute, did'nt want to know any better than he did know, that the Cashier of the Bank was a thick-skull; and he felt very much afraid that the said Cashier had been getting his principals into trouble. Mr. Bite's manner of writing his name was, in Mr. Jenkins' view, proof positive of his lack of capacity; since "nobody in the universal world," as Mr. Jenkins averred, "ever wrote such a hand as that, that know'd anything worth knowing."

But conjectures, however positively advanced, are, after all, not quite satisfactory; and the return of the Commissioners was most anxiously awaited even by the very worthies who knew their business so well.

The sun set most perversely soon, and the light would not stay long after him; and thick darkness settled upon this mundane sphere, and no word transpired from Tinkerville. Morning came, and with it the men of office, but oh! with what lengthened faces!

There were whispers of "an injunction"—horrid sound!—upon the Merchants' and Manufacturers' Bank of Tinkerville.

To picture the dismay which drew into all sorts of shapes the universal face of Montacute, would require a dozen Wilkies.[9] I shall content myself with saying that there was no joking about the matter.

The Commissioners were not very communicative; but in spite of their dignified mystification, something about broken glass and tenpenny nails did leak out before their track was fairly cold.

And where was Harley Rivers? "Echo answers, where?" His dear little wife watered her pillow with her tears for many a night before he returned to Montacute.

It seemed, as we afterwards learned, that the Commissioners had seen some suspicious circumstances about the management of the Bank, and returned with a determination to examine into matters a little more scrupulously. It had been found in other cases that certain "specie-certificates" had been locomotive. It had been rumored, since the new batch of Banks had come into operation, that

> Thirty steeds both fleet and wight
> Stood saddled in the stables day and night—

ready to effect at short notice certain transfers of assets and specie. And in the course of the Tinkerville investigation the Commissioners had ascertained by the aid of hammer and chisel, that the boxes of the "real stuff" which had been so loudly vaunted, contained a heavy charge of broken glass and tenpenny nails, covered above and below with half-

9. Sir David Wilkie (1785–1841), Scottish etcher and painter.

dollars, principally *"bogus."* Alas! for Tinkerville, and alas, for poor Michigan!

The distress among the poorer classes of farmers which was the immediate consequence of this and other Bank failures, was indescribable. Those who have seen only a city panic, can form no idea of the extent and severity of the sufferings on these occasions. And how many small farmers are there in Michigan who have *not* suffered from this cause? . . .

How many settlers who came in from the deep woods many miles distant where no grain had yet grown, after travelling perhaps two or three days and nights, with a half-starved ox-team, and living on a few crusts by the way, were told when they offered their splendid-looking bank-notes, their hard-earned all, for the flour which was to be the sole food of wife and babes through the long winter, that these hoarded treasures were valueless as the ragged paper which wrapped them! Can we blame them if they cursed in their agony, the soulless wretches who had thus drained their best blood for the furtherance of their own schemes of low ambition? Can we wonder that the poor, feeling such wrongs as these, learn to hate the rich, and to fancy them natural enemies? . . .

After public indignation had in some measure subsided, and indeed such occurrences as I have described became too common to stir the surface of society very rudely, Mr. Harley Rivers returned to Montacute, and prepared at once for the removal of his family. I took leave of his wife with most sincere regret, and I felt at the time as if we should never meet again. But I have heard frequently from them until quite lately; and they have been living very handsomely (Mr. Rivers always boasted that he *would* live like a gentleman) in one of the Eastern cities on the spoils of the Tinkerville Wild-cat.

Later Didacticism
The Novel of Education

Maria Cummins

Martha Finley

Susan Warner

THE DIDACTIC FICTION of the mid nineteenth century differs significantly from eighteenth-century didactic fiction. Early fiction warned readers of the perils of seduction and provided racy stories to make the point. The moralistic literature of the nineteenth century, influenced by the beginnings of realism, strives to educate women in preparing themselves for marriage, building a home and family, and developing religious principles. The protagonists are usually children who, as they learn to subdue their strong-willed natures, weep copiously and evoke a similar response from readers. Eventually they overcome the trials of their education and become models of perfection. Moreover, they convert those around them, thereby assuring their own salvation.

Often, as in Susan Warner's *The Wide, Wide World* (1850), Maria Cummins's *The Lamplighter* (1854), and Martha Finley's *Elsie Dinsmore* (1867), the protagonist, orphaned or motherless, must find a surrogate family or series of families in which to mature. The familial model the novels provide is a household in which the father, representative of the Heavenly Father, rules with absolute authority. Sons may challenge the father's word at the risk of disinheritance and separation from the family, but since they can "make their way in the world," they are free to rebel. Wives and daughters, because of their economic dependence, are doomed to submit to every whim of the head of the household. They may hold out against male authority only when it conflicts with Biblical teaching. Even then, they may have to suffer patiently for years before the earthly lord and master comes to see the wisdom of the Heavenly one.

Given this nineteenth-century focus on submission within marriage and the family, it is not surprising that none of the three leading didactic novelists married. What is surprising is that they wrote as they did, encouraging other women to obey God and father. Certainly their religious dedication helped shape their writing. Moreover, all three wrote from economic need and thus conformed to the taste of the times. But these reasons may not fully account for the content of their works. Perhaps, as some recent critics have suggested, they were preaching a more subversive message under the surface. An example from Warner's life supports this conjecture. Warner's first biographer—her sister Anna—remarks in *Susan Warner ("Elizabeth Wetherell")* (see Selected Bibliography) that Warner adored her father, that "she had only one shrine of perfection and it was for him" (p. 109). Yet, a diary entry for February 23, 1859, cited in the biography, reveals Warner's perception of the oppressed state of women: "Got into the cooler little back room and rested with a charming talk with Mrs. Hutton about her reading the W.W.W. [*The Wide, Wide World*] in her kitchen, to her black woman and Irish woman and two little children—all enchained" (p. 387).

Whatever their complex motivation, these authors had an enormous impact on American life. Together, their books covered the experiences of poor and rich, urban and rural, northern and southern peoples.

Susan Warner (1819–1885)

Susan Bogart Warner produced the first American book to sell a million copies. For an author with such a distinction, she lived a quiet and uneventful life. The elder of the two surviving children born to Anna Marsh Bartlett and Henry Whiting Warner of New York City, Warner spent most of her childhood wintering in the city and summering in an historic old house in Canaan, New York. In 1828 shortly after the birth of her sister Anna, her mother died and her father's sister, Frances L. Warner, moved in to watch over the children.

Early in his career Henry Warner was very successful as a lawyer and real estate investor. He moved his family into a series of more and more fashionable homes and provided private tutors for the children. In the panic of 1837 he suffered severe financial reverses that forced the family to move to a simple house on Constitution Island in the Hudson River. From this time onward, Henry Warner's repeated financial mishaps kept the family in poverty.

In 1844 Warner and her sister joined the Mercer Street Presbyterian Church, thereby coming under the influence of its evangelical pastor, Thomas Harvey Skinner. According to biographer and critic Edward Halsey Foster in *Susan and Anna Warner* (see Selected Bibliography), Warner followed Skinner's belief in complete submission to higher authority and Horace Bushnell's teaching that religious conversion results "from a life-long training in Christian principles and attitudes" (p. 39). These beliefs form the underlying philosophy of her works.

In 1849, pressured by the economic conditions of the family and encouraged by her aunt, Warner began writing *The Wide, Wide World*, which she published under the pseudonym Elizabeth Wetherell. The novel was an instant success, and she followed it with *Queechy* (1852) and one or two books every year thereafter. In some of the works, she collaborated with her sister Anna, who also published children's books. Their combined output, including both individually and jointly published books, exceeded 100 volumes.

Warner never reaped the rewards of her literary industry. The return for *The Wide, Wide World* alone could have provided a lifetime of comfort, but her father lost it in one of his unsuccessful projects. Economic pressures often forced her to sell manuscripts, thus foregoing royalty rights. Moreover, Warner, like other writers of her time, fell victim to the lack of international copyright laws.

Susan and Anna Warner lived out their lives on Constitution Island, spending some time teaching Sunday Bible classes to the young men of nearby West Point Military Academy. They were not entirely isolated, as Susan counted among her literary friends Julia Ward Howe and Catharine Maria Sedgwick, whose *A New-England Tale* (1822) seems to have influenced *The Wide, Wide World*.

Selected Bibliography

OTHER WORKS

The Hills of the Shatemuc (1856); *The Old Helmet* (1863); *Melbourne House* (1864); *Daisy* (1868); *A Story of Small Beginnings* (1872); *Diana* (1877); *Bread and Oranges* (1877); *Pine Needles* (1877); *My Desire* (1879); *The End of a Coil* (1880); *Nobody* (1882); *A Red Wallflower* (1884); *Daisy Plains* (1885).

SECONDARY

Foster, Edward Halsey. *Susan and Anna Warner*. Boston: Twayne Publishers, 1978.

[Kirkland, Caroline.] Review of *The Wide, Wide World, Queechy,* and *Dollars and Cents. North American Review* 76 (January 1853): 104–123.

Overmyer, Grace. "Hudson River Bluestockings—The Warner Sisters of Constitution Island." *New York History* 40 (April 1959): 137–158.

Stokes, Olivia E. Phelps. *Letters and Memories of Susan and Anna Bartlett Warner*. New York: G. P. Putnam's Sons, 1925.

Warner, Anna. *Susan Warner ("Elizabeth Wetherell")*. New York: G. P. Putnam's Sons, 1909.

The Wide, Wide World (1850)

An editor at Harper's called it "fudge," and G. P. Putnam published it only at the insistence of his mother. Yet *The Wide, Wide World* went through thirteen editions in two years in the United States and England, was translated into French, German, Swedish, and Italian, and earned popularity second only to that of *Uncle Tom's Cabin*.

While the French critic Hippolyte Taine scorned its content—"the history of the moral progress of a girl of thirteen," American critical response to the novel undoubtedly boosted sales. The *New York Times*'s reviewer commented that "one book like this is not produced in an age," and the Newark *Daily Advertiser* hailed the novel's moral worth, stating that "*The Wide, Wide World* is capable of doing more good than any other work, other than the Bible" (Warner, p. 344; see Selected Bibliography).

Warner's "story"—she did not like the word *novel* applied to her work—covers Ellen Montgomery's life from the age of thirteen, when she is sent to the country to live with her father's sister, Fortune Emerson of Thirlwall, to the age of fifteen, when she goes to live with relatives in Scotland. *The Wide, Wide World* traces Ellen's moral development as she learns to submit to heavenly and earthly authority. For Ellen this lesson is hard, for she, like nearly all of Warner's women, has a strong will and finds it difficult to obey. Nina Baym in *Woman's Fiction* points out, and rightly so, that "more than any of the other women [of her time], Susan Warner dealt with power and the lack of it" (p. 144). Nowhere is this comment so appropriate as when speaking of *The Wide, Wide World*. Not surprisingly, the tomboy Jo weeps over this novel in Louisa May Alcott's *Little Women* (1869).

In addition to instilling principles of obedience, *The Wide, Wide World* also tries to teach the reader how to distinguish good from evil. Warner draws on the nineteenth-century interest in and knowledge of phrenology and physiognomy to impart this lesson. By describing the physical features of characters, she divulges their moral traits. She also uses nature as a teacher. Throughout the novel, characters explicate religious or moral truths, employing flowers, trees, or animals to make a point.

While the pervasive religious content of *The Wide, Wide World* accounts for its initial popularity, its realism assures sustained interest. Henry James, writing in the *Nation* (September 14, 1865), commented favorably on Warner's use of local color and realistic detail in the work. Her description of the flinty country people and their hard physical life counteracts the idyllic pastoral image conveyed by some other nineteenth-century novels. Helen Waite Papashvily in *All the Happy Endings* calls special attention to scenes describing "good eating" and community activities, pointing out that Warner often received requests for "'the receipts for the biscuit on which the cat set his paw'; for the 'splitters,' 'for the cake Alice made'" (p. 7).

As the novel opens, Ellen observes the outside world from the security of her home.

CHAPTER I

.   .   .   .

. . . Ellen betook herself to the window and sought amusement there. The prospect without gave little promise of it. Rain was falling, and made the street and everything in it look dull and gloomy. The foot-passengers plashed through the water, and the horses and carriages plashed through the mud; gayety had forsaken the sidewalks, and equi-pages were few, and the people that were out were plainly there only be-cause they could not help it. But yet Ellen, having seriously set herself to study everything that passed, presently became engaged in her occu-pation; and her thoughts travelling dreamily from one thing to another, she sat for a long time with her little face pressed against the window-frame, perfectly regardless of all but the moving world without.

Daylight gradually faded away, and the street wore a more and more gloomy aspect. The rain poured, and now only an occasional carriage or footstep disturbed the sound of its steady pattering. Yet still Ellen sat with her face glued to the window as if spell-bound, gazing out at every dusky form that passed, as though it had some strange interest for her. At length, in the distance, light after light began to appear; presently Ellen could see the dim figure of the lamplighter crossing the street, from side to side, with his ladder;—then he drew near enough for her to watch him as he hooked his ladder on the lamp-irons, ran up and lit the lamp, then shouldered the ladder and marched off quick, the light glanc-ing on his wet oil-skin hat, rough great coat and lantern, and on the pavement and iron railings. The veriest moth could not have followed the light with more perseverance than did Ellen's eyes—till the lamp-lighter gradually disappeared from view, and the last lamp she could see was lit; and not till then did it occur to her that there was such a place as in-doors.

Ellen soon discovers that she will be thrown into the world. She will live with her Aunt Fortune while her parents travel in Europe, where they hope the mother's health will improve. Fearing that she will not live to see her daughter again, Mrs. Montgomery takes Ellen on a bit-tersweet shopping trip.

The Wide, Wide World (New York: Putnam, 1850 [copyright 1851]), vol. 1, 360 pp.; vol. 2, 330 pp. Excerpts are taken from 1: 9–10, 32–42, 200–201, 218–219, 353–360; 2: 45–46, 222–225.

CHAPTER III

.   .   .   .

"Now, mamma, you look like yourself; I haven't seen you look so well this great while. I'm so glad you're going out again," said Ellen, putting her arms round her; "I do believe it will do you good. Now, mamma, I'll go and get ready; I'll be very quick about it; you shan't have to wait long for me."

In a few minutes the two set forth from the house. The day was as fine as could be; there was no wind, there was no dust; the sun was not oppressive; and Mrs. Montgomery did feel refreshed and strengthened during the few steps they had to take to their first stopping-place.

It was a jeweller's store. Ellen had never been in one before in her life, and her first feeling on entering was of dazzled wonderment at the glittering splendours around; this was presently forgotten in curiosity to know what her mother could possibly want there. She soon discovered that she had come to sell and not to buy. Mrs. Montgomery drew a ring from her finger, and after a little chaffering parted with it to the owner of the store for eighty dollars, being about three-quarters of its real value. The money was counted out, and she left the store.

"Mamma," said Ellen in a low voice, "wasn't that grand-mamma's ring, which I thought you loved so much?"

"Yes, I did love it, Ellen, but I love you better."

"O, mamma, I am very sorry!" said Ellen.

"You need not be sorry, daughter. Jewels in themselves are the merest nothings to me; and as for the rest, it doesn't matter; I can remember my mother without any help from a trinket."

There were tears however in Mrs. Montgomery's eyes, that showed the sacrifice had cost her something; and there were tears in Ellen's that told it was not thrown away upon her.

"I am sorry you should know of this," continued Mrs. Montgomery; "you should not if I could have helped it. But set your heart quite at rest, Ellen; I assure you this use of my ring gives me more pleasure on the whole than any other I could have made of it."

A grateful squeeze of her hand and glance into her face was Ellen's answer.

Mrs. Montgomery had applied to her husband for the funds necessary to fit Ellen comfortably for the time they should be absent; and in answer he had given her a sum barely sufficient for her mere clothing. Mrs. Montgomery knew him better than to ask for a further supply, but she resolved to have recourse to other means to do what she had determined upon. Now that she was about to leave her little daughter, and it might be for ever, she had set her heart upon providing her with certain things which she thought important to her comfort and improvement, and which Ellen would go very long without if *she* did not give them to her, and *now*, Ellen had had very few presents in her life, and those always of the simplest and cheapest kind; her mother resolved that in the midst of the bitterness of this time she would give her one pleasure, if she could; it might be the last.

They stopped next at a bookstore. "O what a delicious smell of new books!" said Ellen, as they entered. "Mamma, if it wasn't for one thing, I should say I never was so happy in my life."

Children's books, lying in tempting confusion near the door, immediately fastened Ellen's eyes and attention. She opened one, and was already deep in the interest of it, when the word "*Bibles*" struck her ear. Mrs. Montgomery was desiring the shopman to show her various kinds and sizes that she might choose from among them. Down went Ellen's book, and she flew to the place, where a dozen different Bibles were presently displayed. Ellen's wits were ready to forsake her. Such beautiful Bibles she had never seen; she pored in ecstasy over their varieties of type and binding, and was very evidently in love with them all.

"Now, Ellen," said Mrs. Montgomery, "look and choose; take your time, and see which you like best."

It was not likely that Ellen's "time" would be a short one. Her mother seeing this, took a chair at a little distance to await patiently her decision; and while Ellen's eyes were riveted on the Bibles, her own very naturally were fixed upon her. In the excitement and eagerness of the moment, Ellen had thrown off her light bonnet, and with flushed cheek and sparkling eye, and a brow grave with unusual care, as though a nation's fate were deciding she was weighing the comparative advantages of large, small, and middle sized;—black, blue, purple, and red;—gilt and not gilt;—clasp and no clasp. Everything but the Bibles before her Ellen had forgotten utterly; she was deep in what was to her the most important of business; she did not see the bystanders smile; she did not know there were any. To her mother's eye it was a most fair sight. Mrs. Montgomery gazed with rising emotions of pleasure and pain that struggled for the mastery, but pain at last got the better and rose very high. "How can I give thee up!" was the one thought of her heart. Unable to command herself, she rose and went to a distant part of the counter, where she seemed to be examining books; but tears, some of the bitterest she had ever shed, were falling thick upon the dusty floor, and she felt her heart like to break. Her little daughter at one end of the counter had forgotten there ever was such a thing as sorrow in the world; and she at the other was bowed beneath a weight of it that was nigh to crush her. But in her extremity she betook herself to that refuge she had never known to fail; it did not fail her now. She remembered the words Ellen had been reading to her but that very morning, and they came like the breath of heaven upon the fever of her soul. "Not my will, but thine be done." She strove and prayed to say it, and not in vain; and after a little while she was able to return to her seat. She felt that she had been shaken by a tempest, but she was calmer now than before.

Ellen was just as she had left her, and apparently just as far from coming to any conclusion. Mrs. Montgomery was resolved to let her take her way. Presently Ellen came over from the counter with a large royal octavo Bible, heavy enough to be a good lift for her. "Mamma," said she, laying it on her mother's lap and opening it, "what do you think of that? isn't that splendid?"

"A most beautiful page indeed; is this your choice, Ellen?"

"Well, mamma, I don't know;—what do you think?"

"I think it is rather inconveniently large and heavy for every day use. It is quite a weight upon my lap. I shouldn't like to carry it in my hands long. You would want a little table on purpose to hold it."

"Well, that wouldn't do at all," said Ellen, laughing; "I believe you are right; mamma; I wonder I didn't think of it. I might have known that myself."

She took it back; and there followed another careful examination of the whole stock; and then Ellen came to her mother with a beautiful miniature edition in two volumes, gilt and clasped, and very perfect in all respects, but of exceeding small print.

"I think I'll have this mamma," said she; "isn't it a beauty? I could put in my pocket, you know, and carry it anywhere with the greatest ease."

"It would have one great objection to me," said Mrs. Montgomery, "inasmuch as I cannot possibly see to read it."

"Cannot you, mamma! But I can read it perfectly."

"Well, my dear, take it; that is, if you will make up your mind to put on spectacles before your time."

"Spectacles, mamma! I hope I shall never wear spectacles."

"What do you propose to do when your sight fails, if you shall live so long?"

"Well, mamma,—if it comes to that,—but you don't advise me then to take this little beauty?"

"Judge for yourself; I think you are old enough."

"I know what you think though, mamma, and I dare say you are right too; I won't take it, though it's a pity. Well, I must look again."

Mrs. Montgomery came to her help, for it was plain Ellen had lost the power of judging amidst so many tempting objects. But she presently simplified the matter by putting aside all that were decidedly too large, or too small, or of too fine print. There remained three, of moderate size and sufficiently large type, but different binding. "Either of these I think will answer your purpose nicely," said Mrs. Montgomery.

"Then, mamma, if you please, I will have the red one. I like that best, because it will put me in mind of yours."

Mrs. Montgomery could find no fault with this reason. She paid for the red Bible, and directed it to be sent home. "Shan't I carry it, mamma?" said Ellen.

"No, you would find it in the way; we have several things to do yet."

"Have we, mamma? I thought we only came to get a Bible."

"That is enough for one day, I confess; I am a little afraid your head will be turned; but I must run the risk of it. I dare not lose the opportunity of this fine weather; I may not have such another. I wish to have the comfort of thinking, when I am away, that I have left you with every-thing necessary to the keeping up of good habits—everything that will make them pleasant and easy. I wish you to be always neat, and tidy, and industrious; depending upon others as little as possible; and careful to improve yourself by every means, and especially by writing to me. I will leave you no excuse, Ellen, for failing in any of these duties. I trust you will not disappoint me in a single particular."

Ellen's heart was too full to speak; she again looked up tearfully and pressed her mother's hand.

"I do not expect to be disappointed, love," returned Mrs. Montgomery.

They now entered a large fancy store. "What are we to get here, mamma?" said Ellen.

"A box to put your pens and paper in," said her mother, smiling.

"O, to be sure," said Ellen, "I had almost forgotten that."

She quite forgot it a minute after. It was the first time she had ever seen the inside of such a store; and the articles displayed on every side completely bewitched her. From one thing to another she went, admir-ing and wondering; in her wildest dreams she had never imagined such beautiful things. The store was fairy-land.

.   .   .   .

Mrs. Montgomery asked to look at writing-desks, and was shown to another part of the store for the purpose. "Mamma," said Ellen, in a low tone, as they went, "you're not going to get me a writing-desk?"

"Why, that is the best kind of box for holding writing materials," said her mother, smiling:—"don't you think so?"

"I don't know what to say!" exclaimed Ellen. "I can't thank you, mamma;—I haven't any words to do it. I think I shall go crazy."

She was truly overcome with the weight of happiness. Words failed her, and tears came instead.

From among a great many desks of all descriptions, Mrs. Montgomery with some difficulty succeeded in choosing one to her mind. It was of mahogany, not very large, but thoroughly well made and finished, and very convenient and perfect in its internal arrangements. Ellen was speechless; occasional looks at her mother, and deep sighs, were all she had now to offer. The desk was quite empty. "Ellen," said her mother, "do you remember the furniture of Miss Allen's desk, that you were so pleased with a while ago."

"Perfectly, mamma; I know all that was in it."

"Well, then, you must prompt me if I forget anything. Your desk will be furnished with everything really useful. Merely showy matters we can dispense with. Now let us see.—Here is a great empty place that I think wants some paper to fill it. Show me some of different sizes if you please."

The shopman obeyed, and Mrs. Montgomery stocked the desk well with letter paper, large and small. Ellen looked on in great satisfaction. "That will do nicely," she said;—"that large paper will be beautiful whenever I am writing to you, mamma, you know, and the other will do for other times when I haven't so much to say; though I am sure I don't know who there is in the world I should ever send letters to except you."

"If there is nobody now, perhaps there will be at some future time," replied her mother. "I hope I shall not always be your only correspondent. Now what next?"

"Envelopes, mamma?"

"To be sure; I had forgotten them. Envelopes of both sizes to match."

"Because, mamma, you know I might, and I certainly shall, want to write upon the fourth page of my letter, and I couldn't do it unless I had envelopes."

A sufficient stock of envelopes was laid in.

.　　.　　.　　.　　.　　.　　.　　.　　.　　.　　.　　.

"Well now we have got all the paper we want, I think," said Mrs. Montgomery; "the next thing is ink,—or an inkstand rather."

Different kinds were presented for her choice.

"O, mamma, that one won't do," said Ellen, anxiously; "you know the desk will be knocking about in a trunk, and the ink would run out, and spoil everything. It should be one of those that shut tight. I don't see the right kind here."

The shopman brought one.

"There, mamma, do you see?" said Ellen; "it shuts with a spring, and nothing can possibly come out; do you see, mamma? You can turn it topsy turvy."

"I see you are quite right, daughter; it seems I should get on very ill without you to advise me. Fill the inkstand, if you please."

"Mamma, what shall I do when my ink is gone? that inkstand will hold but a little, you know."

"Your aunt will supply you, of course, my dear, when you are out."

"I'd rather take some of my own by half," said Ellen.

"You could not carry a bottle of ink in your desk without great danger to everything else in it. It would not do to venture."

"We have excellent ink-powder," said the shopman, "in small packages, which can be very conveniently carried about. You see, ma'am, there is a compartment in the desk for such things; and the ink is very easily made at any time."

"O that will do nicely," said Ellen, "that is just the thing."

"You want to seal your letter before you have written it," said Mrs. Montgomery,—"we have not got the pens yet."

"That's true, mamma; let us have the pens. And some quills too, mamma?"

"Do you know how to make a pen, Ellen?"

"No, mamma, not yet; but I want to learn very much. Miss Pichegru says, that every lady ought to know how to make her own pens."

"Miss Pichegru is very right; but I think you are rather too young to learn. However, we will try. Now here are steel points enough to last you a great while,—and as many quills as it is needful you should cut up for one year at least;—we haven't a pen handle yet."

"Here, mamma," said Ellen, holding out a plain ivory one,—"don't you like this? I think that it is prettier than these that are all cut and fussed, or those other gay ones either."

"I think so too, Ellen; the plainer the prettier. Now what comes next?"

"The knife, mamma, to make the pens," said Ellen, smiling.

"True, the knife. Let us see some of your best pen knives. Now, Ellen, choose. That one won't do, my dear; it should have two blades,—a large as well as a small one. You know you want to mend a pencil sometimes."

"So I do, mamma, to be sure, you're very right; here's a nice one. Now, mamma, the wax."

"There is a box full; choose your own colours." Seeing it was likely to be a work of time, Mrs. Montgomery walked away to another part of the store. When she returned Ellen had made up an assortment of the oddest colours she could find.

"I won't have any red, mamma, it is so common," she said.

"I think it is the prettiest of all," said Mrs. Montgomery.

"Do you, mamma? then I will have a stick of red on purpose to seal to you with."

"And who do you intend shall have the benefit of the other colours?" inquired her mother.

"I declare, mamma," said Ellen, laughing; "I never thought of that; I am afraid they will have to go to you. You must not mind, mamma, if you get green and blue and yellow seals once in a while."

"I dare say I shall submit myself to it with a good grace," said Mrs. Montgomery. "But come, my dear, have we got all that we want? This desk has been very long in furnishing."

.   .   .   .

While Ellen was picking out her seal, which took not a little time, Mrs. Montgomery laid in a good supply of wafers of all sorts; and then went on further to furnish the desk with an ivory leaf-cutter, a paper-folder, a pounce-box, a ruler, and a neat little silver pencil; also, some drawing-pencils, India-rubber, and sheets of drawing paper. She took a sad pleasure in adding everything she could think of that might be for Ellen's future use or advantage; but as with her own hands she placed in the desk one thing after another, the thought crossed her mind how Ellen would make drawings with those very pencils, on those very sheets of paper, which her eyes would never see! She turned away with a sigh, and receiving Ellen's seal from her hand, put that also in its place. Ellen had chosen one with her own name.

"Will you send these things *at once?*" said Mrs. Montgomery; "I particularly wish to have them at home as early in the day as possible."

The man promised. Mrs. Montgomery paid the bill, and she and Ellen left the store.

They walked a little way in silence.

"I cannot thank you, mamma," said Ellen.

"It is not necessary, my dear child," said Mrs. Montgomery, returning the pressure of her hand; "I know all that you would say."

There was as much sorrow as joy at that moment in the heart of the joyfullest of the two.

Ellen arrives at Miss Fortune's and quickly learns that her aunt possesses a cold and brusque nature like that of her father. Aunt Fortune's cruelty is generally psychological rather than physical. She dyes Ellen's white stockings gray, withholds letters received from Ellen's mother, and heaps physical work upon her. When Ellen's independent nature rebels against this treatment, her Bible and hymn book fail to provide the solace and guidance she needs. Ellen finds a counselor in Alice Humphreys, the daughter of a local minister.

CHAPTER XVI

.   .   .   .

"What has brought about this dreadful state of things?" said Alice after a few minutes. "Whose fault is it, Ellen?"

"I think it is aunt Fortune's fault," said Ellen raising her head; "I don't think it is mine. If she had behaved well to me I should have behaved well to her. I meant to, I am sure."

"Do you mean to say you do not think you have been in fault at all in the matter?"

"No, ma'am—I do not mean to say that. I have been very much in fault—very often—I know that. I get very angry and vexed, and sometimes I say nothing, but sometimes I get out of all patience and say things I ought not. I did so to-day; but it is so very hard to keep still when I am in such a passion;—and now I have got to feel so towards aunt Fortune that I don't like the sight of her; I hate the very look of her bonnet hanging up on the wall. I know it isn't right; and it makes me miserable; and I can't help it, for I grow worse and worse every day;—and what shall I do?"

Ellen's tears came faster than her words.

"Ellen, my child," said Alice after a while,—"there is but one way. You know what I said to you yesterday?"

"I know it, but dear Miss Alice, in my reading this morning I came to that verse that speaks about not being forgiven if we do not forgive others; and oh! how it troubles me; for I can't feel that I forgive aunt Fortune; I feel vexed whenever the thought of her comes into my head; and how can I behave right to her while I feel so?"

"You are right there, my dear; you cannot indeed; the heart must be set right before the life can be."

"But what shall I do to set it right?"

"Pray."

"Dear Miss Alice, I have been praying all this morning that I might forgive aunt Fortune, and yet I cannot do it."

"Pray, still, my dear," said Alice, pressing her closer in her arms,—"pray still; if you are in earnest the answer will come. But there is something else you can do, and must do, Ellen, besides praying, or praying may be in vain."

"What do you mean, Miss Alice?"

"You acknowledge yourself in fault—have you made all the amends you can? Have you, as soon as you have seen yourself in the wrong, gone to your aunt Fortune and acknowledged it, and humbly asked her pardon?"

Ellen answered "no" in a low voice.

"Then, my child, your duty is plain before you. The next thing after doing wrong is to make all the amends in your power; confess your fault, and ask forgiveness, both of God and man. Pride struggles against it,—I see yours does,—but my child, 'God resisteth the proud, but giveth grace unto the humble.'"

Ellen burst into tears and cried heartily.

When Ellen apologizes, Aunt Fortune insists that she repeat the apology in front of Abraham Van Brunt, a neighbor who works Miss Fortune's farm and has befriended Ellen.

CHAPTER XVII

.   .   .   .

"Ellen and I had some trouble yesterday," said Miss Fortune, "and she wants to tell you about it."

Mr. Van Brunt stood gravely waiting.

Ellen raised her eyes, which were full, to his face. "Mr. Van Brunt," she said, "aunt Fortune wants me to tell you what I told her last night,—that I knew I behaved as I ought not to her yesterday, and the day before, and other times."

"And what made you do that?" said Mr. Van Brunt.

"Tell him," said Miss Fortune, colouring, "that you were in the wrong and I was in the right—then he'll believe it, I suppose."

"I was wrong," said Ellen.

"And I was right," said Miss Fortune.

Ellen was silent. Mr. Van Brunt looked from one to the other.

"Speak," said Miss Fortune; "tell him the whole if you mean what you say."

"I can't," said Ellen.

"Why, you said you were wrong," said Miss Fortune, "that's only half of the business; if you were wrong I was right; why don't you say so, and not make such a shilly-shally piece of work of it?"

"I said I was wrong," said Ellen, "and so I was; but I never said you were right, aunt Fortune, and I don't think so."

These words, though moderately spoken, were enough to put Miss Fortune in a rage.

"What did I do that was wrong?" she said; "come, I should like to know. What was it, Ellen? Out with it; say everything you can think of; stop and hear it, Mr. Van Brunt; come, Ellen, let's hear the whole!"

"Thank you, ma'am, I've heerd quite enough," said that gentleman, as he went out and closed the door.

"And I have said too much," said Ellen. "Pray, forgive me, aunt Fortune. I shouldn't have said that if you hadn't pressed me so; I forgot myself a moment. I am sorry I said that."

"Forgot yourself!" said Miss Fortune; "I wish you'd forget yourself out of my house. Please to forget the place where I am for to-day, anyhow; I've got enough of you for one while. You had better go to Miss Alice and get a new lesson; and tell her you are coming on finely."

Gladly would Ellen indeed have gone to Miss Alice, but as the next day was Sunday she thought it best to wait. She went sorrowfully to her own room. "Why couldn't I be quiet?" said Ellen. "If I had only held my tongue that unfortunate minute! what possessed me to say that?"

Strong passion—strong pride,—both long unbroken; and Ellen had yet to learn that many a prayer and many a tear, much watchfulness, much help from on high, must be hers before she could be thoroughly dispossessed of these evil spirits. But she knew her sickness; she had applied to the Physician.

At Alice Humphreys's invitation, Ellen spends the Christmas holidays with the Humphreyses family. Alice's brother John, a divinity student, visits home, and Alice gives him to Ellen as a "brother." The Humphreys spend Christmas with the Marshman family, whose cultured elegance contrasts sharply with life at Aunt Fortune's farm. One event of this visit marks a major step in Ellen's moral progress. Sophia Marshman, wishing to keep her guests' children occupied, offers them a bag of colorful morocco leather scraps from which to fashion Christmas gifts.

CHAPTER XXVIII

.   .   .   .

The table was now strewn with pieces of morocco of all sizes and colours, which were hastily turned over and examined with eager hands and sparkling eyes. Some were mere scraps, to be sure; but others showed a breadth and length of beauty which was declared to be "first-rate," and "fine;" and one beautiful large piece of blue morocco in particular was made up in imagination by two or three of the party in as many different ways. Marianne wanted it for a book-cover; Margaret declared she could make a lovely reticule with it; and Ellen could not help thinking it would make a very pretty needle-box, such a one as she had seen in the possession of one of the girls, and longed to make for Alice.

"Well, what's to be done now?" said Miss Sophia,—"or am I not to know?"

"O you're not to know—you're not to know, aunt Sophy," cried the girls;—"you mustn't ask."

.   .   .   .

"Well then I'll take my departure," said Miss Sophia;—"but how will you manage to divide all these scraps?"

"Suppose we were to put them in the bag again, and you hold the bag, and we were to draw them out without looking," said Ellen Chauncey,— "as we used to do with the sugar-plums."

As no better plan was thought of this was agreed upon and little Ellen shutting up her eyes very tight stuck in her hand and pulled out a little bit of green morocco about the size of a dollar. Ellen Montgomery came next; then Margaret, then Marianne, then their mutual friend Isabel Hawthorn. Each had to take her turn a great many times; and at the end of the drawing the pieces were found to be pretty equally divided among the party, with the exception of Ellen, who besides several other good pieces had drawn the famous blue.

"That will do very nicely," said little Ellen Chauncey;—"I am glad you have got that, Ellen. Now, aunt Sophy!—one thing more—you know the silks and ribbons you promised us."

.   .   .   .

"But how shall we do about dividing these?" said little Ellen; "shall we draw lots again?"

"No, Ellen," said Marianne, "that won't do, because we might every one get just the thing we do not want. I want one colour or stuff to go with my morocco, and you want another to go with yours; and you might get mine and I might get yours. We had best each choose in turn what we like, beginning at Isabel."

"Very well," said little Ellen, "I'm agreed."

"Anything for a quiet life," said George Walsh.

But this business of choosing was found to be very long and very difficult, each one was so fearful of not taking the exact piece she wanted most. The elder members of the family began to gather for dinner, and several came and stood round the table where the children were; little noticed by them, they were so wrapped up in silks and satins. Ellen seemed the least interested person at table, and had made her selections with the least delay and difficulty; and now as it was not her turn sat very soberly looking on with her head resting on her hand.

"I declare it's too vexatious!" said Margaret Dunscombe;—"here I've got this beautiful piece of blue satin, and can't do anything with it; it just matches that blue morocco—it's a perfect match—I could have made a splendid thing of it, and I have got some cord and tassels that would just do—I declare it's too bad."

Ellen's colour changed.

"Well, choose, Margaret," said Marianne.

"I don't know what to choose—that's the thing. What can one do with red and purple morocco and blue satin? I might as well give up. I've a great notion to take this piece of yellow satin and dress up a Turkish doll to frighten the next young one I meet with."

"I wish you would, Margaret, and give it to me when it's done," cried little Ellen Chauncey.

"'Tain't made yet," said the other dryly.

Ellen's colour had changed and changed; her hand twitched nervously, and she glanced uneasily from Margaret's store of finery to her own.

"Come, choose, Margaret," said Ellen Chauncey;—"I dare say Ellen wants the blue morocco as much as you do."

"No, I don't!" said Ellen abruptly, throwing it over the table to her;— "take it, Margaret,—you may have it."

"What do you mean?" said the other astounded.

"I mean you may have it," said Ellen,—"I don't want it."

"Well, I'll tell you what," said the other,—"I'll give you yellow satin for it—or some of my red morocco?"

"No,—I had rather not," repeated Ellen;—"I don't want it—you may have it."

"Very generously done," remarked Miss Sophia; "I hope you'll all take a lesson in the art of being obliging."

"Quite a noble little girl," said Mrs. Gillespie.

Ellen crimsoned. "No, ma'am, I am not, indeed," she said, looking at them with eyes that were filling fast,—"please don't say so—I don't deserve it."

"I shall say what I think, my dear," said Mrs. Gillespie smiling "but I am glad you add the grace of modesty to that of generosity; it is the more uncommon of the two."

"I am not modest! I am not generous! you musn't say so," cried Ellen. She struggled; the blood rushed to the surface, suffusing every particle of skin that could be seen;—then left it, as with eyes cast down she went on—"I don't deserve to be praised,—it was more Margaret's than mine. I oughtn't to have kept it at all—for I saw a little bit when I put my hand in. I didn't mean to, but I did!"

Raising her eyes hastily to Alice's face, they met those of John, who was standing behind her. She had not counted upon him for one of her listeners; she knew Mrs. Gillespie, Mrs. Chauncey, Miss Sophia, and

Alice had heard her; but this was the one drop too much. Her head sunk; she covered her face a moment, and then made her escape out of the room before even Ellen could follow her.

There was a moment's silence. Alice seemed to have some difficulty not to follow Ellen's example. Margaret pouted; Mrs. Chauncey's eyes filled with tears, and her little daughter seemed divided between doubt and dismay. Her first move however was to run off in pursuit of Ellen. Alice went after her.

"Here's a beautiful example of honour and honesty for you!" said Margaret Dunscombe, at length.

"I think it is," said John, quietly.

"An uncommon instance," said Mrs. Chauncey.

.   .   .   .

As they were called to dinner Alice and Ellen Chauncey came back; the former looking a little serious, the latter crying, and wishing aloud that all the moroccos had been in the fire. They had not been able to find Ellen. Neither was she in the drawing-room when they returned to it after dinner; and a second search was made in vain. John went to the library which was separate from the other rooms, thinking she might have chosen that for a hiding-place. She was not there; but the pleasant light of the room where only the fire was burning, invited a stay. He sat down in the deep window, and was musingly looking out into the moonlight, when the door softly opened and Ellen came in. She stole in noiselessly, so that he did not hear her, and *she* thought the room empty; till in passing slowly down toward the fire she came upon him in the window. Her start first let him know she was there; she would have run, but one of her hands was caught, and she could not get it away.

"Running away from your brother, Ellie!" said he, kindly; "what is the matter?"

Ellen shrunk from meeting his eye and was silent.

"I know all, Ellie," said he, still very kindly,—"I have seen all;—why do you shun me?"

Ellen said nothing; the big tears began to run down her face and frock.

"You are taking this matter too hardly, dear Ellen," he said, drawing her close to him;—"you did wrong, but you have done all you could to repair the wrong;—neither man nor woman can do more than that."

But though encouraged by his manner, the tears flowed faster than ever.

"Where have you been? Alice was looking for you, and little Ellen Chauncey was in great trouble. I don't know what dreadful thing she thought you had done with yourself. Come!—lift up your head and let me see you smile again."

Ellen lifted her head, but could not her eyes, though she tried to smile.

"I want to talk to you a little about this," said he. "You know you gave me leave to be your brother,—will you let me ask you a question or two?"

"O yes—whatever he pleased," Ellen said.

"Then sit down here," said he, making room for her on the wide window-seat, but still keeping hold of her hand and speaking very gently. "You said you saw when you took the morocco—I don't quite understand—how was it?"

"Why," said Ellen, "we were not to look, and we had gone three times round and nobody had got that large piece yet, and we all wanted it; and I did not mean to look at all, but I don't know how it was just before I shut my eyes I happened to see the corner of it sticking up, and then I took it."

"With your eyes open?"

"No, no, with them shut. And I had scarcely got it when I was sorry for it and wished it back."

"You will wonder at me perhaps, Ellie," said John, "but I am not very sorry this has happened. You are no worse than before;—it has only made you see what you are—very, very weak,—quite unable to keep yourself right without constant help. Sudden temptation was too much for you—so it has many a time been for me, and so it has happened to the best men on earth. I suppose if you had had a minute's time to think you would not have done as you did?"

"No, indeed!" said Ellen. "I was sorry a minute after."

"And I dare say the thought of it weighed upon your mind ever since?"

"Oh yes!" said Ellen;—"it wasn't out of my head a minute the whole day."

"Then let it make you very humble, dear Ellie, and let it make you in future keep close to our dear Saviour, without whose help we cannot stand a moment."

Ellen sobbed; and he allowed her to do so for a few minutes, then said,

"But you have not been thinking much about Him, Ellie."

The sobs ceased; he saw his words had taken hold.

"Is it right," he said softly, "that we should be more troubled about what people will think of us, than for having displeased or dishonoured Him?"

Ellen now looked up, and in her look was all the answer he wished.

"You understand me, I see," said he. "Be humbled in the dust before him—the more the better; but whenever we are greatly concerned, for our own sakes, about other people's opinion, we may be sure we are thinking too little of God and what will please him."

"I am very sorry," said poor Ellen, from whose eyes the tears began to drop again,—"I am very wrong—but I couldn't bear to think what Alice would think—and you—and all of them—"

"Here's Alice to speak for herself," said John.

As Alice came up with a quick step and knelt down before her, Ellen sprang to her neck, and they held each other very fast indeed. John walked up and down the room. Presently he stopped before them.

"All's well again," said Alice, "and we are going in to tea."

Ellen returns home after the holidays. She brings a gift for the "bad" Nancy Vawse, a neighborhood girl Ellen has been trying to convert.

VOL. II

CHAPTER XXXII

.   .   .   .

It was a little hard to go back to Miss Fortune's and begin her old life there. She went on the evening of the day John had departed. They were at supper.

"Well!" said Miss Fortune, as Ellen entered,—"have you got enough of visiting? I should be ashamed to go where I wasn't wanted, for my part."

"I haven't, aunt Fortune," said Ellen.

"She's been nowhere but what's done her good," said Mr. Van Brunt; "she's reely growed handsome since she's been away."

"Grown a fiddlestick!" said Miss Fortune.

"She couldn't grow handsomer than she was before," said the old grandmother, hugging and kissing her little granddaughter with great delight;—"the sweetest posie in the garden she always was!"

Mr. Van Brunt looked as if he entirely agreed with the old lady. That, while it made some amends for Miss Fortune's dryness, perhaps increased it. She remarked, that "she thanked Heaven she could always make herself contented at home;" which Ellen could not help thinking was a happiness for the rest of the world.

In the matter of the collar [a gift Ellen had given Van Brunt], it was hard to say whether the giver or receiver had the most satisfaction. Ellen had begged him not to speak of it to her aunt; and accordingly one Sunday when he came there with it on, both he and she were in a state of exquisite delight. Miss Fortune's attention was at last aroused; she made a particular review of him, and ended it by declaring that "he looked uncommonly dandified, but she could not make out what he had done to himself;" a remark which transported Mr. Van Brunt and Ellen beyond all bounds of prudence.

Nancy's Bible, which had been purchased for her at Randolph, was given to her the first opportunity. Ellen anxiously watched her as she slowly turned it over, her face showing, however, very decided approbation of the style of the gift. She shook her head once or twice, and then said,

"What did you give this to me for, Ellen?"

"Because I wanted to give you something for New Year," said Ellen,—"and I thought that would be the best thing,—if you would only read it,—it would make you so happy and good."

"*You* are good, I believe," said Nancy, "but I don't expect ever to be myself—I don't think I *could* be. You might as well teach a snake not to wriggle."

"I am not good at all," said Ellen,—"we're none of us good,"—and the tears rose to her eyes,—"but the Bible will teach us how to be. If you'll only read it!—please Nancy, do! say you will read a little every day."

"You don't want me to make a promise I shouldn't keep, I guess, do you?"

"No," said Ellen.

"Well, I shouldn't keep that, so I won't promise it; but I tell you what I *will* do,—I'll take precious fine care of it, and keep it always for your sake."

"Well," said Ellen sighing,—"I am glad you will even do so much as that. But Nancy—before you begin to read the Bible you may have to go where you never can read it, nor be happy nor good neither."

Nancy made no answer, but walked away, Ellen thought, rather more soberly than usual.

This conversation had cost Ellen some effort. It had not been made without a good deal of thought and some prayer. She could not hope she had done much good, but she had done her duty. And it happened that Mr. Van Brunt, standing behind the angle of the wall, had heard every word.

At the death of Ellen's parents, Aunt Fortune becomes Ellen's "sole guardian and owner"; she marries Van Brunt, whom Ellen has "converted." Ellen goes to live with the Humphreys family and attempts to fill Alice's place when the latter dies. John returns home to minister to a neighboring community and continue Ellen's education. His guidance so affects her that even when she is summoned to Scotland to live with irreligious relatives, she resists their influence. At the end of the novel the author implies that Ellen will return to America and marry John Humphreys. The following excerpt illustrates John's teaching.

CHAPTER XLV

.   .   .   .

"How eloquent of beautiful lessons all nature would be to us," said John musingly, "if we had but the eye and the ear to take them in."

"And in that way you would heap associations upon associations?"

"Yes; till our storehouse of pleasure was very full."

"You do that now," said Ellen. "I wish you would teach me."

"I have read precious things sometimes in the bunches of flowers you are so fond of, Ellie. Cannot you?"

.   .   .   .

"A bunch of flowers seems to bring me very near the hand that made them. They are the work of his fingers; and I cannot consider them without being joyfully assured of the glory and loveliness of their Creator. It is written as plainly to me in their delicate painting and sweet breath and curious structure, as in the very pages of the Bible; though no doubt without the Bible I could not read the flowers."

"I never thought much of that," said Ellen. "And then you find particular lessons in particular flowers?"

"Sometimes."

"O come here!" said Ellen, pulling him towards the flower-stand,— "and tell me what this daphne is like—you need not see that, only smell it, that's enough;—do John, and tell me what it is like!"

He smiled as he complied with her request, and walked away again.

"Well, what is it?" said Ellen; "I know you have thought of something."

"It is like the fragrance that Christian society sometimes leaves upon the spirit; when it is just what it ought to be."

"My Mr. Marshman!" exclaimed Ellen.

John smiled again. "I thought of him, Ellie. And I thought also of Cowper's lines:—

> " 'When one who holds communion with the skies,
> Has filled his urn where those pure waters rise,
> Descends and dwells among us meaner things,—
> It is as if an angel shook his wings!' "

Ellen was silent a moment from pleasure.

"Well, I have got an association now with the daphne!" she said joyously; and presently added, sighing,—"How much you see in everything, that I do not see at all."

"Time, Ellie," said John;—"there must be time for that. It will come. Time is cried out upon as a great thief; it is people's own fault. Use him but well, and you will get from his hand more than he will ever take from you."

Ellen's thoughts travelled on a little way from this speech [she recalls Alice's death],—and then came a sigh, of some burden, as it seemed; and her face was softly laid against the arm she held.

"Let us leave all that to God," said John gently.

Ellen started. "How did you know—how could you know what I was thinking of?"

"Perhaps my thoughts took the same road," said he smiling. "But Ellie, dear, let us look to that one source of happiness that can never be dried up; it is not safe to count upon anything else."

"It is not wonderful," said Ellen in a tremulous voice,—"if I"—

"It is not wonderful, Ellie, nor wrong. But we, who look up to God as our Father,—who rejoice in Christ our Saviour,—we are happy, whatever beside we may gain or lose. Let us trust him, and never doubt that, Ellie."

"But still"—said Ellen.

"But still, we will hope and pray alike in that matter. And while we do, and may, with our whole hearts, let us leave ourselves in our Father's hand. The joy of the knowledge of Christ! the joy the world cannot intermeddle with, the peace it cannot take away!—Let us make that our own, Ellie; and for the rest put away all anxious care about what we cannot control."

Ellen's hand however did not just then lie quite so lightly on his arm as it did a few minutes ago; he could feel that; and could see the glitter of one or two tears in the moonlight as they fell. The hand was fondly taken in his; and as they slowly paced up and down, he went on in low tones of kindness and cheerfulness with his pleasant talk, till she was too happy in the present to be anxious about the future; looked up again and brightly into his face, and questions and answers came as gayly as ever.

Maria Cummins (1827–1866)

Nathaniel Hawthorne unintentionally immortalized the name of Maria Cummins and the title of her novel, *The Lamplighter* (1854). Cummins and her book had become famous on their own, sales of the novel having reached 40,000 in the first two months after publication and 70,000 in the first year. Nevertheless, it was Hawthorne's remark (see Criticism section) that "America is now wholly given over to a d——d mob of scribbling women," in direct reference to *The Lamplighter*, that assured Cummins a place in American literary history.

Cummins was born in Salem, Massachusetts, the daughter of Maria Franklin Kittredge and David Cummins. She grew up in Salem, spent some time in Springfield, and lived the rest of her life at the Cummins home in Dorchester, where her father was a judge. She became a member of the First Church (Unitarian), where she occasionally taught Sunday school.

Cummins began her education under her father's guidance. Later she attended Mrs. Charles Sedgwick's Young Ladies School in Lenox, Massachusetts. At the Sedgwick school and home, Cummins met Mrs. Sedgwick's sister-in-law, the novelist Catharine Maria Sedgwick, and many other literary men and women. This acquaintance with writers may have instilled in Cummins the idea of becoming an author herself.

In 1854, at the age of twenty-seven, Cummins wrote *The Lamplighter*, which would become, along with *The Wide, Wide World* and *Uncle Tom's Cabin*, one of the three most popular books of the century. Cummins followed her first success with *Mabel Vaughan* (1857). Although this novel is better written than its predecessor, it never attained the popularity of *The Lamplighter*. In fact, none of Cummins's subsequent works equaled the success of her first novel. *Mabel Vaughan* is the story of an heiress's loss of fortune and her subsequent moral growth. *El Fureidis* (1860) relates an exotic Palestinian romance, and *Haunted Hearts* (1864) tells a rather mundane story of the suffering a woman inflicts and suffers as a result of her coquetry.

Besides writing novels, Cummins apparently did some traveling in both America and Europe. The prefaces of her books suggest the American travel. "A Talk About Guides" and "Around Mull," published in the *Atlantic Monthly* in June 1864 and July and August 1865 respectively, deal with European journeys.

Selected Bibliography

SECONDARY

Cummins, Albert. *The Cummins Genealogy*. Montpelier, Vt.: A. O. Cummins, 1904.

Koch, D. A. Introduction to Maria S. Cummins's *The Lamplighter*. New York: Odyssey Press, 1968.

Winslow, Ola Elizabeth. "Maria Susanna Cummins." In *Notable American Women, 1607–1950*, edited by E. T. James, et al, 415–416. Cambridge, Mass.: Harvard University Press, 1971.

The Lamplighter (1854)

The popularity of Maria Cummins's *The Lamplighter* should not have mystified Hawthorne, as he claimed it did. For, as James D. Hart comments in *The Popular Book*, *The Lamplighter* expressed "the thoughts and feelings of the majority" (p. 281) more surely than did Henry David Thoreau's *Walden*, published in the same year. The moralistic story not only follows the development of a young woman from a wild urchin into a polished educator but also traces her growth from one totally ignorant of the existence of God to a converter of hardened unbelievers. Moreover, her experience symbolizes the development of the country as a whole in its pursuit of the Protestant work ethic.

Cummins admittedly patterned *The Lamplighter* on *The Wide, Wide World*. Taking her title, opening passage, and lamplighting motif from Warner's first chapter, Cummins relates how the lamplighter, Trueman Flint, ignites in the orphaned Gerty the latent spark of goodness that brings her to a knowledge of God, the heavenly lamplighter. But although the openings and themes of the books are similar, the novels differ markedly in structure. Ellen Montgomery, the protagonist of *The Wide, Wide World*, moves from city to country in the care of economically secure middle-class people. Her trials come from confrontation with human intransigence and downright cruelty. Gerty, in *The Lamplighter*, rises from slum to mansion, receiving encouragement from many sources along the way. The experiences of *The Wide, Wide World* are typical and probable; those of *The Lamplighter* are so complexly improbable as to bring the novel close to melodrama.

Both Warner and Cummins present worlds in which Providence is unkind to women, but they differ in their visions of woman's role. Nina Baym, in *Woman's Fiction*, notes that while both Warner and Cummins teach the Victorian ideal of feminine submissiveness, Cummins sees this submissiveness as a necessary, but not a natural, female characteristic and as "the means by which a woman can overcome or at least check her chief adversary, God." Baym also holds that Cummins's purpose is "to persuade woman that she is responsible for saving herself and equal to the demand" (p. 166). This feminist tone reveals itself in Gertrude's repeated acts of independence.

The novels also differ in narrative form. Warner's work, although emotionally charged, proceeds in an objective manner, the sermonizing coming from the monologues and dialogues of the characters. Cummins's narrator, especially in the early part of the novel, intrudes into the story to comment on the characters or their actions, as shown by the following passage:

> What then? Is Gertrude a beauty?
> By no means. Hers is a face and form about which there would be a thousand different opinions, and out of the whole number few would pronounce her beautiful. But there are faces whose ever-

varying expression one loves to watch,—tell-tale faces, that speak the truth and proclaim the sentiment within; faces that now light up with intelligence, now beam with mirth, now sadden at the tale of sorrow, now burn with a holy indignation for that which the soul abhors, and now, again, are sanctified by the divine presence, when the heart turns away from the world and itself, and looks upward in the spirit of devotion. Such a face was Gertrude's.

There are forms, too, which, though neither dignified, queenly or fairy-like, possess a grace, an ease, a self-possession, a power of moving lightly and airily in their sphere, and never being in any one's way,—and such a form was Gertrude's.

This excerpt also illustrates Cummins's use of physiognomy to instruct her readers.

As the narrative opens, eight-year-old Gerty waits on the doorstep of Nan Grant's boarding house in the Boston wharf district for the approach of the lamplighter, Trueman Flint. Their encounter initiates Gerty's change from wildness to perfection.

CHAPTER I

> Good God! to think upon a child
> That has no childish days,
> No careless play, no frolics wild,
> No words of prayer and praise!
>
> —Landon.

It was growing dark in the city. Out in the open country it would be light for half an hour or more; but within the close streets where my story leads me it was already dusk. Upon the wooden door-step of a low-roofed, dark, and unwholesome-looking house, sat a little girl, who was gazing up the street with much earnestness. The house-door, which was open behind her, was close to the side-walk; and the step on which she sat was so low that her little unshod feet rested on the cold bricks. It was a chilly evening in November, and a light fall of snow, which had made everything look bright and clean in the pleasant open squares, near which the fine houses of the city were built, had only served to render the narrow streets and dark lanes dirtier and more cheerless than ever; for, mixed with the mud and filth which abound in those neighborhoods where the poor are crowded together, the beautiful snow had lost all its purity.

The Lamplighter (Boston: J. P. Jewett & Co., 1854), 523 pp. Excerpts are taken from 5–8, 132–134, 177–179, 184–186, 503–509.

A great many people were passing to and fro, bent on their various errands of duty or of pleasure; but no one noticed the little girl, for there was no one in the world who cared for her. She was scantily clad, in garments of the poorest description. Her hair was long and very thick; uncombed and unbecoming, if anything could be said to be unbecoming to a set of features which, to a casual observer, had not a single attraction,—being thin and sharp, while her complexion was sallow, and her whole appearance unhealthy.

She had, to be sure, fine, dark eyes; but so unnaturally large did they seem, in contrast to her thin, puny face, that they only increased the peculiarity of it, without enhancing its beauty. Had any one felt any interest in her (which nobody did), had she had a mother (which, alas! she had not), those friendly and partial eyes would perhaps have found something in her to praise. As it was, however, the poor little thing was told, a dozen times a day, that she was the worst-looking child in the world; and, what was more, the worst-behaved. No one loved her, and she loved no one; no one treated her kindly; no one tried to make her happy, or cared whether she were so. She was but eight years old, and all alone in the world.

There was one thing, and one only, which she found pleasure in. She loved to watch for the coming of the old man who lit the street-lamp in front of the house where she lived; to see the bright torch he carried flicker in the wind; and then, when he ran up his ladder, lit the lamp so quickly and easily, and made the whole place seem cheerful, one gleam of joy was shed on a little desolate heart, to which gladness was a stranger; and, though he had never seemed to see, and certainly had never spoken to her, she almost felt, as she watched for the old lamplighter, as if he were a friend.

"Gerty," exclaimed a harsh voice within, "have you been for the milk?"

The child made no answer, but, gliding off the door-step, ran quickly round the corner of the house, and hid a little out of sight.

"What's become of that child?" said the woman from whom the voice proceeded, and who now showed herself at the door.

A boy who was passing, and had seen Gerty run,—a boy who had caught the tone of the whole neighborhood, and looked upon her as a sort of imp, or spirit of evil,—laughed aloud, pointed to the corner which concealed her, and walking off with his head over his shoulder, to see what would happen next, exclaimed to himself, as he went, "She'll catch it! Nan Grant'll fix her!"

In a moment more, Gerty was dragged from her hiding-place, and, with one blow for her ugliness and another for her impudence (for she was making up faces at Nan Grant with all her might), she was despatched down a neighboring alley with a kettle for the milk.

She ran fast, for she feared the lamplighter would come and go in her absence, and was rejoiced, on her return, to catch sight of him, as she drew near the house, just going up his ladder. She stationed herself at the foot of it, and was so engaged in watching the bright flame, that she did not observe when the man began to descend; and, as she was directly in his way, he hit against her, as he sprang to the ground, and she fell upon the pavement. "Hollo, my little one!" exclaimed he, "how's this?" as he stooped to lift her up.

She was upon her feet in an instant; for she was used to hard knocks, and did not much mind a few bruises. But the milk!—it was all spilt.

"Well! now, I declare!" said the man, "that's too bad!—what'll mammy say?" and, for the first time looking full in Gerty's face, he here interrupted himself with, "My! what an odd-faced child!—looks like a witch!" Then, seeing that she looked apprehensively at the spilt milk, and gave a sudden glance up at the house, he added, kindly, "She won't be hard on such a mite of a thing as you are, will she? Cheer up, my ducky! never mind if she does scold you a little. I'll bring you something tomorrow, that I think you'll like, may be; you're such a lonesome sort of a looking thing. And, mind, if the old woman makes a row, tell her I did it.—But did n't I hurt you? What was you doing with my ladder?"

"I was seeing you light the lamp," said Gerty, "and I ain't hurt a bit; but I wish I had n't spilt the milk."

At this moment Nan Grant came to the door, saw what had happened, and commenced pulling the child into the house, amidst blows, threats, and profane and brutal language. The lamplighter tried to appease her; but she shut the door in his face. Gerty was scolded, beaten, deprived of the crust which she usually got for her supper, and shut up in her dark attic for the night. Poor little child! Her mother had died in Nan Grant's house, five years before; and she had been tolerated there since, not so much because when Ben Grant went to sea he bade his wife be sure and keep the child until his return (for he had been gone so long that no one thought he would ever come back), but because Nan had reasons of her own for doing so; and, though she considered Gerty a dead weight upon her hands, she did not care to excite inquiries by trying to dispose of her elsewhere.

When Gerty first found herself locked up for the night in the dark garret (Gerty hated and feared the dark), she stood for a minute perfectly still; then suddenly began to stamp and scream, tried to beat open the door, and shouted, "I hate you, Nan Grant! Old Nan Grant, I hate you!" But nobody came near her; and, after a while, she grew more quiet, went and threw herself down on her miserable bed, covered her face with her little thin hands, and sobbed and cried as if her heart would break. She wept until she was utterly exhausted; and then gradually, with only now and then a low sob and catching of the breath, she grew quite still. By and by she took away her hands from her face, clasped them together in a convulsive manner, and looked up at a little glazed window by the side of the bed. It was but three panes of glass unevenly stuck together, and was the only chance of light the room had. There was no moon; but, as Gerty looked up, she saw through the window shining down upon her *one* bright star. She thought she had never seen anything half so beautiful. She had often been out of doors when the sky was full of stars, and had not noticed them much; but this one, all alone, so large, so bright, and yet so soft and pleasant-looking, seemed to speak to her; it seemed to say, "Gerty! Gerty! *poor* little Gerty!" She thought it seemed like a kind face, such as she had a long time ago seen or dreamt about. Suddenly it flashed through her mind, "Who lit it? Somebody lit it! Some good person, I know! O! how could he get up so high!" And Gerty fell asleep, wondering who lit the star.

Poor little, untaught, benighted soul! Who shall enlighten thee? Thou art God's child, little one! Christ died for thee. Will he not send man or angel to light up the darkness within, to kindle a light that shall never go out, the light that shall shine through all eternity!

The antagonism between Nan and Gerty intensifies until Nan drives the child from her house. True Flint takes Gerty to his home and lavishes his love on her. From him Gerty learns lessons of generosity, and from his neighbors, Mrs. Sullivan and her son William, familial love. Gerty's most important teacher is a blind girl, Emily Graham. When True Flint dies and Willie Sullivan goes to India in the employ of a Mr. Clinton, Emily tries to console Gerty, now Gertrude.

CHAPTER XVII

. . . .

"Miss Emily," said Gertrude, when she had acquainted her with the news, and become again somewhat calm, "how can I bear to have Willie go away? How can I live without Willie? He is so kind, and loves me so much! He was always better than any brother, and, since Uncle True died, he has done everything in the world for me. I believe I could not have borne Uncle True's death if it had not been for Willie; and now how can I let him go away?"

"It is hard, Gertrude," said Emily, kindly, "but it is no doubt for his advantage; you must try and think of that."

"I know it," replied Gertrude,—"I suppose it is; but, Miss Emily, you do not know how I love Willie. We were so much together; and there were only us two, and we thought everything of each other; he was so much older than I, and always took such good care of me! O, I don't think you have any idea what friends we are!"

Gertrude had unconsciously touched a chord that vibrated through Emily's whole frame. Her voice trembled as she answered, "*I*, Gertrude! *not know*, my child! I know better than you imagine how dear he must be to you. *I*, too, had"——then checking herself, she paused abruptly, and there was a few moments' silence, during which Emily got up, walked hastily to the window, pressed her aching head against the frosty glass, and then, returning to Gertrude, said, in a voice which had recovered its usual calmness, "O, Gertrude! in the grief that oppresses you now, you little realize how much you have to be thankful for. Think, my dear, what a blessing it is that Willie will be where you can often hear from him, and where he can have constant news of his friends."

"Yes," replied Gerty; "he says he shall write to his mother and me very often."

"Then, too," said Emily, "you ought to rejoice at the good opinion Mr. Clinton must have of Willie; the perfect confidence he must feel in his uprightness, to place in him so much trust. I think that is very flattering."

"So it is," said Gertrude; "I did not think of that."

"And you have lived so happily together," continued Emily, "and will part in such perfect peace. O, Gertrude! Gertrude! such a parting as that should not make you sad; there are so much worse things in the world. Be patient, my dear child, do your duty, and perhaps there will some day be a happy meeting, that will quite repay you for all you suffer in the separation."

Emily's voice trembled as she uttered the last few words. Gertrude's eyes were fixed upon her friend with a very puzzled expression. "Miss Emily," said she, "I begin to think everybody has trouble."

"Certainly, Gertrude; can you doubt it?"

"I did not use to think so. I knew *I* had, but I thought other folks were more fortunate. I fancied that rich people were all happy; and, though you are blind, and that is a dreadful thing, I supposed you were used to it; and you always looked so pleasant and quiet, I took it for granted nothing ever vexed you now. And then, Willie!—I believed once that nothing could make him look sad, he was always so gay; but when he had n't any place, I saw him really cry; and then, when Uncle True died, and now again to-night, when he was telling me about going away, he could hardly speak, he felt so badly. And so, Miss Emily, since I see that you and Willie have troubles, and that tears will come, though you try to keep them back, I think the world is full of trials, and that everybody gets a share."

"It *is* the lot of humanity, Gertrude, and we must not expect it to be otherwise."

"Then who can be happy, Miss Emily?"

"Those only, my child, who have learned submission; those who, in the severest afflictions, see the hand of a loving Father, and, obedient to his will, kiss the chastening rod."

"It is very hard, Miss Emily."

"It is hard, my child, and therefore few in this world can rightly be called happy; but, if, even in the midst of our distress, we can look to God in faith and love, we may, when the world is dark around, experience a peace that is a foretaste of heaven."

Gertrude does not learn submission easily. Emily Graham and her father assume responsibility for Gertrude and decide to educate her as a teacher, since she will have no dowry and will, therefore, be unable to marry a wealthy man. In return for helping Gertrude, Mr. Graham

expects her absolute submission to his will. When Mrs. Bruce, the
Grahams' housekeeper, inquires about his plans for a trip to the
South, a confrontation between Mr. Graham and Gertrude ensues.

CHAPTER XXI

.   .   .   .

"Mr. Graham," said Mrs. Bruce, "I have been questioning Emily about your visit to the south; and, from the route which she tells me you propose taking, I think it will be a charming trip."

"I hope so, madam,—we have been talking of it for some time; it will be an excellent thing for Emily, and, as Gertrude has never travelled at all, I anticipate a great deal of pleasure for her."

"Ah! then you are to be of the party, Miss Flint?"

"Of course, of course," answered Mr. Graham, without giving Gertrude a chance to speak for herself; "we depend upon Gertrude,—could n't get along at all without her."

"It will be delightful for you," continued Mrs. Bruce, her eyes still fixed on Gertrude.

"I did expect to go with Mr. and Miss Graham," answered Gertrude, "and looked forward to the journey with the greatest eagerness; but I have just decided that I must remain in Boston this winter."

"What are you talking about, Gertrude?" asked Mr. Graham. "What do you mean? This is all news to me."

"And to me, too, sir, or I should have informed you of it before. I supposed you expected me to accompany you, and there is nothing I should like so much. I should have told you before of the circumstances that now make it impossible; but they are of quite recent occurrence."

"But we can't give you up, Gertrude; I won't hear of such a thing; you must go with us, in spite of circumstances."

"I fear I shall not be able to," said Gertrude, smiling pleasantly, but still retaining her firmness of expression; "you are very kind, sir, to wish it."

"Wish it!—I tell you I insist upon it. You are under my care, child, and I have a right to say what you shall do."

Mr. Graham was beginning to get excited. Gertrude and Emily both looked troubled, but neither of them spoke.

"Give me your reasons, if you have any," added Mr. Graham, vehemently, "and let me know what has put this strange notion into your head."

"I will explain it to you to-morrow, sir."

"To-morrow! I want to know now."

Mrs. Bruce, plainly perceiving that a family storm was brewing, wisely rose to go. Mr. Graham suspended his wrath until she and her son had taken leave; but, as soon as the door was closed upon them, burst forth with real anger.

"Now tell me what all this means! Here I plan my business, and make all my arrangements, on purpose to be able to give up this winter to travelling,—and that, not so much on my own account as to give pleasure to both of you,—and, just as everything is settled, and we are almost on the point of starting, Gertrude announces that she has concluded not to go. Now, I should like to know her reasons."

Emily undertook to explain Gertrude's motives, and ended by expressing her own approbation of her course. As soon as she had finished, Mr. Graham, who had listened very impatiently, and interrupted her with many a "pish!" and "pshaw!" burst forth with redoubled indignation.

"So Gerty prefers the Sullivans to us, and you seem to encourage her in it! I should like to know what they've ever done for her, compared with what I have done!"

"They have been friends of hers for years, and, now that they are in great distress, she does not feel as if she could leave them; and I confess I do not wonder at her decision."

"I must say I do. She prefers to make a slave of herself in Mr. W.'s school, and a still greater slave in Mrs. Sullivan's family, instead of staying with us, where she has always been treated like a lady, and, more than that, like one of my own family!"

"O, Mr. Graham!" said Gertrude, earnestly, "it is not a matter of preference or choice, except as I feel it to be a duty."

"And what makes it a duty? Just because you used to live in the same house with them, and that boy out in Calcutta has sent you home a camel's-hair scarf, and a cage-full of miserable little birds, and written you a great package of letters, you think you must forfeit your own interests to take care of his sick relations! I can't say I see how their claim compares with mine. Have n't I given you the best of educations, and spared no expense either for your improvement or your happiness?"

"I did not think, sir," answered Gertrude, humbly, and yet with quiet dignity, "of counting up the favors I had received, and measuring my conduct accordingly. In that case, my obligations to you are immense, and you would certainly have the greatest claim upon my services."

"Services! I don't want your *services*, child. Mrs. Ellis can do quite as well as you can for Emily, or me either; but I like your *company*, and think it is very ungrateful in you to leave us, as you talk of doing."

"Father," said Emily, "I thought the object, in giving Gertrude a good education, was to make her independent of all the world, and not simply dependent upon us."

"Emily," said Mr. Graham, "I tell you it is a matter of feeling,—you don't seem to look upon the thing in the light I do; but you are both against me, and I won't talk any more about it."

So saying, Mr. Graham took a lamp, went to his study, shut the door hard,—not to say slammed it,—and was seen no more that night.

Poor Gertrude! Mr. Graham, who had been so kind and generous, who had seldom before spoken harshly to her, and had always treated her with great indulgence, was now deeply offended. He had called her ungrateful; he evidently felt that she had abused his kindness, and believed that he and Emily stood in her estimation secondary to other, and, as he considered them, far less warm-hearted friends. Deeply wounded and grieved, she hastened to say good-night to the no less afflicted Emily, and, seeking her own room, gave way to feelings that exhausted her spirit, and caused her a sleepless night.

CHAPTER XXII

.   .   .   .

It cannot then be surprising that Gertrude's heart should have almost failed her, when she stood, half an hour before breakfast-time, with the handle of the dining-room door in her hand, summoning all her energies for another meeting with the formidable opposer of her plans. She paused but a moment, however, then opened the door and went in. Mr. Graham was where she expected to see him, sitting in his arm-chair, and on the breakfast-table by his side lay the morning paper. It had been Gertrude's habit, for a year or two, to read that paper aloud to the old gentleman at this same hour, and it was for that very purpose she had now come.

She advanced towards him with her usual "good-morning."

The salutation was returned in a purposely constrained voice. She seated herself, and leaned forward to take the newspaper; but he placed his hand upon it and prevented her.

"I was going to read the news to you, sir."

"And I do not wish to have you read, or do anything else for me, until I know whether you have concluded to treat me with the respect I have a right to demand from you."

"I certainly never intended to treat you otherwise than with respect, Mr. Graham."

"When girls or boys set themselves up in opposition to those older and wiser than themselves, they manifest the greatest disrespect they are capable of; but I am willing to forgive the past, if you assure me, as I think you will after a night's reflection, that you have returned to a right sense of your duty."

"I cannot say, sir, that I have changed my views with regard to what that duty is."

"Do you mean to tell me," asked Mr. Graham, rising from his chair and speaking in a tone which made Gerty's heart quake, in spite of her brave resolutions, "do you mean to tell me that you have any idea of persisting in your folly?"

"Is it folly, sir, to do right?"

"Right!—There is a great difference of opinion between you and me as to what right is in this case."

"But, Mr. Graham, I think, if you knew all the circumstances, you would not blame my conduct. I have told Emily the reasons that influenced me, and she—"

"Don't quote Emily to me!" interrupted Mr. Graham, as he walked the floor rapidly. "I don't doubt she'd give her head to anybody that asked for it; but I hope I know a little better what is due to myself; and I tell you plainly, Miss Gertrude Flint, without any more words in the matter, that if you leave my house, as you propose doing, you leave it with my displeasure; and *that*, you may find one of these days, it is no light thing to have incurred,—unnecessarily, too," he muttered,—"as you are doing."

"I am very sorry to displease you, Mr. Graham, but—"

"No, you're not *sorry*; if you were, you would not walk straight in the face of my wishes," said Mr. Graham, who began to observe the expression of Gertrude's face, which, though grieved and troubled, had in the last few minutes acquired additional firmness, instead of quailing beneath his severe and cutting words;—"but, I have said enough about a matter which is not worthy of so much notice. You can go or stay, as you please. I wish you to understand, however, that, in the former case, I utterly withdraw my protection and assistance from you. You must take care of yourself, or trust to strangers. I suppose you expect your Calcutta friend will support you, perhaps come home and take you under his especial care; but, if you think so, you know little of the world. I daresay he is married to an Indian by this time, and, if not, has pretty much forgotten you."

"Mr. Graham," said Gertrude, proudly, "Mr. Sullivan will not probably return to this country for many years, and I assure you I neither look to him or any one else for support; I intend to earn a maintenance for myself."

"A heroic resolve!" said Mr. Graham, contemptuously, "and pronounced with a dignity I hope you will be able to maintain. Am I to consider, then, that your mind is made up?"

"It is, sir," said Gertrude, not a little strengthened for the dreaded necessity of pronouncing her final resolution by Mr. Graham's sarcastic speeches.

"And you go?"

"I must. I believe it to be my duty, and am therefore willing to sacrifice my own comfort, and, what I assure you I value far more, your friendship."

Mr. Graham did not seem to take the least notice of the latter part of her remark, and before she had finished speaking so far forgot his usual politeness as to drown her voice in the violent ringing of the table-bell.

Gertrude's faithfulness to the Sullivans is ultimately rewarded. During the Grahams' trip, Mr. Graham falls prey to the marriage scheme of the Widow Holbrook, Mr. Clinton's sister-in-law, so the family returns augmented by the new wife and her nieces. While the newlyweds travel in Europe, Gertrude and Emily go to New York. During this trip Gertrude unknowingly meets her father, Philip Amory, who is

Mr. Graham's stepson and Emily's stepbrother and former lover. She also encounters Willie Sullivan, who has returned from India, but he does not recognize her. Believing that he is attached to Isabel Clinton, his employer's daughter, Gertrude does not reveal herself to Willie. After the members of the household return to Boston, a series of revelations and reconciliations occur. Gertrude and Emily are reunited with Philip Amory, their father and lover respectively. As Gertrude visits Uncle True's grave, she is reunited with Willie.

CHAPTER XLIX

. . . [Gertrude] walked on with a pace of whose quickness she was scarcely herself aware, and soon gained the shelter of the heavy pines which bordered the entrance to the cemetery. Here she paused for a moment to enjoy the refreshing breeze that played beneath the branches; and then, passing through the gateway, entered a carriage-road at the right, and proceeded slowly up the gradual ascent. The place, always quiet and peaceful, seemed unusually still and secluded, and, save the occasional carol of a bird, there was no sound to disturb the perfect silence and repose. As Gertrude gazed upon the familiar beauties of those sacred grounds, which had been her frequent resort during several years,—as she walked between beds of flowers, inhaled the fragrant and balmy air, and felt the solemn appeal, the spiritual breathings, that haunted the holy place,—every emotion that was not in harmony with the scene gradually took its flight, and she experienced only that sensation of sweet and half-joyful melancholy which was awakened by the thought of the happy dead.

After a while, she left the broad road which she had been following, and turned into a little by-path. This she pursued for some distance; and then, again diverging through another and still narrower foot-track, gained the shady and retired spot which, partly from its remoteness to the public walks, and partly from its own natural beauty, had attracted her attention and recommended itself to her choice. It was situated on the slope of a little hill; a huge rock protected it on one side from the observation of the passer-by, and a fine old oak overshadowed it upon the other. The iron enclosure, of simple workmanship, was nearly overgrown by the green ivy, which had been planted there by Gertrude's hand, and the moss-grown rock also was festooned by its graceful and clinging tendrils. Upon a jutting piece of stone, directly beside the grave of Uncle True, Gertrude seated herself, as was her wont, and after a few moments of contemplation, during which she sat with her elbow upon her knee and her head resting upon her hand, she straightened her slight figure, sighed heavily, and then, lifting the cover of her basket, emptied her flowers upon the grass, and with skilful fingers commenced weaving a graceful chaplet, which, when completed, she placed upon the grave at her feet. With the remainder of the blossoms she strewed the other mounds; and then, drawing forth a pair of gardening-gloves and a little trowel, she employed herself for nearly an hour among the flowers and vines with which she had embowered the spot.

Her work at last being finished, she again placed herself at the foot of the old rock, removed her gloves, pushed back from her forehead the simple but heavy braids of her hair, and appeared to be resting from her labors.

It was seven years that day since Uncle True died, but the time had not yet come for Gertrude to forget the simple, kind old man. Often did his pleasant smile and cheering words come to her in her dreams; and both by day and night did the image of him who had gladdened and blessed her childhood encourage her to the imitation of his humble and patient virtue. As she gazed upon the grassy mound that covered him, and scene after scene rose up before her in which that earliest friend and herself had whiled away the happy hours, there came, to embitter the otherwise cherished remembrance, the recollection of that third and seldom absent one, who completed and made perfect the memory of their fireside joys; and Gertrude, while yielding to the inward reflection, unconsciously exclaimed aloud, "O, Uncle True! you and I are not parted yet; but Willie is not of us!"

"O, Gertrude," said a reproachful voice close at her side; "is Willie to blame for that?"

She started, turned, saw the object of her thoughts with his mild sad eyes fixed inquiringly upon her, and, without replying to his question, buried her face in her hands.

He threw himself upon the ground at her feet, and, as on the occasion of their first childish interview, gently lifted her bowed head from the hands upon which it had fallen, and compelled her to look him in the face, saying, at the same time, in the most imploring accents, "Tell me, Gerty, in pity tell me why am I excluded from your sympathy?"

But still she made no reply, except by the tears that coursed down her cheeks.

"You make me miserable," continued he, vehemently. "What have I done that you have so shut me out from your affection? Why do you look so coldly upon me,—and even shrink from my sight?" added he, as Gertrude, unable to endure his steadfast, searching look, turned her eyes in another direction, and strove to free her hands from his grasp.

"I am not cold,—I do not mean to be," said she, her voice half-choked with emotion.

"O, Gertrude," replied he, relinquishing her hands, and turning away, "I see you have wholly ceased to love me. I trembled when I first beheld you, so lovely, so beautiful, and so beloved by all, and feared lest some fortunate rival had stolen your heart from its boyish keeper. But even then I did not dream that you would refuse me, at least, a *brother's* claim to your affection."

"I will not," exclaimed Gertrude eagerly. "O, Willie, you must not be angry with me! Let me be your sister!"

He smiled a most mournful smile. "I was right, then," continued he; "you feared lest I should claim too much, and discouraged my presumption by awarding me nothing. Be it so. Perhaps your prudence was for the best; but O, Gertrude, it has made me heart-broken!"

"Willie," exclaimed Gertrude, with excitement, "do you know how strangely you are speaking?"

"Strangely?" responded Willie, in a half-offended tone. "Is it so strange that I should love you? Have I not for years cherished the remembrance of our past affection, and looked forward to our reunion as my only hope of happiness? Has not this fond expectation inspired my labors, and cheered my toils, and endeared to me my life, in spite of its bereavements? And can you, in the very sight of these cold mounds, beneath which lie buried all else that I held dear on earth, crush and destroy, without compassion, this solitary but all engrossing—"

"Willie," interrupted Gertrude, her calmness suddenly restored, and speaking in a kind but serious tone, "is it honorable for you to address me thus? Have you forgotten—"

"No, I have *not* forgotten," exclaimed he, vehemently. "I have not forgotten that I have no right to distress or annoy you, and I will do so no more. But, O, Gerty! my sister Gerty (since all hope of a nearer tie is at an end), blame me not, and wonder not, if I fail at present to perform a brother's part. I cannot stay in this neighborhood. I cannot be the patient witness of another's happiness. My services, my time, my life, you may command, and in my far-distant home I will never cease to pray that the husband you have chosen, whoever he be, may prove himself worthy of my noble Gertrude, and love her one-half as well as I do!"

"Willie," said Gertrude, "what madness is this? I am bound by no such tie as you describe; but what shall I think of your treachery to Isabel?"

"To Isabel?" cried Willie, starting up, as if seized with a new idea. "And has that silly rumor reached *you* too? and did you put faith in the falsehood?"

"Falsehood!" exclaimed Gertrude, lifting her hitherto drooping eyelids, and casting upon him, through their wet lashes, a look of earnest scrutiny.

Calmly returning a glance which he had neither avoided nor quailed under, Willie responded, unhesitatingly, and with a tone of astonishment not unmingled with reproach, "Falsehood?—Yes. With the knowledge you have both of her and myself, could you doubt its being such for a moment?"

"O, Willie!" cried Gertrude, "could I doubt the evidence of my own eyes and ears? Had I trusted to less faithful witnesses, I might have been deceived. Do not attempt to conceal from me the truth to which my own observation can testify. Treat me with frankness, Willie!—Indeed, indeed, I deserve it at your hands!"

"Frankness, Gertrude! It is you only who are mysterious. Could I lay my whole soul bare to your gaze, you would be convinced of its truth, its perfect truth, to its first affection. And as to Isabel Clinton, if it is to her that you have reference, your eyes and your ears have both played you false, if—"

"O, Willie! Willie!" exclaimed Gertrude, interrupting him, "have you so soon forgotten your devotion to the belle of Saratoga; your unwillingness to sanction her temporary absence from your sight; the pain which the mere suggestion of the journey caused you, and the fond impatience which threatened to render those few days an eternity?"

"Stop! stop!" cried Willie, a new light breaking in upon him, "and tell me where you learned all this."

"In the very spot where you spoke and acted. Mr. Graham's parlor did not witness our first meeting. In the public promenade-ground, on the shore of Saratoga lake, and on board the steamboat at Albany, did I both see and recognize you—myself unknown. There too did your own words serve to convince me of the truth of that which from other lips I had refused to believe."

The sunshine which gilds the morning is scarcely more bright and gladsome than the glow of rekindled hope which now animated the face of Willie.

"Listen to me, Gertrude," said he, in a fervent and almost solemn tone, "and believe that in sight of my mother's grave, and in the presence of that pure spirit (and he looked reverently upward) who taught me the love of truth, I speak with such sincerity and candor as are fitting for the ears of angels. I do not question the accuracy with which you overheard my expostulations and entreaties on the subject of Miss Clinton's proposed journey, or the impatience I expressed at parting for her speedy return. I will not pause, either, to inquire where the object of all my thoughts could have been at the time, that, notwithstanding the changes of years, she escaped my eager eyes. Let me first clear myself of the imputation under which I labor, and then there will be room for all further explanations.

"I did, indeed, feel deep pain at Miss Clinton's sudden departure for New York, under a pretext which ought not to have weighed with her for a moment. I did indeed employ every argument to dissuade her from her purpose; and when my eloquence had failed to induce the abandonment of the scheme, I availed myself of every suggestion and motive which might possibly influence her to shorten her absence. Not because the society of the selfish girl was essential, or even conducive, to my own happiness,—far from it,—but because her excellent father, who so worshipped and idolized his only child that he would have thought no sacrifice too great by means of which he could add one particle to her enjoyment, was, at that very time, amid all the noise and discomfort of a crowded watering-place, hovering between life and death, and I was disgusted at the heartlessness which voluntarily left the fondest of parents deprived of all female tending, to the charge of a hired nurse, and an unskillful though willing youth like myself. That eternity might, in Miss Clinton's absence, set a seal to the life of her father, was a thought which, in my indignation, I was on the point of uttering; but I checked myself, unwilling to interfere too far in a matter which came not within my rightful province, and perhaps excite unnecessary alarm in Isabel. If selfishness mingled at all in my views, dear Gerty, and made me over-impatient for the return of the daughter to her post of duty, it was that I might be released from almost constant attendance upon my invalid friend, and hasten to her from whom I hoped such warmth of greeting as I was only too eager to bestow. Can you wonder, then, that your reception struck cold upon my throbbing heart?"

"But you understand the cause of that coldness now," said Gertrude, looking up at him through a rain of tears, which, like a summer sun-shower, reflected itself in rainbow smiles upon her happy countenance. "You know now why I dared not let my heart speak out."

"And this was all, then?" cried Willie; "and you are free, and I may love you still?"

"Free from all bonds, dear Willie, but those which you yourself clasped around me, and which have encircled me from my childhood."

And now, with heart pressed to heart, they pour in each other's ear the tale of a mutual affection, planted in infancy, nourished in youth, fostered and strengthened amid separation and absence, and perfected through trial, to bless and sanctify every year of their after life.

Martha Finley (1828–1909)

Martha Finley, author of one of the most popular nineteenth-century novels set in the South, was actually a northerner. Finley was born in Chillicothe, Ohio, into a family holding strong Presbyterian beliefs. Her parents, Maria Theresa Brown and James Brown Finley, a physician, eventually settled in South Bend, Indiana. Finley was educated in private schools. She followed a teaching career in Indiana country towns and in Phoenixville, Pennsylvania, from 1851 to 1853. Her parents having died by this time, she moved to Philadelphia, where she became associated with the Presbyterian Publications Committee. In 1876 she built a house in Elkton, Maryland, where she lived until her death.

In 1856, under the pseudonym Martha Farquharson (Gaelic for Finley), she sold her first stories to the Presbyterian Board of Publications for use in their Sunday school program. Titles such as *Lame Letty; or, Bear Ye One Another's Burdens* and *Little Joe Carter the Cripple; or Learning to Forgive* suggest the sentimental and didactic nature of the tales. Between 1856 and 1860 Finley wrote twenty-five short tales, a number of which were based on Susan Warner's early books.

Plagued by ill health and failure as a writer of juvenile books, Finley found herself dependent on her stepbrother for support. According to Janet E. Brown in "The Saga of Elsie Dinsmore" (see Selected Bibliography), Finley "prayed for the ability to write a book which would augment her own slender income" (p. 79). She spent the Civil War years at work on the manuscript that her publisher divided into *Elsie Dinsmore* (1867) and *Elsie's Holidays at Roselands* (1868). It was another year after the publication of these volumes before the books caught on. But by 1872 the popularity of the series was assured. Encouraged by her success, Finley went on to write twenty-six more volumes in the series, which in Dodd Mead editions alone sold five million copies and reached an American readership estimated at more than twenty-five million.

The Elsie Dinsmore series represents only a third of Finley's publications. Other works include the Mildred Keith series, seven volumes based on a more realistic world than Elsie's; the Do-Good Library; the Pewt Nest series; and the Finley series. None was so popular as the Elsie Dinsmore series.

Selected Bibliography

OTHER WORKS

Elsie's Motherhood (1876); *Mildred Keith* (1878); *Signing the Contract and What It Cost* (1878); *Mildred at Roselands* (1879); *Elsie's Widowhood* (1880); *Mildred and Elsie* (1881); *Christmas with Grandma Elsie* (1888); *Elsie Yachting with the Raymonds* (1890); *Elsie at the World's Fair* (1894); *Elsie in the South* (1899); *Elsie and Her Namesakes* (1905).

SECONDARY

Brown, Janet E. "The Saga of Elsie Dinsmore." *University of Buffalo Studies* 17 (July 1945): 72–131.

Suckow, Ruth. "Elsie Dinsmore: A Study of Perfection, or How Fundamentalism Came to Dixie." *Bookman* 66 (October 1927): 126–133.

Elsie Dinsmore (1867)

By creating Elsie Dinsmore and the twenty-eight volume series that relates her experiences from youth to old age, Martha Finley won the loyalty of two generations of American readers. But despite her popularity and the fact that she earned a quarter of a million dollars on the Elsie Dinsmore books alone, Finley was ignored by the literary establishment. Critics and editors of juvenile magazines like *St. Nicholas* and *The Youth's Companion* regarded her work as completely inept.

The first really intelligent critique of the Elsie Dinsmore series came from author Ruth Suckow in 1927 (see Selected Bibliography). Although she mocked Elsie's exaggerated perfection, her rigid interpretation of Biblical principles, and her overactive font of tears, Suckow perceived the careful character development and the psycho-sexual interaction that characterize the series. Suckow also recognized how the idealizers of the antebellum South used religious belief to justify white male domination, and she showed how Finley drew on this tradition in creating the Elsie series. Finley was not a southerner, nor had she visited the South when she began the series, but, as Helen Papashvily notes in *All the Happy Endings* (pp. 173–174), this lack of knowledge left her free to spin her tales of plantation life with all the luxury she and her readers could imagine.

Elsie Dinsmore differs in several ways from *The Wide, Wide World* and *The Lamplighter*. Whereas Ellen Montgomery and Gerty Amory struggle to gain economic stability and moral perfection, Elsie emerges from Finley's pen an economically secure model of perfection from the start. Despite that perfection, indeed because of it, Elsie suffers more than her counterparts. The injustice of the trials and punishments laid upon her in spite of her goodness makes her cry even more than Ellen and Gerty. Through her tears, Elsie teaches her readers to endure misunderstanding and neglect while praying for their adversaries.

The primary focus of the first volume, indeed of much of the series, is Elsie's relationship with her father. From birth, Elsie has lived at her paternal grandfather's home, while her father Horace, whom she has never seen, lives and travels abroad. Because his wife died at Elsie's birth, Horace blames Elsie for his loss and will have nothing to do with her. When he returns from Europe, the eight-year-old Elsie's constant question is "Will he love me?" At first he is extremely cold, and Elsie cannot be free and easy with him. He gives commands that seem purely capricious and insists that she obey them without questioning. Gradually she wins his love, and their relationship becomes very intimate and continues so despite Horace's marriage to Rose Allison and Elsie's marriage to Mr. Travilla, Horace's best friend. Elsie seems to become a mother, as Papashvily quips, "by a kind of literary parthenogenesis" (p. 173). She guides her children and grandchildren through various experiences that parallel her own. At Travilla's "convenient" death, she returns to her father, whom she has never really left.

Although the early volumes of the series are totally romantic, later volumes show marks of realism, particularly in the setting. Technology, in the guise of telephone and telegraph, seeps into volume seventeen, *Elsie's Vacation*. Current social issues such as immigration and the feminist movement find their way into conversations, as do other political and cultural changes. But even these bows to reality do not markedly change the romantic idealism of Elsie's story.

An ironic commentary on this idealism is that in the 1940s, according to Janet E. Brown (p. 127; see Selected Bibliography), a number of libraries removed the Elsie Dinsmore books from their children's sections, fearing that Elsie's confrontation with her father on religious matters might lead youngsters to parental disobedience. Finley and her readers would have been appalled that the model Elsie was being perceived as a radical.

In her effort to be perfect, Elsie tries to please her mean relatives. Nevertheless, she becomes the victim of harsh treatment by her step-grandmother and her young aunts and uncles, especially Arthur, who constantly teases and tricks her.

CHAPTER SIXTH

. . . .

But after all, this occurrence [a dangerous carriage ride that drew Elsie and her father together] produced but little change in Elsie's condition; her father treated her a little more affectionately for a day or two, and then gradually returned to his ordinary stern, cold manner; indeed, before the week was out, she was again in sad disgrace.

She was walking alone in the garden one afternoon, when her attention was attracted by a slight fluttering noise which seemed to proceed from an arbor near by, and on hastily turning in to ascertain the cause, she found a tiny and beautiful humming-bird confined under a glass vase; in its struggles to escape it was fluttering and beating against the walls of its prison, thus producing the sound the little girl had heard in passing.

Elsie was very tender-hearted, and could never see any living creature in distress without feeling a strong desire to relieve its sufferings. She knew that Arthur was in the habit of torturing every little insect and bird that came in his way, and had often drawn his persecutions upon herself by interfering in behalf of the poor victim; and now the thought instantly flashed upon her that *this* was some of his work, and that he would return ere long to carry out his cruel purposes. Then at once arose the desire to release the little prisoner and save it further suffering, and

Elsie Dinsmore (New York: M. W. Dodd, 1867), 288 pp. Excerpts are taken from 163–168, 239–242, 244–247, 271–279.

without waiting to reflect a moment she raised the glass, and the bird was gone.

Then she began to think with a little tremor, how angry Arthur would be; but it was too late to think of that now, and after all, she did not stand in very great dread of the consequences, especially as she felt nearly sure of her father's approval of what she had done, having several times heard him reprove Arthur for his cruel practices.

Not caring to meet Arthur then, however, she hastily retreated to the house, where she seated herself in the veranda with a book. It was a very warm afternoon, and that, being on the east side of the house and well protected by trees, shrubbery, and vines, was as cool a spot as could be found on the place.

Arthur, Walter, and Enna sat on the floor playing jack-stones—a favorite game with them—and Louise was stretched full length on a settee, buried in the latest novel.

"Hush!" she said, as Walter gave a sudden shout at a successful toss Enna had just made; "can't you be quiet? Mamma is taking her afternoon nap, and you will disturb her; and, besides, I cannot read in such a noise."

Elsie wondered why Arthur did not go to see after his bird, but soon forgot all about it in the interest with which she was poring over the story of the "Swiss Family Robinson."

The jack-stone players were just finishing their game when they were all startled by the sudden appearance of Mr. Horace Dinsmore upon the scene, asking in a tone of great wrath who had been down in the garden and liberated the humming-bird he had been at such pains to catch, because it was one of a rare species, and he was anxious to add it to his collection of curiosities.

Elsie was terribly frightened, and would have been glad at that moment to sink through the floor; she dropped her book in her lap, and clasping her hands over her beating heart, grew pale and red by turns, while she seemed choking with the vain effort to speak and acknowledge herself the culprit, as conscience told her she ought.

But her father was not looking at her; his eye was fixed on Arthur.

"I presume it was you, sir," he said very angrily, "and if so, you may prepare yourself for either a flogging or a return to your prison, for one or the other I am determined you shall have."

"I didn't *do* it, any such thing," replied the boy, fiercely.

"Of course you will deny it," said his brother, "but we all know that your word is good for nothing."

"Papa," said a trembling little voice, "Arthur did not do it; it was I."

"You," exclaimed her father, in a tone of mingled anger and astonishment, as he turned his flashing eye upon her, "*you*, Elsie! can it be *possible* that this is *your* doing?"

Elsie's book fell on the floor, and, covering her face with both hands, she burst into sobs and tears.

"Come here to me this instant," he said, seating himself on the settee, from which Louise had risen on his entrance. "Come here and tell me what you mean by meddling with my affairs in this way."

"Please, papa, *please*, don't be so very angry with me," sobbed the little girl, as she rose and came forward in obedience to his command; "I didn't know it was your bird, and I didn't mean to be naughty."

"No, you *never mean* to be naughty, according to your own account," he said; "your badness is all accident; but nevertheless, I find you a very troublesome, mischievous child: it was only the other day you broke a valuable vase" (he forgot in his anger how little she had really been to blame for that), "and now you have caused me the loss of a rare specimen which I had spent a great deal of time and effort in procuring. Really, Elsie, I am sorely tempted to administer a very severe punishment."

Elsie caught at the arm of the settee for support.

"Tell me what you did it for; was it pure love of mischief?" asked her father, sternly, taking hold of her arm and holding her up by it.

"No, papa," she answered almost under her breath. "I was sorry for the little bird. I thought Arthur had put it there to torture it, and so I let it go. I did not mean to do wrong, papa, indeed I did not," and the tears fell faster and faster.

"Indeed," said he, "you had no business to meddle with it, let who would have put it there. Which hand did it?"

"This one, papa," sobbed the child, indicating her right hand.

He took it in his and held it a moment, while the little girl stood tremblingly awaiting what was to come next. He looked at the downcast, tearful face, the bosom heaving with sobs, and then at the little trembling hand he held, so soft, and white, and tender, and the sternness of his countenance relaxed somewhat; it seemed next to impossible to inflict pain upon anything so tender and helpless; and for a moment he was half inclined to kiss and forgive her. But no, he had been very much irritated at his loss, and the remembrance of it again aroused his anger, and well-nigh extinguished the little spark of love and compassion that had burned for a moment in his heart. She should be punished, though he would not inflict physical pain.

"See, Elsie," laughed Louise, maliciously, "he is feeling in his pocket for his knife. I suspect he intends to cut your hand off."

Elsie started, and the tearful eyes were raised to her father's face with a look half of terrified entreaty, half of confidence that such *could not* be his intention.

"Hush, Louise!" exclaimed her brother, sternly; "you *know* you are not speaking truly, and that I would as soon think of cutting off my own hand as my child's. You should never speak anything but truth, especially to children."

"I think it is well enough to frighten them a little sometimes, and I thought that was what you were going to do," replied Louise, looking somewhat mortified at the rebuke.

"No," said her brother, "that is a very bad plan, and one which I shall never adopt. Elsie will learn in time, if she does not know it now, that I never utter a threat which I do not intend to carry out, and never break my word."

He had drawn a handkerchief from his pocket while speaking.

"I shall tie this hand up, Elsie," he said, proceeding to do so; "those who do not use their hands aright must be deprived of the use of them. There! let me see if that will keep it out of mischief. I shall tie you up hand and foot before long, if you continue such mischievous pranks. Now go to your room, and stay there until tea-time."

Elsie felt deeply, bitterly disgraced and humiliated as she turned to obey; and it needed not Arthur's triumphant chuckle nor the smirk of satisfaction on Enna's face to add to the keen suffering of her wounded spirit: this slight punishment was more to her than a severe chastisement would have been to many another child; for the very knowledge of her father's displeasure was enough at any time to cause great pain to her sensitive spirit and gentle, loving heart.

Later Elsie's religious principles and her father's "irreligious" commands cross in an incident that nearly takes Elsie's life. After a Sunday dinner at Roselands, Horace's estate, one of his guests asks to hear Elsie play the piano. As Horace prepares to send for his daughter, Elsie's Aunt Adelaide warns him that Elsie will not play and sing for entertainment on the Lord's day. Determined to prove that his daughter will not resist his authority, Horace sends her a message to join the group in the drawing room.

CHAPTER TENTH

.   .   .   .

"Come here, daughter," her father said as she entered the room. He spoke in his usual pleasant, affectionate tone, yet Elsie started, trembled, and turned pale; for catching sight of the group at the piano, and her Aunt Adelaide just vacating the music-stool, she at once perceived what was in store for her.

"Here, Elsie," said her father, selecting a song which she had learned during their absence, and sang remarkably well, "I wish you to sing this for my friends; they are anxious to hear it."

"Will not to-morrow do, papa?" she asked, in a low, tremulous tone.

Mrs. Dinsmore, who had drawn near to listen, now looked at Horace with a meaning smile, which he affected not to see.

"Certainly not, Elsie," he said; "we want it now. You know it quite well enough without any more practice."

"I did not want to wait for *that* reason, papa," she replied in the same low, trembling tones, "but you know this is the holy Sabbath day."

"Well, my daughter, and what of that? *I* consider this song perfectly proper to be sung to-day, and that ought to satisfy you that you will not be doing wrong to sing it: remember what I said to you some weeks ago; and now sit down and sing it at once, without any more ado."

"O papa! I *cannot* sing it to-day; *please* let me wait until to-morrow."

"Elsie," he said in his sternest tones, "sit down to the piano instantly, and do as I bid you, and let me have no more of this nonsense."

She sat down, but raising her pleading eyes, brimful of tears to his face, she repeated her refusal. "Dear papa, I *cannot* sing it to-day. I *cannot* break the Sabbath."

"Elsie, you *must* sing it," said he, placing the music before her. "I have told you that it will not be breaking the Sabbath, and that is sufficient; you must let me judge for you in these matters."

"Let her wait until to-morrow, Dinsmore; tomorrow will suit us quite as well," urged several of the gentlemen, while Adelaide good-naturedly said, "Let me play it, Horace; I have no such scruples, and presume I can do it nearly as well as Elsie."

"No," he replied, "when I give my child a command, it is to be obeyed; I have *said* she should play it, and play it she *must*; she is not to suppose that she may set up her opinion of right and wrong against mine."

Elsie sat with her little hands folded in her lap, the tears streaming from her downcast eyes over her pale cheeks. She was trembling, but though there was no stubbornness in her countenance, the expression meek and humble, she made no movement toward obeying her father's order.

There was a moment of silent waiting: then he said in his severest tone, "Elsie, you shall sit there till you obey me, though it should be until to-morrow morning."

"Yes, papa," she replied in a scarcely audible voice, and they all turned away and left her.

"You see now that you had better have taken my advice, Horace," remarked Mrs. Dinsmore, in a triumphant aside; "I knew very well how it would end."

"Excuse me," said he, "but it has *not* ended; and ere it does, I think she will learn that she has a stronger will than her own to deal with."

Elsie's position was a most uncomfortable one; her seat high and uneasy, and seeming to grow more and more so as the weary moments passed slowly away. No one came near her or seemed to notice her, yet she could hear them conversing in other parts of the room, and knew that they were sometimes looking at her, and, timid and bashful as she was, it seemed hard to bear. Then, too, her little heart was very sad as she thought of her father's displeasure, and feared that he would withdraw from her the affection which had been for the last few months the very sunshine of her life. Besides all this, the excitement of her feelings, and the close and sultry air—for it was a very warm day—had brought on a nervous headache. She leaned forward and rested her head against the instrument, feeling in momentary danger of falling from her seat.

Several hours pass. When the tea-bell rings, Dinsmore stops by to speak to Elsie.

"Elsie," asked her father, coming to her side, "are you ready to obey me now? if so, we will wait a moment to hear the song, and then you can go to your tea with us."

"Dear papa, I cannot break the Sabbath," she replied, in a low, gentle tone, without lifting her head.

"Very well then, I cannot break my word; you must sit there until you will submit; and until then you must fast. You are not only making yourself miserable by your disobedience and obstinacy, Elsie, but are mortifying and grieving *me* very much," he added in a subdued tone, that sent a sharp pang to the loving little heart, and caused some very bitter tears to fall, as he turned away and left her.

The evening passed wearily away to the little girl; the drawing-room was but dimly lighted, for the company had all deserted it to wander about the grounds, or sit in the portico enjoying the moonlight and the pleasant evening breeze, and the air indoors seemed insupportably close and sultry. At times Elsie could scarcely breathe, and she longed intensely to get out into the open air; every moment her seat grew more uncomfortable and the pain in her head more severe: her thoughts began to wander, she forgot where she was, everything became confused, and at length she lost all consciousness.

Several gentlemen, among whom were Mr. Horace Dinsmore and Mr. Travilla, were conversing together on the portico, when they were suddenly startled by a sound as of something falling.

Travilla, who was nearest the door, rushed into the drawing-room, followed by the others.

"A light! quick, quick, a light!" he cried, raising Elsie's insensible form in his arms; "the child has fainted."

One of the others, instantly snatching a lamp from a distant table, brought it near, and the increased light showed Elsie's little face, ghastly as that of a corpse, while a stream of blood was flowing from a wound in the temple, made by striking against some sharp corner of the furniture as she fell.

She was a pitiable sight indeed, with her fair face, her curls, and her white dress all dabbled in blood.

"Dinsmore, you're a brute!" exclaimed Travilla indignantly, as he placed her gently on a sofa.

Horace made no reply, but, with a face almost as pale as her own, bent over his little daughter in speechless alarm, while one of the guests, who happened to be a physician, hastily dressed the wound, and then applied restoratives.

It was some time ere consciousness returned, and the father trembled with the agonizing fear that the gentle spirit had taken its flight.

But at length the soft eyes unclosed, and gazing with a troubled look into his face, bent so anxiously over her, she asked, "Dear papa, are you angry with me?"

"No, darling," he replied in tones made tremulous with emotion, "not at all."

"What was it?" she asked in a bewildered way; "what did I do? what has happened?"

"Never mind, daughter," he said, "you have been ill; but you are better now, so don't think any more about it."

"She had better be put to bed at once," said the physician.

"There is blood on my dress," cried Elsie, in a startled tone; "where did it come from?"

"You fell and hurt your head," replied her father, raising her gently in his arms; "but don't talk any more now."

"Oh! I remember," she moaned, an expression of keen distress coming over her face; "papa—"

"Hush! hush! not a word more; we will let the past go," he said, kissing her lips. "I shall carry you to your room now, and see you put to bed."

He held her on his knee, her head resting on his shoulder, while Chloe prepared her for rest.

"Are you hungry, daughter?" he asked.

"No, papa; I only want to go to sleep."

"There, Aunt Chloe, that will do," he said, as the old nurse tied on the child's night-cap; and raising her again in his arms, he carried her to the bed and was about to place her on it.

"O papa! my prayers first, you know," she cried eagerly.

"Never mind them to-night," said he, "you are not able."

"Please let me, dear papa," she pleaded; "I cannot go to sleep without."

Yielding to her entreaties, he placed her on her knees, and stood beside her, listening to her murmured petitions, in which he more than once heard his own name coupled with a request that he might be made to love Jesus.

As Elsie strives to convert her father, the two draw closer and closer until they resemble lovers rather than father and daughter.

CHAPTER TWELFTH

.   .   .   .

As the hour drew near when her father might reasonably be expected, Elsie took her station at one of the drawing-room windows overlooking the avenue, and the moment the carriage appeared in sight, she ran out and stood waiting for him on the steps of the portico.

Mr. Dinsmore put out his head as they drove up the avenue, and the first object that caught his eye was the fairy-like form of his little daughter, in her blue merino dress, and the golden brown curls waving in the wind. He sprang out and caught her in his arms the instant the carriage stopped.

"My darling, darling child," he cried, kissing her over and over again, and pressing her fondly to his heart, "how glad I am to have you in my arms again!"

"Papa, papa, my own dear, dear papa!" she exclaimed, throwing her arms around his neck, "I'm so happy, now that you have come home safe and well."

"Are you, darling? but I must not keep you out in this wind, for it is quite chilly."

He set her down, and leaving the servant to attend to his baggage, led her into the hall.

"Will you come into the drawing-room, papa?" she said; "there is a bright, warm fire there."

"Is there not one in my dressing-room?" he asked.

"Yes, papa, a very good one."

"Then we will go there. I dare say the rest of the family are in no great hurry to see me, and I want my little girl to myself for half an hour," he said, leading the way up-stairs as he spoke.

They found, as Elsie had reported, a very bright fire in the dressing-room. A large easy chair was drawn up near it, and a handsome dressing-gown and slippers were placed ready for use; all the work of Elsie's loving little hands.

He saw it all at a glance, and with a pleased smile, stooped and kissed her again, saying, "My dear little daughter is very thoughtful for her papa's comfort."

Then exchanging his warm out-door apparel and heavy boots for the dressing-gown and slippers, he seated himself in the chair and took her on his knee.

"Well, daughter," he said, passing his hand caressingly over her curls, "papa has brought you a present. . . .

.   .   .   .

"Take the lid off the band-box first, and see what is there," said her father.

"O papa, how very pretty!" she cried, as she lifted out a beautiful little velvet hat adorned with a couple of ostrich feathers.

"I am very glad it pleases you, my darling," he said, putting it on her head, and gazing at her with proud delight in her rare beauty. "There! it fits exactly, and is very becoming."

Then taking it off, he returned it to the box, and bade her look further.

"I am reserving the present for Christmas," he said, in answer to her inquiring look.

Elsie turned to the trunk again.

"Dear papa, how good you are to me!" she said, looking up at him, almost with tears of pleasure in her eyes, as she lifted out, one after another, a number of costly toys, which she examined with exclamations of delight, and then several handsome dresses, some of the finest, softest merino, and others of thick, rich silk, all ready made in fashionable style, and doing credit to his taste and judgment; and lastly a beautiful velvet pelisse, trimmed with costly fur, just the thing to wear with her pretty new hat.

He laughed and patted her cheek.

"We must have these dresses tried on," he said, "at least one of them; for as they were all cut by the same pattern—one of your old dresses which I took with me—I presume they will all fit alike. There, take this one to mammy, and tell her to put it on you, and then come back to me."

"Oh! I wondered how you could get them the right size, papa," Elsie answered, as she skipped gayly out of the room.

She was back again in a very few moments, arrayed in the pretty silk he had selected.

"Ah! it seems to be a perfect fit," said he, turning her round and round, with a very gratified look.

"Mammy must dress you to-morrow in one of these new frocks, and your pretty hat and pelisse."

Elsie looked troubled.

"Well, what is it?" he asked.

"I am afraid I shall be thinking of them in church, papa, if I wear them for the first time."

"Pooh! nonsense! what harm if you do? This squeamishness, Elsie, is the one thing about you that displeases me very much. But there! don't look so distressed, my pet. I dare say you will get over it by-and-by, and be all I wish; indeed I sometimes think you have improved a little already, in that respect."

Oh! what a pang these words sent to her heart! was it indeed true that she was losing her tenderness of conscience? that she was becoming less afraid of displeasing and dishonoring her Saviour than in former days? The very thought was anguish.

Her head drooped upon her bosom, and the small white hands were clasped convulsively together, while a bitter, repenting cry, a silent earnest prayer for pardon and help went up to Him whose ear is ever open to the cry of His children.

Her father looked at her in astonishment.

"What is it, darling?" he asked, drawing her tenderly toward him, and pushing back the curls from her face; "why do you look so pained? what did I say that could have hurt you so? I did not mean to be harsh and severe, for it was a very trifling fault."

She hid her face on his shoulder and burst into an agony of tears.

"It was not that, papa, but—but—"

"But what, my darling? don't be afraid to tell me," he answered, soothingly.

"O papa! I—I am afraid I don't—love Jesus—as much as I did," she faltered out between her sobs.

"Ah! *that* is it, eh? Well, well, you needn't cry any more. *I* think you are a very good little girl, though rather a silly one, I am afraid, and quite too morbidly conscientious."

He took her on his knee as he spoke, wiped away her tears, and then began talking in a lively strain of something else.

Elsie listened, and answered him cheerfully, but all the evening he noticed that whenever she was quiet, an unusual expression of sadness would steal over her face.

"What a strange child she is!" he said to himself, as he sat musing over the fire, after sending her to bed. "I cannot understand her; it is very odd how often I wound, when I intend to please her."

As for Elsie, she scarcely thought of her new finery, so troubled was her tender conscience, so pained her little heart to think that she had been wandering from her dear Saviour.

But Elsie had learned that "if any man sin, we have an advocate with the Father, Jesus Christ the righteous," and to Him she went with her sin and sorrow; she applied anew to the pardoning, peace-speaking blood of Christ—that "blood of sprinkling that speaketh better things than that of Abel"; and thus the sting of conscience was taken away and her peace restored, and she was soon resting quietly on her pillow, for, "so He giveth His beloved sleep."

Even her father's keen, searching glance, when she came to him in the morning, could discover no trace of sadness in her face; very quiet and sober it was, but entirely peaceful and happy, and so it remained all through the day. Her new clothes did not trouble her; she was hardly conscious of wearing them, and quite able to give her usual solemn and fixed attention to the services of the sanctuary.

"Where are you going, daughter?" Mr. Dinsmore asked, as Elsie gently withdrew her hand from his on leaving the dining-room.

"To my room, papa," she replied.

"Come with me," he said; "I want you."

"What do you want me for, papa?" she asked, as he sat down and took her on his knee.

"What for? why to keep, to love, and to look at," he said laughing. "I have been away from my little girl so long, that now I want her close by my side, or on my knee, all the time. Do you not like to be with me?"

"*Dearly* well, my own darling papa," she answered, flinging her little arms round his neck, and laying her head on his breast.

He fondled her, and chatted with her for some time, then, still keeping her on his knee, took up a book and began to read.

Elsie saw with pain that it was a novel, and longed to beg him to put it away, and spend the precious hours of the holy Sabbath in the study of God's word, or some of the lesser helps to Zion's pilgrims which the saints of our own or other ages have prepared. But she knew that it would be quite out of place for a little child like her to attempt to counsel or reprove her father; and that, tenderly as he loved and cherished her, he would never for one moment allow her to forget their relative positions.

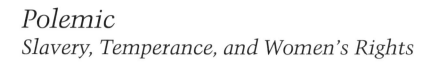

Polemic
Slavery, Temperance, and Women's Rights

Caroline Chesebro'

Sara Willis Parton [Fanny Fern]

Caroline Lee Whiting Hentz

Metta Fuller Victor

BY THE MIDDLE of the nineteenth century, nearly every phase of American life showed the effects of the reform movements that had begun in the 1830s and 1840s. Slavery, temperance, and women's rights topped the list of causes that found advocates among women fiction writers.

When the Fugitive Slave Law passed in 1850, Harriet Beecher Stowe received a letter from her sister-in-law urging her to write more on the subject of slavery: "Hattie, if I could use the pen as you can, I would write something to make this whole nation feel what an accursed thing slavery is." A few months later Stowe set to work on the novel that began running serially in the *National Era* in June of 1851. *Uncle Tom's Cabin*, possibly the most important book yet published in America, immediately won a wide readership. No doubt the novel appealed to Stowe's contemporaries, as it does to readers today, because it so vividly depicts the physical, emotional, and mental torture suffered by the slaves.

But the success of *Uncle Tom's Cabin* in its time can also be attributed to its adherence to the conventions of the didactic novel. Stowe's fundamental argument against slavery is not the cruelty and injustice of the system but its destruction of the family. The emphasis in *Uncle Tom's Cabin* on the sanctity of the family unit and the necessity of religious faith reveals the novel's close relationship to such didactic works as *Elsie Dinsmore, The Wide, Wide World*, and *The Lamplighter*. Like Elsie, Little Eva converts her father to Christianity, and like Ellen Montgomery, she redeems a bad little girl through the power of Christian love; like Gertie, Uncle Tom learns to submit, forgive his oppressors, and await his reward from the lamplighter in the sky.

By the time *Uncle Tom's Cabin* appeared in book form in 1852, proslavery forces were ready with responses. More than a score of novelists attempted to refute Stowe's work. Among the dozen women who sought to defend the southern system was the popular novelist Caroline Lee Hentz, a native of Massachusetts, who had lived most of her adult life in the South. Although her novel *The Planter's Northern Bride* (1854) appealed to many southerners, neither she nor any of the others who attempted to counteract Stowe gained a strong following for their proslavery works. Stowe's novel, on the other hand, was credited by some with having started the Civil War and has been translated throughout the world.

The story of slavery had been told repeatedly, long before the didactic novelists chose to challenge or defend it. The first slave narrative, *Adam Negro's Tryall* (1703), came out just two years after the first abolitionist pamphlet, Samuel Sewell's *The Selling of Joseph*. From that time until Harriet Brent Jacobs published her *Incidents in the Life of a Slave Girl* (1861), the narratives developed from straightforward adventure stories to sophisticated indictments of the slave system. Jacobs's account, probably the most extensive and polished of those written by women, may eventually become as well known as Frederick Douglass's. Jacobs's experiences, as well as her analysis of the evils of the system, strongly support Stowe's interpretation.

Like slavery, intemperance was perceived as carrying many other evils in its train. Excessive drinking was charged with fomenting violence, causing poverty, disrupting families, fostering juvenile delinquency, and generally disrupting civic life. The initial temperance document came from the pen of Dr. Benjamin Rush in 1815. Lyman Beecher and other clergy influenced by Rush moved to halt intemperance, and by 1846 the movement had gained international proportions. Temperance advocates welcomed novelists into the ranks early, and by mid century many novels by women included a drunken father, husband, son, or brother who brought disgrace to the family and ruin to himself. Metta Fuller Victor's *The Senator's Son* (1853) illustrates the trend of these works.

The abolition and temperance movements inadvertently precipitated the development of the women's rights movement. Prevented from speaking at abolition meetings either here or abroad, women gathered at Seneca Falls in 1848 to discuss their own oppression. When they were suppressed by temperance leaders at the national convention of temperance societies in Albany, New York, in 1852, the women withdrew and formed the Women's State Temperance Association. Female novelists supported women's rights in several ways: by creating independent heroines and allowing them to succeed; by placing arguments for women's rights in the mouths of powerful protagonists, as Caroline Chesebro' does in *Isa, a Pilgrimage* (1852); and by aggressively challenging the male establishment as Sara Parton ("Fanny Fern") does in *Ruth Hall* (1855).

Caroline Lee Whiting Hentz (1800–1856)

Although she was born in New England, Caroline Lee Hentz became a leading writer of the plantation romance and literary champion of the southern social and economic system. Descended from Samuel Whiting, the first minister of Lynn, Massachusetts, Hentz was born to Colonel John Whiting and Orpha Danforth of Lancaster, Massachusetts, the youngest of their eight children. Hentz developed her literary interests early, reading widely in her father's library. Reportedly, she wrote poems and a tragedy before the age of twelve and a novel in her teens. As an adult, she composed easily, even in the midst of family or friends or with someone peering over her shoulder.

In 1824 she married Nicholas Marcellus Hentz, a linguist who worked with George Bancroft at the Round Hill School in Northampton, Massachusetts. An intelligent but highly nervous and jealous person, Nicholas Hentz repeatedly withdrew from situations in which he felt insecure. His first move was to the University of North Carolina, Chapel Hill, where he became professor of modern languages and belles-lettres. By this time, the couple's first child had died, and Hentz had given birth to three other children. In 1830 the Hentzes moved to Covington, Kentucky, where they started a boarding school for young women. Subsequently, they established similar schools in Cincinnati, Ohio; Florence, Tuscaloosa, and Tuskeegee, Alabama; and Columbus, Georgia. Although these changes in residence were disruptive, they gave Hentz the wide experience from which she depicted southern life.

While living in Covington, Hentz received a prize of $500 for *De Lara; or, the Moorish Bride; a Tragedy* (1843), which had successful runs at theaters in Boston and Philadelphia. During her stay in Cincinnati, she attended meetings of the Semi-Colon Club, a literary group that gave her much attention and encouragement and where she probably met the young Harriet Beecher, whose *Uncle Tom's Cabin* she would one day try to refute.

Hentz's association with a Colonel King, another of the Semi-Colons, precipitated the family's departure from Cincinnati in 1834. When King expressed his admiration for Hentz in a note, her husband intercepted her response, created a scene, and immediately moved the family to Florence, Alabama. During the nine-year stay in the frontier town, Hentz participated in managing and teaching at the school and bore her last child. While living in Tuscaloosa, Hentz gained wide recognition through her stories serialized in the Philadelphia *Saturday Courier* and later collected in *Aunt Patty's Scrap Bag* (1846).

Early in 1849, while conducting the school in Columbus, Georgia, both Hentzes became ill, Nicholas's health failing completely. After her recovery, Hentz continued to operate the school for a time, but after 1851, she supported the family entirely by writing. Her first novels, *Linda; or, The Young Pilot of Belle Creole* (1850) and *Rena; or the Snow Bird* (1851) belong to this period. In 1852 Hentz moved the family to Marianna, Florida, where her two older children resided. Within five years, while caring for her sick husband, Hentz published four novels, including *The Planter's Northern Bride* (1854), and collected and published four volumes of her shorter pieces. Hentz visited the East two years before her death, which preceded that of her husband by one year.

Selected Bibliography

OTHER WORKS
The Mob Cap; and Other Tales (1850); *Eoline; or, Magnolia Vale* (1852); *Marcus Warland; or, The Long Moss Spring. A Tale of the Old South* (1852); *Robert Graham* (1855); *Courtship and Marriage; or, The Joys and Sorrows of American Life* (1856); *Ernest Linwood* (1856); *Love After Marriage; and Other Stories of the Heart* (1857).

SECONDARY
Brevard, Caroline M. *Library of Southern Literature* 6 (1907): 2375–2379.
Ellison, Rhoda C. Introduction to *The Planter's Northern Bride*, vii–xxii. Chapel Hill: University of North Carolina Press, 1970.
———. "Mrs. Hentz and the Green-Eyed Monster." *American Literature* 22 (November 1950): 345–350.
Papashvily, Helen W. *All the Happy Endings*. New York: Harper and Brothers, 1956.

The Planter's Northern Bride (1854)

When Caroline Lee Hentz's *The Planter's Northern Bride* appeared in 1854, it was only one of dozens of responses to Harriet Beecher Stowe's *Uncle Tom's Cabin*. Even so, its readability placed it among the most popular of the rebuttals in both the North and South. The people of Columbus, Georgia, where Hentz was living at the time of publication, were so delighted that they presented her with $200 and a piece of jewelry. Sarah Josepha Hale, editor of *Godey's Lady's Book*, praised the mediating value of the work and described Hentz as a thoughtful person who, having lived in the North, West, and South, had "learned the wisdom of loving her whole country above any particular state or section." The New York *Mirror* pictured Hentz as a "dove of peace to every fireside in the Union" (Rhoda C. Ellison, Introduction to *The Planter's Northern Bride*, p. xv; see Selected Bibliography).

Hentz repeatedly fostered this image of herself as a mediator. In her "Address to the Reader" of *Marcus Warland* (1852), her first defense of slavery, she identified herself as "a native of the North and a dweller of the South with affections strongly clinging to both." In the preface to *The Planter's Northern Bride*, she again assumes the posture of the northerner whose wide experience in the South supports the evidence she presents. She asserts furthermore, that were she under oath she would affirm that during her residence in the South she "never *witnessed* one scene of cruelty or oppression, never beheld a chain or a manacle, or the infliction of a punishment more severe than parental authority would be justified in applying to filial disobedience or transgression."

The idea that slavery provides security dominates Hentz's vision. She makes characters repeatedly affirm and demonstrate that sensitive masters and mistresses represent the majority of slaveholders and that they care for their slaves not only during their productive years but also when they become old or ill. Thus she portrays the slaves as much better off than northerners who work unreasonable hours for inadequate wages and lose their jobs when sickness or old age overtakes them. Early in the novel, Betsy, a northern servant, converses with a slave: " 'Talk about the black folks at the South having such a dreadful time!' muttered Betsy, half to herself and half to him. 'I want to know who has an easier time than this fellow? If I hadn't more to do, I should get so lazy I'd want somebody to laugh for me. I'm ten times more of a slave, this minute, than you are, and have been all my life'" (p. 174).

Other dimensions of Hentz's argument illustrate her paternalistic stance. She has her characters show that slaves would be quite content were it not for abolitionists who hold out to them promises of money and jobs that can never be attained. Mr. and Mrs. Softly—caricatures of the Stowes—who entice the greedy Crissy from her mistress, coerce her when she wavers, and finally abandon her to her own devices, exemplify Hentz's view of abolitionists. Hentz's characters also criticize the evils provoked by those who stir up insurrections, thereby bringing about a "blood bath" for both North and South.

Moral and religious issues also figure in Hentz's rationale. She castigates the English for their self-righteousness in criticizing the South, pointing out that it was English slave traders who first brought the Negroes to America. Having made this accusation, Hentz attempts to show that even from this evil, Divine Providence can bring good. Her central male character, Russell Moreland, who has inherited his slaves, theorizes that Providence is working through slavery to bring the pagan Africans to the knowledge of Christianity. Concomitantly, Moreland contends that God put the color barrier between the races and meant it to keep them separate.

Hentz opens her novel in New England, where Russell Moreland, a wealthy southern planter, falls in love with the beautiful Eulalia Hastings. Moreland immediately wins the admiration of the entire Hastings family. Even Squire Hastings, abolitionist educator, lecturer, and editor of the Emancipator, *enjoys the company of the southerner. At their second encounter, the two men discuss the slavery issue heatedly.*

CHAPTER III

.   .   .   .

"Well, let us begin the combat by one plain, positive question?" said Mr. Hastings, his keen black eyes sparkling like ignited coals. "Do you justify slavery?"

"Were you to ask me if I justified the *slave trade,*—that traffic forced upon us, by that very British government which now taunts and upbraids us with such bitterness and rancour for the institution whose cornerstone itself has laid,—I would answer *No!* but if you mean the involuntary slavery which surrounds me and my brethren of the South, I reply, I can justify it; we had no more to do with its existence than our own. We are not responsible for it, though we are for the duties it involves, the heaviest perhaps ever imposed upon man."

"Do you assert that you are not responsible for its *continuance;* that you have not the power to break the chains another's hand has forged; to restore the freedom which was as much the birthright of their ancestors as your own?"

"We have the *power* to do many things which reason and right forbid. We have the power to cast thousands of helpless, ignorant, reckless be-

The Planter's Northern Bride (Philadelphia: Parry and M'Millan, 1854), 579 pp. Excerpts are taken from 1: 82–86, 108–110, 201–204; 2: 32–35, 202–204, 207–210, 265–268.

ings on their own resources, or to commit them to the tender mercies of those who, while they rave of their injuries, hold out no hand to redress them; but we believe it our duty to take care of them, to make the life of servitude, which seems their present destiny, as much as possible a life of comfort and enjoyment; and, while we reap the benefit of their labour and the fruit of their toil in their day of vigour, to nurse them in sickness, provide for them in old age, and save them from the horrors and miseries of want."

"I should like to know how many masters believe this their duty," interrupted Mr. Hastings; "or, believing it, fulfil the obligations you have described. I should like to have you explain the tales of cruelty and suffering, the cries of anguish that have rent the very heavens, and moved the spirit of men to a resistance that can never again be subdued to passiveness."

"That there are hard and cruel masters," replied Moreland; "that there is in consequence much suffering and wrong, I grieve to acknowledge; for wherever human nature exists, man has abused his privileges, and the cry of human suffering pierces the ear of the Almighty. But no sufferings which they can possibly endure, no degradation to which they are ever forced in their present condition, can compare to the misery, the degradation and hopelessness of their lot, in their native Africa, where they are doomed to a slavery more galling than imagination can conceive, and steeped in a superstition so dark and loathsome that the soul shudders at the contemplation. Have you never read of the hecatombs of human victims slaughtered at the grave of a barbarian chief, or the shrieks and groans of wives, sacrificed with the most terrific rites, to the manes[1] of their husbands? I will not speak of the horrors of cannibalism. There is no need of calling up such revolting images. I only wished to present before you a faint picture of the native African, and contrast it with even the most degraded of our Southern slaves."

.   .   .   .

"Indeed!" replied Moreland, "I am astonished that you do not question the justice and mercy of God, in creating this subservient and benighted race, with lineaments so devoid of beauty and grace, and swathing them in a skin, whose hue is the blackness of darkness, marking a boundary line between us, as distinct, yea, more distinct than that which severs the noonday from midnight. The mulatto, in whose veins the blood of the white man is flowing and brightening their dusky tide, partakes of the beauty and intelligence of our race,—but take the native African, examine his lineaments, features, and peculiar characteristics, and say if he came from the hands of God in a state of equality with ourselves, endowed with equal physical and intellectual powers, intended for our bosom companions and familiar friends."

1. Spirits of the dead.

"If you are about to hide yourself in the counsels of the Almighty," cried Mr. Hastings, with increasing excitement of manner, "I give up the discussion. I see you close up every avenue to conviction, and indulge in a sophistry I consider unworthy of an honest, upright mind. Sir, we might talk in this way for six thousand years without changing my immutable conviction, that, as long as you allow the existence of slavery, you are living in sin and iniquity, that you are violating the laws of God and man, incurring the vengeance of heaven, and the retributions of eternity. I use strong language, sir, for the occasion justifies it. I am a philanthropist, sir, a champion of truth, and I have sworn to defend it at any sacrifice, yea, that of life itself, if the offering be required."

"But if you could be convinced," said Moreland, becoming more calm and energetic as his opponent grew fiery and vehement, "that, by your premature efforts, and overheated zeal, you increase the evils, which time alone can remedy; that you only rivet more closely the bonds you rashly attempt to wrench asunder by the hand of violence; that, instead of being the friends, you are in reality the worst enemies of the bondman whose cause you espouse; that, by adopting a kinder, more rational course, you would find in us co-labourers and brethren, instead of antagonists; if you could be convinced of all this, sir, would you not lay down your weapons, and reflect on the consequences that may flow from your present course of action?"

"I never can be convinced, sir; it is utterly impossible. I know that I am right, and that you are wrong. This conviction is one of those first, great truths, which are learned by intuition, not by the slow process of reasoning. God is both the teacher and the judge. You are wasting breath, sir. I am sorry to inform you of it, but you are wasting much precious breath on me."

Despite their numerous arguments, Moreland continues to visit Squire Hastings's home. Even when Moreland reveals that he is a divorced man with a small daughter, the Hastings family receives him. Eventually, with Eulalia's permission, he asks the Squire for her hand and is flatly refused.

CHAPTER IV

. . . "Is it your inexorable resolution that I shall not wed your daughter?"

"It is."

Moreland laid his hand on the latch and was passing out, when Mr. Hastings added, with an entire change of manner—"I am sorry to part with one unpleasant feeling on either side. I do not wish to give you pain. You have paid my daughter a great compliment, which we shall all appreciate. You must perceive that I am actuated by principle alone. I am a poor man, and you are rich. Were my judgment to be influenced by personal accomplishments, yours would be irresistible. I have but one objection, but that is insurmountable. Were you an humble missionary to some heathen land, I would give her to you in the name of the living God; I would give her as the firstling of my flock; I would devote her as a lamb without spot or blemish, to a good and glorious cause."

"I look upon myself as a missionary," replied Moreland, with a kindling countenance. "I look upon every master and mistress in our Southern land, as missionaries appointed to civilize and christianize the sons and daughters of Africa. To them Ethiopia is stretching out its sable hands, and through them they are lifted to God. If all the efforts of all the missionaries in our country were concentrated in the dark regions of Africa, they could not, judging of the success of their labours elsewhere, make one-tenth part of the number of converts that are found in our households and plantations. In our towns and villages, the churches of the negroes rise side by side with our own. Their prayers of faith, their hymns of praise, ascend on the same breeze, and are borne upward to the same heaven. Once more, then, I entreat you, give me your daughter, and look upon her evermore as the wife of a Christian missionary."

"I cannot consent to evil that good may come," was the emphatic reply. "But one condition I will make. Liberate your slaves; remove the curse from your household and your land; come to me with a pure, unburdened conscience, and I will oppose no barrier to your love."

"I have offered many of them their freedom, on condition that they go to Liberia, but they will not listen to the proposition. And I cannot, even to secure Paradise itself, cast upon the Northern world the large family dependent upon me for comfort and support. Under such circumstances, the freedom for which you plead would be their direst curse, instead of their greatest blessing. I believe, in God's good time, the day of liberation will come, if man will wait his leading. No, sir, I cannot accede to your proposition; nor is it from mercenary motives that I refuse. Heaven knows I am above such considerations. If I can purchase happiness only at the sacrifice of duty, then I must be for ever wretched."

"May you live to have very different ideas of duty from what now govern you! You have decided the question yourself, and I am glad of it. You can no longer reproach me for destroying the happiness of Eulalia."

"You might have spared me that," exclaimed Moreland, with irrepressible bitterness. Then, fearing to trust himself to say more in his present maddened state of feeling, he made a silent bow and left the house.

Moreland, who is a very strong-willed person, has a violent physical reaction to the refusal. According to the doctor, he comes close to death. Eulalia also becomes ill. As soon as she is able, she enlists the aid of the minister, Dr. Ellery, who persuades Hastings not to stand between the lovers.

As the newlyweds travel to Georgia, Moreland attempts to prepare
his northern bride for her new life in slave territory and particularly
in her own home.

CHAPTER VIII

.   .   .   .

"I have no misgivings for them [the slaves]," answered Moreland;
"they will adore you as a mistress, and rejoice under your firm, yet gentle sway. You have every attribute to win their admiration, as well as
their love. The negro has an intense appreciation of beauty and grace,
and feels the influence of mental superiority. I know you better than you
know yourself, my too self-distrusting bride. There is a greal deal of latent energy reposing under those downy flakes of gentleness, and should
occasion require, it will wake and astonish yourself by its power. I fear
but one thing."

"And what is that?" asked Eulalia.

"Your own repugnance to the African race. You must struggle with
this from the first, and it will surely be overcome. It is of unnatural
birth—born of prejudice and circumstance. The few specimens you have
seen of the negroes have been of the most repulsive kind. It is certainly a
strong argument in favour of their condition at the South, that the free
negro is generally far more degraded, more low in the scale of being,
than the slave. The air of freedom, which gives luxuriant growth to his
vices, does not foster his peculiar virtues. His social character degener-
ates. The philanthropists who interest themselves so much in his destiny at home, leave him to his own resources when brought within the
sphere of their assistance. They will not hold social communion with
one on whom God has affixed the seal of a darker dispensation. At a distance, they stretch out their arms, and call him brother, and exclaim,
'Are we not the children of the same Father?' but when near, they forget
the ties of consanguinity, and stand back with a *holier than thou* written on their brows."

"My father doth not so," said Eulalia, with earnestness; "he took one
of these wandering Parias by the hand, and, making no distinction of
colour, treated him as a companion and friend. I tried to imitate his example, for I believed it my duty; but I cannot express the abhorrence I
felt, the struggle of principle with inclination."

"And how was your father's kindness repaid?"

"I am sorry to say, with insolence and ingratitude. When we ascertained his true character, I was glad to believe that it was an instinctive
horror of vice which I felt, instead of a loathing for his kind."

"My dear Eulalia, God never intended that you and I should live on
equal terms with the African. He has created a barrier between his race
and ours, which no one can pass over without incurring the ban of society. The white woman who marries a negro, makes herself an outcast,

a scorn, and a byword. The white man who marries a negress forfeits his position as a gentleman, and is excluded from the social privileges of his brethren. This is the result of an inherent principle of the human breast, entwined, like conscience, with our vitality, and inseparable from it. The most ultra Northern philanthropist dare not contradict this truth. He may advocate amalgamation with his lips, but in his heart, he recoils from it with horror. He would sooner see a son or daughter perish beneath the stroke of the assassin than wedded to the African, whom he professes to look upon as his equal and his friend. Nature has marked a dividing line, as distinct as that which separates the beasts of the field, the birds of the air, and the fishes of the sea. And why should any one wish to violate this great law of nature,—this principle of homogeneousness? The negro feels the attraction of his kind, and forms, like ourselves, congenial ties."

"But, alas!" exclaimed Eulalia, "how often are those ties broken by the rude hand of violence and oppression. How many heart-strings are bruised and torn by the stroke of the auctioneer's hammer. This is an evil which, kind and feeling as you are, you must deplore."

"I do; and it is one which good masters avert, in every possible manner. It is an evil which has never yet approached my plantation or household, and never shall, unless necessity lays its iron hand upon me."

"Ah! if all masters were like you, slavery would be robbed of its terrors and its gloom."

"I am no better than the majority, perhaps not as good. I know of some bad masters, and, what is still worse, bad mistresses; but public opinion brands them with its curse."

Upon arriving at her southern home, Eulalia finds everything as Moreland had described it. The slaves rejoice at Moreland's return and respond lovingly to his beautiful northern bride. When Moreland takes Eulalia for her first visit to the plantation, she begins to be impressed with and converted to his point of view.

VOL. II

CHAPTER I

.   .   .   .

And now for the first time she realized that she was the wife of a Southern planter.

All around, far as the eye could reach, rich, rolling fields of cotton, bearing the downy wealth of the South, stretched out a boundless ocean of green, spotted with white, like the foam of the wave. Long rows of whitewashed cabins, extending back of the central building, whose superior style of architecture distinguished it as the master's mansion, exhibited some black sign at every door, to show the colour of the occupants. Though it wanted something of the usual time, as Moreland wished Eulalia to witness a true plantation scene before the duskiness of twilight, he ordered the bugle blast to sound which called the labourers home, and its echoes rolled over the whitened plains with clear and sweet reverberations. Soon, returning in grand march from the fields, came the negroes, poising on their heads immense baskets brimming with the light and flaky cotton. Little children, looking very much like walking semicolons, toddled along, balancing their baskets also, with an air of self-importance and pride. Eulalia gazed with a kind of fascination on the dark procession, as one after another, men, women, and children, passed along to the gin house to deposit their burdens. It seemed as if she were watching the progress of a great eclipse, and that soon she would be enveloped in total darkness. She was a mere speck of light, in the midst of shadows. How easy it would be to extinguish her! She recollected all the horrible stories she had heard of negro insurrections, and thought what an awful thing it was to be at the mercy of so many slaves, on that lonely plantation. When she saw her husband going out among them, and they all closed round, shutting him in as with a thick cloud, she asked herself if he were really safe. Safe! Napoleon, in the noonday of his glory, surrounded by the national guard, was not more safe—more honoured or adored. They gathered round him, eager to get within reach of his hand, the sound of his voice, the glance of his kind, protecting, yet commanding eye. More like a father welcomed by his children than a king greeted by his subjects, he stood, the centre of that sable ring. Eulalia thought she had never seen him look so handsome, so noble, so good. She had never felt so proud of being his wife. An impression of his power, gently used, but still manifest, produced in her that feeling of awe, softened by tenderness, so delicious to the loving, trusting heart of woman. He appeared to her in a new character. She had known him as the fond, devoted bridegroom; now he was invested with the authority and responsibility of a master. And she must share that responsibility, assist him in his duties, and make the welfare, comfort, and happiness of these dependent beings the great object of her life. He had twined round her the roses of love, but she was not born to sit idly in a bower and do nothing for those who were toiling for her. He had adorned her with the gems of wealth, but she must not live in selfish indulgence while the wants of immortal souls were pressing upon her, while the solemn warning "Thou must give an account of thy stewardship" was ringing in her soul.

Never before had she made an elaborate comparison between the white and the black man. She had so often heard her father say that they were born equal—equal in mind, body, and soul, having only the accidental difference of colour to mark them—that she had believed it, and loathed herself for the feeling of superiority over them which she could not crush. But as she looked at her husband, standing in their midst, the representative of the fair sons of Japheth, wearing on his brow the signet of a loftier, nobler destiny, every lineament and feature expressive of intellect and power, and then at each of that dark, lowly throng, she felt a conviction that freedom, in its broadest latitude, education, with its most exalted privileges, could never make them equal to him.

In succeeding days Eula, as she asks Moreland to call her, visits the cabins and wins the love of the slaves. She sings for the dying Dilsey and attends her funeral, at which Moreland renews his pact with his slaves.

During the second year of their marriage the Morelands receive a visitor from the North, the Reverend Mr. Brainard, who claims to be a Methodist minister and to know Squire Hastings. Moreland hires him to give a series of sermons at the plantation. One by one, beginning with the preacher Paul, Brainard incites the slaves against their master. Before the insurrection can be carried out, Moreland learns of it, goes to the plantation with his whole household, and, standing beside Dilsey's grave, confronts his slaves.

CHAPTER IX

.   .   .   .

"More than two years have passed," said Moreland, his eyes glancing from face to face, calmly and gravely, as he spoke, "since I stood on this spot, on which the grave-clods had just been thrown, and you all stood around me then, just as you are gathered now. At that hour, I renewed the vows of protection and kindness to you which I uttered, when a boy, in the ear of a dying mother. I told you, if I ever proved unkind, unjust, and tyrannical, if I ever forgot my duties to you as a master and a friend, to meet me here, in this solemn enclosure, and remind me of what I then said. You all promised then, to continue faithful, trustworthy, and obedient, and, judging of the future by the past, I believed you. And yet," he added, his voice deepening into sternness and his eye kindling with indignation, "you have basely deceived me; you have been listening to a traitor and a villain, and plotting against your master and your friend. Under pretence of worshipping God, you have been engaged in the service of Satan, and doing the work of devils. I know all your horrible plans. I know what holiday frolics you are preparing. Which of you has a word to say in his defence? Which of you can look me in the face and say he does not deserve the severest punishment, for treachery and ingratitude to a master as kind and forbearing as I have ever been? Paul, you have taken upon you the office of a preacher of the gospel of peace, who, on all occasions, are the voice of your brethren; look up, speak, and if you have one word to say in your justification and theirs, let us hear it, and hear it quickly."

"No, massa!" cried Paul, slowly raising his head, without lifting his eyes; "got noting to say—noting—only Massa Brainard."

"Poor, deluded creatures!" said Moreland, "poor, blind tools of an artful, selfish, false, and cold-hearted hypocrite, who cares no more for you than the grass you are trampling under your feet. I pity you; for I sent the wretch in your midst, believing him to be a man of God. He has beguiled you with promises of freedom. What is the freedom he can offer you? Nothing but poverty, degradation, and sorrow. If you could compare your condition with those of the free coloured people at the North, you would shudder to think of all that you have escaped. Listen! You are slaves, and I am free; but I neither made you slaves nor myself a free man. We are all in the condition in which we were born. You are black, and I am white; but I did not give you those sable skins, nor myself this fairer complexion. You and I are as God Almighty made us, and, as I expect to give an account of the manner in which I fulfil my duties as a master, so you will be judged according to your fidelity, honesty, and uprightness as servants. The Bible says—'Can the Ethiopian change his skin?' No, he cannot! but there is no reason why he should have a black heart, because his skin is black. Free! how willingly would I make you free this moment, if, by so doing, I could make you better and happier! Free! I would to heaven you were all free,—then I, too, should be free from a burden made intolerable by your treachery and ingratitude! I would rather, ten thousand times, cultivate these broad fields myself, than be served by faithless hands and false, hollow hearts. I have hands that can work. I would do it cheerfully, if labour was the portion God had assigned me in this world. Better, far better, the toiling limbs, than the aching heart!"

.   .   .   .

"Oh, massa!" exclaimed Paul,—completely subdued and melted, and sinking down on his knees, right on the grave of Dilsy,—"forgive us! Don't send us away! Trust us once more! We've ben 'ceived by Satan, and didn't know what we were doing!"

The moment Paul prostrated himself before his master, all but *one* followed his example, entreating for pardon, and imploring with tears and sobs not to be sent away from him. Vulcan, the blacksmith, stood firm and unmoved as the anvil in his forge. All his dark and angry passions had been whetted on the edge of the murderous weapons hidden beneath his shop, and made red hot by the flames of the midnight furnace. His stubborn knees refused to bend, and a sullen cloud added luridness to his raven-black face.

Moreland and he stood side by side;—all the rest were kneeling. The beams of the departing sun played in golden glory round the brow of Moreland; the negro seemed to absorb the rays,—he looked of more intense, inky blackness.

"Vulcan!" said his master, "if you expect my forgiveness, ask it. Dare to resist me, and you shall feel the full weight of my indignation."

"I'm my own master," cried the blacksmith, in a morose, defying tone. "I ain't a gwine to let no man set his feet on my neck. If the rest are a mind to be fools, let 'em!" and he shook his iron hand over the throng, and rolled his bloodshot eyes, like a tiger ready to spring from its lair.

The face of Moreland turned pale as marble, and lightnings kindled in his eyes. To brute force and passion he had nothing to oppose but moral courage and undaunted will; but he paused not to measure his strength with the muscles swelling out, like twisting serpents, in the negro's brandished arm. Laying his right hand commandingly on his shoulder, he exclaimed:—

"There is but one master here. Submit to his authority, or tremble for the consequences!"

Suddenly wrenching his shoulder from the hand that grasped it, the blacksmith leaped forward, and seizing his master in his gigantic arms, was about to hurl him to the ground, when a tremendous blow on the back of his head laid him prostrate and stunned at Moreland's feet. So sudden had been the attack, so instantaneous the release, that Moreland was hardly conscious how it had been effected, till the sight of Paul, standing with dilated nostrils and panting chest over the fallen giant, and brandishing with both hands a massy rail, which had been lying at the foot of the grave, made him aware who his deliverer was.

"Let me kill 'em, massa—let me kill 'em," cried Paul, swinging the rail above his head, and planting his foot on the broad breast of the rebel.

"Stop!" cried Moreland; "in the name of God, stop! He may be dead already! Let him be carried to the guard-house and there taken care of. Give him in charge to the overseer."

Four of the stoutest negroes sprang forward, eager to show their re-covered zeal and loyalty, and lifted up the heavy mass of insensible flesh, which they would have beaten to jelly in their indignation, so powerful was the reaction of their feelings.

"Paul," said Moreland, holding out his hand, "true and faithful servant yet! Let the past be forgotten, or remembered only to forgive!"

"Oh! dear massa!" cried Paul, dropping the rail, and throwing his arms round Moreland's shoulders, he wept and sobbed like a child,—"you're safe and alive yet! Bless a Lord Almighty! Paul's heart always was right, but he got a mighty poor head of hisn."

Moreland remembers his promise to Squire Hastings to bring Eula home for a visit. Shortly after the Morelands arrive in the North, an announcement is posted in the town concerning a lecture by a Mr. Howard who would be accompanied by a recently escaped slave. As might be expected, Mr. Howard turns out to be Brainard and his companion Vulcan, whom Moreland had freed and dismissed. Moreland comes forward and exposes the deceiver and surprisingly wins the support of Squire Hastings. By uniting her husband and father, the "Northern Bride" becomes a mediator between North and South. As the following scene opens, Moreland speaks.

CHAPTER X

.   .   .   .

". . . This man is a vile imposter. Pretending to be a minister of God, he introduced himself into my household, and, under the cloak of religion, plotted the most damning designs. I received him as a friend, cherished him as a brother, and obtained for him the confidence of a generous and trusting community. I blush for my own weakness; I pity the delusion of others. As to the horrible charges he has brought against me and my Southern brethren, I scorn to deny them. If you could believe such atrocities of *any* man, your good opinion would be valueless to me. That you can believe them of *me*, knowing me, as most of you now do, I know it is impossible. Had he been less malignant, he had done me more evil."

"I have spoken the truth, and nothing but the truth," interrupted Brainard, grinding his teeth with suppressed rage; "our black brother can bear witness to all I have declared."

But "our black brother" did not seem disposed to back his falsehoods with the boldness he had anticipated. Though brute force, roused by long continued excitement, had once triumphed over moral cowardice, it gave him no sustaining influence now, and he shrunk and quailed before the thrilling eye of his deserted and injured master. The influence of early habits and feelings resumed its sway, and gleamings of his better nature struggled through the darkness of falsehood and treachery. Notwithstanding the bluntness of his perceptions, he felt the power of Moreland's moral superiority over Brainard, and when he found himself called upon to confirm his unblushing lies in the pure light of his master's countenance, a sudden loathing for the white man who could stoop to such degradation, filled his mind; and a strong desire for the favour he had forfeited and the place he had lost, stirred his heart.

"Speak, Vulcan!" cried Moreland, who had marked the changes of his dark face with intense interest, "speak! and in the presence of an all-hearing God, say if this man utters the truth, or I."

"You, massa, you!" burst spontaneously from the lips of the negro, and it seemed as if a portion of blackness rolled away from his face, with the relieving consciousness of having borne testimony to the truth.

"Villain!" cried Brainard,—stamping his foot, and turning fiercely on the blacksmith,—"villain, you lie! you and your master—"

"Order, order!" exclaimed Mr. Hastings, who had been terribly agitated during this scene. Before he could add another syllable, Moreland, with one bound, stood upon the platform, and seizing Brainard by the arm, gave him a downward swing that sent him reeling against the living wall below. The act was instantaneous as lightning, and the mimic thunder of the pounding sticks followed the flash. Brainard could not, at any time, compete in strength with Moreland, and now, when indignation nerved the arm of the latter, it seemed to have a giant's sinews.

Conscious of a great revulsion of feeling in the audience, since Vulcan's testimony against him, he began to feel the insecurity of his situation. Turning in desperation to the platform, like an animal at bay,

"Sir," said he, addressing Mr. Hastings, "I appeal to you for redress, and protection from insult and outrage. I appeal to this whole assembly, as a stranger foully wronged. I appeal to Northern justice, for defence against Southern insolence and aggression."

For one moment, there was a breathless stillness, awaiting the reply of Mr. Hastings. The face of Moreland crimsoned, and his heart throbbed audibly. Would Eulalia's father throw the shield of his protection round this man? If so, they must be for ever separated.

"Sir," cried Mr. Hastings,—coming forward and speaking with emphasis, though in an agitated voice,—"I have no protection to offer an imposter and a liar. This people have no redress for one who insults them by asking it, in the face of such a shameful detection. He shall find to his cost, that Northern justice will protect the South from aggressions and slanders like his!"

A deafening shout went up as Mr. Hastings concluded, showing how warmly public sentiment was now enlisted in the cause of Moreland. Moreland, relieved from an intolerable dread, involuntarily grasped the hand of his father-in-law, and pressed it with more cordiality than he had ever felt before.

Harriet Brent Jacobs (1818–1896)

"I was born a slave; but I never knew it until six years of happy child-hood had passed away," Harriet Brent Jacobs writes in *Incidents in the Life of a Slave Girl* (1861), published under the pseudonym Linda Brent. There is little information available on Jacobs except what she presents in this narrative, which may or may not be a literal account of her life.

According to Jacobs, she was born in 1818, the great granddaughter of a South Carolina planter. Until the age of six she lived with her parents and a younger brother identified as William in the text. Her father, a skilled carpenter, had contracted with his owner to support himself and his family and to pay her $200 a year. He tried repeatedly to purchase his children, but she would never agree to sell them. When Jacobs was six, her mother died and the child was taken into her mistress's house. There her mistress taught her to read and spell, skills for which she later said she was grateful. When Jacobs was twelve, her mistress died, leaving the slave to a five-year-old niece.

Jacobs spent the next six years of her life in the home of her owner's parents, where she was constantly harassed by the master, a doctor, and hated by the mistress. Jacobs's greatest source of protection was her maternal grandmother, a freed slave who was highly respected by everyone in the town. At the age of eighteen, Jacobs became pregnant by a white man other than her master and was driven out of the house. She took refuge with her grandmother, where she remained until she escaped to the North at the age of twenty-seven.

In the North, Jacobs supported herself and her two children by working as a nurse for the children of a wealthy Bostonian who purchased her freedom. With the encouragement of Lydia Maria Child, who edited *Incidents*, Jacobs allowed her narrative to be published in 1861. She died in 1896.

Selected Bibliography

SECONDARY
Heddin, Raymond. "The American Slave Narrative: The Justification of the Picaro." *American Literature* 53 (January 1982): 630–645.

Incidents in the Life of a Slave Girl (1861)

Like authors of seduction novels and captivity narratives, Harriet Brent Jacobs begins her preface by asserting the truth of her story: "Reader, be assured this narrative is no fiction. I am aware that some of my adventures may seem incredible; but they are, nevertheless, strictly true." She notes that names of people and places have been changed throughout but only (as earlier didactic writers claimed) to prevent identification of actual persons.

Jacobs had a compelling reason for calling her narrative "strictly true": she was undertaking the task of informing the women of the North of the condition of two million women in bondage in the South. She did not want readers to think she had exaggerated the evils of slavery; in fact, she notes, "my descriptions fall far short of the facts."

Most likely the incidents Jacobs relates were strictly true; however, the narrative shows an artist at work in the skillful arrangement of events and the carefully created suspense and dramatic tension. Whether *Incidents* should be considered autobiography, fictionalized autobiography, or autobiographical fiction, it is more powerfully written than many novels of the time, including Harriet E. Adams Wilson's recently discovered *Our Nig* (1859), considered the first novel published by a black woman.

The content of *Incidents* forms a vivid contrast to the subject matter of *The Planter's Northern Bride* and other novels written in defense of slavery. In *Incidents* Jacobs recounts inhumane physical tortures she witnessed and endured, and she describes the ingenious plans for escape devised by family, friends, and sympathizers. She also explains the illogical aspects of the slave system, pointing out how ownership embroiled the whites in personal and economic entanglements from which they did not know how to escape. Perhaps Jacobs's most significant contribution to the slave narrative tradition is her skill in depicting the pervasiveness and intensity of sexual harassment in the lives of black women. Her account of the doctor's persistence in tormenting her, personally and through her family, remains in the reader's memory long after the book has been put aside.

The narrative opens with the account of Linda Brent's early life with her parents and the story of her grandmother's life. Her mother's death results in Linda's being taken into the home of the mistress who teaches her to read and spell; the death of that mistress brings about Linda's removal to the home of Dr. and Mrs. Flint, the parents of her five-year-old owner. In the Flint house Linda suffers from the jealousy of Mrs. Flint and sexual harassment by Dr. Flint. Linda's most serious troubles begin in her fifteenth year.

V

The Trials of Girlhood

During the first years of my service in Dr. Flint's family, I was accustomed to share some indulgences with the children of my mistress. Though this seemed to me no more than right, I was grateful for it, and tried to merit the kindness by the faithful discharge of my duties. But I now entered on my fifteenth year—a sad epoch in the life of a slave girl. My master began to whisper foul words in my ear. Young as I was, I could not remain ignorant of their import. I tried to treat them with indifference or contempt. The master's age, my extreme youth, and the fear that his conduct would be reported to my grandmother, made him bear this treatment for many months. He was a crafty man, and resorted to many means to accomplish his purposes. Sometimes he had stormy, terrific ways, that made his victims tremble; sometimes he assumed a gentleness that he thought must surely subdue. Of the two, I preferred his stormy moods, although they left me trembling. He tried his utmost to corrupt the pure principles my grandmother had instilled. He peopled my young mind with unclean images, such as only a vile monster could think of. I turned from him with disgust and hatred. But he was my master. I was compelled to live under the same roof with him—where I saw a man forty years my senior daily violating the most sacred commandments of nature. He told me I was his property; that I must be subject to his will in all things. My soul revolted against the mean tyranny. But where could I turn for protection? No matter whether the slave girl be as black as ebony or as fair as her mistress. In either case, there is no shadow of law to protect her from insult, from violence, or even from death; all these are inflicted by fiends who bear the shape of men. The mistress, who ought to protect the helpless victim, has no other feelings towards her but those of jealousy and rage. . . .

. . . My master met me at every turn, reminding me that I belonged to him, and swearing by heaven and earth that he would compel me to submit to him. If I went out for a breath of fresh air, after a day of unwearied toil, his footsteps dogged me. If I knelt by my mother's grave, his dark shadow fell on me even there. The light heart which nature had given me became heavy with sad forebodings. The other slaves in my master's house noticed the change. Many of them pitied me; but none dared to ask the cause. They had no need to inquire. They knew too well the guilty practices under that roof; and they were aware that to speak of them was an offence that never went unpunished.

I longed for some one to confide in. I would have given the world to have laid my head on my grandmother's faithful bosom, and told her all my troubles. But Dr. Flint swore he would kill me, if I was not as silent

Incidents in the Life of a Slave Girl ed. by L. Maria Child (Boston: Published for the Author, 1861), 306 pp. Excerpts are taken from 44–47, 51–52, 118–120, 154–156, 173–177, 185–186, 233–236, 300–303.

as the grave. Then, although my grandmother was all in all to me, I feared her as well as loved her. I had been accustomed to look up to her with a respect bordering upon awe. I was very young, and felt shame-faced about telling her such impure things, especially as I knew her to be very strict on such subjects. Moreover, she was a woman of a high spirit. She was usually very quiet in her demeanor; but if her indignation was once roused, it was not very easily quelled. I had been told that she once chased a white gentleman with a loaded pistol, because he insulted one of her daughters. I dreaded the consequences of a violent outbreak; and both pride and fear kept me silent. But though I did not confide in my grandmother, and even evaded her vigilant watchfulness and inquiry, her presence in the neighborhood was some protection to me. Though she had been a slave, Dr. Flint was afraid of her. He dreaded her scorching rebukes. Moreover, she was known and patronized by many people; and he did not wish to have his villainy made public. It was lucky for me that I did not live on a distant plantation, but in a town not so large that the inhabitants were ignorant of each other's affairs. Bad as are the laws and customs in a slaveholding community, the doctor, as a professional man, deemed it prudent to keep up some outward show of decency.

.   .   .   .

VI
The Jealous Mistress

.   .   .   .

I had entered my sixteenth year, and every day it became more apparent that my presence was intolerable to Mrs. Flint. Angry words frequently passed between her and her husband. He had never punished me himself, and he would not allow any body else to punish me. In that respect, she was never satisfied; but, in her angry moods, no terms were too vile for her to bestow upon me. Yet I, whom she detested so bitterly, had far more pity for her than he had, whose duty it was to make her life happy. I never wronged her, or wished to wrong her; and one word of kindness from her would have brought me to her feet.

After repeated quarrels between the doctor and his wife, he announced his intention to take his youngest daughter, then four years old, to sleep in his apartment. It was necessary that a servant should sleep in the same room, to be on hand if the child stirred. I was selected for that office, and informed for what purpose that arrangement had been made. By managing to keep within sight of people, as much as possible, during the day time, I had hitherto succeeded in eluding my master, though a razor was often held to my throat to force me to change this line of policy. At night I slept by the side of my great aunt, where I felt safe. He was too prudent to come into her room. She was an old woman, and had been

in the family many years. Moreover, as a married man, and a professional man, he deemed it necessary to save appearances in some degree.
But he resolved to remove the obstacle in the way of his scheme; and he
thought he had planned it so that he should evade suspicion. He was
well aware how much I prized my refuge by the side of my old aunt, and
he determined to dispossess me of it. The first night the doctor had the
little child in his room alone. The next morning, I was ordered to take
my station as nurse the following night. A kind Providence interposed
in my favor. During the day Mrs. Flint heard of this new arrangement,
and a storm followed. I rejoiced to hear it rage.

*When Linda falls in love with a young free-born carpenter, Dr. Flint
refuses to allow the man to buy her freedom. Eventually the young
man goes off to claim an inheritance, and Linda, knowing Dr. Flint's
determination to keep her, bids her lover not to return. After the young
man's departure, Flint presses Linda harder to agree to become his
mistress, promising to set her up in a house of her own.*

*At this time Linda begins to receive attention from a Mr. Sands, a
"white unmarried gentleman," who, realizing the pressure under
which she is living in the Flint household, takes advantage of her need
for a friend. Linda succumbs to his attentions. When she becomes
pregnant, she is driven from the Flint household and takes shelter
with her grandmother. Enraged at the birth of her son, which he sees
as concrete evidence of Linda's rejection of him, Flint continues to
refuse to sell her. Despite the humiliation that her alliance with Sands
has brought upon her, Linda continues the relationship.*

XIV
Another Link to Life

.   .   .   .

When Dr. Flint learned that I was again to be a mother, he was exasperated beyond measure. He rushed from the house, and returned with a
pair of shears. I had a fine head of hair; and he often railed about my
pride of arranging it nicely. He cut every hair close to my head, storming
and swearing all the time. I replied to some of his abuse, and he struck
me. Some months before, he had pitched me down stairs in a fit of passion; and the injury I received was so serious that I was unable to turn
myself in bed for many days. He then said, "Linda, I swear by God I will
never raise my hand against you again;" but I knew that he would forget
his promise.

After he discovered my situation, he was like a restless spirit from the
pit. He came every day; and I was subjected to such insults as no pen can
describe. I would not describe them if I could; they were too low, too
revolting. I tried to keep them from my grandmother's knowledge as

much as I could. I knew she had enough to sadden her life, without having my troubles to bear. When she saw the doctor treat me with violence, and heard him utter oaths terrible enough to palsy a man's tongue, she could not always hold her peace. It was natural and motherlike that she should try to defend me; but it only made matters worse.

When they told me my new-born babe was a girl, my heart was heavier than it had ever been before. Slavery is terrible for men; but it is far more terrible for women. Superadded to the burden common to all, *they* have wrongs, and sufferings, and mortifications peculiarly their own.

Dr. Flint had sworn that he would make me suffer, to my last day, for this new crime against *him*, as he called it; and as long as he had me in his power he kept his word. On the fourth day after the birth of my babe, he entered my room suddenly, and commanded me to rise and bring my baby to him. The nurse who took care of me had gone out of the room to prepare some nourishment, and I was alone. There was no alternative. I rose, took up my babe, and crossed the room to where he sat. "Now stand there," said he, "till I tell you to go back!" My child bore a strong resemblance to her father, and to the deceased Mrs. Sands, her grandmother. He noticed this; and while I stood before him, trembling with weakness, he heaped upon me and my little one every vile epithet he could think of. Even the grandmother in her grave did not escape his curses. In the midst of his vituperations I fainted at his feet. This recalled him to his senses. He took the baby from my arms, laid it on the bed, dashed cold water in my face, took me up, and shook me violently, to restore my consciousness before any one entered the room. Just then my grandmother came in, and he hurried out of the house. I suffered in consequence of this treatment; but I begged my friends to let me die, rather than send for the doctor. There was nothing I dreaded so much as his presence. My life was spared; and I was glad for the sake of my little ones. Had it not been for these ties to life, I should have been glad to be released by death, though I had lived only nineteen years.

Finally, Flint gives Linda the choice of becoming his mistress or going as a slave to his son's plantation. She chooses the latter as a means of escaping his constant harassment. From time to time she returns to her grandmother's at night to visit her children, whose freedom she is determined to obtain. When she learns that the children are to be brought to the plantation to keep her "contented," she runs away and hides with a friend who lives near her grandmother's home. Later a white woman, eager to help Linda escape to the North, arranges to shelter her. Linda's escape from the plantation causes her family much suffering.

XVIII
Months of Peril

.   .   .   .

I was daily hoping to hear that my master had sold my children; for I knew who was on the watch to buy them. But Dr. Flint cared even more for revenge than he did for money. My brother William, and the good aunt who had served in his family twenty years, and my little Benny, and Ellen, who was a little over two years old, were thrust into jail, as a means of compelling my relatives to give some information about me. He swore my grandmother should never see one of them again till I was brought back. They kept these facts from me for several days. When I heard that my little ones were in a loathsome jail, my first impulse was to go to them. I was encountering dangers for the sake of freeing them, and must I be the cause of their death? The thought was agonizing. My benefactress tried to soothe me by telling me that my aunt would take good care of the children while they remained in jail. But it added to my pain to think that the good old aunt, who had always been so kind to her sister's orphan children, should be shut up in prison for no other crime than loving them. I suppose my friends feared a reckless movement on my part, knowing, as they did, that my life was bound up in my children. I received a note from my brother William. It was scarcely legible, and ran thus: "Wherever you are, dear sister, I beg of you not to come here. We are all much better off than you are. If you come, you will ruin us all. They would force you to tell where you had been, or they would kill you. Take the advice of your friends; if not for the sake of me and your children, at least for the sake of those you would ruin."

Poor William! He also must suffer for being my brother. I took his advice and kept quiet. My aunt was taken out of jail at the end of the month, because Mrs. Flint could not spare her any longer. She was tired of being her own housekeeper. It was quite too fatiguing to order her dinner and eat it too. My children remained in jail, where brother William did all he could for their comfort. Betty [Linda's friend] went to see them sometimes, and brought me tidings. She was not permitted to enter the jail; but William would hold them up to the grated window while she chatted with them. When she repeated their prattle, and told me how they wanted to see their ma, my tears would flow. Old Betty would exclaim, "Lors, chile! what's you crying 'bout? Dem young uns vil kill you dead. Don't be so chick'n hearted! If you does, you vil nebber git thro' dis world."

When the doctor returns from New York, he sells Linda's brother William and her children. Unknown to him, the trader who bought them was in Sands's employ. When the children are returned to their grandmother, the doctor becomes enraged. He renews the search for Linda. When danger of discovery threatens, she leaves her haven dressed as a sailor. After several days in the swamp and nights aboard a boat an-chored nearby, she is returned to her grandmother's house.

XXI
The Loophole of Retreat

A small shed had been added to my grandmother's house years ago. Some boards were laid across the joists at the top, and between these boards and the roof was a very small garret, never occupied by any thing but rats and mice. It was a pent roof, covered with nothing but shingles, according to the southern custom for such buildings. The garret was only nine feet long and seven wide. The highest part was three feet high, and sloped down abruptly to the loose board floor. There was no admission for either light or air. My uncle Phillip, who was a carpenter, had very skillfully made a concealed trap-door, which communicated with the storeroom. He had been doing this while I was waiting in the swamp. The storeroom opened upon a piazza. To this hole I was conveyed as soon as I entered the house. The air was stifling; the darkness total. A bed had been spread on the floor. I could sleep quite comfortably on one side; but the slope was so sudden that I could not turn on the other without hitting the roof. The rats and mice ran over my bed; but I was weary, and I slept such sleep as the wretched may, when a tempest has passed over them. Morning came. I knew it only by the noises I heard; for in my small den day and night were all the same. I suffered for air even more than for light. But I was not comfortless. I heard the voices of my children. There was joy and there was sadness in the sound. It made my tears flow. How I longed to speak to them! I was eager to look on their faces; but there was no hole, no crack, through which I could peep. This continued darkness was oppressive. It seemed horrible to sit or lie in a cramped position day after day, without one gleam of light. Yet I would have chosen this, rather than my lot as a slave, though white people considered it an easy one; and it was so compared with the fate of others. I was never cruelly over-worked; I was never lacerated with the whip from head to foot; I was never so beaten and bruised that I could not turn from one side to the other; I never had my heel-strings cut to prevent my running away; I was never chained to a log and forced to drag it about, while I toiled in the fields from morning till night; I was never branded with hot iron, or torn by bloodhounds. On the contrary, I had always been kindly treated, and tenderly cared for, until I came into the hands of Dr. Flint. I had never wished for freedom till then. But though my life in slavery was comparatively devoid of hardships, God pity the woman who is compelled to lead such a life!

My food was passed up to me through the trap-door my uncle had contrived; and my grandmother, my uncle Phillip, and aunt Nancy would seize such opportunities as they could, to mount up there and chat with me at the opening. But of course this was not safe in the daytime. It must all be done in darkness. It was impossible for me to move in an erect position, but I crawled about my den for exercise. One day I hit my head against something, and found it was a gimlet. My uncle had left it sticking there when he made the trap-door. I was as rejoiced as Robinson Crusoe could have been at finding such a treasure. It put a lucky thought into my head. I said to myself, "Now I will have some light. Now I will see my children." I did not dare to begin my work during the daytime, for fear of attracting attention. But I groped round; and having found the side next the street, where I could frequently see my children, I stuck the gimlet in and waited for evening. I bored three rows of holes, one above another; then I bored out the interstices between. I thus succeeded in making one hole about an inch long and an inch broad. I sat by it till late into the night, to enjoy the little whiff of air that floated in. In the morning I watched for my children. The first person I saw in the street was Dr. Flint. I had a shuddering, superstitious feeling that it was a bad omen. Several familiar faces passed by. At last I heard the merry laugh of children, and presently two sweet little faces were looking up at me, as though they knew I was there, and were conscious of the joy they imparted. How I longed to *tell* them I was there!

My condition was now a little improved. But for weeks I was tormented by hundreds of little red insects, fine as a needle's point, that pierced through my skin, and produced an intolerable burning. The good grandmother gave me herb teas and cooling medicines, and finally I got rid of them. The heat of my den was intense, for nothing but thin shingles protected me from the scorching summer's sun. But I had my consolations. Through my peeping-hole I could watch for the children, and when they were near enough, I could hear their talk. Aunt Nancy brought me all the news she could hear at Dr. Flint's. From her I learned that the doctor had written to New York to a colored woman, who had been born and raised in our neighborhood, and had breathed his contaminating atmosphere. He offered her a reward if she could find out any thing about me. I know not what was the nature of her reply; but he soon after started for New York in haste, saying to his family that he had business of importance to transact.

.   .   .   .

Autumn came, with a pleasant abatement of heat. My eyes had become accustomed to the dim light, and by holding my book or work in a certain position near the aperture I contrived to read and sew. That was a great relief to the tedious monotony of my life. But when winter came, the cold penetrated through the thin shingle roof, and I was dreadfully chilled. The winters there are not so long, or so severe, as in northern latitudes; but the houses are not built to shelter from cold, and my little den was peculiarly comfortless. The kind grandmother brought me bed-clothes and warm drinks. Often I was obliged to lie in bed all day to keep comfortable; but with all my precautions, my shoulders and feet were frostbitten. O, those long, gloomy days, with no object for my eye to rest upon, and no thoughts to occupy my mind, except the dreary past and the uncertain future! I was thankful when there came a day sufficiently mild for me to wrap myself up and sit at the loophole to watch the passers by.

XXIII
Still in Prison

. . . .

I suffered much more during the second winter than I did during the first. My limbs were benumbed by inaction, and the cold filled them with cramp. I had a very painful sensation of coldness in my head; even my face and tongue stiffened, and I lost the power of speech. Of course it was impossible, under the circumstances, to summon any physician. My brother William came and did all he could for me. Uncle Phillip also watched tenderly over me; and poor grandmother crept up and down to inquire whether there were any signs of returning life. I was restored to consciousness by the dashing of cold water in my face, and found myself leaning against my brother's arm, while he bent over me with streaming eyes. He afterwards told me he thought I was dying, for I had been in an unconscious state sixteen hours. I next became delirious, and was in great danger of betraying myself and my friends. To prevent this, they stupefied me with drugs. I remained in bed six weeks, weary in body and sick at heart. How to get medical advice was the question. William finally went to a Thompsonian doctor,[1] and described himself as having all my pains and aches. He returned with herbs, roots, and ointment. He was especially charged to rub on the ointment by a fire; but how could a fire be made in my little den? Charcoal in a furnace was tried, but there was no outlet for the gas, and it nearly cost me my life. Afterwards coals, already kindled, were brought up in an iron pan, and placed on bricks. I was so weak, and it was so long since I had enjoyed the warmth of a fire, that those few coals actually made me weep. I think the medicines did me some good; but my recovery was very slow. Dark thoughts passed through my mind as I lay there day after day. I tried to be thankful for my little cell, dismal as it was, and even to love it, as part of the price I had paid for the redemption of my children. Sometimes I thought God was a compassionate Father, who would forgive my sins for the sake of my sufferings. At other times, it seemed to me there was no justice or mercy in the divine government. I asked why the curse of slavery was permitted to exist, and why I had been so persecuted and wronged from youth upward. These things took the shape of mystery, which is to this day not so clear to my soul as I trust it will be hereafter.

1. Practitioner of the curative method patented by Samuel Thomson (1769–1843), a botanic physician. The spelling is erroneous.

*Linda remains in the attic area with only brief respites in the store-
room. Although Sands has promised to free William and the children,
he has not done so. When he goes North, taking William with him,
William escapes to freedom. Later Sands, who was elected to Congress, takes Linda's daughter Ellen with him to Washington and then
sends her to Brooklyn to live with a cousin. The night before Ellen's
departure for Washington, Linda risks going to her old room and having Ellen brought to her. The child never breathes a word to anyone,
even her brother, about having seen her mother.*

*After remaining seven years in the shed, Linda receives word
through a friend Peter that there is a way for her to escape to the
North by boat. She takes leave of her son and grandmother.*

XXIX
Preparations for Escape

.   .   .   .

I made all my arrangements to go on board as soon as it was dusk. The
intervening time I resolved to spend with my son. I had not spoken to
him for seven years, though I had been under the same roof, and seen
him every day, when I was well enough to sit at the loophole. I did not
dare to venture beyond the storeroom; so they brought him there, and
locked us up together, in a place concealed from the piazza door. It was
an agitating interview for both of us. After we had talked and wept together for a little while, he said, "Mother, I'm glad you're going away. I
wish I could go with you. I knew you was here; and I have been *so* afraid
they would come and catch you!"

I was greatly surprised, and asked him how he had found it out.

He replied, "I was standing under the eaves, one day, before Ellen went
away, and I heard somebody cough up over the wood shed. I don't know
what made me think it was you, but I did think so. I missed Ellen, the
night before she went away; and grandmother brought her back into the
room in the night; and I thought maybe she'd been to see *you*, before she
went, for I heard grandmother whisper to her, 'Now go to sleep; and remember never to tell.'"

I asked him if he ever mentioned his suspicions to his sister. He said
he never did; but after he heard the cough, if he saw her playing with
other children on that side of the house, he always tried to coax her
round to the other side, for fear they would hear me cough, too. He said
he had kept a close lookout for Dr. Flint, and if he saw him speak to a
constable, or a patrol, he always told grandmother. I now recollected
that I had seen him manifest uneasiness, when people were on that side
of the house, and I had at the time been puzzled to conjecture a motive
for his actions. Such prudence may seem extraordinary in a boy of twelve
years, but slaves, being surrounded by mysteries, deceptions, and dan-

gers, early learn to be suspicious and watchful, and prematurely cautious and cunning. He had never asked a question of grandmother, or uncle Phillip, and I had often heard him chime in with other children, when they spoke of my being at the north.

I told him I was now really going to the Free States, and if he was a good, honest boy, and a loving child to his dear old grandmother, the Lord would bless him, and bring him to me, and we and Ellen would live together. He began to tell me that grandmother had not eaten any thing all day. While he was speaking, the door was unlocked, and she came in with a small bag of money, which she wanted me to take. I begged her to keep a part of it, at least, to pay for Benny's being sent to the north; but she insisted, while her tears were falling fast, that I should take the whole. "You may be sick among strangers," she said, "and they would send you to the poorhouse to die." Ah, that good grandmother!

For the last time I went up to my nook. Its desolate appearance no longer chilled me, for the light of hope had risen in my soul. Yet, even with the blessed prospect of freedom before me, I felt very sad at leaving forever that old homestead, where I had been sheltered so long by the dear old grandmother; where I had dreamed my first young dream of love; and where, after that had faded away, my children came to twine themselves so closely round my desolate heart. As the hour approached for me to leave, I again descended to the storeroom. My grandmother and Benny were there. She took me by the hand, and said, "Linda, let us pray." We knelt down together, with my child pressed to my heart, and my other arm round the faithful, loving old friend I was about to leave forever. On no other occasion has it ever been my lot to listen to so fervent a supplication for mercy and protection. It thrilled through my heart, and inspired me with trust in God.

Peter was waiting for me in the street. I was soon by his side, faint in body, but strong of purpose. I did not look back upon the old place, though I felt that I should never see it again.

After several narrow escapes, Linda reaches the North. There she is united with Ellen, and eventually the grandmother sends Benjamin to her. Even though all three are now in free territory, the Flints continue to pursue her. After nearly being caught, Linda agrees to let Mrs. Bruce, for whom she works, purchase her freedom from the Flints through their son-in-law Mr. Dodge.

XLI
Free at Last

.   .   .   .

Without my knowledge, Mrs. Bruce employed a gentleman in New York to enter into negotiations with Mr. Dodge. He proposed to pay three hundred dollars down, if Mr. Dodge would sell me, and enter into obligations to relinquish all claim to me or my children forever after. He who called himself my master said he scorned so small an offer for such a valuable servant. The gentleman replied, "You can do as you choose, sir. If you reject this offer you will never get any thing; for the woman has friends who will convey her and her children out of the country."

Mr. Dodge concluded that "half a loaf was better than no bread," and he agreed to the proffered terms. By the next mail I received this brief letter from Mrs. Bruce: "I am rejoiced to tell you that the money for your freedom has been paid to Mr. Dodge. Come home to-morrow. I long to see you and my sweet babe."

My brain reeled as I read these lines. A gentleman near me said, "It's true; I have seen the bill of sale." "The bill of sale!" Those words struck me like a blow. So I was *sold* at last! A human being *sold* in the free city of New York! The bill of sale is on record, and future generations will learn from it that women were articles of traffic in New York, late in the nineteenth century of the Christian religion. It may hereafter prove a useful document to antiquaries, who are seeking to measure the progress of civilization in the United States. I well know the value of that bit of paper; but much as I love freedom, I do not like to look upon it. I am deeply grateful to the generous friend who procured it, but I despise the miscreant who demanded payment for what never rightfully belonged to him or his.

I had objected to having my freedom bought, yet I must confess that when it was done I felt as if a heavy load had been lifted from my weary shoulders. When I rode home in the cars I was no longer afraid to unveil my face and look at people as they passed. I should have been glad to have met Daniel Dodge himself; to have had him seen me and known me, that he might have mourned over the untoward circumstances which compelled him to sell me for three hundred dollars.

. . . .

My grandmother lived to rejoice in my freedom; but not long after, a letter came with a black seal. She had gone "where the wicked cease from troubling, and the weary are at rest."

Time passed on, and a paper came to me from the south, containing an obituary notice of my uncle Phillip. It was the only case I ever knew of such an honor conferred upon a colored person. It was written by one of his friends, and contained these words: "Now that death has laid him low, they call him a good man and a useful citizen; but what are eulogies to the black man, when the world has faded from his vision? It does not require man's praise to obtain rest in God's kingdom." So they called a colored man a *citizen*! Strange words to be uttered in that region!

Reader, my story ends with freedom; not in the usual way, with marriage. I and my children are now free! We are as free from the power of slaveholders as are the white people of the north; and though that, according to my ideas, is not saying a great deal, it is a vast improvement in *my* condition. The dream of my life is not yet realized. I do not sit with my children in a home of my own. I still long for a hearthstone of my own, however humble. I wish it for my children's sake far more than for my own. But God so orders circumstances as to keep me with my friend Mrs. Bruce. Love, duty, gratitude, also bind me to her side. It is a privilege to serve her who pities my oppressed people, and who has bestowed the inestimable boon of freedom on me and my children.

It has been painful to me, in many ways, to recall the dreary years I passed in bondage. I would gladly forget them if I could. Yet the retrospection is not altogether without solace; for with those gloomy recollections come tender memories of my good old grandmother, like light, fleecy clouds floating over a dark and troubled sea.

Metta Fuller Victor (1831–1885)

One of the most prolific of nineteenth-century literary women, Metta Victoria Fuller Victor wrote over fifty novels, contributed frequently to periodicals, worked as an editor, and bore nine children. Victor was a "westerner" born near Erie, Pennsylvania, the daughter of Adonijah Fuller and Lucy Williams. She was educated at a female seminary in Wooster, Ohio, where her parents moved when she was eight. Victor started writing as a child; she was only thirteen when a local paper printed one of her stories, fifteen when the New York *Home Journal* began to accept her poetry on a regular basis.

In 1848 Victor moved to New York with her older sister, Frances, who was also an aspiring writer. Befriended by Rufus Griswold, N. P. Willis, and other editors, the sisters concentrated their efforts on poetry. They appeared as "Sisters of the West" in Griswold's well-known anthology *The Female Poets of America* (1848), and they were joint authors of *Poems of Sentiment and Imagination* (1851). But neither sister pursued a career as a poet. Frances Fuller married and spent most of her life in Nebraska, California, and Oregon, where she pioneered in writing histories of the West. Victor turned to fiction and quickly established herself as a best-selling author. She followed her first temperance novel, *The Senator's Son* (1853), with a second, *Fashionable Dissipations* (1854), and then an attack on polygamy and Mormon religion, *Mormon Wives* (1856).

She entered a new phase in her career in 1856 when she married Orville Victor, an editor and friend of Rufus Griswold. Orville Victor became the general editor of the famous series of "dime novels" published by Beadle and Adams: pocket-sized paperbacks that sold for a dime. They had to be short and simple, filled with adventure, and concerned with some aspect of American pioneer life. Any author in the series was guaranteed a vast audience in the 1860s and early 1870s, when the dime novels sold by the millions. Metta Fuller Victor wrote some of the most popular titles, such as Dime Novel No. 4, *Alice Wilde, the Raftsman's Daughter* (1860), and No. 10, *The Backwoods' Bride* (1861). Her most popular contribution was No. 33, *Maum Guinea, and Her Plantation "Children"* (1861), a tale of slave life that was praised by Lincoln and sold 100,000 copies.

In the 1870s Victor changed her subject matter and style to accord with public taste, just as she had done in each previous decade of her career. When the reputation of the dime novel declined, she wrote sketches and stories in a lighter vein. She exploited the popularity of humorous treatments of childhood with such works as *A Bad Boy's Diary* (1880), *A Naughty Girl's Diary* (1884), and *A Good Boy's Diary* (1885). Nevertheless, Victor failed to match her earlier successes. Even though many of her books were still in print at the time of her death, an obituary writer called her "comparatively unknown to the present generation."

Victor wrote under a variety of names, including George E. Booram, Corinne Cushman, Eleanor Lee Edwards, Walter T. Gray, Rose Kennedy, and Seeley Regester.

Selected Bibliography

OTHER WORKS
Miss Slimmen's Window (1859); *The Dead Letter* (1866); *The Blunders of a Bashful Man* (1881).

SECONDARY
Johannsen, Albert. *The House of Beadle and Adams*, 2:278–285. Norman: University of Oklahoma Press, 1950.
Simmons, Michael. "*Maum Guinea*: or, A Dime Novelist Looks at Abolition." *Journal of Popular Culture* 10 (Summer 1976–1977): 81–87.

The Senator's Son (1853)

The full title of Metta Fuller Victor's novel reads *The Senator's Son, or, The Maine Law; A Last Refuge; A Story Dedicated to the Law-Makers*. The subtitles would have made it clear to Victor's contemporaries that she was advocating total abstinence from alcohol. Maine had, in 1851, banned the sale of wine and strong liquors, and statewide prohibition laws came to be known as "Maine laws." Victor, like most temperance novelists, states her purpose explicitly in a preface to the novel; she hopes to portray "the mournful ruins of humanity, caused by Intemperance" in order to hasten "the ultimate triumph of the Maine Liquor Law, through the length and breadth of our fair land."

Modern critics like Edmund Pearson in *Queer Books* and Herbert Ross Brown in *The Sentimental Novel in America, 1789–1860* ridicule all temperance novels without exception simply because they advocate temperance. In Victor's time, however, the temperance movement was widespread. In the 1830s the American Temperance Union could claim a membership of some 5,000 local organizations and one and a half million individuals. By the 1850s there were at least fifteen strong temperance journals. Nor was Maine the only dry state; between 1850 and 1869, thirteen states, or more than one-third of the Union, adopted statewide prohibition laws. Temperance novels were an acceptable, indeed a preferred, form of propaganda for the cause. In 1836 the American Temperance Union formally endorsed fiction as a weapon in the movement. Victor was simply repeating a standard argument when she noted in her preface that the "evils of society" can be portrayed more effectively in novels than by "dull argument and dry statistics." Many well-known writers wrote fiction to advance the temperance cause. Walt Whitman contributed *Franklin Evans, or The Inebriate* (1842), and Timothy Shay Arthur, the most popular novelist of the 1840s, wrote several temperance stories. His *Ten Nights in a Bar-Room*, published the year after Victor's first novel, had a sensational success, its sales and notoriety in the 1850s being second only to *Uncle Tom's Cabin*.

The Senator's Son is a typical temperance novel. It has the usual "first glass to grave" structure (following the gradual downfall of the drunkard) and the usual authorial preaching interspersed with melodramatic incidents (most often violent deaths that are the result of drinking). Victor includes a good deal of violence, even though she avoids the more gruesome details found in some temperance novels, such as descriptions of alcoholics' deteriorating "innards" and accounts of their deaths by spontaneous combustion and other bizarre means; Brown notes one drunken character who stumbled into a ravine and "falling headlong he burst asunder in the midst, and all his bowels gushed out" (p. 220).

But if temperance novelists had some latitude in portraying the horrible effects of drinking, they needed to be careful when suggesting the causes. The connections Victor makes in the passages below between drinking and politics and drinking and the city are not atypical but press the point a bit strongly. Most temperance novelists advocated total abstinence from alcohol and believed abstinence could occur only if alcohol were unavailable, in other words, prohibited by legislation. Thus, one could not propose a simple cure like staying out of politics or living in the country. Victor gets around the problem by asserting that her protagonist, Parke Madison, cannot restrain himself when liquor is available anywhere. She represents alcoholism as an inherited disease; Parke's father was an alcoholic, so when Parke drank his first glass of wine at age four, he was doomed. At the end of the novel, Victor poses the question of what will happen to Parke's little son. Only if Maine laws win throughout the country, will he have a chance to escape his father's fate.

Victor does not consider the future of Parke's daughter, for she assumed, along with her contemporaries, that men drank and women suffered. It was clearly concern over the victimization of women and children that attracted women to the temperance cause. Men had launched the movement, and they controlled it until the second wave of temperance agitation after the Civil War and the founding of the Women's Christian Temperance Union in 1874. Women, however, began to join the movement in large numbers during the late 1840s and 1850s; the reason, Barbara Epstein argues in *The Politics of Domesticity*, was that the temperance question allowed women to discuss a range of issues about family life without challenging the family structure or attacking the male sex in general. The temperance issue highlighted women's vulnerable position within the family—their inability to protect themselves and their children from physical abuse, their lack of economic control, their frequent isolation and loneliness. *The Senator's Son* has Parke's wife Lucy facing all these problems, and in fact, the novel focuses less on Parke himself than on the ruin he inflicts on his wife, mother, sister, and daughter. In this emphasis on the female victims of male alcoholism, the temperance cause intersects with that of women's rights.

Parke Madison, son of a senator, drinks for the first time at age four when he gets into some wine left over from a dinner party. His mother stops serving wine, but the senator soon forces her to resume. While in Washington the senator drinks to excess and is murdered by another senator he had insulted when drunk. As Parke grows up, he drinks increasingly and is expelled from college. His mother dies, seemingly from anxiety, after having extracted a deathbed promise from Parke that he will remain sober. Parke's companions, especially a false friend named Alfred Clyde who loves Parke's sister Alice, tempt him into breaking the vow. When Parke is drunk, Alfred tricks him into forging a check and then threatens him with exposure unless Alice will save him. Alice has to marry Alfred and lead a miserable life. Parke reforms and marries Lucy Van Duyn; they have a daughter and move to the country, where Parke stays dry for four years.

CHAPTER IX

. . . .

It was a time of great political excitement. Parke, now developed into the full grown man, with established views and active purposes, was not contented with devoting all his energies, talents, and education to farming. Though his farm was a model, exhibiting all the latest improvements, and cultivated upon scientific principles; though it was the admiration of the country around, and though it brought him an income amply sufficient for a generous and elegant way of living, he was not content. He had plenty of leisure, since he was only the head, not the hands, of his farm, to turn his attention to other pursuits; and the Senator's son, following in the path marked out by his father, was fast becoming ambitious of political distinction.

His wife had a dread of this. To her, who had always lived in the country, there seemed no life so free, so happy, so virtuous, so healthy as country-life; no occupation so pleasant as the cultivation of land. She did not see how there could be any tameness, any want of variety in avocations which brought one continually to observe the changes and endless industry of nature. . . .

. . . .

. . . She thought that no one could accuse her husband of an inactive or useless existence if he employed it only in such occupations as their present position suggested. She had reason to dread his being drawn into political whirlpools. She was suspicious of the strength of his resolutions; and had no cause to think but that the country would be just as safe if her husband took no part in its debates. Feverish, unhealthy, and dangerous seemed to her the ambition which was coming over him; the country was safer without him than he was with it. Therefore, by all the tact and power of affection, she endeavored to divert his mind from its tendencies. But Parke was determined not to be satisfied with a wife, a baby, a home, and a farm. Politics seem in this country frequently to take the shape of a fever, which disturbs the quiet operations of the physical and mental powers, exciting the brain to a kind of delirium which for the time destroys its finely-balanced qualities. Mental blindness; a strange inability to discern truth from falsehood; an insane conception that our institutions are tottering into the gulf of their opponent's treachery, and will soon fall unless *they* rush to the rescue and make columns of support out of themselves; an itching at their fingers-ends to dabble in the spoils, and a burning desire for office, are some of the symptoms apparent in many of the victims of this disease.

The Senator's Son, or The Maine Law; A Last Refuge; A Story Dedicated to the Law-Makers (Cleveland, Ohio: Tooker & Gatchel, 1853), 291 pp. Excerpts are taken from 205–206, 209–213, 217–220, 222–231, 234–235, 267–271.

Parke Madison had not the fever in such a violent degree. He did not care about the emoluments, nor think the sudden dissolution of the Union at hand; but there were some principles he desired to see advocated, some more he wished to uphold; and as he felt himself competent to speak on certain questions, he was bound to make himself heard. The honor paid to the talents of his father encouraged him to believe that he could achieve eminence in the same path.

Upon the day which is introduced in the beginning of this chapter, he had gone to New York to join his party in a great outbreak of enthusiasm; he spoke, and was loudly applauded; the excitement of the day was followed by a supper given by the leaders to one of the great men, and to which Mr. Madison of course must remain.

The supper at the Astor was faultless, the wines were such as great men may drink without doing injustice to their taste, the remarks were profound, disinterested, and logical. Under the influence of the champagne and the speeches the country came very near being saved! But, alas, for one of its eloquent friends! Parke Madison, the generous, the witty, the earnest, the well-meaning, could control others better than he could himself. Forever striving after the right, and forever falling! That fatal weakness of resolution broke down this evening as it had done in days gone by. Not more surely will a moth always flutter into destruction when a lamp is by, than he would be tempted to excess by a scene like this. He knew it before he placed himself in the way of temptation; but his ardent temperament was already excited beyond prudence by the events of the day. He attended the feast given to the great man, and became intoxicated in his honor.

Lucy followed the suggestion of her house-keeper, and drank her tea, but it was with very little relish. She then returned to a charming employment, which was that of sketching little Carrie as she lay asleep in her crib. She was intending to surprise Parke with a birth-day present of the picture, painted on ivory, and handsomely set. The dimpled arm tossed up beside the rosy cheeks, the golden lashes, and the still more golden curls, the pouting, parted lips, made a fine subject for the mother artist. She drew the outlines and drapery, after which she laid her work aside in order to do the coloring by the nicer light of day. It was the usual hour of retiring; she no longer expected her husband that night, but she could not go to bed as long as there was a possibility of his returning. She hemmed a little on a piece of cambric, she played a short time on her guitar, she tried to get interested in a book, but her mind was uneasy, and she could not amuse it. At twelve o'clock, weary but nervous, she retired to short slumbers and disturbing dreams. It was her first night of watching for a dissipated husband, but it was not her last.

At noon, of the following day, Mr. Madison came home. He thought that his secret was safe from his wife. He greeted her gayly, and with many excuses for not sending her word that he should remain in town over night, he kissed Carrie, sat her upon his knee, and proceeded to astonish and delight her with the gift of her first doll-baby. But the quick eye of affection detected the lurking shame in his glance, its ear pined with the nervous hastiness of the first greeting; and in his kiss, despite of the frequent confection he had been eating, remained the feverish complaint of an ill-used stomach. Lucy kept her wretched discovery to herself, and abated nothing of her gentle welcome. She would not humble the pride of her husband, by allowing him to know that she was conscious of his error. But when she found him more absorbed than ever in politics, and bent upon walking right into the net—that he was restless until the next day came for a public excitement, and that he spent more than half of his time in the city, she was obliged to remonstrate. Such remonstrance might rather be called the very gentleness of entreaty. It was with threads of silver and gold that she endeavored to keep him within the sacred circle of home, where the evil genii that surrounded him in the outer air could not intrude.

The worm of the still, when its eye is once fastened upon a victim, must exercise a fascination more alluring than the dreaded enchantments of the rattle-snake. Else how could it draw Parke Madison, held back as he was by past experience, by a wife like Lucy, a sister like Alice; how could it draw him from the holiness of his hearth-stone, downwards to the old desperation of excess?

Upon that birthday, when Lucy designed to surprise him with the exquisitely-finished portrait of Carrie asleep, he came home, for the first time, in a disgraceful condition. Hitherto he had carefully remained away until in a fit state to return to his family. It happened that Mrs. Madison had company. Mrs. Van Duyn was out, with an old friend from Philadelphia, a lady of such mind and attainments as secured for her the love and respect of whatever circle she adorned with her presence. She had always made a pet of Lucy, who, in her girlhood, had once or twice visited her in her own city. Now she had come to see what kind of a home the fair girl had to boast of, what kind of a husband, and what kind of a baby; for she had heard a great deal about all of these, but she had not beheld with her own eyes the prosperity of this beautiful branch of the fatherland vine.

When they first arrived Mr. Madison was not at home. Lucy gave them a cheerful welcome. There was not even a shadow upon her brow that day, for Parke had been so good for the past week, and she had so pleased herself with thoughts of the present she had as a surprise for him, that her brown eyes were seldom brighter, or her cheeks more glowing.

.   .   .   .

The three ladies had such a social and happy afternoon, as confidential chit-chat among a kindly friend, a proud grand-mother, a joyous mother, and a good-natured little one ought to make. . . .

The lamps were lighted before the sound of a carriage rolling up to the door, and of steps in the hall, told Lucy that her husband had returned. A rich color rushed into her cheek, and her dark eyes lighted up. Mrs.

Smythe smiled secretly to observe the unconscious pride and brilliancy that came over her demeanor. Lucy was indeed proud of her husband, not only of his beauty and accomplishments, but of that eloquence of conversation and grace of manner which he had inherited from his father. She arose as he came into the apartment, but hesitated as she was about to advance to meet him.

"Lute, my love!" he began, in no very dulcet voice, "how do you do? Gen. Taylor will be President as sure as—ah! Mrs. Van Duyn!" he shook hands with her gaily.

She was astonished at his flushed face and disorderly air; but as Lucy made no move to do so, she presented him to her friend.

"Mrs. Smythe—Smythe! you are not the person who makes shirts for me, by that name? ah, no! I remember now—from Philadelphia? I beg your pardon—how well you are looking—extremely well! I think I never saw you looking so finely, Madam."

"I presume you never did," replied that lady, not daring to glance towards the young wife, whose face had grown pale, and who stood motionless as if from alarm.

He took a chair and sat down confidentially near her.

"Would you ever have thought Old Whitey's prospects were so favorable?" he asked, in a muddled tone. "I've a bet of two thousand against one thousand that he will never sit in the Presidential chair."

"I dare say you will win," replied his guest, a flash of humor breaking through her gravity. "We have never elevated horses to that dignity yet; though it has been aspired to by a still inferior animal."

"'My horse! my horse! a kingdom for my horse!' says Hudibras. So there, Madam, was a man who was willing to give his horse a kingdom, if we are not. But you are right, I intended to speak of Old Whitey—not his master."

"Ah?" was all his companion ventured to say.

Mrs. Van Duyn was sitting opposite, her face burning with indignation and surprise. Poor Lucy retreated into the nursery, where she sank down upon the bed, and burst into tears of mortification. Was this the husband she had arisen in such a glow of pride to present to her old friend? Bitter was her humiliation; but humiliation is not the worst suffering of a drunkard's wife; and if we pity her now, we shall have more to pity her for bye-and-bye.

"It seems to me that you are hardly yourself, Sir, this evening," observed his mother-in-law, coldly.

"Why—no—I am not. At least I thought that I was not a short time ago," he replied, looking at her comically. "I imagined that I was a bottle of champagne which the Whigs and Locos were playing a game of 'brag' for. As I was only a bottle of wine they thought nothing of my looking over, and from where I sat on the table, I could see the Old General cheating furiously: I tried to inflate myself enough to get the cork out of my mouth, so that I could cry out 'fraud! treason!' and in trying to do it I upset myself—crash! fizz!—I was a bottle of spilled champagne, not worth quarreling about. I had no hopes of ever getting myself together again, when John picked me up and put me, not in the broken bottle, but on my seat. You see, the roads were so confounded rough, and he had driven over a stone and jostled me off!"

He told this little story with great spirit. The two ladies glanced at each other as if not knowing whether to laugh or cry.

"Are you satisfied now of your identity?" inquired Mrs. Smythe, after a pause. "I suspect that you hold more champagne now than a steady, respectable bottle should do."

"You wrong me, Mrs. Brown," he replied, with an air of dignity that would have been superb upon a sober man. "There no doubt appears something peculiar in my manner, but it is owing to the excitement of the times. I have taken a glass once or twice to-day with a few of my friends—but the condition of our party demanded it. When the interests of the country are at stake a man must not stand—"

"Nor fall—" suggested Mrs. Smythe.

"There you have me again. You are witty, Mrs. Brown," with an admiring bow: "no, he must not fall, as I did once to-day; but he must not stand upon trifles. It is against my principles to touch any kind of intoxicating beverage. I swore to my dear Lucy, before I was married, that I never would 'toy with the dangerous flame;' did I not, my love?" he turned to where his wife had stood, but she was gone; "and I am bound to keep my promise sacredly after the first Tuesday in November. . . ."

Parke continues his drunken talk and then falls asleep during dinner.

Of course the presentation of the portrait had to be delayed until morning. Something of the mortification which had tortured Lucy the preceding evening was now endured by Parke, as he, with a faint recollection of his yesterday's absurdities, was obliged to be present at breakfast. He would have given half his farm to be a hundred miles away from the reproachful glance of Mrs. Van Duyn's eye, as she took his hand at meeting. He felt that he had wounded the mother through her child's heart—that beloved child whom he had taken from her, to cherish with a husband's fondness. Lucy was all kindness; and Mrs. Smythe appeared to have forgotten the manner in which their acquaintance was made. The remembrance to him was intolerable; hearing that the guests designed returning home that afternoon, he made an errand to town, that he might be relieved from that society which would have been so agreeable but two days ago; resolved not to return until they had departed.

There was a silent language in the embrace Mrs. Van Duyn gave her daughter at parting—unutterable love, the wish to avert danger, to protect from coming sorrow. It brought the quick drops to Lucy's eyes, but she bravely drove them back.

"Mrs. Smythe," she said, "you must forgive Mr. Madison for my sake. It is his first offence, and I am determined that it shall be his last."

She smiled, but it did not hide the quiver of her lips.

That night, again, Parke did not return home.

From that time began for Lucy Madison the untold miseries of an inebriate's wife. It had been hard and bitter for a sister to wear out the midnight hours in waiting—to wear out her hopes in watching—to wear out her heart in sorrow; but a sister's wretchedness cannot be that of a wife's. She looked upon her child with mingled feelings; it was her consolation and her trouble. Its pretty ways wiled her of many a weary hour; but thoughts of its future, as cursed by an unhappy father, gave her many another sleepless one. It was with no tender thrill of joy that she found, before the winter was past, that she had the promise of again becoming a mother. Ah, no! why should she desire children? that they might grow up ashamed, with an inheritance of vice? Her spirits ebbed to the lowest tide, but she never for a moment gave up to despair. Parke, wavering and unsteady as he was, could not have had a companion more purposed for his good. With all her affection, Lucy had her mother's indomitable soul, her noble pride and persevering energy. When she saw that he neglected his farm affairs, and that his carelessness was taken advantage of by his men, she, herself, stepped forward to the rescue of their falling fortunes, and made their people feel that there was still a head at work, if it was a woman's head. One third of their beautiful estate went immediately after election into the hands of those with whom he had betted. This loss was not sufficient to diminish any of their comforts—it only foreboded troubles that were yet to come.

A few months of dissipation produced their usual effects upon Parke. His nerves, unstrung by excess, grew irritable, and as a natural consequence his temper grew harsh and fretful. His remorse did not tend to sooth them, and the result was coldness and unkindness towards his wife. In vain she tried now to wile him back to his former self with the sweetness of her guitar, and the still softer music of her voice. In vain that she strove to keep him at home by making their artless daughter the pretty pleader. His every-day stimulus was brandy now; and it eat into his heart and brain as well as his stomach. It preyed upon those nice perceptions and glowing imaginations which once added such spirit to his character; it gnawed ceaselessly at those heart-strings once so finely strung to the lightest touch of love, until they mouldered one by one, and when Lucy would have wakened their melody as of old, there was silence where once was sweetest sound. It inflamed the coarser passions of his nature, those which could endure the fiery lash; but his more delicate sensibilities fell and perished under the infliction. There grew less and less in him to love. It was not only that harshness and moodiness repelled her affection; when Lucy looked for those qualities which had won her passionate regard, they were gone. Gone the soul-beaming glance—gone the glory and purity of intellectual gifts—gone the gentleness of manner—gone the playful fancy—gone the tender and reverential admiration of her wifely excellence! In their place, the sullen and abashed look, the dull and diseased mind, the reckless hardness of actions, the senseless gayety startling at times out of stupidity, the cowardly coldness on the maudlin caress.

It takes more than a few months of trial to wear out a woman's endurance. Lucy's devotion was more than ever, if her affection was somewhat less. She loved him for what he had been and for what she still hoped he would yet be. She loved him as the love of her youth, her husband, and the father of Carrie. A protector he had ceased to be, and had become instead a persecutor.

.   .   .   .

. . . God, who knows the heart, knows that Parke had hours of deep repentance, of mental agony; and that Lucy knew of these, and pitied while she blamed, and loved while she pitied. To others and to herself she urged, in extenuation, his inherited defects of energy and passion for stimulating drink, and they were good excuses as far as they went. She cried out as Parke's mother and sister, as he himself, had done—

"Since he cannot control himself, why is there no power that can be brought to bear to prevent this worst of self-murders?" In her anguish there was evidence that no sophistry, no policy of state, could refute. If any one had asked her in such moments "if the traffick in intoxicating drinks was an evil?" she would have gazed at him in astonishment. If he had went on with his questions and enquired "whether it was right to prohibit evil by law?" she would still have regarded these simple propositions, already decided in the hearts of every drunkard's wife and child and friend, and of every drunkard himself, as so established in the affirmative as to require no answer. She would not have stopped to enquire, "Will it add to or take away from the income of this Government?" but she would have stretched out her hands to the nation and cried,

"Give me my husband! give me back my husband!"

One pleasant day in September, Lucy sat by the window in that west room where Parke's mother had died, and which was always the pleasantest of summer rooms. In her lap was a variety of Carrie's out-grown baby-clothes which she was preparing for the expected little stranger. A tear would occasionally steal slowly down her cheek and drop upon her work, as she mused upon the past, and with what different and happier emotions she had first fashioned those fine cambrics, soft flannels, and dainty embroideries.

Carrie sat on a footstool by her side, with a huge needle, a long thread, and a wee-bit of cloth, taking her first lesson in the womanly-accomplishment of sewing.

Suddenly she hushed her childish prattle, for she heard her father coming around the portico with hasty steps.

"Curse it!" he was swearing to himself, "that dog Dixon has cheated me out of five hundred dollars—I know he has; and he's so cursed impudent about it, too! I'll not have him on this farm another year—no! he shall leave, if he goes to perdition!"

He came into his wife's presence and commenced his complaints. He was not intoxicated, though he had been drinking some. She ventured a remonstrance, when he swore that he would discharge his farmer; for she knew that Dixon would do better than anybody else, even if he did not always do right, and she told him so.

"What do you women know about that?" he asked, with contempt. "Here, Carrie, come to your father!"

Mrs. Madison thought that she had had good opportunities for learning something of his affairs, but she said nothing. Carrie was hiding behind her chair, regarding her father fearfully, one eye just visible through Lucy's net-work of braided hair. She hesitated to obey his command, which was spoken in no gentle tone.

"What are you skulking there for? are you afraid of me? This is some of your work, Mrs. Madison, teaching our child to dislike me! I will have no such actions in a daughter of mine. When I call her, she shall come; and without turning white, either."

He was terribly out of humor, and as he approached the trembling little girl, Lucy was afraid that he would lay violent hands upon her. She stood up, and pushed Carrie behind her.

"Parke! what do you mean? I have taught your child no disobedience. You know very well that she has reason to be afraid of you. It is you who have taught her this fear."

"Is she to witness your disrespect, Madam, and to think that you are going to interfere with my commands?"

He put out his hand, not to strike, but to thrust her rudely to one side. In her present condition she was not strong; she staggered and dropped to the floor, bruising her temple against the window-casement. Ashamed and alarmed, her husband raised her, and found that she had fainted. At that moment his sister Alice confronted him. She had rode out from town upon horseback to enquire after Lucy's health, and coming silently up the greensward had dismounted and entered the house without being perceived. She stood in the door during this brief scene. When she stepped forward to the wife's aid, her face was colorless, and her eyes flashed with a fire that had never been kindled in their depths before.

"Go!" she said, in a clear, ringing voice, "leave her with me! You are unfit to render assistance here."

She took the sufferer from him, as if she had the strength of a giant, laid her tenderly upon the lounge, dipped her handkerchief in a pitcher of ice-water which stood upon the table, bathing that bruised forehead and wiping the blood which trickled slowly from the temple. He lingered until Lucy opened her eyes, and then retreated from the room. With mechanical composure, Alice continued her efforts, until consciousness had fully returned and Lucy made an effort to sit up.

"I am not hurt," she said, "I was only stunned for a moment. He did not intend to hurt me—I know he didn't—but I was so weak. Now, Alice, do not tell mother."

Alice upbraids Parke and insists on taking Lucy to her mother.

By her directions the family carriage was prepared as comfortably as possible, and Lucy placed therein. Carrie and a trunk of clothing followed. Lucy was loth to go. She felt as if she ought to go, out of consideration for her own comfort; but she could not endure to leave her husband to his own unhappy society. Parke saw them depart from the parlor-window; Alice riding her pony close by the carriage, looking in and talking to its occupants. Should he let them go? it was his right and privilege to recall his wife and child and compel them to obedience. The terror which came over him when he saw Lucy lying senseless before him, recurred to his mind; how should he answer for himself, that to-morrow he might not again be as much of a brute, or perhaps a murderer? How could he give surety for the conduct of a madman? and did he not make a madman of himself every day?

He turned from the window, as the carriage slowly rolled away, and walked rapidly back and forth, such fire scorched his brain, such red shapes swam before his eyes, such hideous images thronged his mind, that he was seized with a fear of a drunkard's mania. Was *that* madness coming upon him, too? with a cry between a groan and shriek he rushed out of the house and ran towards the grove. Anywhere, anywhere, out into the open air where no eye could behold him, nor ear take note of his distress. He fled along; in gaining the grove, he had to cross the stream which wound through the meadow. Late rains had swelled it to quite a little river. As his foot lingered on the log which spanned it, a new sound confused him—"Anywhere—anywhere *out of the world!*" rang through his ear; he obeyed the cunning suggestion and sprang into the stream. He fell face downwards, sank, and rose again struggling. He struck out his hands, but they clutched not even a straw. Demons were shouting in his ears and sitting upon his breast. Off! off! would they not release him from their dreadful weight upon his bosom? no! they laughed and roared, and their pressure grew intolerable. Then they slowly swam away, leaving him floating upon a cloud airily through the sky, and Lucy singing her cradle-songs to Carrie, close by his side.

Parke loses the farm and Lucy's baby dies. Parke reforms again and is reunited with Lucy and Carrie. They move West, where Parke resumes drinking and Lucy has to support the family by painting. A son is born. When Parke, in a drunken rage, throws a kettle of boiling water and badly burns Carrie, Lucy and the children leave him for good. Parke becomes a vagrant and dies during a fit of delirium tremens. On the election day shortly before his death, he is asked whether he intends to vote for the Maine law.

CHAPTER XI

. . . [Parke's] countenance had a pallor and ghostliness unlike the bloated red of his companions. He was leaning against an awning-post when they addressed him; he straitened himself up and advanced a step or two; a flush came into his haggard cheeks, and he spoke in a clear, round tone which startled them.

"I am no longer fit to address gentlemen; but if you wish to know whether I intend to vote for the Maine Law or not, I answer that if I live to go to the polls again, I shall vote for it. Do you want to know my reasons? I, too, have spent my three hundred a night on champagne-suppers—I say it to my disgrace—not boastingly. I was intended to be a pretty fine man! God gave me talent, an eloquent tongue, and a generous, affectionate heart. He gave me, too, a christian mother, and a sister!—a sister worthy of the best man that ever lived. My father bequeathed me wealth and a good name. But he bequeathed me, too, that weakness which made him "tarry long at the wine," and which, at last, led directly to his murder, as some of you may have heard. Well! what has this inclination led me into? After years of ambitious study it sent me disgraced from college—it led me into all the accompanying temptations of a city, and destroyed my mother's health with anxiety and sorrow. Upon that beloved mother's dying requirement I vowed to never again taste wine, and it led me to break that vow. It led me to commit forgery; and that beautiful, that angelic sister of whom I scarcely dare speak, to save me from a prison, made the sacrifice I demanded of her, and married the villain in whose power I was. I wooed and won a noble, true-hearted and lovely woman, and it led me to blast her happiness, to inflict upon her poverty, disgrace, and wordless wretchedness—it led me to nearly murder my only and innocent little daughter; she wears upon her once charming face the scars which tell of a father's fiendishness. This passion has made a pauper of me; it has caused me to break the most powerful chains that were ever woven by the love of friends, the pride of position, the desire to be a good man; it has brought me days of anguish, such as I pray God none of you may ever feel; it has gnawed my heart out with remorse, and yet drawn me on with its burning fascination into this depth of degradation. It has killed my pride—destroyed my intellect—hardened my heart—ruined my soul! In my extreme youth, when I lifted the sparkling goblet to my lips, I laughed and said—"I can take care of myself!—it is nobody's business but my own!" *Now*, I would go down on my knees to the world if it would stretch out its hand and save me. I ask of the law, of you who make the law, to save me from this monster which preys upon human hearts. Hercules was sent out to slay the Nemean lion, and to kill the dreaded boar of Erymanthus, but what were their ravages to that of this passion for strong drink, that such thousands of your fellow-creatures have to struggle with![1] Will you

1. Parke refers here to the Twelve Labors of Hercules. Punished with temporary insanity by the Goddess Hera, Hercules killed his wife and sons. To remove his guilt he

aid them? will you send out the Hercules of the law to protect them? or shall they all perish, as I am perishing? Heaven knows I have fought until I have fainted many times, and yet I am a victim. You may throw a class of men out of employment, but if they make their living out of the blood and tears of the hearts of wives and children, why should they not abandon the unholy work, and turn to more righteous gains? The serpents prey upon frogs, the frogs upon spiders, the spiders upon flies, but need man to prey upon the weaknesses of his brothers, in order to find food? If you throw this grog-shop across the way out of business, and in return gain three honest, industrious, and peaceable citizens, who are now its patrons and the pest of society, can you answer whether you gain or lose? You may say that rich men can procure their costly wines and privately poison themselves, and teach their children to do the same, even if you should have this law. The rich are not the largest class of any community; and if they refuse to be benefited, shall the other classes all suffer for want of that protection which their need demands? When they have sunk as low as I, they will not refuse this rope which is thrown to keep them from drowning. If every man in this State, who could not pay five dollars for a bottle of wine twice or thrice a week, was to stand up with steady hand, undimmed eye, clear voice, and dignified demeanor, before the rich, free from all marks of this vice, those who now grow pompous over their costly decanters, would be ashamed of the wine-odor in their breath and its flush upon their cheek.

"Speak! gentlemen, I cannot speak what I feel! My mother is dead—my sister's heart is broken—my wife has gone from me to struggle alone against poverty and woe—my children are afraid of me—they tremble at the mention of my name—they too are gone, and I am left to my fate. My fortune is gone—my health is gone—my religion, my talents, my happiness. It is this passion which has stolen all; now that I am weak and forlorn, incapable of taking care of myself, have you not the heart of humanity enough to try to obtain for me my rights? I charge you to do it! in the name of all the misery I have inflicted and endured—in the name of christian charity—in the name of a DYING SOUL!—will you serve me? Will you save my soul? I know that Satan is bound to obtain it; he has visited me as plainly as ever he did the disordered fancy of Old Peter; but if you do your best you may cheat him of his gains. Will you do it?"

He stretched out his hands for a moment.

As a lamp that has burned nearly out suddenly lifts itself into temporary brilliancy, after it is apparently extinguished, his mind had once more startled into life. The group regarded him with astonishment. He had not made exactly that expression of his sentiments which they an-

---

was given twelve all-but-impossible tasks, among which were to kill the Nemean lion and the boar of Mount Erymanthus; to bring back the stag with the golden horns, the Minoan bull, the mares of Diomedes, the Golden Apples; and to clean the Augean stables in a day.

ticipated. The flame blazed up a moment, betraying the shattered and ruined condition of the lamp, and sank back into darkness. His strength was overtasked by the sudden excitement, and, as his arms fell to his side, he dropped fainting to the ground. After the little tumult attending his recovery had subsided, the crowd dispersed, satisfied for that day with what they had heard about the Maine Law.

Caroline Chesebro' (1825 – 1873)

Among the women writers of the 1850s, Caroline Chesebrough, or Chesebro', the name under which she wrote and is known, is something of an enigma. Although she never attained a large following, she succeeded in keeping her fiction before the public for a twenty-year period, won favor with the better critics of the times, and still arouses interest in readers who come across her work today.

Biographers provide slim information about Chesebro'. They identify her parents as Nicholas G. and Betsey Kimball Chesebrough of Canandaigua, New York, where Chesebro' was born in 1825. Chesebro' received her education at the Canandaigua Seminary, began writing stories and articles for *Graham's* and *Holden's Dollar Magazine* in 1848, and subsequently placed work in *Harper's, Putnam's, Knickerbocker, Atlantic Monthly,* and *Appleton's Journal.* Within a score of years, she produced twenty volumes of fiction, including short stories and novels for both young readers and adults.

Chesebro's first volume of fiction, *Dream-Land by Daylight* (1852), contains stories previously published in magazines. The critic who reviewed the volume for *Harper's* (February 1852) saw in her work "unmistakable evidence of originality of mind, an almost superfluous depth of reflection for the department of composition to which it is devoted" (p. 274). But he thought her lack of grace and fluency would make her unpopular.

Boldness of subject matter marks all of Chesebro's early works, especially *Isa, a Pilgrimage* (1852), excerpted here. In *The Children of Light* (1853), also unorthodox, two strong women—one a traditional and one a "new" woman—finding that the men in their lives prefer passive and pliable mates, turn to each other for support. *Getting Along: A Book of Illustrations* (1855) examines the motivations underlying women's commitment to marriage. It is intended to illustrate how men seek to dominate the women in their lives, especially if those women are gifted, and how women dedicated to others can find a life of service rewarding only if the work they undertake is satisfying.

After the appearance of *Philly and Kit* (1856), Chesebro' retired from publishing for seven years. By 1863, when she brought out *Peter Carradine, or The Martindale Pastoral,* Chesebro' seems to have come to terms with the views of her time. Gone are the radical ideas of her earlier works, as she presents women finding happiness in service while impressing their moral visions on the world around them.

Chesebro's fiction for young readers follows conventional patterns of the 1850s. The children suffer from homelessness, poverty, and spiritual and emotional deprivations. One of the most intense stories, "A Story of a Cross," dramatizes a child's emotional speculation about her own cross as she watches shadows forming crosses on the walls of her room.

Chesebro' remained unmarried throughout her life and spent her last eight years teaching rhetoric and composition at Packer Collegiate Institute, Brooklyn, New York. During this period she lived with her brothers and sister at Pierpont on the Hudson, where she died in 1873.

Selected Bibliography

OTHER WORKS

The Little Cross-Bearers (1854); *The Beautiful Gate, and Other Stories* (1855); *Victoria, or The World Overcome* (1856); *The Sparrow's Fall* (1863); *Amy Carr* (1864); *The Fishermen of Gamp's Island* (1865); *The Glen Cabin* (1865); *The Foe in the Household* (1871).

SECONDARY

Baym, Nina. *Woman's Fiction.* Ithaca, N.Y. and London: Cornell University Press, 1978.

Brown, Herbert Ross. *The Sentimental Novel in America, 1789–1860.* Durham, N.C.: Duke University Press, 1940.

Douglas, Ann. *The Feminization of American Culture.* New York: Alfred A. Knopf, 1977.

Hart, John Seely. *A Manual of American Literature.* Philadelphia: Eldredge and Bros., 1873.

"Literary Notices" [Review of *Dream-land by Daylight*]. *Harper's* 4, no. 20 (February 1852): 274.

"Literary Notices" [Review of *Isa, A Pilgrimage*]. *Harper's* 4, no. 24 (May 1852): 853.

[Obituary—Caroline Chesebro']. *Packer [Institute] Quarterly*, 1873: 90–95.

Isa, A Pilgrimage (1852)

Isa, a Pilgrimage, Caroline Chesebro's first and most daring novel, opens with a situation that might have made it a best seller: an orphan rescued from the poorhouse is growing up as the favored child in a comfortable household; she displays uncommon intellectual, physical, and personal gifts and is winning the love of her patron's son. But here Chesebro' departs from the pattern and turns her novel into what the *Harper's* (May 1852) critic called a "successful specimen of a quite difficult species" but a "too sombre creation" (p. 853).

Chesebro' depicts Isa as a freethinker who reaches that philosophical stance while living in a devout household where the son is a ministry student. Isa's turn from religion to rationalism subsequently leads her to socialism, feminism, and rejection of the marriage contract. Chesebro' heightens Isa's iconoclasm by contrast, introducing a sub-plot. Mary Irving, another gifted woman, follows the traditional religious path, remains faithful in marriage despite temptations, and apparently dies a Christian martyr.

Structurally, the novel combines sections from Isa's journal, the journal of Weare Dugganne (the son of her patron), and third-person narration. The juxtaposition of these differing points of view does not seem as unusual today as it did in 1852, but it complicates the novel, forcing the reader to shift perspective in order to perceive the author's intent. Chesebro' wishes the reader to see Isa as a clear-thinking woman who refuses to be molded by traditional religious, social, and political thought, a woman strong enough to follow through on the choices she makes and sufficiently gifted to succeed in a male-dominated world.

In only one way does Isa seem no better off than her traditional counterpart: she substitutes her philosophical mentor and lover Alanthus Stuart for the Christian God. With this exception, Chesebro' draws Isa as a woman of the future; she presents her as a person who consciously works for a society that will nourish women, one who sustains her vision of the strength of the human will with more hope than most Christians face heaven.

Before dubbing *Isa* "sombre," the *Harper's* writer gave it a sensitive reading. He found Isa's pilgrimage centered on "an abnormal spiritual experience, showing the perils of entire freedom of thought in a powerful, original mind, during the state of intellectual transition between attachment to tradition and the supremacy of individual conviction." He praised Chesebro's firmness in handling "the interior world—the world of consciousness, of reflection, of passion." John Seely Hart included Chesebro' in the 1873 edition of *A Manual of American Literature,* noting her insight into human emotions. But critical recognition did not make *Isa* popular. Chesebro's bold thought and unorthodox style were simply premature.

The novel opens with Isa Lee's journal account of her adoption from the poorhouse by Mrs. Dugganne and her son Weare. From her earliest consciousness, Isa senses her difference from others. But in the generally favorable conditions of the household, she develops quickly. Mrs. Dugganne teaches her to read and to fill the daughterly role. Occasional visits by Mr. Dugganne, a drunkard, frighten Isa but do not retard her progress. His early death benefits the entire family. Under Mrs. Dugganne's tutelage, Isa advances both spiritually and intellectually. In an early journal entry she analyzes her relationship to Mrs. Dugganne and Weare.

CHAPTER I

". . . I am certainly to her now, and always have been, to some extent, a daughter. The service demanded of me is only such as might be asked of a daughter, less than is required of many a child, and I am well aware that many a daughter has never felt the love, the filial gratitude, which the love and friendship of Mrs. Dugganne has inspired in me. I must, in some sense, have taken the place of a child in her heart, or she could never have done for me all she has. I do not well understand how this relationship existing between us now, was brought about. Did she, on the day of my great rescue from that first remembered home, design this high place for me, or rather me for it? I know, or, at least, it is in my power to conceive, how, once entered into, this relation maintains itself. But what good angel inspired her at first (before she knew me for what I am) with the belief that I was worthy of exaltation into her love and favor? Weare Dugganne, could you not answer me? Has the mother, in her maternal fondness, looked through your eyes? Has she reposed confidence in one whom she believes her son trusts to the utmost? Can it be so?—

"We were always much together, Weare and I. She never obstructed our intercourse. It early grew to be as free as that existing between brother and sister; yet it was not such—no, for we have made a study of each other's nature and character as brothers and sisters never do, in a wholly critical mood. They, I believe, are content to love with the heart—they do not call in the aid of the understanding. After all, we were never as brother and sister.

.   .   .   .

I have not given him the affection called fraternal—or not that merely: I never have found myself voiceless, will-less, trembling before him, as

Isa, A Pilgrimage (New York: Redfield, 1852), 320 pp. Excerpts are taken from 34–35, 37–40, 42–43, 45–46, 55, 139–143, 160–166, 169–171, 181–183, 312–314, 316–320.

though I had in him a master—as it is said women often find to be true
of the men they love. I believe, indeed, that when we were younger, I
could understand him much more readily and intimately than now; for
since my own knowledge of self, and this new ambition has roused to
life within me, and my nature has begun to unfold itself from the very
Heart of Life, I have found myself at times looking with wonder on him.
It almost seems as though I had passed beyond him—as though I were
standing in a new light—as though, in looking backward and forward, I
were gazing through a new medium, and not with my old understanding. An impeding something—and what, what is it?—has grown up
within me. I do not see, as once, with his eyes. There seems to be a necessity laid upon us, compelling us to differ. We certainly are not one.

"At my dear mother-friend's suggestion, which she gave, I know, because she perceived my earnest inclination, I have begun to read more
closely, to study more intensely, and there has been, in consequence, an
entire change in the current of my thoughts. Is it because they rest less
often on him, the real, and turn more frequently to the imaginative and
the abstract? Are my thoughts, then, becoming alienated from him? Nay!
Could ambition destroy love?

. . . .

Our ambition, I am convinced, became first aroused in these multi-
tudinous discussions—my ambition rather. I am not certain that he has
what is called ambition; but there has certainly been with both of us an
earnest and an honest desire to improve ourselves. An unbounded desire
to learn all things has marked my way as a student thus far, and so it has
marked his. The attainments we made, of themselves, served to excite
us mutually.

"We have had extraordinary discussions; and some of them of such a
nature that they must with us be endless. Our restlessness has done for
each other that which time usually accomplishes for the student. We
have developed each other's intellects, have forced each other on to con-
clusions we might otherwise have been years in reaching; and now, here
I have fallen on this word, this strange word, LOVE . . . !

"Baffled and awed by its mystic sound, my heart, soul, and mind, repeat it, hour by hour. I can not make out the meaning of the word when
it points toward him. Why have I not, or rather, why can I not, why
should I not, go to him, and argue, as in other matters, about its nature?
Why is it, that we have never once by chance, touched on this word love,
LOVE?"

*Weare, writing in his journal, comments on Isa's ambition. He wor-
ries about it, fearing that she has totally lost her faith.*

CHAPTER II

. . . .

"What surprises me, of all things, is Isa's entire consciousness of ability. This does not reveal itself, as ordinarily in boys and girls, by an obtrusive self-confidence, but in a never-failing readiness to attempt all things. There is no shrinking back. Yet it is not boldness in any common presentiment. The working of this girl's spirit is a phenomenon.

"I begin to think her ambition exceeds all I have ever observed in my contemplations of human nature. It is not of the usual nature of ambition, but of a spirit that strikes me as almost unpardonable in a woman. I am convinced, however, that her aim is not simply to exceed others; or, at least, it is not so much that, as an endeavor to educate every power and capacity of her mind. To strengthen it to the utmost possible degree, is her endeavor. Every day proves it; by incessant vigilance she is learning to master herself; is she doing this that she may in turn master others? Mother would smile at the apparent absurdity of such a question relative to a girl of eighteen years; but is it an irrelevant or idle question when connected with Isa? She surprises every one by her diligence, and the celerity with which she masters the principles of whatever comes under her notice. I am well convinced that few things or ideas within the grasp of mortal mind are too deep for her. It would seem a happy thing for her, had she less of talent, or less of beauty; but it could not be the wish of any wise person to repress the unfoldings of her genius, or to repel her to a lower grade of society again; indeed, she could not be repelled, save by miracle.

. . . .

"We were conversing of the government of God (and it is singular that she should so persist in discussing such a point); in the excitement of our conversation she called me puritanic, and asked me why it was that I suffered myself to be bound by 'such exceedingly narrow, timid views,' as I always advanced—why I did not at once give myself liberty of unlimited range of vision, and, without fear, study and search into all things. I knew very well what she meant, and exclaimed solemnly, 'What! the deep things of God? There is a bar across that path. We must not go beyond it. We have no right to attempt to penetrate the Holy of Holies. We must not seek to pierce that veil which in mercy to our weakness, screens the presence and the power of Jehovah.'

" 'It is a cowardly argument at best,' she replied with emphasis. 'There is no limit given but that which our own will regulates. No other voice than man's own mental capacity, ever said, *thus far, no farther.* I can readily imagine how one with sufficient perseverance, energy, and courage, might pierce and solve all mystery, and stand, yes, even in the flesh, stand face to face with spirit.' "

. . . .

"'And have you gone so far as to question God? Will he be inquired of by creatures such as we? Isa, this human life will not see the termination of our grand duty of striving to enter in at the strait gate. It may not be till eternal ages have rolled on, that we shall in any degree accomplish that command, 'Be ye perfect.'

"'You assume one thing, and not another!—time, and not power! How ridiculous! how unjust! What right have you to assume one and not the other?'

"'A very clear right, Isa—that of reason.'

"'Well, what is reason?'

"'The light given us.'

"'What gives the light? who gives it? where does it come from?'

"'God.'

"She seemed not to hear my answer, but went on speaking with increased vehemence."

When Weare professes his love, Isa, who is determined to become a writer, rejects him although she loves him. Shaken by her rejection, Weare attacks her heretical reading, especially her study of Alanthus Stuart's works, and her interest in the supremacy of the human will. Once she has achieved some success as a writer, Isa receives an invitation from Mr. Warren, the editor of the Guardian, *to make her home with him and his wife. In time Isa assumes co-editorship of the journal with Stuart. At a party, Mrs. Warren asks Isa's help in arguing for women's rights with General S——, a prominent political figure.*

CHAPTER IX

.   .   .   .

". . . Isa—Miss Lee, your aid! We must be slaves, or else put down as mischief-makers, must we! Why, looking upon it only in one light, what a breach of gallantry is such a statement as that!"

Isa would fain have replied in the same gay strain these friendly combatants had used, but she felt it to be impossible. To this very subject her attention had in divers ways been directed, her soul had been wholly and earnestly roused by it. And, notwithstanding, she had heard it discussed and supported by ignorant fanatics, though she had seen such agitators exposing themselves to just and scorching ridicule, her eyes had nevertheless been keen of sight to pierce through all masqueradings; she had seen what woman's wrongs were, and knew how they were borne, and so she felt herself compelled to say, gravely:—

"When such a subject is brought up for discussion, I never can speak excepting with earnestness. I must honestly say what I think. Pardon me, Mrs. Warren, for being so miserable a champion—but you know I have but recently come into the field—and I would be prudent—I had rather not commit myself."

"In short, you won't combat!" exclaimed Mrs. Warren.

"What we *want*, is your honest opinion, young lady," said the old soldier, with bland dignity, and gallant kindness.

"Do speak, Isa," said Mrs. Warren; but just at that moment she was called away. An awkward silence ensued, during which her opponent was evidently expecting an answer. Isa struggled with herself as she noticed this, and finally managed to say:—

"It only seems to me, sir, that such a question as this of woman's rights, could never have been so fiercely agitated, so widely, and with such earnest force, if woman's wrongs had not in the first place suggested it."

"With all deference, madam, has not a little ambition among a few restless mortals set the ball rolling? Would you not find this to be the exact state of the case, if you looked thoroughly into it? It strikes me that this same ambition to get up excitement, and to keep it up, has kept this question in agitation so long—much in the way you know that our words affect the sea of air around us; as the naturalists say they do."

"A cause that is not supported by, or founded in a living truth, must die."

"Precisely; and may not that 'living truth' be just this: AMBITION? sheerest vanity? I confess to but little sympathy with fanatics myself. I believe there is no God, but God—but I'm not disposed to say that every new leader, party, or sect, produced, is his prophet."

"As any one may plainly see," pronounced the musical voice of Mrs. Roderick Irving, who just then joined them; "I see, moreover, that you have not the better part of this argument, General S——, which I am very glad to see. Can you not valiantly beat a retreat? If I am not mistaken, your opinions are fast getting to be mutinous! Are all your sympathies against the struggling, the poor, blind, struggling?"

"Yes, assuredly. What business have the blind to struggle? they must be led. And, moreover, Mrs. Irving, I never yet learned how to 'beat a retreat;' and you will agree with me I am quite too old to learn now. Continue the argument, Miss Lee," he said, with a tone and look, which had unconsciously become extremely commanding.

Isa had conquered the agitation which she felt at first, and she had taken a bold resolve to teach her listeners a lesson, if that, indeed, were possible.

"Was there ever a cause of vital importance," she asked, glancing from Mrs. Irving to the general, with a sincere and trustful look, "agitated among men and women, when some of its supporters did not carry their prejudices in favor of it to a fanatical extreme, or when some among its opponents did not carry their prejudices against it to as great an extreme? Notwithstanding all you say of ambition being the support of this cause, I must hold to the belief that you will never find an unimportant, weak, and causeless cause making such commotion among people, high and low, wise and ignorant, weak and clear headed reasoners. I do not think, sir, that it will be either in your power or your wisdom to affirm long, that this question springs from a trivial point. For my part, I am proud to confess to practical faith in the poet's assertion, that

> "Woman's best is unbegun;
> Her advent, yet to come!"

Isa's listeners had heard her with a courteous gravity and interest. The general, a great admirer of beauty wherever he found it, was thinking, while she spoke with such subdued yet evident enthusiasm, how very lovely she was, and Mrs. Irving listened with an emotion that almost betrayed itself in tears.

"Well said, Miss Lee! Now, general!" exclaimed Mrs. Warren, joining them at that moment.

"Your arguments are forceful, I admit it," said the old man, thus appealed to. "But, pardon me; what would your convictions in regard to this subject lead you *to do*, Miss Lee?"

"That I know not, as yet. My duty, I trust, as it should appear to me."

"Good! Your zeal is really according to knowledge. You will become no public lecturer; no ridiculous, ranting—"

"You forget. She has not promised as much. Besides, she does not need to be a lecturer. Miss Lee wields a pen!"

Isa develops a strong friendship with the gifted young singer, Mary (Mrs. Roderick) Irving. Mary, unlike Isa, lacks the courage to develop her talent and remain independent. Trapped in a loveless marriage, which she chose instead of a career, Mary feels degraded. She and Isa become close friends. Their conversations point up their likenesses and differences. Mary speaks.

CHAPTER XI

.   .   .   .

"I am glad you have discovered my soul's secret. But do not flatter yourself that such revelation of one's inner nature is only made in song. I too have looked into your soul. And I have frequently longed to tell you of it. I rejoice that you have placed yourself in a position that enables me to say this much to you without fear. Tell me, is there not one picture you are given to drawing, on which you invariably expend your utmost power?"

"What is it?"

"A struggling and lonely human heart, supported by WILL through the extremes of suffering and misfortune. Patient, content to struggle, determined to accomplish:—is not this your highest, most exalted idea of heroism? Oh, how I wish I had known you before—before it was too late!"

Mary spoke with startling vehemence, and her listener turned away to conceal her emotion, and her joy. She had not been deceived; that voice had in its tone of revealment, a

> "Behold, and see
> What a great heap of grief lay hid in me!"

She gave her hand to the timid questioner, who had suddenly become so bold, and said softly:—

"My sister—Mary."—

The words acted like a charm on Mary Irving. Her diffidence and hesitancy were thrown aside as a mask; the shadows which seemed for ever folding over her eyes—her sad, "pathetic eyes"—cleared away; there was sunshine in her face. Hastening to the piano, she poured forth her joy, not with words, but in a glad and solemn chant. As she turned again from the instrument, she threw herself at Isa's feet, and her heart sped through its open doors. She spoke with the utmost truth of word, look, and expression:—

"When compelled to make use of this gift as a means of living, I was weak; I faltered, fainted, failed, in my purpose. A door of escape opened. I rushed through it, never thinking or caring whether light or darkness were beyond . . I met my reward—I found that there are two kinds of poverty in this world, and that the last is infinitely worse than the first. Let no one say there is not a worse thing than hunger, and nakedness, and the isolation caused by such poverty. You do not believe that, do you?"

"So far from it, I know to the contrary; Mary I have tried both kinds of poverty."

"But—but—but—"

"Yes—" said Isa, as hesitatingly, interrupting her friend in the endeavor she was making to express the thought; "I *am* free, but as yet I am hardly convinced as to whether it is my salvation, or madness, and ruin, to be so."

"Think it is your salvation! Oh, believe it! Don't let your mind harbor another idea."

"Do you admire that character you say I am so given to drawing, of a struggling and patient heart?"

"Yes; as I admire the sketches of angels my own fancy furnishes. But it is so much easier to say than to do! Have you not always found it so? I have never encountered a perfect mortal yet, have you?"

"Yes—and one who had grown perfect through fiery trial."

"A woman then! I have a presentiment. Yet tell me, why do you so often represent woman as gifted especially with the hero nature?"

"Does not woman deserve to be so represented? Where, in this world, in this generation, will you find the spirit so alive—so thoroughly alive, as in her?"

"Alas, I do not know. I had almost begun to think that all sorts of heroism had died out from among us."

"Look about you—look within you! Look, but not with the eyes of sense—think of all that woman is doomed by nature, by society, by custom, to endure. Do you not see the evidences of a divine patience? and that you know is 'all the passion of great hearts.'"

"I grant it to a degree. I do see this 'divine patience.' I should feel proud, indeed, if I could see as you do, and so grant it wholly. But can one really do so who takes the present for what it is, unillumined by the great hope of what it will be? Only see of what society is made!"

"Yes—I do see. Society is a masked ball—and the music is discordant, and can hardly in this life be otherwise than so. But it may be less discordant, more harmonious. And the beatings of woman's heart must make it so; for these beatings give the key-notes to the tunes of life! You are not to judge, you know, by the triflers among women—say what people will, they are few in comparison with the earnest hearts, the striving minds, the effectual workers.

.   .   .   .

"Love is nothing, if it be not worship, you know," said Isa. Mary reflected a moment, and said:—

"Your pardon, but it strikes me love can exist, and yet be nothing *like* worship. How else can the unworthy be loved?—they *are* loved. No one would think of worshipping a bad man or a bad woman, while such may, after all, be the objects or recipients of very strong affection."

"Love is not animal passion; it is not that principle which leads people to live together oftentimes in perfect peace and comfort. Mary, love is not love, if it be not devotion."

"Then love is sinful—it must be so."

"Most assuredly not."

"What! Do you not believe that there is only One to whom worship should be rendered? Would you apply the same word to our bond of fellowship with man, and with God? A friend, a companion, a husband, or a wife, may be inexpressibly dear, may be necessary perhaps to the truest happiness in this life. It seems to me so. But how *can* you say that man or woman worship is not sinful?"

"I do not probably understand the word SIN in the way you do. For the rest, I should say such worship is not sinful, simply because—it is among the possibilities."

.   .   .   .

"Since not one in ten thousand, I will venture to say, ever conceived of marriage as you do, tell me, pray, what think you of the institution as a general thing?"

"We are progressive. The institution was well enough for the people of past ages; but its necessity and its power have gone by: it is, therefore, now become a bond too galling, too oppressive. In ninety-nine cases out of a hundred, people assuming matrimonial vows, especially women, sell their birthright of freedom for a mess of pottage. In its present state, as an institution, marriage is not a holy thing—it is an abomination."

"Tell me," said Mrs. Irving, with hesitating but painful earnestness, "if you were bound to another, and found out that the tie was for you an abomination, the covenant awfully ridiculous, what would you do?"

"Break the bond without delay. To me it would be a 'sin' to bear, or to endure it."

"Have you imagined what would ensue, if people dared to do this—if all dared who had the inclination, I mean?"

"No: when there is so much that must be thought of, it is scarcely worth while to brood over the effects of imaginary events. The earth, recollect, is peopled with cowards. If it were not so, if all bound in the shackles of marriage dared to speak, to break their bonds, to be free again, I suppose the very virtue that inspired the unhappy to free themselves, put into vigorous circulation by such act of voluntary divorcement, would of itself produce a better state of things."

"You do not reflect that the virtuous would hardly be swiftest to break such ties, even if the precedent were established."

"Yes, yes! I am sure of that. The vicious are weak, and it is not they who are oftenest truly and consciously unhappy."

"I have misunderstood you all along, then; you do not think it is a crowning glory to endure wrong patiently—to suffer and bear in quiet?"

"No, I have not affirmed that. We are constituted to enjoy intellectual freedom to the utmost. What were life worth to me—to you—without this consciousness? Would you exist without it? How can one enjoy this life himself, or promote any of its best interests, if a low, narrow, abominable, carking care, or grief, or oppression, of another's imposing, of a miserable domestic nature, is for ever souring the life, drying up the fountains of the soul—destroying her best powers—lowering, preventing, annulling her aspirations? How is one to learn, to discover and develop, the immeasurable capacities of the soul or heart, if a grief, that false pride makes nameless, is pressing continually upon it, hiding the light of truth from it, or utterly distorting it? If one would LIVE, one must have freedom. I can conceive of nothing called life worthy the name, without it. Annihilation were better than such existence."

During this period Isa becomes a committed socialist and takes Stuart as her political and philosophical guide. He seems to be the man-angel in a dream she once related to Mrs. Dugganne, who repeats it to Weare.

CHAPTER XII

.　.　.　.　.　.　.　.　.　.　.　.　.　.

"*She* called me *mother*, Weare, when she commenced telling it as she has several times of late. I was quite proud to hear her. 'Mother,' she said, 'I was out on a wild sea last night, in an awful storm. Such blackness of darkness! I could feel the darkness, and imagine how it might have been felt in Egypt. I was in a ship, pacing to and fro, when I heard a cry, suddenly. I ran with others to the deck, and saw a huge mountain bearing down directly upon us. If you could only conceive the confusion there was among us! the screaming, and praying, the rushing backward and forward across the ship!'—'And what were *you* doing all this while?' I asked. 'I caught hold of a spar, and then felt myself safe,' she said; 'so I stood and watched the coming of the iceberg. I never in my life saw anything so beautiful. All at once the clouds separated, the moon appeared, and flooded the immense mountain with light; it shone like a diamond in the light. I was so absorbed in its beauty that I entirely forgot the danger. Then, just as the vessel and iceberg came in contact, I saw a figure perched upon the summit of the ice. It looked like an angel—yet like a man; just as I caught sight of him, my eyes were riveted by his gaze—he seemed to be looking me through and through, with such eyes as I never saw in any human being's head. Then came the crash!—it seems to me now as though I heard distinctly as I did in the dream—three sounds, only three, the breaking of the ship—the one shout, GOD! that went up from the crowd on board like the appealing cry of an individual—the other sound . . it was the strangest burst of laughter, coming from the man-angel on the rock. As I floated away, his laugh seemed to run through me like electricity, and in a perfect ecstacy of joy, I joined him in the shout.'"

When the Guardian *is sold, Isa and Stuart continue their intellectual revolution by writing books. Isa's works become popular, but as their radical content increases, the critics condemn the "immoral and dangerous doctrines." Rejecting the institution of marriage, Isa and Stuart choose to live together, but social pressure forces them to seek peace abroad. Finally, Isa and Stuart return to the States, where Isa dies. When on her deathbed she experiences the iceberg dream again, Isa does not hear the laughter she had heard previously, for by this time even in her subconscious she regards the human as supreme and therefore not evil when it trusts itself rather than the deity. The question the reader faces at the end is whether Isa is right in her belief or whether she has been destroyed by Stuart, as Dugganne believes. Stuart and Isa converse for the last time.*

CHAPTER XII

.   .   .   .

"Isa," he said, "how marvellous a mystery is this life! Oh, that you might abide here yet longer! That we might together solve this wondrous problem! You and I have gone far; and it seems to me, that if we made but *one* other step of progress, our hands would rest upon the key, which, turned in its lock, would unveil to our eyes every mystery of nature. Remain with me! Go on with me! we have only begun to accomplish!"

He was endeavoring to perform a miracle by his own energy of will, communicated to gesture, voice, and glance—to arouse her, and restore her to health! And for an instant she did seem fired with new life; but it was only for an instant that they were unconscious of the madness of his words. She struggled to arise, but fell back in the endeavor. Looking up into his face, she smiled, and said: "Not yet; but together we *will* soon unveil the mystery! Stuart, do you believe that man will yet discover how to master death?"

"I have no doubt of it, Isa. This it is which makes the thought of parting with you terrible—this shocking waste of life! oh, to the future generations with whom death shall no longer be a necessity, but merely a choice, what madmen, what blind idiots, we shall seem."

"Stuart . . ."

"Well, Isa."

"Would death with you be a choice, if you became his master?"

"Yes," he answered her in deep emotion. "The world will have lost all its charm to me, Isa, when you go from it."

"But you will be content to labor still for the advancement of the people? You will not let your soul stay in its grand progress! You will not suffer your voice to fail, Stuart, you will not?"

"Not till I am lying here, in this room, upon this bed where you lie, my head upon this pillow that supports your head—then my voice may fail, my hand will falter, but my work will be all accomplished."

"Who will watch beside you then, as you watch over me?—who"—As she spoke, a light tap at the door was made. Stuart was so absorbed by her words that he did not hear it; but Isa caught the sound, and, thinking it was the physician or the servant, said, "Come in."

To their surprise a stranger entered; he was, however, no stranger to Isa, the dying woman: ay, though it was long since she had looked upon the figure that advanced into the room, muffled as it was against the cold, she knew Weare Dugganne, and a faint cry of surprise broke from her. He went up to her without ceremony, and said:—

"I heard you were ill, Isa. Forgive my coming here, if my presence pains you: I was compelled to come."

"You heard I was dying," she said, gazing on his care-worn and haggard face, not with the anxiety of one who longed to hear her conviction refuted, but with the steadfast, tender gaze of one who felt that she was looking on a long-absent and dear friend for the last time; then she added quietly:—

"It is strange that you should meet for the first time here to-night. He heard I was dying, and came! I hardly deserved as much from him. This is Weare Dugganne, Alanthus Stuart."

.   .   .   .

There was a silence, and the two men saw that rapid changes were passing in Isa: they saw it with emotion—what varied emotion! Her face grew very pale, and her body was in a constant shiver: yet she was not trembling with fear.

Stuart looked at Dugganne, and his glance had a world of meaning in it. He sat down on the bedside, and, taking Isa's hands in his, he pressed them fervently. She looked up into his face as if she understood his movement—as though his soul had asked her soul a question; and she said:—

"No, Stuart, I do not fear to die."

Yet to Dugganne she looked not so much like Isa, the fearless, dauntless woman he had known, as the confiding child whose teacher was beside her, and who had ceased to believe all save what that teacher told her.

"For the last time— —do you anticipate annihilation, Isa?"

He said it so tenderly that Weare could scarcely believe the words issued from him. He leaned forward, and looked with scrutiny on Stuart's countenance—and Stuart's face was not averted, but Dugganne was baffled in his attempt to read if this strange man were making of that death-hour a time for triumph over him. If Stuart were seeking to assure himself, or Isa, or to prove before him that the woman's faith was enough to die by, Dugganne could not tell.

"No," said Isa, in reply, "THERE IS NO ANNIHILATION. I have never for a moment imagined that there is. I am going within the veil—you will follow me. I shall wait just beyond the point on which your eyes are fixed now. I will not go further until you join me, Alanthus."

.   .   .   .

"Isa," said Stuart, "I will meet you THERE. We shall never be separated after that re-union. Perish the dream that death is anything but change! Long ago, I told you that I had my guardian-angel! She is being now withdrawn from the sight of these eyes, but to my inward vision she stands revealed for ever! You will not even for a second be conscious of separation, Isa; nor shall I. When others might because of their spirits' apathy, be conscious of loss, we shall be aware of immeasurable gain! I shall know of you as near—you will constantly behold your soul's husband and our child. You will be near me for ever and for ever. While I remain on earth, to guide and guard me, since our spirits are proved so inevitably ONE. We have never been so entire, complete an existent, as we yet shall be. Perfect, eternal, beautiful, shall our union be, my beloved, my beloved! In the day-time and the night, in bitterest need, in loneliness, in desertion, in danger, wherever I go, whatever I do, you will be with me! I am above the world!" His voice grew fainter, and lower; he bent over her more closely, and whispered in her ear while her eyes and her smile were upon him, until the beating of her heart was imperceptible, and he believed she breathed no longer. For a moment after he thought that she was dead his head bent upon her breast, but not one sigh escaped him—not one tear fell.

Suddenly she moved again; she looked upon Dugganne—her lips parted, and she cried out, "GOD!"

There was another apparent departure of the spirit, and another re-awakening—"STUART, LET US GO," she said softly, and her last look was a smile on him.

"Dugganne," Stuart said, at length, to the pale, motionless man beside him; "Dugganne, how beautiful is that change which we call death! I have lost her daily presence of the body—oh, how I have gained thus in nearness of soul! She is dwelling in me now! Our union is complete and eternal!"

He spoke as though forgetful of the thoughts and emotions which his heart-broken listener had so plainly revealed since he came there. And Dugganne passionately exclaimed in answer:—

"May God, whom you have denied, pardon you, Stuart, for your cruelty and blasphemy! You have ruined an immortal soul!"

His voice proclaimed no anger, but it trembled with the passion of grief; and when he had finished speaking he bent hastily over the lifeless body—he did as she had done, in days long gone, to him—repeatedly pressed his lips to her forehead, and before Stuart could speak again, DUGGANNE HAD DEPARTED FROM ISA LEE'S PRESENCE FOR EVER.

Sara Willis Parton (1811–1872)

Best known by her pseudonym, "Fanny Fern," Sara Willis Parton collected an unusual number of names: Grata Payson Sara Willis Eldredge Farrington Parton. Her father, Nathaniel Willis, named her "Grata Payson" after the mother of a minister he admired; when the rest of the family objected, she was called "Sara" after her mother, whom she preferred to her harsh, narrowly religious father. The Willis family moved from Portland, Maine, to Boston, where Nathaniel established a religious newspaper and later founded the well-known *Youth's Companion*. Parton attended Boston schools and then Catharine Beecher's seminary in Hartford, Connecticut, at the time when Harriet Beecher was student teacher. Both Beechers remembered her as a mischievous student, more fond of pranks than schoolwork, who nonetheless wrote witty essays.

In 1837 Parton married Charles Eldredge, a bank cashier. She lived happily for a few years but in the mid 1840s suffered the deaths of her mother, the eldest of her three daughters, and her husband. Reduced to relative poverty, with only grudging support from her father and in-laws, Parton married Samuel Farrington, a Boston merchant. He promptly deserted her, and when she failed to earn a living either teaching or sewing, she had to give up one of her daughters to her in-laws. In desperation she began to write short sketches under the name "Fanny Fern." By 1851 she was placing her essays in small Boston magazines; in 1853 she collected them as *Fern Leaves from Fanny's Portfolio*. *Fern Leaves* became an instant best seller, and Parton followed it with two more series of essays and an autobiographical novel, *Ruth Hall* (1855).

Although *Ruth Hall* caused a scandal when the author's identity was discovered and the villains in the novel were recognized as her relatives, "Fanny Fern" was achieving the security she had long sought. She reclaimed her daughter, moved to New York, and started to write for the *New York Ledger* at the extravagant sum of $100 a week. She made a third marriage, to the biographer James Parton, and spent the rest of her years quietly producing her weekly column for the *Ledger*.

In *Folly As It Flies* (1859) and succeeding collections of Parton's essays, the sentimentality and heavy-handed satire of her early work gives way to relaxed, humorous philosophizing. Parton also broadens her range of subject matter, depicting economic conditions in New York, and becomes more direct and outspoken in her championship of women. Her advice to women in her early essays was to "wear the mask of submission," but by the end of the 1850s she came to support the women's rights movement and encourage her readers to seek suffrage and wider fields of endeavor.

Selected Bibliography

OTHER WORKS

Fern Leaves From Fanny's Portfolio, 2d ser. (1854); *Little Ferns for Fanny's Little Friends* (1854); *Rose Clark* (1856); *Fresh Leaves* (1857); *Ginger-Snaps* (1870); *Caper-Sauce* (1872); *Fanny Fern: A Memorial Volume,* edited by James Parton (1873).

SECONDARY

Adams, Florence Bannard. *Fanny Fern; or a Pair of Flaming Shoes.* Privately printed, 1966.

The Life and Beauties of Fanny Fern. New York: H. Long and Brother, 1855.

McGinnis, Patricia I. "Fanny Fern, American Novelist." *Biblion* 2 (Spring 1969): 2–37.

Schlesinger, Elizabeth Bancroft. "Fanny Fern: Our Grandmothers' Mentor." *New York Historical Society Quarterly* 38 (October 1954): 501–519.

Wood, Ann D. "The 'Scribbling Women' and Fanny Fern: Why Women Wrote." *American Quarterly* 23 (Spring 1971): 3–24.

Ruth Hall (1855)

Ruth Hall was Sara Parton's revenge. Based very closely on her own experience as she viewed it, the novel recounts the struggles of a widow to support herself and her children. Ruth Hall finds few opportunities open to women and is treated shabbily by her relatives, who can tolerate neither a passive dependent nor the successful writer Ruth finally becomes. The relatives are clearly recognizable as Parton's own: Dr. and Mrs. Hall, the villains who plot to get Ruth's daughters, are the author's in-laws; Mr. Ellet, Ruth's miserly father, is the author's father. Parton reserved her strongest attack for her brother, N. P. Willis, a well-known poet and editor in New York. Although he published the fiction of several women writers, such as Grace Greenwood and Fanny Forester, Willis had refused Parton's appeal to help her launch a literary career. According to Parton, he pronounced her writing vulgar and advised her to make shirts for a living. In *Ruth Hall*, Parton satirizes Willis as Ruth's poet brother "Apollo Hyacinth," a selfish dandy and social climber.

Much to Parton's surprise, *Ruth Hall* created a sensation in the literary world. Parton had apparently thought herself protected by her pseudonym and failed to anticipate that her identity would be discovered and the family quarrel aired in public. Naturally, Victorian critics considered it unladylike to pillory one's relatives in a novel; they deplored the "unfemininely bitter wrath and spite" and concluded that Parton had "demeaned herself as no right-minded woman should have done" (*Putnam's Monthly*, February 1855, p. 216). Soon after the publication of *Ruth Hall*, there appeared the anonymously authored *Life and Beauties of Fanny Fern* (1855), denouncing Parton as a spendthrift and ingrate to her family. The book claimed that she began her writing career in an elegant apartment rather than the slum depicted in *Ruth Hall*.

The response to Parton's novel was not, however, uniformly negative. Nathaniel Hawthorne admired it and made Parton the one exception to his sweeping indictment of his female rivals as a "d----d mob of scribbling women." But most critics attacked *Ruth Hall* for the same reason Hawthorne praised it: its lack of "female delicacy." In the first half of the novel, Ruth is an acceptable heroine: a loving wife and mother and, after her husband dies, a passive victim. Most of the time she seems incapacitated by tears and headaches. But, as Ruth embarks on her writing career, she becomes more and more aggressive until she is "sharp," a "regular businesswoman." According to one of Parton's contemporaries, she metamorphoses into "Ruthless Hall."

Any work from the 1850s in which a woman openly expresses anger and ambition is bound to be interesting. Unfortunately, the style and structure of *Ruth Hall* may inhibit the reader. While Parton had a talent for the short, informal essay, she could not sustain a long work of fiction. In *Rose Clark* (1856), her second and last novel, new plots and characters succeed each other in a bewildering fashion. *Ruth Hall*, with its ready-made autobiographical structure, has more unity but is still

awkward and disjointed. The author's sentimentality also poses a problem. While the passion of her indictment of society makes the novel appealing, Parton sometimes, as in the first selection below, drowns the
reader in a bath of tears.

*The first quarter of the novel describes Ruth's happy marriage to
Harry Hall. Except for the death of one of her daughters and the fault-
finding and nosiness of her in-laws, Ruth's life is idyllic. Then Harry
dies of typhus fever, leaving Ruth and the two remaining daughters
penniless. Neither the Halls nor Ruth's father will agree to support the
family.*

CHAPTER XXXIV

The day was dark and gloomy. Incessant weeping and fasting had brought
on one of Ruth's most violent attacks of nervous headache. Ah! where
was the hand which had so lately charmed that pain away? where was
the form that, with uplifted finger and tiptoe tread, hushed the slightest sound, excluded the torturing light, changed the heated pillow, and
bathed the aching temples? Poor Ruth! nature had been tasked its utmost with sad memories and weary vigils, and she sank fainting to the
floor.

Well might the frightened children huddle breathless in the farther
corner. The coffin, the shroud, and the grave, were all too fresh in their
childish memory. Well might the tearful prayer go up to the only Friend
they knew,—"Please God, don't take away our mamma too."

Ruth heard it not; well had she *never* woke, but the bitter cup was not
yet drained.

"Good morning, Ruth," said her father, (a few hours after,) frowning
slightly as Ruth's pale face, and the swollen eyes of her children, met his
view. "Sick?"

"One of my bad headaches," replied Ruth, with a quivering lip.

"Well, that comes of excitement: you should n't get excited. I never
allow myself to worry about what can't be helped; this is the hand of
God, and you ought to see it. I came to bring you good news. The doctor
[her father-in-law] has very generously offered to take both your children
and support them. It will be a great burden off your hands; all he asks in
return is, that he shall have the entire control of them, and that you
keep away. It is a great thing, Ruth, and what I did n't expect of the doctor, knowing his avaricious habits. Now you'll have something pleasant
to think about, getting their things ready to go; the sooner you do it the
better. How soon, think?"

Ruth Hall: A Domestic Tale of the Present Time (New York: Mason Brothers, 1855),
400 pp. Excerpts are taken from pages 128–131, 132–135, 139, 220–223, 230–234,
250–254, 256, 330–333.

"I can *never* part with my children," replied Ruth, in a voice which, though low, was perfectly clear and distinct.

"Perfect madness," said her father, rising and pacing the floor; "they will have a good home, enough to eat, drink, and wear, and be taught—"

"To disrespect their mother," said Ruth, in the same clear, low tone.

"Pshaw," said her father impatiently; "do you mean to let such a trifle as that stand in the way of their bread and butter? I'm poor, Ruth, or at least I *may* be to-morrow, who knows? so you must not depend on me; I want you to consider that, before you refuse. Perhaps you expect to support them yourself; you can't do it, that's clear, and if you should refuse the doctor's offer, and then die and leave them, he would n't take them."

"Their *Father in Heaven* will," said Ruth. "He says, 'Leave thy fatherless children with me.'"

"Perversion of Scripture, perversion of Scripture," said Mr. Ellet, foiled with his own weapons.

Ruth replied only with her tears, and a kiss on each little head, which had nestled up to her with an indistinct idea that she needed sympathy.

"It is of no use getting up a scene, it won't move me, Ruth," said Mr. Ellet, irritated by the sight of the weeping group before him, and the faint twinges of his own conscience; "the doctor *must* take the children, there's nothing else left."

"Father," said Ruth, rising from her couch and standing before him; "my children are all I have left to love; in pity do not distress me by urging what I can never grant."

"As you make your bed, so lie in it," said Mr. Ellet, buttoning up his coat, and turning his back upon his daughter.

It was a sight to move the stoutest heart to see Ruth that night, kneeling by the side of those sleeping children, with upturned eyes, and clasped hands of entreaty, and lips from which no sound issued, though her heart was quivering with agony; and yet a pitying Eye looked down upon those orphaned sleepers, a pitying Ear bent low to list to the widow's voiceless prayer.

CHAPTER XXXV

"Well, Mis. Hall, you have got your answer. Ruth won't part with the children," said the doctor, as he refolded Mr. Ellet's letter.

"I believe you have lived with me forty years, come last January, have n't you, doctor?" said his amiable spouse.

"What of that? I don't see what that remark is going to fetch up, Mis. Hall," said the doctor. "You are not as young as you might be, to be sure, but I'm no boy myself."

"There you go again, off the track. I did n't make any allusion to my age. It's a thing I *never* do. It's a thing I never wish *you* to do. I repeat, that I have lived with you these forty years; well, did you ever know me back out of anything I undertook? Did you ever see me foiled? That letter makes no difference with me; Harry's children I'm determined to have, sooner or later. What can't be had by force, must be had by strategem. I propose, therefore, a compromise, (*pro-tem*). You and Mr. Ellet had better agree to furnish a certain sum for awhile, for the support of Ruth and her children, giving her to understand that it is discretionary, and may stop at any minute. That will conciliate Ruth, and will *look* better, too.

"The fact is, Miss Taffety told me yesterday that she heard some hard talking about us down in the village, between Mrs. Rice and Deacon Gray (whose child Ruth watched so many nights with, when it had the scarlet fever). Yes, it will have a better look, doctor, and we can withdraw the allowance whenever the 'nine days' wonder' is over. These people have something else to do than to keep track of poor widows."

"I never supposed a useless, fine lady, like Ruth, would rather work to support her children than to give them up; but I don't give her any credit for it now, for I'm quite sure it's all sheer obstinacy, and only to spite us," continued the old lady.

"Doctor!" and the old lady cocked her head on one side, and crossed her two forefingers, "whenever—you—see—a—blue-eyed—soft-voiced—gentle—woman,—look—out—for—a—hurricane. I tell you that placid Ruth is a smouldering volcano."

"That tells the whole story," said the doctor. "And speaking of volcanoes, it won't be so easy to make Mr. Ellet subscribe anything for Ruth's support; he thinks more of one cent than of any child he ever had. I am expecting him every moment, Mis. Hall, to talk over our proposal about Ruth. Perhaps you had better leave us alone; you know you have a kind of irritating way if anything comes across you, and you might upset the whole business. As to my paying anything towards Ruth's board unless he does his full share, you need n't fear."

"Of course not; well, I'll leave you," said the old lady, with a sly glance at the china closet, "though I doubt if *you* understand managing him alone. Now I could wind him round my little finger in five minutes if I chose, but I hate to stoop to it, I so detest the whole family."

"I'll shake hands with you there," said the doctor; "but that puppy of a Hyacinth is my *especial* aversion, though Ruth is bad enough in her way; a mincing, conceited, tip-toeing, be-curled, be-perfumed popinjay—faugh! Do you suppose, Mis. Hall, there *can* be anything in a man who wears fancy neck-ties, a seal ring on his little finger, and changes his coat and vest a dozen times a day? No; he's a sensuous fop, that tells the whole story; ought to be picked up with a pair of sugar-tongs, and laid carefully on a rose-leaf. Ineffable puppy!"

"They made a great fuss about his writings," said the old lady.

"*Who* made a fuss? Fudge—there's that piece of his about 'The Saviour'; he describes him as he would a Broadway dandy. That fellow is all surface, I tell you; there's no depth in him. How should there be? Is n't he an Ellet? but look, here comes his father."

Mr. Ellet refuses to commit himself, and the Halls give Ruth a pit-
tance, hoping she will have to relinquish her children. Ruth fails to
get a teaching position or to earn enough money sewing.

CHAPTER XXXVI

In a dark, narrow street, in one of those heterogeneous boarding-houses
abounding in the city, where clerks, market-boys, apprentices, and sewing-
girls, bolt their meals with railroad velocity; where the maid-of-all-work,
with red arms, frowzy head, and leathern lungs, screams in the entry for
any boarder who happens to be inquired for at the door; where one plate
suffices for fish, flesh, fowl, and dessert; where soiled table-cloths, sticky
crockery, oily cookery, and bad grammar, predominate; where greasy
cards are shuffled, and bad cigars smoked of an evening, you might have
found Ruth and her children.

CHAPTER LVI

.   .   .   .

. . . Just then a carrier passed on the other side of the street with the
morning papers, and slipped one under the crack of the house door
opposite.

A thought! why could not Ruth write for the papers? How very odd it
had never occurred to her before? Yes, write for the papers—why not?
She remembered that while at boarding-school, an editor of a paper in
the same town used often to come in and take down her compositions in
short-hand as she read them aloud, and transfer them to the columns of
his paper. She certainly *ought* to write better now than she did when an
inexperienced girl. She would begin that very night; but where to make
a beginning? who would publish her articles? how much would they pay
her? to whom should she apply first? There was her brother Hyacinth,
now the prosperous editor of the Irving Magazine; oh, if he would only
employ her? Ruth was quite sure she could write as well as some of his
correspondents, whom he had praised with no niggardly pen. She would
prepare samples to send immediately, announcing her intention, and offering them for his acceptance. This means of support would be so congenial, so absorbing. At the needle one's mind could still be brooding
over sorrowful thoughts.

Ruth counted the days and hours impatiently, as she waited for an answer. Hyacinth surely would not refuse *her* when in almost every number of his magazine he was announcing some new contributor; or, if *he*
could not employ her *himself*, he surely would be brotherly enough to
point out to her some one of the many avenues so accessible to a man of
extensive newspaperial and literary acquaintance. She would so gladly

support herself, so cheerfully toil day and night, if need be, could she only win an independence; . . . and then she rose and walked the floor in her impatience; and then, her restless spirit urging her on to her fate, she went again to the post office to see if there were no letter. How long the clerk made her wait! Yes, there *was* a letter for her, and in her brother's hand-writing too. Oh, how long since she had seen it!

Ruth heeded neither the jostling of office-boys, porters, or draymen, as she held out her eager hand for the letter. Thrusting it hastily in her pocket, she hurried in breathless haste back to her lodgings. The contents were as follows:

"I have looked over the pieces you sent me, Ruth. It is very evident that writing never can be *your* forte; you have no talent that way. You may possibly be employed by some inferior newspapers, but be assured your articles never will be heard of out of your own little provincial city. For myself I have plenty of contributors, nor do I know of any of my literary acquaintances who would employ you. I would advise you, therefore, to seek some *unobtrusive* employment. Your brother,

"Hyacinth Ellet."

A bitter smile struggled with the hot tear that fell upon Ruth's cheek. "I have tried the unobtrusive employment," said Ruth; "the wages are six cents a day, Hyacinth;" and again the bitter smile disfigured her gentle lip.

"No talent!"

"At another tribunal than his will I appeal."

"Never be heard of out of my own little provincial city!" The cold, contemptuous tone stung her.

"But they shall be heard of;" and Ruth leaped to her feet. "Sooner than he dreams of, too. I *can* do it, I *feel* it, I *will* do it," and she closed her lips firmly; "but there will be a desperate struggle first," and she clasped her hands over her heart as if it had already commenced; "there will be scant meals, and sleepless nights, and weary days, and a throbbing brow, and an aching heart; there will be the chilling tone, the rude repulse; there will be ten backward steps to one forward. *Pride* must sleep! but—" and Ruth glanced at her children—"it shall be *done*. They shall be proud of their mother. *Hyacinth shall yet be proud to claim his sister.*"

"What is it, mamma?" asked Katy, looking wonderingly at the strange expression of her mother's face.

"What is it, my darling?" and Ruth caught up the child with convulsive energy; "what is it? only that when you are a woman you shall remember this day, my little pet;" and as she kissed Katy's upturned brow a bright spot burned on her cheek, and her eye glowed like a star.

Ruth has to give up her older daughter, Katy, to the Halls, but she begins to write and seeks a publisher.

CHAPTER LIX

"Is this 'The Daily Type' office?" asked Ruth of a printer's boy, who was rushing down five steps at a time, with an empty pail in his hand.

"All you have to do is to ask mem. You've got a tongue in your head, have n't ye? women folks generally has," said the little ruffian.

Ruth, obeying this civil invitation, knocked gently at the office door. A whir of machinery, and a bad odor of damp paper and cigar smoke, issued through the half-open crack.

"I shall have to walk in," said Ruth, "they never will hear my feeble knock amid all this racket and bustle;" and pushing the door ajar, she found herself in the midst of a group of smokers, who, in slippered feet, and with heels higher than their heads, were whiffing and laughing, amid the pauses of conversation, most uproariously. Ruth's face crimsoned as heels and cigars remained in *statu quo*, and her glance was met by a rude stare.

"I called to see if you would like a new contributor to your paper," said Ruth; "if so, I will leave a few samples of my articles for your inspection."

"What do you say, Bill?" said the person addressed; "drawer full as usual, I suppose, is n't it? more chaff than wheat, too, I'll swear; don't want any, ma'am; come now, Jo, let's hear the rest of that story; shut the door, ma'am, if you please."

"Are you the editor of the 'Parental Guide'?" said Ruth, to a thin, cadaverous-looking gentleman, in a white neck-cloth, and green spectacles, whose editorial sanctum was not far from the office she had just left.

"I am."

"Do you employ contributors for your paper?"

"Sometimes."

"Shall I leave you this MS. for your inspection, sir?"

"Just as you please."

"Have you a copy of your paper here, sir, from which I could judge what style of articles you prefer?"

At this, the gentleman addressed raised his eyes for the first time, wheeled his editorial arm-chair round, facing Ruth, and peering over his green spectacles, remarked:

"Our paper, madam, is most em-phat-i-cal-ly a paper devoted to the interests of religion; no frivolous jests, no love-sick ditties, no fashionable sentimentalism, finds a place in its columns. This is a serious world, madam, and it ill becomes those who are born to die, to go dancing through it. Josephus remarks that the Saviour of the world was never known to smile. *I* seldom smile. Are you a religious woman, madam?"

"I endeavor to become so," answered Ruth.

"V-e-r-y good; what sect?"

"Presbyterian."

At this the white neck-clothed gentleman moved back his chair:

"Wrong, madam, all wrong; I was educated by the best of fathers, but he was *not* a Presbyterian; his son is not a Presbyterian; his son's paper sets its face like a flint against that heresy; no, madam, we shall have no occasion for your contributions; a hope built on a Presbyterian foundation, is built on the sand. Good morning, madam." . . .

Ruth could not but acknowledge to herself that she had thus far met with but poor encouragement, but she knew that to climb, she must begin at the lowest round of the ladder. It were useless to apply to a long-established leading paper for employment, unless endorsed by some influential name. Her brother had coolly, almost contemptuously, set her aside; and yet in the very last number of his Magazine, which accident threw in her way, he pleaded for public favor for a young actress, whom he said had been driven by fortune from the sheltered privacy of home, to earn her subsistence upon the stage, and whose earnest, strong-souled nature, he thought, should meet with a better welcome than mere curiosity. "Oh, why not one word for me?" thought Ruth; "and how can I ask of strangers a favor which a brother's heart has so coldly refused?"

It was very disagreeable applying to the small papers, many of the editors of which, accustomed to dealing with hoydenish contributors, were incapable of comprehending that their manner towards Ruth had been marked by any want of that respectful courtesy due to a dignified woman. From all such contact Ruth shrank sensitively; their free-and-easy tone fell upon her ear so painfully, as often to bring the tears to her eyes. Oh, if Harry—but she must not think of him.

The next day Ruth wandered about the business streets, looking into office-entries, reading signs, and trying to gather from their "know-nothing" hieroglyphics, some light to illumine her darkened pathway. Day after day chronicled only repeated failures, and now, notwithstanding she had reduced their already meagre fare, her purse was nearly empty.

Mr. Lescom, editor of the Standard, *accepts some of Ruth's articles, and she commences her business education.*

CHAPTER LXIV

"I have good news for you," said Mr. Lescom to Ruth, at her next weekly visit; "your very first articles are copied, I see, into many of my exchanges, even into the ____, which seldom contains anything but politics. A good sign for you Mrs. Hall; a good test of your popularity."

Ruth's eyes sparkled, and her whole face glowed.

"Ladies *like* to be praised," said Mr. Lescom, good-humoredly, with a mischievous smile.

"Oh, it is not that—not that, sir," said Ruth, with a sudden moistening of the eye, "it is because it will be bread for my children."

Mr. Lescom checked his mirthful mood, and said, "Well, here is something good for me, too; a letter from Missouri, in which the writer says, that if "Floy" (a pretty *nom-de-plume* that of yours, Mrs. Hall) is to be a contributor for the coming year, I may put him down as a subscriber, as well as S. Jones, E. May, and J. Noyes, all of the same place. That's good news for *me*, you see," said Mr. Lescom, with one of his pleasant, beaming smiles.

"Yes," replied Ruth, abstractedly. She was wondering if her articles were to be the means of swelling Mr. Lescom's subscription list, whether *she* ought not to profit by it as well as himself, and whether she should not ask him to increase her pay. She pulled her gloves off and on, and finally mustered courage to clothe her thought in words.

"Now that's just *like* a woman," replied Mr. Lescom, turning it off with a joke; "give them the least foot-hold, and they will want the whole territory. Had I not shown you that letter, you would have been quite contented with your present pay. Ah! I see it won't do to talk so unprofessionally to you; and you need n't expect," said he, smiling, "that I shall ever speak of letters containing new subscribers on your account. I could easily get you the offer of a handsome salary by publishing such things. No—no, I have been foolish enough to lose two or three valuable contributors in that way; I have learned better than that, 'Floy';" and taking out his purse, he paid Ruth the usual sum for her articles.

Ruth bowed courteously, and put the money in her purse; but she sighed as she went down the office stairs. Mr. Lescom's view of the case was a business one, undoubtedly; and the same view that almost any other business man would have taken, viz.: to retain her at her present low rate of compensation, till he was necessitated to raise it by a higher bid from a rival quarter. And so she must plod wearily on till that time came, and poor Katy must still be an exile; for she had not enough to feed her, her landlady having raised the rent of her room two shillings, and Ruth being unable to find cheaper accommodations. It *was* hard, but what could be done? Ruth believed she had exhausted all the offices she knew of. Oh! there was one, "The Pilgrim;" she had not tried there. She would call at the office on her way home.

The editor of "The Pilgrim" talked largely. He had, now, plenty of contributors; he did n't know about employing a new one. Had she ever written? and *what* had she written? Ruth showed him her article in the last number of "The Standard."

"Oh—hum—hum!" said Mr. Tibbetts, changing his tone; "so you are 'Floy,' are you?" (casting his eyes on her.) "What pay do they give you over there?"

Ruth was a novice in business-matters, but she had strong common sense, and that common sense said, he has no right to ask you that question; don't you tell him; so she replied with dignity, "My bargain, sir, with Mr. Lescom was a private one, I believe."

"Hum," said the foiled Mr. Tibbetts; adding in an under-tone to his partner, "sharp that!"

"Well, if I conclude to engage you," said Mr. Tibbetts, "I should prefer you would write for me over a different signature than the one by which your pieces are indicated at The Standard office, or you can write exclusively for my paper."

"With regard to your first proposal," said Ruth, "if I have gained any reputation by my first efforts, it appears to me that I should be foolish to throw it away by the adoption of another signature; and with regard to the last, I have no objection to writing exclusively for you, if you will make it worth my while."

"Sharp again," whispered Tibbetts to his partner.

The two editors then withdrawing into a further corner of the office, a whispered consultation followed, during which Ruth heard the words, "Can't afford it, Tom; hang it! we are head over ears in debt now to that paper man; good articles though—deuced good—must have her if we dispense with some of our other contributors. We had better begin low though, as to terms, for she'll go up now like a rocket, and when she finds out her value we shall have to increase her pay, you know."

(Thank you, gentlemen, thought Ruth, when the cards change hands, I'll take care to return the compliment.)

In pursuance of Mr. Tibbetts' shrewd resolution, he made known his "exclusive" terms to Ruth, which were no advance upon her present rate of pay at The Standard. This offer being declined, they made her another, in which, since she would not consent to do otherwise, they agreed she should write over her old signature, "Floy," furnishing them with two articles a week.

Ruth accepted the terms, poor as they were, because she could at present do no better, and because every pebble serves to swell the current.

Months passed away, while Ruth hoped and toiled. "Floy's" fame as a writer increasing much faster than her remuneration. There was rent-room to pay, little shoes and stockings to buy, oil, paper, pens, and ink to find; and now autumn had come, she could not write with stiffened fingers, and wood and coal were ruinously high, so that even with this new addition to her labor, Ruth seemed to retrograde pecuniarily, instead of advancing; and Katy still away! She must work harder—harder.

.   .   .   .

Ruth's brother, Hyacinth, saw "Floy's" articles floating through his exchanges with marked dissatisfaction and uneasiness. That she should have succeeded in any degree without his assistance, was a puzzle, and the premonitory symptoms of her popularity, which his weekly exchanges furnished, in the shape of commendatory notices, were gall and wormwood to him. *Something* must be done, and that immediately. Seizing his pen, he despatched a letter to Mrs. Millet, which he requested her to read to Ruth, alluding very contemptuously to Ruth's articles, and begging her to use her influence with Ruth to desist from scribbling, and seek some other employment. *What* employment, he did not condescend to state; in fact, it was a matter of entire indifference to him, provided she did not cross his track. Ruth listened to the contents of the letter, with the old bitter smile, and went on writing.

When John Walter of the Household Messenger *(in real life Robert Bonner of the* New York Ledger*) offers Ruth a large salary to write exclusively for his paper, she triumphantly quits Mr. Lescom and Mr. Tibbetts. Ruth takes advantage of an offer to publish her articles as a book; she confidently refuses to sell the copyright and asks for a percentage of the sales.*

CHAPTER LXXVII

And now our heroine had become a regular business woman. . . . The little room was littered with newspapers, envelopes, letters opened and unopened, answered and waiting to be answered. One minute she might be seen sitting, pen in hand, trying, with knit brows, to decipher some horrible cabalistic printer's mark on the margin of her proof; then writing an article for Mr. Walter, then scribbling a business letter to her publishers, stopping occasionally to administer a sedative to Nettie, in the shape of a timely quotation from Mother Goose, or to heal a fracture in a doll's leg or arm. Now she was washing a little soiled face, or smoothing little rumpled ringlets, replacing a missing shoe-string or pinafore button, then wading through the streets while Boreas[1] contested stoutly for her umbrella, with parcels and letters to the post-office, (for Ruth must be her own servant,) regardless of gutters or thermometers, regardless of jostling or crowding. What cared she for all these, when Katy would soon be back—poor little patient, suffering Katy? Ruth felt as if wings were growing from her shoulders. She never was weary, or sleepy, or hungry. She had not the slightest idea, till long after, what an incredible amount of labor she accomplished, or how her *mother's heart* was goading her on.

.   .   .   .

Publication day came at last. There was *the* book. Ruth's book! Oh, how few of its readers, if it were fortunate enough to find readers, would know how much of her own heart's history was there laid bare. Yes, there was the book. She could recall the circumstances under which each separate article was written. Little shoeless feet were covered with the proceeds of this; a little medicine, or a warmer shawl was bought with that. This was written, faint and fasting, late into the long night; that composed while walking wearily to or from the offices where she was employed. One was written with little Nettie sleeping in her lap; another still, a mirthful, merry piece, as an escape-valve for a wretched

1. The Greek personification for the North Wind.

heartache. Each had its own little history. Each would serve, in after-
days, for a land-mark to some thorny path of by-gone trouble. Oh, if the
sum of prosperity, after all, should gild these rugged paths! Some virtues—many faults—the book had—but God speed it, for little Katy's
sake!

The Halls and Ruth's father and brother are duly humbled by her
success. Ruth gets Katy back and moves to Mr. Walter's city. The cli-
max of the book comes in the following brief passage.

CHAPTER LXXXIX

.   .   .   .

"'Floy,'" said Mr. Walter, taking a package from his pocket, "I have
obeyed your directions, and here is something which you may well be
proud of;" and he handed Ruth a paper. It ran thus:

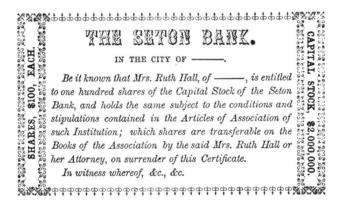

"There," said Mr. Walter, laughing, "imagine yourself, if you can, in
that dismal attic one year ago, a bank-stock holder! Now confess that
you are proud of yourself."

Criticism

NATHANIEL HAWTHORNE'S COMPLAINT to his publisher about the "damned mob of scribbling women" is the best known critical statement about early American women writers. But Hawthorne's hostility was shared by many, if not most, of the reviewers and critics of the day. Scribbling women might be praised and encouraged only if they kept within prescribed limits—if they placed their domestic duties above writing, took care not to "unsex" themselves, and produced "morally elevating" work. Above all, they had to restrict themselves to "the sphere in literature peculiarly woman's," as one critic put it, that is, children's books and "light" literature (fiction and poetry). Mr. Abbot, in the second selection below, is willing to patronize women writers but quick to threaten them if they should forget their place and "advocate their own claims or be each other's champions."

Ann Douglas describes the reaction of literary women to male hostility in the elaborate rationale they created to justify their writing. In the portion of the article not included here, she discusses Fanny Fern as an exception to the general rule in her failure to disguise her "unfeminine" ambition and delight in economic success. Yet even Fanny Fern was capable of defensive statements like "a woman may be literary, and yet feminine and lovable; content to find her greatest happiness in the charmed circle of Home" (*Fern Leaves from Fanny's Portfolio*, 1853). The 1860 article by Mary E. Bryan, which directly protests the limitations imposed on women writers, was highly unusual for its time.

Alexander Cowie, Helen Papashvily, Nina Baym, and Jane P. Tompkins attempt to characterize the "domestic" or "sentimental" fiction written by women in the first half of the nineteenth century. Cowie's amusing recipe for a domestic novel typifies the patronizing attitude of modern literary historians and their conclusion that the novels teach "submission to suffering." Papashvily was the first critic to detect a note of rebellion, but she does not support her thesis that "the domestic novels were handbooks of . . . feminine revolt." She implies, but does not demonstrate, that women were revenging themselves against men by placing women at the center of their fiction and by writing anti-war and temperance novels. Baym's *Woman's Fiction* (1978) was the first sustained analysis of early-nineteenth-century women's fiction. In the selection included here, she describes the basic story told by many of the novels and explains the balance of submission and rebellion in the authors' philosophy. Baym does not see "literary greatness" in any of the works she discusses, but Tompkins takes a different approach, one that may become the trend of future criticism. She defends sentimental fiction and finds positive value in novels such as Susan Warner's *The Wide, Wide World* (1850).

Nathaniel Hawthorne
Letters to William D. Ticknor (1854–1857)

Liverpool, Feb. 17th, '54

Dear Tick—

Thank you for the books and papers. Those are admirable poems of Mrs. Howe's,[1] but the devil must be in the woman to publish them. It seems to me to let out a whole history of domestic unhappiness. What a strange propensity it is in these scribbling women to make a show of their hearts, as well as their heads, upon your counter, for anybody to pry into that chooses! However, I, for one, am much obliged to the lady, and esteem her beyond all comparison the first of American poetesses. What does her husband think of it?

Liverpool, Jany 19th, '55

Dear Ticknor,

I am sorry to have given a false alarm; but as it turns out, I shall have no occasion to draw on you at present—having a good portion of the requisite amount on hand, and supplying the rest by drafts on the State Department for advances made. I shall lose nothing by this investment; and as to your advice not to lend any more money, I acknowledge it to be good, and shall follow it so far as I can and ought. But when the friend of half my lifetime asks me to assist him, and when I have perfect confidence in his honor, what is to be done? Shall I prove myself to be one of those persons who have every quality desirable in friendship, except that they invariably fail you at the pinch? I don't think I can do that; but, luckily, I have fewer friends than most men, and there are not a great many who can claim anything of me on that score.

.   .   .   .

. . . I shall spend a year on the Continent, and then decide whether to go back to the Wayside, or to stay abroad and write books. But I had rather hold this office[2] two years longer; for I have not seen half enough of England, and there is the germ of a new Romance in my mind, which will be all the better for ripening slowly. Besides, America is now wholly given over to a d____d mob of scribbling women, and I should have no chance of success while the public taste is occupied with their trash— and should be ashamed of myself if I did succeed. What is the mystery of these innumerable editions of the Lamplighter, and other books neither

Letters of Hawthorne to William D. Ticknor, 1851–1864 (Newark, New Jersey: Carteret Book Club, 1910). Excerpts are taken from 1: 29–30, 73–75, 76–78; 2: 50, 55–56.

1. Julia Ward Howe (1819–1910), poet and author of "Battle Hymn of the Republic." Her husband, Samuel Gridley Howe, director of the Perkins Institute for the Blind, disapproved of her literary career.

2. Hawthorne was serving as American consul in Liverpool.

better nor worse?—worse they could not be, and better they need not be, when they sell by the 100,000.

Liverpool, Febry 2d, 1855

Dear Ticknor,

.   .   .   .

In my last, I recollect, I bestowed some vituperation on female authors. I have since been reading "Ruth Hall"; and I must say I enjoyed it a good deal. The woman writes as if the devil was in her; and that is the only condition under which a woman ever writes anything worth reading. Generally women write like emasculated men, and are only to be distinguished from male authors by greater feebleness and folly; but when they throw off the restraints of decency, and come before the public stark naked, as it were—then their books are sure to possess character and value. Can you tell me anything about this Fanny Fern? If you meet her, I wish you would let her know how much I admire her.

I don't think of anything more to say, just now.

Truly yours,
Nath[1] Hawthorne.

Liverpool, April 24th, '57

Dear Ticknor,

.   .   .   .

I enclose a critique of a volume of poems by Mrs. Howe; and the writer (Mr. Bright of this town) wished it to be sent to her. I read her play, (and thank you for it,) but her genius does not appear to be of the dramatic order. In fact, she has no genius or talent, except for making public what she ought to keep to herself—viz. her passions, emotions, and womanly weaknesses. "Passion Flowers"[3] were delightful; but she ought to have been soundly whipt for publishing them.

Liverpool, June 5th, 1857

Dear Ticknor,

Since my last, Mrs. Hawthorne and I have been on a very pleasant tour to some of the eastern counties of England, and returned only a day or two since. . . .

.   .   .   .

. . . Everything that I see in my travels goes down into my journal; and I have now hundreds of pages, which I would publish if the least of them were not too spicy. But Mrs. Hawthorne altogether excels me as a writer of travels. Her descriptions are the most perfect pictures that ever

---

3. Howe's first book of verse, published anonymously in 1854.

were put on paper; it is a pity they cannot be published; but neither she nor I would like to see her name on your list of female authors.

How is Grace Greenwood?[4] I saw a paragraph in the Post, some months ago, stating that she had stabbed a man. If so, I suppose she may be now in the States Prison; but I think there must have been some mistake—at least, I hope so.

4. Pseudonym of Sara Jane Clarke Lippincott (1823–1904), popular journalist and writer of children's books. Hawthorne's reference to her stabbing a man is intended as a joke.

A. W. Abbot
"Female Authors" (1851)

It is apparent to any one who will take the trouble to look over the books which make up the burden of a bookseller's counter, that it has become a wonderfully common piece of temerity for a lady to make a book. Apart from the consideration, that a female author puts much of her personal individuality into her book, being more prone to express emotions than ideas, it may be said that in taking *any* public stand for praise or blame, a woman risks more than a man. From the time when the boy finds himself struggling among fifty or a hundred other boys, to find the level accorded to his measure of strength, tact, and talent, till the day when the man must cope with men in the crowded avenues to fame and wealth,—he is sheltered by no prescriptive immunities. Whatever he may say, do, or indite, he knows he must be responsible for, and wince at no consequences; for any extraordinary exhibition of sensitiveness on his part brings, in natural course, an uncommon exercise of any means of attrition in the power of his merciless fellows. As it was in urchinhood, so it is in graver and wiser years. If he *will* speak his honest mind on an exciting topic, he must have no fear of brickbat or more unsavory missile, (we speak metaphorically, of course); he must wrap himself in a tough integument of indifference, and stand his ground— rhinoceros-like—between the spear-thrusts of ignorant prejudice on the one hand and hard common sense on the other, eternally contending for the verdict of public opinion. To prepare a woman for her peculiar sphere, none of these hardening influences are at work; her sensibility is but too much protected, too fondly cultivated, in the shelter of home. To most women, therefore, even fame, except so far as it bears the character of sympathy and moral approbation, is more an annoyance than a pleasure. Fame is hardly ever her object in taking up the pen; and she is even surprised and wounded by criticism on mere literary defects, having expected from the world in general the indulgent sympathy which she has found among partial friends. She would fain be allowed to draw upon her imagination and her feelings without the chill fear of a sneer, and, addressing the heart, would be judged only by the heart. She writes her book as she writes a letter, and expects a response in the spirit of it. But if she writes to the public without some acquaintance with the humor of that cool and impartial personage, she may be grieved by an admonition to study logic, to cut off the nib of her pen and buy some blacker ink, if she would have anybody read her communications who has any thing else to do. . . .

We trust the appetite for bookmaking notoriety is not so alarmingly on the increase among our fair friends, as from the mere number of

North American Review 72 (January 1851): 151–153; 163–164.

names we might forbode. In many of these female authors we recognize an earnest and holy spirit and true aim, inconsistent with a petty love of display. We need not as yet surely deprecate this appetite as a new and higher form of the childish (shall we be pardoned if we say, feminine) desire for personal admiration. As we read, we feel that the desire of success, in many cases, must be the pure prayer for power to do good; if it looks to earthly approbation, it is for encouragement, and a deeper conviction of truth than can be felt without sympathy. We can allow women to covet praise while they shrink from admiration.

.   .   .   .

Female authorship being quite too common in these latter days to strike the world agape, nobody dreams of being eclipsed and envious. A man must fill an exceedingly small space in his own opinion, who could not afford not to be jealous of the amount of approbation that follows the most successful effort of his wife's pen, so long as her dabbling in ink does not involve his domestic comfort. Neither need he trouble himself about her temerity. Minerva's helmet and sword are a joke, and her shield is only useful to lean upon. Her fair face softens all manly hearts. He who should put her arms to the proof, even in a just cause, would cut but a sorry figure. Whoever it may be that she may have broken her reed lance upon, he can but shrug his shoulders, and leave her in possession of the field.

It is the custom to praise lady authors, even those who suffer much under parlor criticism from their own sex. It must be a very uncommon merit or demerit, which receives any thing like discriminating retribution in the court of letters, if a lady claims the award. Her book receives no more just meed than the "Very well—exceedingly well, indeed," bestowed by a smiling school-committee man upon a smart school-girl's theme, after a whispered agreement, that with some pruning and a little more thought, it would be really a surprising achievement *for a girl*. The blushing smile of girlhood is a very pretty and pleasant thing to look upon; and, under the circumstances, to throw a damper upon harmless vanity, by pointing out an exuberance to be restrained, or a more vigorous tone of thought to be wrought for, is hardly worth the while. And thus the enterprises of full-fledged ambition among the scribbling fair, are dealt with by good-natured critics. If they have the good fortune to be brought under notice at all, they are the theme of neatly turned compliments and ingenious congratulations.

But evils are likely to grow out of such a half contemptuous leniency; and it may not be so easy to repair as it might have been to prevent them. A wholesome dread of satire may in time be a necessary curb upon the shrewish element in the feminine character; for why should a scolding pen find more toleration than a scolding tongue? Indeed, if every vixenish impulse is to be allowed to seize upon the press, by way of speaking-trumpet, and when we stop our ears, hold down our heads, and run, we must find home taunts upon our most defenceless follies and sins, mocking us in derisive echoes, before us and behind us and on every side; if we are to be overtaken, and branded, and cruelly mauled, without judge or jury, or a chance for defence or deprecation; if we must stand and take this clapper-clawing from fair, but not gentle, hands, under the eyes of the amused public, who, if they interfere at all, pelt either party at random, or both, to make justice sure and prevent brawls in the open thoroughfare in future,—is it not high time there was a police to come to the rescue? Shall we be pilloried without authority, put in the stocks with no warrant but an individual will, that there may be unbounded liberty in the republic of letters? A despotism were better, unless public opinion be strong enough to keep the peace. . . .

Having so many agreeable books upon our shelves, for which we have to thank and to love gentle authors, we have, perhaps, cherished too comfortable a confidence that the prevalence of good taste would bar the entrance of the Amazonian mania into literature, at least in any offensive form. With about as much of faith and of dread as was excited in our courageous hearts by the cry of epidemic hydrophobia, which, some time since, caused such a massacre of four-footed innocents, did we hear the rumors of a rage for public speech and action, and for turning the world inside out and upside down, which certain "strong-minded women" were proclaimed to be afflicted withal. We believed the hue and cry had arisen through a groundless panic. If there be such a mania, and it come hither also, we can only say, that for our own household we should much prefer the advent of the cholera. We should shudder if we observed any alarming symptoms in our immediate vicinity, or the presence of any exciting cause. As we look abroad, we see only a chivalrous disposition, not merely to respect the rights, but to uphold the privileges, of the fair sex, which makes it, in our view, altogether unnecessary that they should advocate their own claims or be each other's champions.

Ann Douglas Wood
"The 'Scribbling Women' and Fanny Fern:
Why Women Wrote" (1971)

. . . Sarah Hale cautioned aspiring poetesses in her *Lady's Magazine*, a precursor of *Godey's*:

> The path of poetry, like every other path in life, is to the tread of woman, exceedingly circumscribed. She may not revel in the luxuriance of fancies, images and thoughts, or indulge in the license of choosing themes at will, like the Lords of creation.[1]

"Grace Greenwood," born Sara Clarke, a popular authoress of the day, wrote spirited, occasionally unconventional sketches and stories, but when she came to describe what "true feminine genius" should be, she slipped into line behind Mrs. Hale. In her first collection of sketches, *Greenwood Leaves*, she explains that "true feminine genius is ever timid, doubtful, and clingingly dependent; a perpetual childhood. A true woman shrinks instinctively from greatness." Carried away for a moment in praising "the joys of creation" and "the heaven-born soul of song," she soon retreats, and cautions, "but this is for the *masters* of the lyre; it can never be felt by woman with great intensity; at least, can never satisfy her."[2]

Both Sarah Hale, one of the most successful editors in mid-19th century America, and Grace Greenwood, a noted abolitionist and lecturer, were urging other women to do as they said, not as they did. Why? The half-conscious purpose behind their rationale is given away by the graceful references both of them make to the "Lords of creation" and the "*masters* of the lyre" who are to have privileges of creativity denied to women. These two women are assuaging a half-felt sense that they as writers are threatening to men,[3] that they will be seen as women who have left the world of home to challenge the exclusive right of men to the joys of intellectual and emotional self-expression, and even to compete directly with them, as Hawthorne knew they did, for a limited literary market. If the emergence of a group of feminine writers who threatened to corner the market alarmed men, it alarmed the women as well. The women writers themselves wanted to have their cake and eat it too: stay "feminine" and write successful best sellers. On one level, this de-

American Quarterly 23 (Spring 1971): 5–13.

1. *Lady's Magazine*, 2 (1829), 142. See also her *Woman's Record* (New York: Harper & Brothers, 1876), which discusses many women writers from this angle.—[Author's note, as are subsequent notes to this selection.]

2. *Greenwood Leaves* (Boston: Ticknor, Reed, and Fields, 1850), pp. 310–12. Grace Greenwood was capable of satirizing the kind of literature this critique produced (see *Greenwood Leaves*, pp. 303–8), but not of altering the critique.

3. Helen Papashvily treats the anti-men aspect of this literature as do William R. Taylor and Christopher Lasch, "'Two Kindred Spirits': Sorority and Family in New England, 1839–1846," *New England Quarterly*, 36 (1963), 231–41.

sire was rooted in shrewd analysis: "feminine" books got better reviews from male reviewers. On another, it genuinely expressed their own ambivalent guilt that they were not leaving the field to the "lords of creation," but taking it over, and enjoying the conquest. As a result of this complex pattern of motives and reactions, most of the women writers of the day, like Sarah Hale and Grace Greenwood, subscribed to a rationale, heartily supported by their male reviewers, that attempted to prove how justifiable, innocuous and even elevating their work was.

Literary duties, these women assured their readers, need not and did not draw them from their proper "sphere" of home. Their hearts remained there, not in their books. Catharine Maria Sedgwick, one of the most popular and interesting American writers of the 1820s and 1830s, undeservedly neglected today, can assure her friends that her books "constitute no portion of my happiness"—this she found rather in the "dearest relations of life." In fact, cooking was the only accomplishment of which she admitted to being vain.[4] Mrs. Hale loved to satirize the "would-be-literary lady" who affected to "despise the dull routine of domestic duties her sex enjoined upon her."[5] Indeed, domestic cares apparently could provide the sort of artistic "inspiration" suitable to woman. Mrs. A. D. T. Whitney, who rivaled Louisa May Alcott in her popularity with female readers, showed in a novel called *The Other Girls* (1873) how a young maid becomes a successful poetess, but still refuses to quit her cooking and cleaning, because, as she tells her mistress, "'The best and brightest things I've ever thought have come into my head over the ironing-board or the bread-making.'"[6]

Women in becoming writers were not leaving the home for the market place, according to this reasoning, but bringing the home *into* the market. Men's concerns, such as politics, were not suitable subjects for lady writers, as Mrs. Hale rather pointedly reminded the noted abolitionist writer Lydia Maria Child: "The precepts and examples of the Saviour should be the guide of woman's benevolent efforts. In no case did He lend aid or encouragement to the agitation of political questions."[7] Women were to eschew direct criticism of the *status quo*, Mrs. Hale argued, in favor of a quiet transmutation and sanctification of life by the "painting of domestic scenes and *deep* emotions."[8] As a result, ladies were urged toward children's literature, books on child care and household management, and works of sensibility steeped in depoliticized and lofty patriotism and misty, death-oriented and nonsectarian religious fervor. . . .

.   .   .   .

4. Mary E. Dewey, *Life and Letters of Catharine M. Sedgwick* (New York: Harper & Brothers, 1871), pp. 250, 330.
5. "Sketches of American Characters, No. 7: The Belle and the Bleu," *Lady's Magazine*, 1 (1828), 305.
6. *The Other Girls* (Boston: J. R. Osgood and Company, 1873), p. 434.
7. *Woman's Record*, p. 620.
8. *Lady's Magazine*, 2 (1829), 143.

In masking and hallowing their activity, these women writers reached
the paradoxical point where, by a mysterious transmutation, they were
somehow hardly writing at all. As they told it, they stumbled accidentally on the stanzaic or novel form in the course of musing about "domestic scenes and deep emotions," and picked it up, not really knowing
what they had. Caroline Lee Hentz, a popular southern novelist of the
day, can hardly explain what she is doing in her book *Ernest Linwood*,
and has to ask herself:

> Book! Am I writing a book? No, indeed! This is only a record of my
> heart's life, written at random and carelessly thrown aside, sheet
> after sheet, sibylline leaves from the great book of fate. The wind
> may blow them away, a spark consume them. I may myself commit
> them to the flames. I am tempted to do so at this moment.[9]

Needless to say, she overcame the temptation. Mrs. Sigourney was said
to write in the same unwitting way, naturally heedless of any sense of
literary form. A contemporary lauded her because, "ever hurrying along
on some urgent errand of affection or duty," she never worried about the
"mere style of her expression" or her "literary reputation."[10]

What is happening is clear: women's motives in writing are being
stripped of all their aggressive content, until the woman writer seems
practically anesthetized, or rather hypnotized, responding only to the
calls of home and God, calls so close to her instinctive womanly nature
that she hardly needs consciously to hear them. She writes because she
cannot help it, and is apt, like the consumptive young poetess Lucretia
Davidson, to appear "the inhabitant of another sphere" as she writes.[11]
Whittier explains why he could not discourage the budding writer Alice
Cary, who was later to become New York's best known poetess, when
she first appeared on his doorstep:

> Foredoomed to song, she seemed to me;
> I queried not with destiny . . . .
> What could I other than I did?
> Could I a singing-bird forbid?
> Deny the wind-stirred leaf? Rebuke
> The music of the forest brook?[12]

Such descriptions give the whole mystique in a nutshell. The woman
writer is hardly a flesh-and-blood competitor in a literary market, but a
songbird, a leaf, or, like Lucretia Davidson, the inhabitant of another

9. *Ernest Linwood* (Boston: J. P. Jewett and Company, 1856), p. 69.
10. The Rev. E. B. Huntingdon, "Lydia H. Sigourney," in *Eminent Women of the Age*
(Hartford, Conn: Betts, 1869), p. 96.
11. Catharine M. Sedgwick, "Lucretia Mott Davidson," *The Library of American Biography*, ed. Jared Sparks, 7 (Boston: Hilliard, Gray, and Co., 1837), p. 238.
12. Quoted in Mary Clemmer Ames, *A Memorial of Alice and Phoebe Cary* (New
York: Hurd and Houghton, 1874), p. 27.

sphere altogether. Nor is she a willful creator, bent on self-expression; rather she is "foredoomed to song," a suffering instrument for the still, sad music of humanity. All her writing is, in a sense, automatic writing, and, hence, not only inevitable, but holy. When Harriet Beecher Stowe finally announced that "God wrote" *Uncle Tom's Cabin*, she was putting herself in a long-standing tradition. . . .

Women were not only forced into writing, but they were then frequently forced into print. A woman writer was particularly admirable if, like the young and sickly poetess Martha Day, daughter of President Day of Yale, she "aimed rather to repress than to cultivate her poetic genius."[13] Her journals and poetic works were published only posthumously, by an adoring and grieving family. This situation seemed so ideal that Mrs. Sigourney made use of it in a fictionalized work called *Lucy Howard's Journal*, published in 1857. The public is only allowed the chance to peruse the exemplary, chaste and retiring thoughts of this young housewife because she died and her husband felt he could not, in all good conscience, withhold such a source of inspiration from the world. In fact, if the lady were living at publication date, one could often assume that, as in the case of Lydia Maria Child or Catharine Maria Sedgwick, relatives had urged or even betrayed her into print.[14]

The most delicate aspect of this whole rationale was that which dealt with the economic motives of the woman writer. As Helen Papashvily has pointed out in her valuable study, *All the Happy Endings*, many women writers were widows, suddenly forced to support themselves and their children, or women otherwise unexpectedly robbed of male support.[15] The situation here was very complex. On the one hand, economic necessity was a better excuse for writing than a sheer burning unladylike desire for self-expression. On the other hand, it was, as we have seen, taboo for the lady writers to appear to be what Hawthorne realized they were: shrewd competitors in the literary market. . . . Various women writers took different ways of repressing awareness, in their readers and in themselves, of this facet of their literary activity. The widowed Mrs. Hale, . . . engages in her literary and editorial work, a pursuit "foreign to the usual character and occupations of her sex," only in order to "obtain the means of supporting and educating her children in some measure as their father would have done."[16] Clearly anxious that she has somehow usurped her husband's role, she stresses that her only real source of happiness in her fame is the sweet thought "that *his* name bears the celebrity."[17] Yet she is not above using her declared maternal motivation for a

13. "Literary Remains of Martha Day," *Lady's Magazine*, 7 (1834), 278.
14. See Dewey, pp. 150–51, and Margaret Farrand Thorp, *Female Persuasion* (New Haven: Yale Univ. Press, 1949), pp. 216–18.
15. Papashvily, p. xvi. For some contemporary evidence, see Hale, *Woman's Record*, *passim*; Gordon S. Haight, *Mrs. Sigourney: The Sweet Singer of Hartford* (New Haven: Yale Univ. Press, 1930), p. 36.
16. *Lady's Magazine*, 4 (1831), 3–4.
17. *Woman's Record*, p. 687.

shrewd bit of advertising: the public is given the "surest pledge" that she will deserve its patronage: "The guaranty of a mother's affection."[18] She is indeed having her cake and eating it too.

The financial imperative offering itself as the maternal (or sometimes filial) impulse, mysteriously disconnected from what Mrs. Hale gingerly refers to here as "pecuniary remuneration," makes a frequent appearance in this literature. Above all, a woman writer was not to display her economic need. If she did, she was clearly threatening, reminding an absent husband or a neglectful father, or men in general, of their failure to support her in the graceful domestic sphere for which she was presumably formed, and implying that she might now actively take from them what they refused to give. "Fanny Forrester," born Emily Chubbuck, a popular New York writer of the 1840s, who later became the third Mrs. Judson and a missionary to Burma, provides a telling example of the advertising techniques an impoverished woman writer might employ. Raised in New Hampshire by a father lacking in all "practical shrewdness and energy," she knew poverty young. She later recalled digging "broken wood out of the snow" to keep her family from freezing, and she started work at eleven in a woolen factory (p. 20).[19] Not surprisingly, she combined, as her biographer recorded, "shrinking sensitiveness" with the "masculine energy of action" (p. 54) her father so notably lacked. She early took over his role as breadwinner for the family. While teaching young ladies at the Utica Female Seminary in New York, she began to write pious Sunday school tales that found a small but dependable market. Her assessment of her motives given to friends was candid in the extreme: she planned to sell "brains for money" (p. 57). Although she was proud of the "iron" toughness she had gained in her struggles with a harsh world, she felt there was "little of the poetry of life" left in her (p. 48). Indeed, she occasionally felt that writing had become "such a matter-of-fact dollars and cents business" with her, that she hated her pen: "Oh, there is nothing," she exclaimed to a sympathetic correspondent, "like coining one's brain into gold—no, bread—to make the heart grow sick" (p. 72).

Yet when she entered the New York market by submitting two trial sketches to Nathaniel Willis' *New York Mirror*, the organ of New York's would-be fashionables, this impoverished schoolteacher publicly denied all pretensions to being a "blue," and coyly explained that, although her friend "Bel" had urged her to pretend poverty to win sympathy, she has decided to tell the "truth"—she is a charming young thing who simply wants a little cash for a new hat! She prefers to disarm her readers and Willis with a false confession of feminine frivolity rather than to expose a need and a determination which would be seen as unfeminine. Her

---

18. "The Beginning," *Lady's Magazine*, 2 (1829), 5.

19. This and all subsequent references about Emily Chubbuck's life will be to A. C. Kendrick, *The Life and Letters of Emily C. Judson* (New York: Sheldon & Company, 1860).

subsequent sketches of the woman artist all deal with girls who are a compound of Little Eva and Ariel, wandering amongst dense mists of poetry and totally eschewing any aspect, economic or otherwise, of the real world.[20] She herself became a romantic figure whose consumption was seen, not as a badge of poverty and overwork, but of poetic genius. An admiring sister poetess spoke of the "shadow wan and deep" on her brow, her "hollow temples" with their "darker violet veins," and her "fairy feet," falling "faint and low / As the feathery flakes of the drifting snow."[21]

No one should or could minimize the fact that dying poetesses and consumptive storytellers were hardly a figment of the feminine imagination: they existed, in staggering numbers, and were as genuine a part of the feminine experience as the hearth and altar which provided the chief themes of these women's work. Yet it is equally undeniable that these facts of life also yielded a complex symbolic value and served an important double function. The consumptive ladies, for example, presented a tacit reproach to a masculine world that murderously trampled on their delicate sensibilities, and yet, at the same time, their wan faces and decaying limbs hinted that if they had offended by their literary ambitions, at least they were dying for it. The reality of this guilt as a component of the woman writer's psyche seems undeniable. Grace Greenwood wrote a long and fascinating story for the *Atlantic Monthly* in 1859 called "Zelma's Vow," probably based in part on her own unhappy marital experiences.[22] Zelma, a noble but wild English girl of gypsy descent runs away from her foster father's home with a younger actor. He turns out to be worthless, selfish and flagrantly unfaithful, and when she herself becomes a great actress, he is bitterly and undeservedly jealous of her. In fact, interestingly enough, it is precisely his scorn of her capacities which stings her "like a lash" into her first triumph (p. 333). On stage, she plays a character in Congreve's *The Mourning Bride* who defies and triumphs over the character her husband plays, but off-stage, she is at once, "the loving wife, yearning for one proud smile, one tender word" (p. 334). The split between the artist and the wife, one aggressive and defiant, the other asking to be forgiven for her aggression and defiance, could not be clearer. As her acting, to which she allegedly turns for "consolation" for his coldness, improves, his grows worse and worse. In some psychic fashion, she is sapping him of his vitality, and finally, he dies. Although Grace Greenwood has given us no overt hint that Zelma is in any way to blame, she clearly *feels* that her heroine is guilty, for the rest of the story is concerned with Zelma's deterioration as an actress and as a woman. Dying of consumption, she is reduced to playing in

20. See particularly "Ida Ravelin," "The Poetess" and "Dora," in her collection of sketches, *Alderbrook* (Boston: W. D. Ticknor & Company, c. 1846).
21. Kendrick, p. 121.
22. See Thorp, pp. 157 ff. All references to "Zelma's Vow" will be to the *Atlantic Monthly*, 4 (1859), 73–84, 327–44.

cheap, provincial theaters. In a terrible scene, after accidentally using her husband's skull as a stage prop in a scene from Rowe's *Fair Penitent*, she dies murmuring, "he will forgive me . . . when he sees that all the laurels have dropped away" (p. 344).

This guilt and the kind of soft-pedaling and blurring it imposed on the woman writer's need to express and finance herself were of course evidences of deep-rooted alienation and of genuine psychological conflict within these women, but, in a curious way, the resulting rationale, as I have suggested, also furthered their original impulse. Authoresses like Sarah Hale and Fanny Forrester presumably unconsciously believed that they could succeed better, be more assertive economically, by hiding behind a conventional "feminine" façade. Hence, the importance of the rationale for strategic as well as psychic reasons was very great. It enabled hundreds of women to write without understanding all the frightening and unacceptable implications of their desire to do so, and it helped them make a profit from their writing as well. So it is hardly surprising to find one woman author after another, from Lydia Maria Child to Harriet Beecher Stowe, subscribing in large measure to the Hale doctrine, no matter how outspoken or even subversive her own work might be.

Mary E. Bryan
"How Should Women Write?" (1860)

The idea of women writing books! There were no prophets in the days of King John to predict an event so far removed from probability. The women of the household sat by their distaffs, or toiled in the fields, or busied themselves in roasting and brewing for their guzzling lords. If ever a poetic vision or a half-defined thought floated through their minds, they sang it out to their busy wheels, or murmured it in rude sentences to lull the babies upon their bosoms, or silently wove it into their lives to manifest itself in patient love and gentleness. And it was all as it should have been; there was need for nothing more. Physical labor was then all that was required of woman; and to "act well her part," meant but to perform the domestic duties which were given her. Life was less complex then than now—the intellectual part of man's twofold nature being but unequally developed, while the absence of labor-saving implements demanded a greater amount of manual toil from men as well as from women.

It is different now. Modern ingenuity and Protean appliances of machinery have lessened the necessity of actual physical labor; and, in the constant progress of the human race, new fields have been opened, and new social needs and requirements are calling for workers in other and higher departments.

There is a cry now for intellectual food through the length and breadth of the land. The old oracles of the past, the mummied literary remains of a dead age, will not satisfy a generation that is pressing so vigorously forward. They want books imbued with the strong vitality and energy of the present. And as it is a moving, hurrying, changing time, with new influences and opinions constantly rising like stars above the horizon, men want books to keep pace with their progress—nay, to go before and guide them, as the pillar of fire and cloud did the Israelites in the desert. So they want books for every year, for every month—mirrors to "catch the manners living as they rise," lenses to concentrate the rays of the new stars that dawn upon them.

There is a call for workers; and woman, true to her mission as the helpmeet for man, steps forward to take her part in the intellectual labor, as she did when only manual toil was required at her hands. The pen has become the mighty instrument of reform and rebuke; the press is the teacher and the preacher of the world; and it is not only the privilege, but the duty of woman to aid in extending this influence of letters, and in supplying the intellectual demands of society, when she has been

Southern Field and Fireside 1 (January 1860). Reprinted in *Southland Writers: Biographical and Critical Sketches of the Living Female Writers of the South*, ed. Ida Raymond [Mary T. Tardy], vol. 2 (Philadelphia: Clexton, Remson & Haffelfinger, 1870), 664–668.

endowed with the power. Let her assure herself that she has been called to the task, and then grasp her pen firmly, with the stimulating consciousness that she is performing the work assigned to her.

Thus is apparent what has been gradually admitted, that it is woman's duty to write—but how and what? This is yet a mooted question. Men, after much demur and hesitation, have given women liberty to write; but they cannot yet consent to allow them full freedom. They may flutter out of the cage, but it must be with clipped wings; they may hop about the smooth-shaven lawn, but must, on no account, fly. With metaphysics they have nothing to do; it is too deep a sea for their lead to sound; nor must they grapple with those great social and moral problems with which every strong soul is now wrestling. They must not go beyond the surface of life, lest they should stir the impure sediment that lurks beneath. They may whiten the outside of the sepulchre, but must not soil their kidded hands by essaying to cleanse the inside of its rottenness and dead men's bones.

Nature, indeed, is given them to fustianize over, and religion allowed them as their chief capital—the orthodox religion, that says its prayers out of a prayer-book, and goes to church on Sabbaths; but on no account the higher, truer religion, that, despising cant and hypocrisy, and scorning forms and conventionalisms, seeks to cure, not to cloak, the plague-spots of society—the self-forgetting, self-abnegating religion that shrinks not from following in the steps of Christ, that curls not its lip at the touch of poverty and shame, nor fears to call crime by its right name, though it wear a gilded mask, nor to cry out earnestly and bravely, "Away with it! away with it!" No! not such religion as this. It is *unfeminine;* women have no business with it whatever, though they may ring changes as often as they please upon the "crowns of gold," the "jasper walls," and "seraph harps."

Having prescribed these bounds to the female pen, men are the first to condemn her efforts as tame and commonplace, because they lack earnestness and strength.

If she writes of birds, of flowers, sunshine, and *id omne genus*, as did Amelia Welby, noses are elevated superbly, and the effusions are said to smack of bread and butter.

If love, religion, and domestic obligations are her theme, as with Mrs. Hentz, "namby-pamby" is the word contemptuously applied to her productions. If, like Mrs. Southworth, she reproduces Mrs. Radcliffe in her possibility—scorning romances, her nonsensical clap-trap is said to be "beneath criticism;" and if . . . she gossips harmlessly of fashions and fashionables, of the opera and . . . of watering-places, lectures, and a railroad trip, she is *"pish"*-ed aside as silly and childish; while those who seek to go beyond the boundary-line are put down with the stigma of *"strong-minded."* Fanny Fern, who, though actuated by no fixed purpose, was yet more earnest than the majority of her sisterhood, heard the word hissed in her ears whenever she essayed to strike a blow at the root of social sin and inconsistency, and had whatever there was of noble and philanthropic impulse in her nature annihilated by the epithets of "bold" and "indelicate," which were hurled at her like poisoned arrows.

It will not do. Such dallying with surface-bubbles, as we find in much of our periodical literature, might have sufficed for another age, but not for this. We want a deeper troubling of the waters, that we may go down into the pool and be healed. It is an earnest age we live in. Life means more than it did in other days; it is an intense reality, crowded thick with eager, questioning thoughts and passionate resolves; with burning aspirations and agonized doubts. There are active influences at work, all tending to one grand object—moral, social, and physical advancement. The pen is the compass-needle that points to this pole. Shall woman dream on violet banks, while this great work of reformation is needing her talents and her energies? Shall she prate prettily of moonlight, music, love, and flowers, while the world of stern, staring, pressing realities of wrong and woe, of shame and toil, surrounds her? Shall she stifle the voice in her soul for fear of being sneered at as *strong-minded*, and shall her great heart throb and heave as did the mountain of Æsop, only to bring forth such insignificant mice—such productions—more paltry in purpose than in style and conception—which she gives to the world as the offspring of her brain?

It will not long be so. Women are already forming higher standards for themselves, learning that genius has no sex, and that, so the truth be told, it matters not whether the pen is wielded by a masculine or a female hand. The active, earnest, fearless spirit of the age, which sends the blood thrilling through the veins of women, will flow out through their pens, and give color to the pictures they delineate, to the principles they affirm. Literature must embody the prominent feeling of the age on which it is engrafted. It is only an isolated, excepted spirit, like Keats's, which can close its eyes to outward influences, and, amid the roar of gathering political storms, and the distant thunderings of the French Revolution, lie down among the sweet, wild English flowers, and dream out its dream of the old Greek beauty.

How should a woman write? I answer, as men, as all should write to whom the power of expression has been given—*honestly and without fear*. Let them write what they feel and think, even if there be errors in the thought and the feeling—better that than the lifeless inanities of which literature, and especially periodical literature, furnishes so many deplorable samples.

Our opinions on ethical and social questions change continually as the mind develops, and the light of knowledge shines more broadly through the far-off opening in the labyrinth of inquiry through which we wander seeking for truth. Thus, even when writers are most honest, their opinions, written at different times, often appear contradictory. This the discerning reader will readily understand. He will know that in ascending the ladder, upon whose top the angels stand, the prospect widens and changes continually as newer heights are won. Emerson, indeed, tells us that "a foolish consistency is the hobgoblin of little minds. With consistency, a great soul has simply nothing to do. Speak what you think now in hard words; and to-morrow, speak what to-morrow thinks in hard words again, though it contradict everything you said to-day." This is strong—perhaps too unqualified; but even inconsistency is better than the dull, donkey-like obstinacy which refuses to move from one position, though the wooing spirit of inquiry beckon it onward, and winged speculation tempt it to scale the clouds.

Still, there should be in writing, as in acting, a fixed and distant purpose to which everything should tend. If this be to elevate and refine the human race, the purpose will gradually and unconsciously work out its own accomplishment. Not, indeed, through didactic homilies only; every image of beauty or sublimity crystallized in words, every philosophic truth, and every thought that has a tendency to expand the mind or enlarge the range of spiritual vision, will aid in advancing this purpose, will be as oil to the lamp we carry to light the footsteps of others.

As to the subjects that should be written upon, they are many and varied; there is no exhausting them while nature teems with beauty—while men live, and act, and love, and suffer—while the murmurs of the great ocean of the *Infinite* come to us in times when the soul is stillest, like music that is played too far off for us to catch the tune. Broad fields of thought lie before us, traversed, indeed, by many feet, but each season brings fresh fruits to gather and new flowers to crop.

Genius, like light, shines upon all things—upon the muck-heap as upon the gilded cupola.

As to the wrong and wretchedness which the novelist lays bare—it will not be denied that such really exists in this sin-beleaguered world. Wherefore shrink and cover our eyes when these social ulcers are probed? Better earnestly endeavor to eradicate the evil, than seek to conceal or ignore its existence. Be sure this will not prevent it eating deeper and deeper into the heart.

Genius, when true and earnest, will not be circumscribed. No power shall say to it: "Thus far shalt thou go, and no farther." Its province is in part, to daguerreotype the shifting influences, feelings, and tendencies at work in the age in which it exists—and sin, and grief, and suffering, as well as hope, and love, and joy, and star-eyed aspiration, pass across its pages as phantoms across the charmed mirror of the magician. Genius thrills along "the electric chain wherewith we are darkly bound," from the highest to the lowest link of the social ligature; for true genius is Christ-like; *it scorns nothing*; calls nothing that God made common or unclean, because of its great yearning over mankind, its longing to lift them up from the sordid things of sense in which they grovel to its own higher and purer intellectual or spiritual atmosphere. The noblest woman of us all, Mrs. Elizabeth Browning, whom I hold to have written, in "Aurora Leigh," the greatest book of this century,—the greatest, not from the wealth of its imagery, or the vigor of its thoughts, but because of the moral grandeur of its purpose,—Mrs. Browning, I say, has not shrunk from going down, with her purity encircling her, like the halo around the Saviour's head, to the abodes of shame and degradation for material to aid in elucidating the serious truths she seeks to impress for sorrowful examples of the evils for which she endeavors to find some remedy. She is led to this through that love which is inseparable from the higher order of genius. That noblest form of genius which generates the truest poetry—the poetry of feeling rather than of imagination—warm with human life, but uncolored by voluptuous passion—is strongly connected with love. Not the sentiment which dances through the world to the music of marriage-bells; but that divine, self-ignoring, universal love of which the inspired apostle wrote so burningly, when, caught up in the fiery chariot of the Holy Ghost, he looked down upon the selfish considerations of common humanity: the love (or charity) "which beareth all things, endureth all things, which suffereth long and is kind,"— the love which, looking to heaven, stretches its arms to enfold the whole human brotherhood.

This is the love which, hand in hand with genius, is yet to work out the redemption of society. I have faith to believe it; and sometimes, when the tide of hope and enthusiasm is high, I have thought that woman, with the patience and the long-suffering of her love, the purity of her intellect, her instinctive sympathy and her soul of poetry, might be God's chosen instrument in this work of gradual reformation, this reconciling of the harsh contrasts in society that jar so upon our sense of harmony, this righting of the grievous wrongs and evils over which we weep and pray, this final uniting of men into one common brotherhood by the bonds of sympathy and affection.

It may be but a Utopian dream; but the faith is better than hopelessness; it is elevating and cheering to believe it. It is well to aspire, though the aspiration be unfulfilled. It is better to look up at the stars, though they dazzle, than down at the vermin beneath our feet.

Alexander Cowie
"The Domestic Sentimentalists and Other Popular Writers" (1948)

.   .   .   .

The domestic novel had reciprocal relationships with various other forms of fiction. A precise definition is therefore difficult, but for the moment the domestic novel may be roughly defined, in its first phase at least, as an extended prose tale composed chiefly of commonplace household incidents and episodes casually worked into a trite plot involving the fortunes of characters who exist less as individuals than as carriers of moral or religious sentiment. The thesis of such a book is that true happiness comes from submission to suffering. In its purest strain the domestic novel relied far more on religious sentiment than on romantic love, but as time went on the latter greatly increased its ratio and even an erotic element (for which the author acknowledged no responsibility) became dimly apparent between the lines. Other variations occur from author to author, but enough homogeneity obtains in the genre to give some validity to the following receipt to make a domestic novel.

First, take a young and not-too-pretty child about ten years old. Boys are possible, but girls are to be preferred, for the author and the increasing majority of women readers will be more at home in the detail. Make sure that the child is, or shortly will be, an orphan. If the mother is still living, put her to death very gradually in a scene of much sorrow and little physical suffering, uttering pious hopes and admonitions to the last. The father presumably died years ago under circumstances not well known. Now put the child under the care of a shrewish aunt, who resents being obliged to take care of her dead brother's brat. If it has been impossible to remove the father as suggested above, a reasonably good compromise will be to have him make a second marriage with a frivolous, heartless society woman. In an emergency a cruel housekeeper will do. The child is now unhappy, undernourished, and underprivileged. She is exposed to the taunts of snobbish little rich girls. It is essential that she accidentally overhear unkind comments on her awkward clothes, rustic manners, bad behavior, or even her family honor. Slander may be used freely for spicing the plot. The child's behavior may in fact be actually bad in the beginning. She may "sass" her aunt. She may even shy a stone through a window. But her worst sin is her "pride." Now introduce a young woman living not far away, who embodies all Christian virtues, especially humility. Let this lady kiss, pray over, and cry with the heroine at intervals of from three to four pages. The lady may or may not be blind; at any rate she has had her sorrows and she is destined to die

Chapter 10 in *The Rise of the American Novel* (New York: American Book Co., 1948), 413–415.

about two-thirds of the way through the book of badly diagnosed tuber-culosis. She will die at sunset—without a struggle. She is going home. Tears which have been flowing freely now practically inundate the book. The girl's only remaining friends are an eccentric (Barkis-like) teamster, and a wealthy (Cheeryble-like) merchant who now and then gives her a lollipop.[1] In the meantime she has learned to subdue her pride and to submit graciously to the suffering which is the lot of all mortals in this shabby world. You may end your story here if you will, with the child on the verge of adolescence; but it is preferable to carry on a few years in order that the heroine may be menaced by a proud, handsome, moody, Rochester-like man aged about thirty who has traveled and sinned (very vaguely) in the Orient. He at first scarcely notices the meek little girl, but her bright spirit and vaguely referred to physical charms finally force him to admit to himself that he must have her. If it weren't for Queen Victoria, he would try to seduce her, but as it is he is reduced to proposing marriage. To his astonishment she refuses. This sends him darkly off on more travels. The girl meanwhile has learned to support herself by teaching, acting as governess, or writing, and she talks rather briskly about independence for women. Let her endure many trials and perform many pious acts. Monotony may be broken by a trip to Saratoga or by the introduction of some physical peril such as a carriage accident, an attack by a mad dog, or a fire. One day the moody man comes back, and finds her sitting in a cemetery. He proposes again and is accepted. Don't be alarmed at this: his pride has been humbled, too, and he is now reformed. He may even become a minister—but he has plenty of money. For her part, the heroine now drops all fantastic notions of female inde-pendence, for she realizes that a woman's greatest glory is wifely submis-sion. The acid aunt either dies or experiences a change of heart toward the heroine. In the latter case she may be married off to the neighboring teamster (blacksmith will do). The wealthy merchant turns out to be the heroine's father: he wasn't really lost at sea! Everybody is now happy in a subdued, Christian sort of way.

1. The references are to characters in novels by Charles Dickens; Barkis is the oblig-ing carrier in *David Copperfield* (1849–1850), and the Cheerybles are wealthy mer-chants who befriend the hero of *Nicholas Nickleby* (1839).

Helen Waite Papashvily
All the Happy Endings (1956)

. . . [B]asically the domestic novels were ever the same. The center of interest was the home although that edifice might range from one of Mrs. E.D.E.N. Southworth's noble English castles to the tastefully adorned wigwam of Malaeska in Mrs. Ann Stephens' book of the same name. The common woman was always glorified, her every thought, action, gesture, chance word fraught with esoteric meaning and far-reaching influence; her daily routine of cooking, washing, baking, nursing, scrubbing imbued with dramatic significance; her petty trials and small joys magnified to heroic proportions.

There were no historical figures, few excursions into the past or the future. Their own world and the immediate present occupied readers and writers exclusively.

The authors of the domestic novel shared curiously similar backgrounds. Almost all were women of upper-middle-class origin who began very early in life to write, frequently under pressure of sudden poverty. Several published while still in their teens (usually a temperance tale). A majority lived or visited in the South. Most important for many of these women, somewhere, sometimes, someplace in her past some man—a father, a brother, a husband, a guardian—had proved unworthy of the trust and confidence she placed in him. This traumatic experience, never resolved, grew into a chronic grievance.

The small crimes of men—their propensity to make noise and dirt and war and trouble—the insensitivity, the violence, the lust inherent in the masculine character might sometimes be overlooked, but readers and writers and their unifying symbol, the heroines, could never forget how a man boasted and swaggered and threatened and promised and commanded—nor ever forgive that in the end he failed.

No man, fortunately for his peace of mind, ever discovered that the domestic novels were handbooks of another kind of feminine revolt— that these pretty tales reflected and encouraged a pattern of feminine behavior so quietly ruthless, so subtly vicious that by comparison the ladies at Seneca appear angels of innocence.

Even so astute an observer as Vernon K. Parrington could dismiss the sentimental novel as weak "cambric tea." Like the rest of his sex, he did not detect the faint bitter taste of poison in the cup nor recognize that these books were rather a witches' broth, a lethal draught brewed by women and used by women to destroy their common enemy, man.

It is not to be imagined that the ways and means of correcting a long list of feminine grievances were communicated on a conscious level. The link between reader and writer forged by every popular book is a

(New York: Harper and Brothers, 1956), xvi–xvii.

mystic one. The writer may not know all he has said; the reader all he has heard; yet they understand each other perfectly.

Nineteenth-century women, if they were to achieve freedom in what seemed to them a hostile world, needed direction, inspiration, appreciation, reassurance, a sense of self-importance and a group unity, a plan of action.

The Seneca Falls Convention supplied this to a few women but uncounted hundreds and thousands more found *their* Declaration of Rights, *their* Statement of Intentions within the pages of the domestic novel.

Nina Baym
Woman's Fiction (1978)

. . . The many novels all tell, with variations, a single tale. In essence, it is the story of a young girl who is deprived of the supports she had rightly or wrongly depended on to sustain her throughout life and is faced with the necessity of winning her own way in the world. This young girl is fittingly called a heroine because her role is precisely analogous to the unrecognized or undervalued youths of fairy tales who perform dazzling exploits and win a place for themselves in the land of happy endings. She also fits the pattern of comic hero, whose displacement indicates social corruption and whose triumph ensures the reconstruction of a beneficent social order. In Jungian perspective, her story exemplifies the difficult but successful negotiation of the undifferentiated child through the trials of adolescence into the individuation of sound adulthood. The happy marriages with which most—though not all—of this fiction concludes are symbols of successful accomplishment of the required task and resolutions of the basic problems raised in the story, which is in most primitive terms the story of the formation and assertion of a feminine ego.

.   .   .   .

[The story] exists in two parallel versions. In one, the heroine begins as a poor and friendless child. Most frequently an orphan, she sometimes only thinks herself to be one, or has by necessity been separated from her parents for an indefinite time. In the second, the heroine is a pampered heiress who becomes poor and friendless in midadolescence, through the death or financial failure of her legal protectors. At this point the two plots merge, for both show how the heroine develops the capacity to survive and surmount her troubles. At the end of the novel she is no longer an underdog. The purpose of both plots is to deprive the heroine of all external aids and to make her success in life entirely a function of her own efforts and character. The idea that a woman's identity or place in life is a function of her father's or husband's place is firmly rejected, not merely on idealistic but also on realistic grounds. If the orphan's rags-to-riches story caught one aspect of American life and faith, the heiress's riches-to-rags caught another. As some moved up, others fell down. When men fell, their dependent women fell with them. Several women authors began their careers as a direct result of financial catastrophe in their families; as we will see, the Panic of 1837 created a large new group of women authors. Their novels showed how women were forced to depend on themselves. They asserted that women had to be prepared for both economic and emotional self-support, but promised

(Ithaca, N.Y.: Cornell University Press, 1978), 11–12; 35–40; 48–50.

that the sex was equal to the challenge, even that the challenge could become an opportunity.

There are two kinds of heroine in this novel, the flawless and the flawed. The flawless are those who already possess the emotional strength and stability to function effectively when adversity strikes. The flawed are those whose characters are defective, so that triumph in adversity becomes a matter of self-conquest as well as conquest of the other. Some novels present more than one heroine. A flawed and a flawless heroine may counterpoint one another. Again, two kinds of flaws will be opposed, such as excessive dependency against excessive self-will. The overly dependent woman has to acquire firmness, the self-willed woman learns to bend so as not to break. The idea of what is, and what is not, a flaw varies according to the perspective of the individual author, yet all agree that some degree of self-control is a moral and practical necessity while total self-abnegation is suicidal. The writers' conviction that character had to adjust to limiting circumstances, their belief that suffering and hardship could not be avoided in any human life, and their strenuous insistence that such trials, because they called out otherwise dormant abilities, could become occasions for "perfecting" the character imply a deeply Victorian world view. This view is radically unlike the postmodern sensibility with its stress on the immediate, the physical, and the expressive as well as its return to the pre-Victorian infatuation with pure feeling conceptualized as identical to virtue. Hence the implications of the authors' message, evolved within such a view, may strike today's reader as inhibiting rather than liberating as they were meant to be.

The novels were Victorian also in their perception of the self as a social product, firmly and irrevocably embedded in a social construct that could destroy it but that also shaped it, constrained it, encouraged it, and ultimately fulfilled it. They told stories about the emergent self negotiating amidst social possibilities, attempting to assert and maintain a territory within a social space full of warring claims. The process was fatiguing and frustrating, but none of these authors proposed the Huck Finn solution of abandoning "sivilization" because none of them could imagine the concept of self apart from society. If critics ever permit the woman's novel to join the main body of "American literature," then all our theories about American fiction, from Richard Chase's "romance" to Richard Poirier's "world elsewhere" to Carolyn Heilbrun's "masculine wilderness" will have to be radically revised.

The heroine's "self" emerges concurrently with her growth from child to adult; as child and woman her chief relations are with those more powerful than she. We find two basic power situations: either those who have authority over the child abuse it (much the more common situation) or they are fair but unsympathetic and uncongenial. These two situations confront the child with somewhat different problems, but in both of them there are invariable conditions: home life is not happy, the

child is not loved or valued, those who should love and nurture her instead exploit or neglect her. Home is more a detention camp than a
"walled garden," sharing with that popular image only the walls. The
romances make the point through fathers who lock up their daughters;
the realistic novels prefer to show the daily wearing down of neglected
and overworked orphans. The heroine's problem in these situations is,
indeed, basic; it is to endure until she comes of age and at the same time
to grow so that when she comes of age she will be able to leave the unfriendly environment and succeed on her own. She must learn to strike
a balance between total submission, which means self-denial to the
point of death, and an equally suicidal defiance. She has to learn how to
comply as a practical necessity, without being violated. Compliance and
inner independence are equally necessary for life.

.   .   .   .

As her kin fail her, the heroine meets people in the community who
support, advise, and befriend her. Occasionally they intercede to remove
her from the unfriendly environment. As an adult, she continues to rely
on them and often returns the favors they have done her. In novel after
novel, a network of surrogate kin gradually defines itself around the heroine, making hers the story not only that of a self-made woman but that
of a self-made or surrogate family. Most of these novels conclude with a
marriage that represents the institutionalizing of such families, for the
heroine's new home includes not only her husband but all her other inti-
mates as well. And her final "domesticity" is defined as her relations
with all these adults, rather than as childbearing and childrearing, for
the novels rarely follow the heroine past the threshold of motherhood.
Lip service was certainly paid to motherhood as the crown of woman's
joys, and no author had the courage to suggest that children might be
more burdensome than pleasurable; yet the plots make it absolutely
clear that although children may be necessary for a woman's happiness,
they are not necessary for her identity—nor is a husband.

Between her unhappy childhood and the conclusion, the heroine experiences an interlude during which she must earn her own living. Generally she turns to some form of teaching. The heiress fallen on hard
times has ladylike accomplishments in which she can now instruct others; the exploited orphan has stolen enough time from her duties to acquire a rudimentary education that she can now pass on. In this time of
her life, whether through misunderstanding or other cause, the heroine is
without a suitor and resigns herself to a life without marriage. She stays
aloof from the husband hunting of her peers, preferring, in an oft-repeated
phrase, "honest independence" to a mercenary marriage. She often rejects eligible suitors for reasons that, though sometimes far-fetched, require her to confront and accept the likelihood of spinsterhood. Although almost all the heroines do eventually marry, the stories assert
that marriage cannot and should not be the goal toward which women
direct themselves, that neither its inevitability nor its permanence can

be assumed, and that a commercial marriage is worse by far than a single life. This message is reinforced by the important background role played by unmarried or widowed women. The proliferation and variety of such characters evokes a world in which marriage may be only an episode in a woman's life; everywhere the heroine encounters women of all ages without husbands. Few characters in this literature receive the same respect and affection as does the kind, strong-hearted widow who has brought up stable children and still finds time to mother the heroine. Too, the predominance of woman characters in most of this fiction suggests that women perceived themselves to be living in a world mostly populated by members of their own sex and recognized that, on a day-to-day basis, relations with their own sex constituted the texture of their lives.

The men in this fiction are less important to the heroine's emotional life than women. Chiefly, they are the controllers and dispensers of money, and in this way the ultimate though sometimes remote shapers of women's lives. The heiress cannot possess her wealth directly but must maneuver with men. If orphaned, she must deal with the cupidity of her guardians and suitors. An heiress with parents must combat her father's plans to dispose of her wealth, plans that generally include the disposal of her person. An heiress who is suddenly impoverished becomes so through the gambling habits of a brother or (a larger form of the same vice) the speculating habits of a father. In many novels, death of the father reveals what is called "an embarrassed state of affairs" plunging a comfortable and unprepared family into poverty. When the mother—an eighteenth-century passive and dependent woman—cannot deal with the situation, the more flexible and enterprising daughter takes charge. The brother, who ought to guide the straitened family, is absent or unable to rise above entrenched habits of idleness and attitudes of snobbery. Gambling tempts him as well as drink, and soon he becomes another of his sister's dependents. If the father survives his bankruptcy, the heroine supports him too; in effect she becomes the head of the family whatever its circumstances. But she goes beyond taking her father's place. She brings into being a new kind of family life, organized around love rather than money. Money subsides into its adjunct function of ensuring domestic comfort.

. . . [T]hese writers were thinking about a social reorganization wherein their special concept of home was projected out into the world. They recognized that home and the world were different, but unlike many male theorists of the day (and in contradistinction to the interpretation that later generations have put on them) they did not really see these as "separate spheres." Their depiction of home life showed the home thoroughly penetrated at every point by the world, dominated by man, the world's ambassador, and vulnerable to the various empty temptations of wealth as well as the possibility of poverty. If worldly values could dominate the home, perhaps the direction of influence could be reversed so that home values dominated the world. Since they identified home values with basic human values, they saw this as a reformation of America into a society at last responsive to truly human needs, a fulfillment of the original settlers' dreams.

Now in this view "home" is not a space but a system of human relations; still it is in the family enclosure that such a system can most quickly be put into practice and, since new human beings are trained there, can be lastingly learned. Woman, if she can preside over the home space, will then be not out of the world but at the very center of it. When accepting, as one's basic relation to another, obligation rather than exploitation, doing another good rather than doing him in; when books and conversation and simple comfort seem superior to ostentation and feverish pleasure—then, our authors believed, a true social revolution will have taken place, American life will have been transformed. . . .

Thus our authors imagined that if each woman rose to the opportunity that history was putting in her hands, the opportunity to develop herself as worthy representative of domestic values, then women collectively would make a peaceful revolution. The decade of the 1850s was the high point of their fiction because the motives of self-development and social reform could run together so smoothly. Women could change others by changing themselves, and the phrase "woman's sphere is in the home" could appear to mean "woman's sphere is to reform the world." Some of the authors liked to use Pascal's circle, whose center was everywhere and circumference nowhere, as the image of woman's "sphere." Nor did these women couch their reforming intentions in the language of nostalgia, although in fiction of the twenties and thirties one finds a certain longing for colonial austerity. Most authors felt that the domestic institution under whose banner they were crusading was, like woman's expanding self-confidence and self-esteem, something entirely new.

The course of history dictated that the crusade for domesticity, unlike that for woman's parity with men, would be short-lived. The liberal women who began their writing careers after the Civil War found the redemptive possibilities of enlightened domesticity to be no longer credible. The Civil War had demonstrated the feebleness of the affectional model of human relationships, and the Gilded Age affirmed profit as the motive around which all of American life was to be organized. Home now became a retreat, a restraint and a constraint, as it had not appeared to be earlier; to define it as woman's sphere was now unambiguously to invite her to absent herself permanently from the world's affairs. . . . Hence, after the Civil War, the idea of expanding woman and her world began to oppose the domestic ideology rather than cooperate with it. Women continued to write, in ever greater numbers, but the "woman's novel"—that is, the novel designed to succeed with a mass audience of literate women—changed its form and ideology.

Jane P. Tompkins
"The Other American Renaissance" (1985)

[According to modern critical tradition] the "great" figures of the 1850's, a period known to us now as the "American Renaissance," were a handful of men who refused to be taken in by the pieties of the age. Disgusted by the cliches that poured from the pens of the "scribbling women," these men bore witness to a darker reality, which the mass of readers could not face. While successful female authors told tearful stories about orphan girls whose Christian virtue triumphed against all odds, the truly great writers—Poe, Hawthorne, Melville, Emerson, Thoreau—dared, according to Henry Nash Smith, to "explore the dark underside of the psyche," and to tackle "ultimate social and intellectual issues." And because they repudiated the culture's dominant value-system they were, in Perry Miller's words, "crushed by the juggernaut" of the popular sentimental novel.[1] The sentimental writers, on the other hand, were sadly out of touch with reality. What they produced, says Smith, was a literature of "reassurance," calculated to soothe the anxieties of an economically troubled age. To the "Common Man and Common Woman," fearful of challenge or change, they preached a "cosmic success story," which promised that the practice of virtue would lead to material success. Their subject matter—the tribulations of orphan girls—was innately trivial; their religious ideas were "little more than a blur of good intentions"; they "feared the probing of the inner life," and above all were committed to avoiding anything that might make the "undiscriminating mass" of their middle-brow readers "uncomfortable."[2]

Those judgments are, in fact, amplified versions of what Hawthorne and Melville said about their sentimental rivals, whom they hated for their popular and critical success. My purpose here is to challenge that description of sentimental novels and to argue that their exclusion from the canon of American literature has been a mistake. For it seems to me that . . . modern scholars ought to pay attention to a body of work which was so enormously influential and which drew so vehement a response from those who—successfully as it turned out—strove to suppress it.

. . . .

Chapter 3 in *Sensational Designs: The Cultural Work of American Fiction, 1790–1860* (New York: Oxford University Press, 1985). Excerpts were taken from ms. 108–109; 110–112; 114–116; 127; 130–134.
1. Henry Nash Smith, "The Scribbling Women and the Cosmic Success Story," *Critical Inquiry*, 1 (September, 1974): 47–49; *Democracy and the Novel* (New York: Oxford University Press, 1978), p. 12; Perry Miller, "The Romance and the Novel," *Nature's Nation* (Cambridge, Mass.: Belknap Press of Harvard University Press, 1967), pp. 255–256.—[Author's note, as are subsequent notes to this selection; ellipses ours.]
2. Smith, *Democracy and the Novel*, pp. 13–15.

. . . The impact of sentimental novels is directly related to the cultural context that produced them. And once one begins to explore this context in even a preliminary way, the critical practice which assigns Hawthorne and Melville the role of heroes, the sentimental novelists the role of villains, and the public the role of their willing dupes, loses its credibility. The one great fact of American life during the period under consideration was, in Perry Miller's words, the "terrific universality" of the revival.[3] Sentimental fiction was perhaps the most influential expression of the beliefs that animated the revival movement and had shaped the character of American life in the years before the Civil War. Antebellum critics and readers did not distinguish sharply between fiction and what we would now call religious propaganda. [Susan] Warner, for instance, never referred to her books as "novels" but called them stories, because, in her eyes, they functioned in the same way as Biblical parables, or the pamphlets published by the American Tract Society; that is, they were written for edification's sake and not for the sake of art, as we understand it. The highest function of any art, for Warner as for most of her contemporaries, was the bringing of souls to Christ. Like their counterparts among the evangelical clergy, the sentimental novelists wrote to educate their readers in Christian perfection and to move the nation as a whole closer to the City of God. They saw their work as part of a world-historical mission, but in order to understand the nature of their project one has to have some familiarity with the cultural discourse of the age for which they spoke.

The best place to begin is with a set of documents that, as far as I know, have never made their way into criticism of American Renaissance literature: the publications of the American Tract Society, one of the five great religious organizations of the Evangelical United Front.[4] . . . The literature of the American Tract Society, the first organization in America to publish and distribute the printed word on a mass scale, is a testament both to the faith of evangelical Christians—to the shape of their dreams—and to what they experienced as everyday reality. It is only by attempting to see reality as they did that one can arrive at a notion of what gave sentimental fiction its tremendous original force.

.   .   .   .

. . . In one Tract Society report the Visiter [to homes of the poor] records that a young woman who was dying of pulmonary consumption became concerned at the eleventh hour about the condition of her soul and asked for spiritual help. "She was found by the Visiter," the report reads, "supplied with a number of tracts, and kindly directed to the Sav-

3. Perry Miller, *The Life of the Mind in America from the Revolution to the Civil War* (New York: Harcourt Brace and World, 1965).
4. This is the term given to the movement by Charles Foster in his excellent account, *An Errand of Mercy: The Evangelical United Front, 1790–1837* (Chapel Hill: The University of North Carolina Press, 1960).

iour of sinners. Some of her relatives—they cannot be called friends—attempted to impede the Visiter's way to her bedside, and would often present hinderances which she could not remove. God, however, showed himself strong in her behalf. . . . For some time clouds hung over her mind, but they were at length dispelled by the sun of righteousness. . . . As she approached the hour which tries men's souls, her strength failed fast; her friends gathered around her; . . . and while they were engaged in a hymn her soul seemed to impart unnatural energy to her emaciated and dying body. To the astonishment of all, she said to her widowed mother, who bent anxiously over her, 'Don't weep for me, I shall soon be in the arms of my Saviour.' She prayed fervently, and fell asleep in Jesus."[5]

Like all the fiction we label "sentimental," this narrative blots out the uglier details of life and cuts experience to fit a pattern of pious expectation. The anecdote tells nothing about the personality or background of the young woman, fails to represent even the barest facts of her disease or of her immediate surroundings. For these facts, the report substitutes the panaceas of Christian piety—God's mercy on a miserable sinner, the tears and prayers of a deathbed conversion, "falling asleep" in Jesus. Its plot follows a prescribed course from sin to salvation. But what is extraordinary about this anecdote is that it is not a work of fiction but a factual report. Though its facts do not correspond to what a twentieth-century observer would have recorded, had he or she been at the scene, they faithfully represent what the Tract Society member saw. Whereas a modern social worker would have noticed the furniture of the sick room, the kind of house the woman lived in, her neighborhood, would have described her illness, its history and course of treatment, and sketched in her socio-economic background and that of her relatives and friends, the Tract Visiter sees only a spiritual predicament: the woman's initial "alarm," the "clouds . . . that hung over her mind," God's action on her heart, the turn from sin to righteousness. Whereas the modern observer would have structured the events in a downward spiral, as the woman's condition deteriorated from serious to critical, and ended with her death, the report reverses that progression. Its movement is upward, from "thoughtlessness" to "conviction," to "great tranquility, joy, and triumph."[6]

The charge twentieth-century critics have always levelled against sentimental fiction is that it presents a picture of life so oversimplified and improbable, that only the most naive and self-deceiving reader could believe it. But the sense of the real which this criticism takes for granted is not the one that the readers of sentimental novels had. Their assumptions are the same as those that structured the events of the report I have just quoted. . . .

.   .   .   .

5. New York City Tract Society, *Eleventh Annual Report* (New York, 1837), pp. 51–52.
6. Ibid.

. . . When critics dismiss sentimental fiction because it is out of touch with reality, they do so because the reality *they* perceive is organized according to a different set of conventions for constituting experience. For while the attack on sentimental fiction claims for itself freedom from the distorting effects of a naive religious perspective, the real naivete is to think that that attack is launched from no perspective whatsoever, or that its perspective is disinterested and not culture-bound in the way the sentimental novelists were. The popular fiction of the American Renaissance has been dismissed primarily because it follows from assumptions about the shape and meaning of existence that we no longer hold. But once one has a grasp of the problems these writers were trying to solve, their solutions do not seem hypocritical or shallow, unrealistic or naive; on the contrary, given the social circumstances within which they had to work, their prescriptions for living seem at least as heroic as those put forward by the writers who said, "No, in thunder."

Tompkins goes on to argue that "the practice of submission, which looks like slavery to us, became, in the context of evangelical Christianity, the basis for a claim to mastery," just as "confinement to the home, which looks to us like deprivation, became a means of personal fulfillment." Her approach is illustrated by her comments on the opening chapters of Susan Warner's The Wide, Wide World.

. . . The fact is that American women simply could not assume a stance of open rebellion against the conditions of their lives for they lacked the material means of escape or opposition. They had to stay put and submit. And so the domestic novelists made that necessity the basis on which to build a power structure of their own. Instead of rejecting the culture's value system outright, they appropriated it for their own use, subjecting the beliefs and customs that had molded them to a series of transformations that allowed them both to fulfill and transcend their appointed roles.

The process of transformation gets underway immediately in Warner's novel when the heroine, Ellen Montgomery, a child of ten, learns that her mother is about to leave on a long voyage for the sake of her health and that she will probably never see her mother again. The two have been weeping uncontrollably in one another's arms, when Mrs. Montgomery recollects herself and says: "Ellen! Ellen! listen to me . . . my child this is not right. Remember, my darling, who it is that brings this sorrow upon us,—though we *must* sorrow, we must not rebel."[7] Ellen's mother, who has been ordered to go on this voyage by her husband and her physician, makes no attempt to change the situation. She accepts the features of her life as fixed and instructs her daughter to do the same. The message of this scene, and of most sentimental fiction, is "though

7. Elizabeth Wetherell (Susan Warner), *The Wide, Wide World*, 2 vols, in 1 (1851); rept. J. P. Lippincott and Co., 1886), I, 12.

we *must* sorrow, we must not rebel." This message can be understood in one of two ways. The most obvious is to read it as an example of how this fiction worked to keep women down. This reading sees women as the dupes of a culture which taught them that disobedience to male authority was a "sin against heaven."[8] When mothers teach their daughters to interpret the commands of husbands and fathers as the will of God, they make rebellion impossible, and at the same time, hold out the false hope of a reward for suffering, since, as Mrs. Montgomery says, "God sends no trouble upon his children but in love."[9] In this view, religion is nothing but an opiate for the oppressed and a myth which served the rulers of a "Puritanical" and "trading nation." In this view, the sentimental novelists, to use Ann Douglas's phrase, did "the dirty work" of their culture by teaching women how to become the agents of their own subjection.[10]

The problem with this reading is that it is too simplistic. The women in these novels make submission "their boast" not because they enjoy it but because it gave them another ground on which to stand, a position that, while it fulfilled the social demands placed upon them, gave them a place from which to launch a counter-strategy against their worldly masters that would finally give them the upper hand. Submission, as it is presented throughout this novel, is never submission to the will of a husband or father, though that is what it appears to be on the surface; submission is first of all a self-willed act of conquest of one's own passions. Mrs. Montgomery tells Ellen that her tears of anger are "not right," that she must "command" and "compose" herself, because, she says, "You will hurt both yourself and me, my daughter, if you cannot."[11] Ellen will hurt herself by failing to submit because her submission is not capitulation to an external authority but the mastery of herself, and therefore, paradoxically, an assertion of autonomy.[12] In its definition of power relations, the domestic novel operates here, and elsewhere, according to a principle of reversal whereby what is "least" in the world's eyes becomes "greatest" in its perspective. So "submission" becomes "self-conquest" and doing the will of one's husband or father brings an access of divine power. By conquering herself in the name of the highest possible authority, the dutiful woman merges her own authority with God's. When Mrs. Montgomery learns that her husband and doctor have ordered her to part from Ellen, she says to herself "Not my will, but thine be done."[13] By making themselves into the vehicles of God's will,

8. Rev. Orville Dewey, *A Discourse Preached in the City of Washington, on Sunday, June 27th, 1852* (New York: Charles S. Francis and Company, 1852), p. 13. . . .

9. Warner, *The Wide, Wide World*, I, 13.

10. Ann Douglas, *The Feminization of American Culture* (New York: Alfred A. Knopf, 1977), p. 11.

11. Warner, *The Wide, Wide World*, I, 13.

12. Tocqueville describes the process of moral education of American women in very much the same terms. . . . *Democracy in America*, II, 210, 212.

13. Warner, *The Wide, Wide World*, I, 35.

these female characters become nothing in themselves but all-powerful in relation to the world. By ceding themselves to the source of all power, they bypass worldly (male) authority and, as it were, cancel it out. The ability to "submit" in this way is presented, moreover, as the special prerogative of women, transmitted from mother to daughter. As the women in these novels teach one another how to "command" themselves, they bind themselves to one another and to God in a holy alliance against the men who control their material destinies. Thus, when Mr. Montgomery refuses his wife the money to buy Ellen a parting gift, it is no accident that she uses her own mother's ring to make the purchase; the ring symbolizes the tacit system of solidarity that exists among women in these books. Nor is it an accident that the gift Mrs. Montgomery gives her daughter is a Bible. The mother's Bible-gift, in sentimental literature, is invested with supernatural power because it testifies to the reality of the spiritual order where women hold dominion over everything by virtue of their submission on earth.

Bibliography

Works asterisked are directly about eighteenth- and nineteenth-century women's literature; works not asterisked provide general background on the topic.
    Works solely about individual authors are not included here; rather, they appear in the selected bibliographies appended to the biographical sections.

Allen, Richard. "If You Have Tears: Sentimentalism as Soft Romanticism." *Genre* 8 (June 1975): 119–145.
American Women Writers: A Critical Reference Guide from Colonial Times to the Present. 4 vols. Edited by Lina Mainiero and Langdon Lynne Faust. New York: Frederick Ungar Publishing Co., 1979–1982.
Barnett, Louise K. *The Ignoble Savage: American Literary Racism, 1790–1890.* Westport, Conn.: Greenwood Press, 1975.
Baym, Nina. "Melodramas of Beset Manhood: How Theories of American Fiction Exclude Women Authors." *American Quarterly* 33 (Summer 1981): 123–139.
———. "Portrayal of Women in American Literature, 1790–1870." In *What Manner of Woman: Essays on English and American Life and Literature,* edited by Marlene Springer, 211–234. New York: New York University Press, 1977.
*———. *Woman's Fiction: A Guide to Novels by and about Women in America 1820–1870.* Ithaca, N.Y. and London: Cornell University Press, 1978.
Beard, Mary Ritter. "American Women and the Printing Press." *Annals of the American Academy of Political and Social Science* 143 (May 1929): 195–206.
Benson, Mary Sumner. *Women in Eighteenth-Century America: A Study of Opinion and Social Usage.* New York: Columbia University Press, 1935.
Blair, Walter. *Native American Humor.* New York: American Book Co., 1937.
*Bode, Carl. "The Scribbling Women: The Domestic Novel Rules the 'Fifties." In *The Anatomy of American Popular Culture, 1840–1861,* 169–187. Berkeley and Los Angeles: University of California Press, 1959.
Branch, Edward Douglas. *The Sentimental Years, 1836–1860.* New York: D. Appleton-Century Co., 1934.
Brooks, Van Wyck. *The Flowering of New England, 1815–1865.* New York: E. P. Dutton and Co., 1936.
*Brown, Herbert Ross. "Sex and Sensibility" and "Home Sweet Home." In *The Sentimental Novel in America, 1789–1860,* 101–165; 281–322. Durham, N.C.: Duke University Press, 1940.
Browne, Anita, ed. *The 100 Best Books by American Women, 1833–1933.* Chicago: Associated Authors Service, 1933.
Bruère, Martha Bensley, and Beard, Mary Ritter, eds. *Laughing Their Way: Women's Humor in America.* New York: Macmillan Co., 1934.
Carroll, Berenice A., ed. *Liberating Women's History.* Urbana: University of Illinois Press, 1976.
Coad, Oral Sumner. "The Gothic Element in American Literature before 1835." *Journal of English and Germanic Philology* 24, no. 1 (1925): 72–93.

Conrad, Susan Phinney. *Perish the Thought: Intellectual Women in Romantic America, 1830–1860.* New York: Oxford University Press, 1976.

Cott, Nancy F. *The Bonds of Womanhood: "Woman's Sphere" in New England 1780–1835.* New Haven, Conn.: Yale University Press, 1977.

*Cowie, Alexander. "The Domestic Sentimentalists and Other Popular Writers (1850–1870)." In *The Rise of the American Novel,* 412–446. New York: American Book Co., 1948.

*———. "The Vogue of the Domestic Novel, 1850–1870." *South Atlantic Quarterly* 41 (October 1942): 416–424.

Davidson, Cathy N. "Mothers and Daughters in the Fiction of the New Republic." In *The Lost Tradition: Mothers and Daughters in Literature,* edited by Cathy N. Davidson and E. M. Broner, 115–127. New York: Frederick Ungar Publishing Co., 1980.

Deegan, Dorothy Yost. *The Stereotype of the Single Woman in American Novels.* New York: Columbia University Press, 1951.

Dexter, Elisabeth Anthony. "With Tongue, Pen, and Printer's Ink." In *Colonial Women of Affairs: A Study of Women in Business and the Professions in America before 1776,* 126–179. Boston and New York: Houghton Mifflin Co., 1924.

*Donovan, Josephine. "Toward the Local Colorists: Early American Women's Tradition." In *New England Local Color Literature: A Women's Tradition,* 25–37. New York: Frederick Ungar Publishing Co., 1983.

Douglas, Ann [Ann Douglas Wood]. *The Feminization of American Culture.* New York: Alfred A. Knopf, 1977.

———. "Heaven Our Home: Consolation Literature in the Northern United States, 1830–1880." *American Quarterly* 26 (December 1974): 496–515.

———. "The Literature of Impoverishment: The Women Local Colorists in America 1865–1914." *Women's Studies* 1, no. 1 (1972): 3–40.

———. "Mrs. Sigourney and the Sensibility of the Inner Space." *New England Quarterly* 45 (June 1972): 163–181.

Doyle, Mildred D. *Sentimentalism in American Periodicals, 1741–1800.* New York: New York University Press, 1944.

Dubois, Ellen. *Feminism and Suffrage: The Emergence of an Independent Women's Movement in America, 1848–1869.* Ithaca, N.Y.: Cornell University Press, 1978.

Earle, Alice Morse. "Early Prose." In *Early Prose and Verse,* edited by Alice Morse Earle and Emily Ellsworth Ford, 3–103. New York: Harper and Brothers, 1893.

Epstein, Barbara Leslie. *The Politics of Domesticity.* Middletown, Conn.: Wesleyan University Press, 1981.

Ernest, Joseph M., Jr. "Whittier and the 'Feminine Fifties.'" *American Literature* 28 (March 1956–January 1957): 184–196.

Fiedler, Leslie. *Love and Death in the American Novel.* New York: Criterion Books, 1960.

Flexner, Eleanor. *Century of Struggle: The Woman's Rights Movement in the United States.* Cambridge, Mass.: Harvard University Press, 1959.

*Forrest, Mary [Julia Deane Freeman]. *Women of the South Distinguished in Literature.* New York: Charles B. Richardson, 1865.

Foster, Edward Halsey. *The Civilized Wilderness: Backgrounds to American Romantic Literature, 1817–1860.* New York: Free Press, 1975.

*Frederick, John T. "Hawthorne's 'Scribbling Women.'" *New England Quarterly* 48 (June 1975): 231–240.

Gaines, Francis Pendleton. *The Southern Plantation*. New York: Columbia University Press, 1924.

*Garrison, Dee. "Immoral Fiction in the Late Victorian Library." *American Quarterly* 28 (Spring 1976): 71–89.

*Geary, Susan. "The Domestic Novel as a Commercial Commodity: Making a Best Seller in the 1850's." *Papers of the Bibliographical Society of America* 70 (July–September 1976): 365–395.

Goodwin, Etta Ramsdell. "The Literary Women of Washington." *Chautauquan* 27 (September 1898): 579–586.

*Habegger, Alfred. *Gender, Fantasy, and Realism in American Literature*. New York: Columbia University Press, 1982.

Hale, Sarah Josepha. *Woman's Record; or, Sketches of All Distinguished Women, from the Creation to A.D. 1854*. New York: Harper and Brothers, 1855.

*Hart, James D. "Home Influence." In *The Popular Book: A History of America's Literary Taste*, 85–105. New York: Oxford University Press, 1950.

Hart, John Seely. *A Manual of American Literature*. Philadelphia: Eldredge and Bros., 1873.

*———. *The Female Prose Writers of America. With Portraits, Biographical Notices, and Specimens of Their Writings*. Philadelphia: E. H. Butler and Co., 1852.

Hartman, Mary, and Lois W. Banner, eds. *Clio's Consciousness Raised*. New York: Harper and Row, Publishers, 1974.

Henneman, John Bell. *The Nineteenth Century Woman in Literature*. N.p. [1892].

Higginson, Thomas Wentworth. "Woman in Literature." In *Woman: Her Position, Influence, and Achievement Throughout the Civilized World*, edited by William C. King, 493–505. Springfield, Mass.: King-Richardson Co., 1901.

*Hilldrup, Robert Le Roy. "Cold War against the Yankees in the Antebellum Literature of Southern Women." *North Carolina Historical Review* 31 (July 1954): 370–384.

*Hofstader, Beatrice. "Popular Culture and the Romantic Heroine." *American Scholar* 30 (Winter 1960–1961): 98–116.

Howe, Daniel Walker. "American Victorianism as a Culture." *American Quarterly* 27 (December 1975): 507–532.

Hubbell, Jay B. *The South in American Literature, 1607–1900*. Durham, N.C.: Duke University Press, 1954.

*Hull, Raymona E. "'Scribbling' Females and Serious Males: Hawthorne's Comments from Abroad on Some American Authors." In *The Nathaniel Hawthorne Journal 1975*, edited by C. E. Frazer Clark, Jr., 35–58. Englewood, Colo.: Microcard Editions Books, 1975.

*Jehlen, Myra. "Archimedes and the Paradox of Feminist Criticism." *Signs* 6 (Summer 1981): 575–601.

Johannsen, Albert. *The House of Beadle and Adams and Its Dime and Nickel Novels*. 2 vols. Norman: University of Oklahoma Press, 1950.

*Kelley, Mary. "The Literary Domestics: Private Woman on a Public Stage." In *Ideas in America's Cultures*, edited by Hamilton Cravens, 83–102. Ames: Iowa State University Press, 1982.

*———. *Private Woman, Public Stage: Literary Domesticity in Nineteenth-Century America*. New York: Oxford University Press, 1984.

*———. "The Sentimentalists: Promise and Betrayal in the Home." *Signs* 4 (Spring 1979): 434–446.

Kirkland, Joseph. "Realism versus Other Isms." *Dial*, 16 February 1893, 99–101.

Kolb, Harold H., Jr. *The Illusion of Life: American Realism as a Literary Form.* Charlottesville: University Press of Virginia, 1969.

*Kolba, Ellen D. "Stories for Sale." *English Journal* 69 (October 1980): 37–40.

Kolodny, Annette. *The Land Before Her: Fantasy and Experience of the American Frontiers, 1630–1860.* Chapel Hill and London: University of North Carolina Press, 1984.

Lerner, Gerda. "The Lady and the Mill Girl: Changes in the Status of Women in the Age of Jackson." *American Studies* 10 (Spring 1969): 5–15.

Levy, David W. "Racial Stereotypes in Antislavery Fiction." *Phylon* 26 (Summer 1970): 265–279.

"The Literary Lady." In *The Genteel Female: An Anthology,* edited by Clifton Joseph Furness, 256–266. New York: Alfred A. Knopf, 1931.

Loshe, Lillie Deming. *The Early American Novel.* New York: Columbia University Press, 1907.

McDowell, Tremaine. "Sensibility in the Eighteenth Century American Novel." *Studies in Philology* 24 (July 1927): 383–402.

MacLeod, Anne Scott. *A Moral Tale: Children's Fiction and American Culture 1820–1860.* Hamden, Conn.: Shoe String Press, Archon Books, 1975.

*McNall, Sally Allen. *Who Is in the House: A Psychological Study of Two Centuries of Women's Fiction in America, 1795 to the Present.* New York: Elsevier North-Holland, 1981.

Manley, Seon, and Belcher, Susan. *O, Those Extraordinary Women: or the Joys of Literary Lib.* Philadelphia: Chilton Book Co., 1972.

*Manthorne, Jane. "The Lachrymose Ladies." *Horn Book* 43 (June 1967): 375–384; (August 1967): 501–513; (October 1967): 622–630.

Moers, Ellen. "Money, the Job, and Little Women." *Commentary* 55 (January 1973): 57–65. [Discussion in ibid. (May 1973): 26.]

———. "Women's Lit: Profession and Tradition." *Columbia Forum* 1 (Fall 1972): 27–34.

Mott, Frank Luther. *Golden Multitudes: The Story of Best Sellers in the United States.* New York: Macmillan Co., 1947.

———. *A History of American Magazines.* Vol. 1, 1741–1850, New York: D. Appleton and Co., 1930. Vol. 2, 1850–1865, Cambridge, Mass.: Harvard University Press, 1938.

Noel, Mary. *Villains Galore.* New York: Macmillan Co., 1954.

*Nye, Russel B. "The Novel as Dream and Weapon: Women's Popular Novels in the 19th Century." *Historical Society of Michigan Chronicle* 11 (4th Quarter 1975): 2–16.

———. *Society and Culture in America, 1830–1860.* New York: Harper and Row, Publishers, 1974.

———. *The Unembarrassed Muse: The Popular Arts in America.* New York: Dial Press, 1970.

O'Neill, William. *Everyone Was Brave: A History of Feminism in America.* Chicago: Quadrangle Books, 1969.

Orians, G. Harrison. "Censure of Fiction in American Romances and Magazines, 1789–1810." *PMLA* 52 (March 1937): 195–214.

*Papashvily, Helen Waite. *All the Happy Endings: A Study of the Domestic*

Novel in America, the Women Who Wrote It, the Women Who Read It, in the Nineteenth Century. New York: Harper and Brothers, 1956.

Parker, Gail. "Introduction." In *The Oven Birds: American Women on Womanhood, 1820–1920,* edited by Gail Parker. Garden City, N.Y.: Doubleday and Company, 1972.

*"A Patchwork Piece: The Nineteenth-century American Women's Fiction Project." *Women's Studies Quarterly* 10 (Fall 1982): 35–40.

Pattee, Fred Lewis. *The Feminine Fifties.* New York: D. Appleton-Century Co., 1940.

———. *First Century of American Literature.* New York: D. Appleton-Century Co., 1935.

Pearce, Roy Harvey. *The Savages of America.* Baltimore: Johns Hopkins Press, Rev. ed., 1965.

Pearson, Edmund. *Queer Books.* Garden City, N.Y.: Doubleday, Doran and Co., 1928.

Petter, Henri. *The Early American Novel.* Columbus: Ohio State University Press, 1971.

*Rather, Lois. "Were Women Funny? Some 19th Century Humorists." *American Book Collector* 21 (February 1971): 5–10.

*Raymond, Ida [Mary T. Tardy]. *The Living Female Writers of the South.* Philadelphia: Claxton, Remson and Haffelfinger, 1872.

*———. *Southland Writers: Biographical and Critical Sketches of the Living Female Writers of the South. With Extracts from Their Writings.* 2 vols. Philadelphia: Claxton, Remson and Haffelfinger, 1870.

*Robbins, Alice Wellington. "The Humor of Women." *Critic,* 28 June 1884, 301–302.

*———. "Women's Sense of Humor." *Critic,* 29 March 1884, 145–146.

Rosenfelt, Deborah S. "The Politics of Bibliography: Women's Studies and the Literary Canon." In *Women in Print I,* edited by Joan E. Hartman and Ellen Messer–Davidow, 11–35. New York: Modern Language Association, 1982.

Rourke, Constance. *The Roots of American Culture.* New York: Harcourt, Brace and Co., 1942.

Ruoff, John C. "Frivolity to Consumption: or, Southern Womanhood in Antebellum Literature." *Civil War History* 18 (September 1972): 213–229.

Rusk, R. L. *The Literature of the Middle Western Frontier.* 2 vols. New York: Columbia University Press, 1925–1926.

*Sanborn, Kate, ed. *The Wit of Women.* New York: Funk and Wagnalls Co., 1885.

Satterwaite, Joseph. "The Tremulous Formula: Form and Technique in *Godey's* Fiction." *American Quarterly* 8 (Summer 1956): 99–113.

*Smith, Harrison. "Feminism and the Household Novel." *Saturday Review,* 30 March 1957, 22.

*Smith, Henry Nash. "The Scribbling Women and the Cosmic Success Story." *Critical Inquiry* 1 (September 1974): 47–70.

———. *Virgin Land: The American West as Symbol and Myth.* Cambridge, Mass.: Harvard University Press, 1950.

*Smith, Leslie. "Through Rose-Colored Glasses: Some American Victorian Sentimental Novels." In *New Dimensions in Popular Culture,* edited by Russel B. Nye, 90–106. Bowling Green, Ohio: Bowling Green University Popular Press, 1972.

Smith, Thelma M. "Feminism in Philadelphia, 1790–1850." *Pennsylvania Magazine of History and Biography* 68 (July 1944): 243–268.

Smith-Rosenberg, Carroll. "The Female World of Love and Ritual: Relations between Women in Nineteenth-Century America." *Signs* 1 (Autumn 1975):
1–30.

———. "The Hysterical Woman: Sex Roles and Role Conflict in Nineteenth-
Century America." *Social Research* 39 (Winter 1972): 631–678.

Smith-Rosenberg, Carroll, and Rosenberg, Charles. "The Female Animal: Medical and Biological Views of Woman in Nineteenth-Century America." *Journal of American History* 60 (September 1973): 332–356.

*"Some 'Lady Novelists' and Their Works: As Seen from a Public Library." *Lit-
erary World*, 3 June 1882, 184–186.

Stanford, Ann. "Images of Women in Early American Literature." In *What Manner of Woman: Essays on English and American Life and Literature*,
edited by Marlene Springer, 184–210. New York: New York University
Press, 1977.

Stearns, Bertha Monica. "New England Magazines for Ladies, 1830–1860."
New England Quarterly 3 (October 1930): 627–656.

Stern, Madeleine B., ed. *Publishers for Mass Entertainment in Nineteenth Century America*. Boston: G. K. Hall and Co., 1980.

*Suckow, Ruth. "Literary Soubrettes." *Bookman* 63 (July 1926): 517–519.

Tandy, Jeannette Reid. "Pro-Slavery Propaganda in American Fiction of the
Fifties." *South Atlantic Quarterly* 21 (January 1922): 41–50; (April 1922):
170–178.

Taylor, William R., and Lasch, Christopher. "Two 'Kindred Spirits': Sorority and
Family in New England, 1839–1846." *New England Quarterly* 36 (March
1963): 23–41.

*Thompson, Adele E. "Woman's Place in Early American Fiction." *Era* 12 (November 1903): 472–474.

Thompson, Ralph. *American Literary Annuals and Gift Books, 1825–1865*.
New York: H. W. Wilson Co., 1936.

*Tompkins, Jane P. *Sensational Designs: The Cultural Work of American Fic-
tion, 1790–1860*. New York: Oxford University Press, forthcoming.

*———. "Sentimental Power: *Uncle Tom's Cabin* and the Politics of Literary
History." *Glyph* 8 (1981): 79–102.

Tutwiler, Julia R. "The Southern Woman in New York." *Bookman* 18 (February
1904): 624–634; 19 (March 1904): 51–58.

*Urann, C. A. "Early Women Writers in America." *Chautauquan* 30 (January
1900): 377–380.

Van Doren, Carl. *The American Novel, 1789–1939*. New York: Macmillan Co.,
1947.

*Voloshin, Beverly R. "A Historical Note on Women's Fiction: A Reply to An-
nette Kolodny." *Critical Inquiry* 2 (Summer 1976): 817–820.

*———. "The Limits of Domesticity: The Female *Bildungsroman* in America,
1820–1870." *Women's Studies* 10, no. 3 (1984): 283–302.

Wasserstrom, William. *Heiress of All the Ages: Sex and Sentiment in the Genteel Tradition*. Minneapolis: University of Minnesota Press, 1959.

Wegelin, Oscar. *Early American Fiction: 1774–1830*. New York: Peter Smith,
1929.

Welter, Barbara. "The Cult of True Womanhood, 1820–1860." *American Quarterly* 18 (Summer 1966): 151–174.

———. *Dimity Convictions: The American Woman in the Nineteenth Century*. Athens: Ohio University Press, 1976.

Wharton, Edith. *A Backward Glance*. New York: D. Appleton-Century Co.,
    1934.
Wright, Lyle H. "A Statistical Survey of American Fiction, 1774–1850." *Hunt-*
    ington Library Quarterly 2 (April 1939): 309–318.
*Wood, Ann Douglas. "The 'Scribbling Women' and Fanny Fern: Why Women
    Wrote." *American Quarterly* 23 (Spring 1971): 3–24.

Available Editions of Works Excerpted

ABBREVIATIONS

ACS   American Culture Series. Ann Arbor: University Microfilms.

APS3 American Periodical Series 3. Ann Arbor: University Microfilms.

EAI   Early American Imprints. Ann Arbor: University Microfilms.

WS   Wright Series. Glen Rock, N.J.: Research Publications (microfilm) and
      Louisville, Ky.: Lost Cause Press (microfiche).

Bleecker, Ann Eliza. *The Posthumous Works*. Repr. of 1793 ed. New York:
    Irvington Publishers, $15.00. *The History of Maria Kittle*. Repr. of 1797 ed.
    New York: Garland Publishing, $44.00. New York: Irvington Publishers,
    $15.00. ACS. EAI. WS.
Child, Lydia Maria. *Hobomok*. Repr. of 1824 ed. New York: Irvington Pub-
    lishers, $16.50. ACS. WS.
Cummins, Maria. *The Lamplighter*. Repr. of 1854 ed. New York: Irvington Pub-
    lishers, $19.50. St. Clair Shores, Mich.: Scholarly Press, $30.00. ACS.
Finley, Martha. *Elsie Dinsmore*. Repr. of 1896 ed. Philadelphia: N. W. Ayer and
    Son, Publishers, $24.00. Cutchogue, N.Y.: Buccaneer Press, $17.95.
Foster, Hannah. *The Coquette*. Repr. of 1797 ed. St. Clair Shores, Mich.: Schol-
    arly Press/Somerset, $39.00. New Haven, Conn.: New College/University
    Press, $9.95; pap. $6.95. EAI. WS.
Hale, Sarah Josepha. *Northwood*. Facs. ed. 1852. Philadelphia: N. W. Ayer and
    Son, Publishers, $21.00. Repr. of 1852 ed. Chicago: Johnson Publishing Co.
    $32.00. WS.
Hentz, Caroline Lee. *The Planter's Northern Bride*. WS.
Jacobs, Harriet Brent. *Incidents in the Life of a Slave Girl*. New York: Harcourt
    Brace Jovanovich/Harbrace, $4.95. Repr. of 1861 ed. New York: AMS Press,
    $12.00. Facs. ed. Philadelphia: N. W. Ayer and Son, Publishers, $13.75. St.
    Clair Shores, Mich.: Scholarly Press, $12.50. WS.
Kirkland, Caroline. *A New Home—Who'll Follow?* New Haven, Conn.: New
    College/University Press, $5.95. Repr. of 1839 ed. New York: Irvington Pub-
    lishers, $18.50. New York: AMS Press, $37.50. ACS. WS.
Parton, Sara Willis. *Ruth Hall*. WS.
Rowson, Susanna. *Charlotte Temple*. New Haven, Conn.: New College/Univer-
    sity Press, $4.95. Repr. of 1794 ed. St. Clair Shores, Mich.: Scholarly Press/
    Somerset, $19.00. ACS. EAI. WS.
Sedgwick, Catharine Maria. *Hope Leslie; or, Early Times in the Massachusetts*.
    Repr. of 1827 ed. New York: Irvington Publishers, $19.50. ACS. WS.
Southworth, E.D.E.N. *The Hidden Hand*. ACS. APS3.
Tenney, Tabitha. *Female Quixotism*. Repr. of 1801 ed. $37.50. New York: AMS
    Press, $37.50. ACS. EAI. WS.
Victor, Metta Fuller. *The Senator's Son*. WS.
Warner, Susan. *The Wide, Wide World*. Repr. of 1851 ed. St. Clair Shores,
    Mich.: Scholarly Press/Somerset, $59.00. WS.
Whitcher, Frances Miriam. *The Widow Bedott Papers*. ACS. APS3.

Wilson, Augusta Evans. *St. Elmo*. Repr. of 1896 ed. Laurel, N.Y.: Lightyear Press, $17.25. Philadelphia: N. W. Ayer and Son, Publishers, $32.00. Cutchogue, N.Y.: Buccaneer Press, $19.95. ACS.

Wood, Sally. *Dorval*. Repr. of 1801 ed. New York: AMS Press, $37.50.

Index

Illustration Credits